RACIAL REALIGNMENT

PRINCETON STUDIES IN AMERICAN POLITICS:
HISTORICAL, INTERNATIONAL, AND
COMPARATIVE PERSPECTIVES

IRA KATZNELSON, ERIC SCHICKLER, MARTIN SHEFTER,
AND THEDA SKOCPOL, SERIES EDITORS

A list of titles in this series appears at the back of the book

RACIAL REALIGNMENT

The Transformation of American Liberalism, 1932–1965

Eric Schickler

PRINCETON UNIVERSITY PRESS
PRINCETON AND OXFORD

Copyright © 2016 by Princeton University Press

Published by Princeton University Press, 41 William Street, Princeton,
New Jersey 08540

In the United Kingdom: Princeton University Press, 6 Oxford Street,
Woodstock, Oxfordshire OX20 1TW

press.princeton.edu

All Rights Reserved

ISBN 978-0-691-15387-2

ISBN (pbk.) 978-0-691-15388-9

British Library Cataloging-in-Publication Data is available

This book has been composed in Sabon

Printed on acid-free paper. ∞

Printed in the United States of America

1 3 5 7 9 10 8 6 4 2

Contents

PART 3
THE NATIONAL PARTIES RESPOND

Illustrations

FIGURES

Table

Acknowledgments

THIS BOOK WOULD not have come together without the help of many colleagues, both at Berkeley and across the country.

The project depended on several major, collaborative data collection efforts. Brian Feinstein, who started out as a research assistant but soon became a coauthor, played a pivotal role in putting together the collection of state party platforms that launched the project (see Feinstein and Schickler, "Platforms and Partners: The Civil Rights Realignment Reconsidered," *Studies in American Political Development*, 2008). This database serves as one of the foundations for chapter 7. Kathryn Pearson's discovery of discharge petitions in the National Archives provided a second, invaluable data source, which Pearson, Feinstein, and I drew on in an article revisiting the congressional side of the civil rights realignment ("Shifting Partisan Coalitions: Support for Civil Rights in Congress, 1933–1972," *Journal of Politics*, 2010). The analysis in chapter 8 relies heavily on this database. A third critical data source is a compendium of hundreds of public opinion polls from the 1930s and 1940s. The National Science Foundation has funded a decade-long collaboration with Adam Berinsky, which has involved cleaning, recoding, and devising weights for these early surveys (NSF Political Science Program Grants SES-0550431 and SES-1155143). A team of collaborators and research assistants brought these data to fruition, which serves as the basis for chapters 5 and 6.

Special thanks are due to Ira Katznelson, who was the first to suggest that the initial research on the civil rights realignment at the state and congressional levels could serve as the basis for a book that might make a broader contribution to the study of political change. Throughout the process, Katznelson was a source of insight and advice, commenting on both individual papers and the manuscript as a whole. Robert Mickey, David Mayhew, Richard Valelly, and Anthony Chen each also deserve special acknowledgment for offering terrific comments both as I first launched the book project and several years later as I completed the manuscript.

As the project developed, I received useful comments and feedback from numerous colleagues, including Richard Bensel, David Karol, Frances Lee,

Paul Pierson, Paul Sniderman, John Zaller, Kathleen Bawn, Christopher Baylor, Richard Beth, Dan Carpenter, Ted Carmines, Jack Citrin, Chris Deering, Erik Engstrom, Kathleen Frydl, Paul Frymer, Sean Gailmard, Alan Gerber, John Gerring, Don Green, John Griffin, Rodney Hero, Jeff Jenkins, Samuel Kernell, Thad Kousser, John Lapinski, Taeku Lee, Gabe Lenz, Robert Lieberman, Nolan McCarty, Suzanne Mettler, Sid Milkis, Hans Noel, Kevin Quinn, Jas Sekhon, Daniel Schlozman, Merrill Shanks, Robert Shapiro, John Sides, Theda Skocpol, Laura Stoker, Vanessa Tyson, Robert Van Houweling, Lynn Vavreck, Dorian Warren, Greg Wawro, and Vesla Weaver. I thank Thomas Ogorzalek, John Lapinski, Scott Adler, and John Wilkerson for generously sharing their congressional data.

Several current and former graduate students also played a critical role in the project. Devin Caughey made major contributions as a research assistant and as a collaborator on several related projects. Devin's innovative method for estimating the dynamics of state- and group-level opinion provided a key resource for the analyses in chapters 5 and 6. In addition to providing sterling research assistance, Ruth Bloch Rubin generously shared several critical "finds" from her dissertation research in the archives of southern members of Congress. Emily Hertz deserves special thanks for her superb work as a research assistant and as a commenter on each chapter of the manuscript; Hertz's contributions in helping me think through the structure of the argument and presentation in each chapter constituted the kind of wise feedback one expects from a senior colleague rather than a second-year Ph.D. student.

I also benefited from excellent research assistance from Sara Chatfield, Michael Dougal, Jake Grumbach, Peter Hanson, Erin Hartman, John Henderson, Adrienne Hosek, Tony Huynh, Morris Levy, Mark Oleszek, Eleanor Powell, Arman Rezaee, Adam Silver, Alex Theodoridis, Joseph Warren, Nicole Fox Wilcoxon, and Ian Yohai. Berkeley undergraduates Mariam Azhar, Sean Diament, Lena Ghamrawi, Deepa Kollipara, and Raquel Pelke also provided important research help.

I am grateful to Eric Crahan at Princeton University Press for his guidance and his encouragement of the project throughout the process. I also thank Chuck Myers, who was the editor at Princeton when I first framed the initial book prospectus for an advance contract.

Finally, my deepest gratitude goes to Terri Bimes, Sam Schickler, and Lea Schickler, for their unending love and support. It is to them that this book is dedicated (though I suspect Lea and Sam would not forgive me if I did not mention Wilbur's name as well).

RACIAL REALIGNMENT

CHAPTER 1

Introduction

TODAY POLITICAL OBSERVERS take for granted the idea that Democratic partisanship, economic liberalism, and racial liberalism cohere under a common programmatic banner, just as Republican partisanship is associated with economic conservatism and greater resistance to government programs to redress problems of racial inequality. But the emergence of these linkages is a relatively recent phenomenon. Prior to the 1930s Republican elites provided greater (if often only tepid) support for civil rights than did their Democratic counterparts. By the mid-1960s, however, Democratic partisanship and economic liberalism were clearly identified with civil rights support and Republican conservatism had become identified with greater opposition to governmental action to redress racial inequalities. This book aims to explain the dynamics of this momentous transformation.

The partisan transformation on race is often depicted as an elite-led, center-driven shift that occurred in the 1960s, breaking apart the New Deal coalition that had dominated American politics for more than a generation. By contrast, I show that the realignment began with mass and midlevel party actors, that it was rooted in state and local politics rather than in Washington, DC, and that much of the important work was complete by the mid-1940s. In doing so, I aim to provide a new way of thinking about the nature of the New Deal coalition and of the political significance of New Deal liberalism more generally. This account also has important implications for theories of political parties and of political change in the United States. Thus the civil rights realignment is important both in its own right and as a window into the workings of the American political system more broadly.

THE CONVENTIONAL VIEW OF THE
CIVIL RIGHTS REALIGNMENT

Although scholars have studied the civil rights realignment from a wide variety of angles, three related claims have shaped the prevailing understanding of its dynamics. The first claim is that national party elites played the decisive role in driving the change in each party's stance. Edward Carmines and James Stimson's pathbreaking study, *Issue Evolution: Race and the Transformation of American Politics*, put forward the argument that the two parties took similar positions straddling (and often avoiding) civil rights in the 1940s and 1950s, with Republicans if anything a bit to the left of their Democratic counterparts.[1] The critical break point arrived when Lyndon Johnson and Barry Goldwater took sharply different stands on the Civil Rights Act of 1964. As Thomas Edsall and Mary Edsall put it, "Goldwater ... publicly defined the Republican Party as anti–civil rights with his opposition to the Civil Rights Act of 1964.... Johnson, conversely, firmly established the commitment of the Democratic Party to civil rights."[2] Once national party leaders made this dramatic break, party activists followed their lead, polarizing on civil rights policy, and the mass public gradually followed along.[3] Indeed, the civil rights case is often taken as a leading example of the idea that public opinion generally follows cues from national party elites, with mass partisans polarizing on issues when these elites provide clear, distinct cues.[4]

This reshuffling of party coalitions launched the post–New Deal party system in which Democrats were identified with African Americans and racial liberalism, while Republicans were associated with racial conservatism.[5] Lyndon Johnson's often-cited observation after he signed the Civil Rights Act that "we have delivered the South to the Republican Party for your lifetime and mine" nicely set the stage for the view that elite choice at a critical moment drove the racial realignment.[6]

Second, national political actors take center stage in this story, in part because federalism is understood to be a key blockage preventing action on civil rights. Federalism gave southerners secure control of law enforcement and the means of coercion in their region while allowing southern elites to appeal to the rhetoric of states' rights to justify their discriminatory policies. Federalism also meant that state party competition often focused on local issues, with the result that many northern state Democratic parties consisted of inward-looking political machines with little commitment to programmatic liberalism.[7] Change had to come from the top down because only nationally oriented political actors had the capacity and (eventually) the will to move policy on racial issues. The civil rights movement figures into this story as an important source of pressure on these national political elites, but the crucial step was to persuade top party leaders based in Washington that they needed to act.

Third, leading accounts of the civil rights realignment date the partisan transformation to the 1960s. This focus on the 1960s as a "critical juncture" is not confined to works that embrace the elite-led view of the realignment. For example, Doug McAdam and Karina Kloos's *Deeply Divided: Racial Politics and Social Movements in Post-War America* does an excellent job of tracing the creative role of the civil rights movement in generating the partisan landscape that has dominated American politics for the past fifty years. Yet they too accept the idea that the 1960s constitute the critical moment for the realignment, arguing that "the GOP was, in the aggregate, far and away more progressive on civil rights issues" than the Democrats at the start of the decade. A "seismic" shift occurred during "a fairly short span of time in the early to mid-'60s" when the civil rights movement and segregationist countermovement "decisively altered the partisan geography of the United States and in the process pushed the national Democratic and Republican parties sharply to the left and right respectively."[8]

In sum, the conventional account treats the civil rights realignment as the disruption of one stable partisan alignment—rooted in the avoidance of racial issues—and its replacement by another alignment in which race played a defining role. The critical decisions driving this process occurred in the 1960s as national party elites grappled with the question of how to respond to pressure from civil rights activists and their opponents. The choices made at the center then reverberated throughout the political system, gradually remaking both parties at the mass and middle levels.

THE CIVIL RIGHTS REALIGNMENT: CONSTITUENCIES, LOCALLY ROOTED POLITICIANS, AND TIMING

In contrast to the conventional account, this book argues that the partisan realignment on civil rights was rooted in changes in the New Deal coalition that emerged in the mid- to late 1930s, not the 1960s. Rather than realignment starting in Washington and diffusing out and down, state parties and locally oriented rank-and-file members of Congress provided a key mechanism for pro–civil rights forces—which first entered the New Deal coalition in the 1930s—to capture the Democratic Party from below. Far from spearheading the realignment, national party elites—that is, the leaders of political institutions of national scope, such as the president, top congressional leaders, and national party chairmen—feared the disruptive potential of civil rights issues for their respective partisan coalitions. As a result, these national leaders generally sought to straddle the civil rights divide and were actually among the last to move.

Constituency-Level Changes

Changes in the constituency base of the Democratic Party that took place in the 1930s set in motion the partisan realignment on race. While the New Deal's economic programs originally drew African Americans and Congress of Industrial Organizations (CIO) unions to the Democratic Party, their entry into the party coalition—and the reaction that entry provoked from southern Democrats—established important linkages between civil rights liberalism and New Deal liberalism that reverberated through the midlevels of the party and eventually forced the hand of top national leaders.

African Americans had voted Republican for decades but received little in return for their loyalty. By contrast, even as core features of the New Deal accommodated racial discrimination, Roosevelt's program offered real benefits to many northern African Americans, particularly when compared with the Hoover administration's dismal record. Recognizing these gains, African Americans voted decisively for Roosevelt in 1936 and stuck with the president for the remainder of his term. The emergence of African Americans as a potentially important source of votes for northern Democrats gave at least some rank-and-file Democratic politicians an incentive to show concern for civil rights.[9]

While the number of northern states and congressional districts with a substantial African American population in the 1930s and early 1940s was modest, the meteoric rise of the CIO gave African Americans an important ally within the Democratic coalition. Before the formation of the CIO in 1935, the American Federation of Labor (AFL)–dominated labor movement had a poor record on civil rights. But from early on, the CIO stood out among white-led organizations in its support for civil rights. Even as rank-and-file union workers often shared in the racial prejudice that was prevalent in their communities, the union's leaders and organizers made racial equality a key facet of their program. This support was rooted both in the union's internal organizing imperatives and in its broader programmatic vision. The CIO's leaders and organizers believed that African American support was crucial for the union's prospects in industrial workplaces in which replacement workers were a constant threat. At the same time, many of these same union officials had roots in left-wing political movements committed to the idea that racial divisions undermined the class consciousness required to fight economic exploitation. These interests and beliefs led the CIO to fuse concerns about class and race, arguing that the cause of economic justice required an encompassing labor movement willing to use governmental power to tackle the mutually reinforcing problems of economic and racial inequality.

This fusion was especially important as observers on all sides quickly recognized that the CIO had developed into the central mobilization instrument outside the Democratic Party itself on behalf of liberalism. The CIO became the leading symbol—both for supporters and for opponents—of the most ambitious strands of New Deal liberalism in the United States, urging congressional Democrats and the executive branch to move to the left across a range of policies.[10] The CIO's outspoken civil rights advocacy meant that the group most associated with an expansive reading of the New Deal's goals was also associated with the civil rights cause.

These two constituency shifts provoked a furious reaction among south-ern Democrats, which had equally important implications for the future of New Deal liberalism. Southern Democrats had provided critical backing for the first and second New Deal.[11] But many southern politicians viewed Afri-can Americans' incorporation into both the Democratic Party and the labor movement as an existential threat to the racially oppressive "southern way of life."[12] Southern Democrats were soon the most consequential opponents of labor-sponsored expansions of the New Deal, cooperating with Republicans to push investigations and legislation that sought to undermine organized labor, and along with it, the liberal agenda more generally. Southern Demo-crats' fierce opposition both to the CIO and to civil rights meant that African Americans were no longer isolated claimants: their political enemies were in-creasingly identified as a crucial enemy of liberal advances, not just on civil rights but across a range of policy domains, including especially labor policy.

These changes gradually reshaped the meaning of New Deal liberalism. A new political alignment took shape in which the supporters of an ambitious reading of the New Deal's promise—CIO unions and African Americans, along with Jews and urban liberals more generally—found themselves op-posed by southern Democrats who viewed both the CIO and African Amer-icans as mortal threats. This alignment reached all the way down to the mass level of the parties, as economically liberal white northern Democrats were substantially more likely to back key civil rights initiatives by about 1940 than were economically conservative Republicans. The mass- and group-level developments had important implications for politicians: for Repub-licans to make civil rights their issue, they would have had to overcome the skepticism of their own economically conservative core partisans. For northern Democrats to skirt the issue, they would have had to ignore the views of their own core partisans—economic liberals and the growing num-ber of African American Democrats.

Federalism and Geographical Decentralization

Northern state parties and rank-and-file members of Congress responded to these new constituency dynamics long before national party elites did.[13] Tra-ditionally, liberals have interpreted the history of civil rights as the classic example of why one should be suspicious of states' rights and local politics. This analysis suggests that may be too hasty. While federalism and geo-graphic representation certainly facilitated the development of the Jim Crow South, they also helped to precipitate its downfall. Locally rooted politicians played a crucial role as intermediaries between constituency-based pressures and elite decision-making arenas in the civil rights realignment.[14]

The nationally oriented party leaders who had the greatest stake in main-taining the Democrats' North-South coalition were generally slow to respond when advocates attempted to graft civil rights onto New Deal liberalism. But the independent power base of state and local parties and the election of House members through separate geographic districts channeled constituency pressure for civil rights, without requiring an immediate showdown with national party leaders. Even as many national political elites sought to avoid the civil rights issue, movement activists could appeal to rank-and-file members of Congress, mayors and other local officials, and state and local parties, each of which had its own, partly independent power base and constituency. These locally rooted politicians then contributed to civil rights activists' efforts to raise the salience of the issue.[15]

Specifically, Democratic partisanship and economic liberalism became associated with civil rights support among northern members of the House of Representatives starting in the late 1930s. By the end of World War II a substantial gap in civil rights support separated northern Democrats and economic liberals from northern Republicans and economic conservatives. Northern state Democratic parties displayed a similar pattern, adopting platforms and pursuing policies that were to the left of their GOP counterparts on civil rights by the mid-1940s, with the gap increasing gradually in the ensuing years. These midlevel party actors proved far more responsive to pressure to support civil rights than did most top national elites, who were preoccupied with holding together the increasingly precarious North-South coalition forged by Roosevelt.[16]

Federalism and the decentralized system of electing members of Congress thus provided key institutional mechanisms to facilitate the gradual incorporation of civil rights into the mainstream of the Democratic Party, undermining the implicit deal among national political leaders that had been a key foundation of the party for decades. Much like abolitionism in the 1830s–1840s and the currency issue in the 1870s–1880s, efforts by national party leaders to block a new issue ultimately failed and party lines were reshuffled.[17] Congress and state parties emerge from this case as potential vehicles for new interests to gain access; localism and geographic-based districts are often seen as bastions of conservatism, but in this case they provided institutional footholds for civil rights liberals.

Midlevel party actors also played an important role in the GOP's transformation on race. Growing southern Democratic disaffection with New Deal liberalism stirred Republican hopes of a realignment more than two decades before Barry Goldwater entered the political scene. The appeals to states' rights and limited government that became a staple of conservative Republican attacks on the New Deal in the 1930s were well suited to wooing southern Democrats worried about the threat posed by the CIO's brand of liberalism. But the moderate leaders atop the national GOP were wary of the implications of a wholesale alliance with southern conservatives. As a result, Republican presidential candidates generally sought to sidestep civil rights in the 1940s and 1950s.

Developments below the top leadership, however, gradually tilted the balance within the GOP in favor of racial conservatives during the 1940s and 1950s. Rank-and-file northern Republicans in Congress—facing little or no constituency pressure to back civil rights—drifted away from their earlier advocacy of civil rights legislation and even made common cause with southerners in fighting strong fair-employment practices legislation in the 1940s. At the state level, President Dwight Eisenhower's party-building efforts in the South—which aimed to create a suburban, moderate organization in his image—ironically created a new power base for his conservative rivals within the party. The Goldwater movement had deep roots in these earlier shifts within the party, which opened a pathway for racial conservatives to gain the upper hand and bring to fruition the long-standing conservative goal of drawing disaffected southern Democrats into the GOP.

For both Democrats and Republicans, the ability of state party organizations and rank-and-file members of Congress to adopt their own positions provided a mechanism for the parties' existing and new coalition partners and ideological allies to gain a power base at the local level in advance of capturing the national party as a whole. The leaders of social movements and their interest group allies need not first win over national party leaders in order to transform party politics. Rather, at least in the case of civil rights, a series of victories at the state level paved the way for a national realignment. The federal nature of American parties and, relatedly, the existence of important offices controlled by lower-level units thus emerge as key elements in the civil rights realignment.[18]

Timing

Rather than viewing the 1960s as the critical moment in the partisan realignment on race, I argue that much of the political work involved in bringing racial liberalism into the Democratic program was undertaken decades earlier. Efforts by the CIO, African American activists, and other urban liberals starting in the mid- to late 1930s had remade the Democratic Party, so that economic liberalism, Democratic partisanship, and support for civil rights were connected at both the mass and midlevels of the party throughout the North by the mid-1940s.

But winning over northern state parties and members of Congress was not itself sufficient to transform national alignments. A complete takeover of the national Democratic Party required overcoming the resistance not just of southern party leaders but also of the nationally oriented officials atop the party structure. With a few exceptions, top party leaders struggled mightily to tamp down the pressure to take a clear stand on civil rights. From 1944 to 1956, rank-and-file Democratic activists and convention delegates had been to the left of national leaders on civil rights, yet party elites generally succeeded in avoiding adoption of a platform or nomination of a presidential candidate that would alienate southern conservatives.

But civil rights movement activists—often acting in tandem with midlevel party actors—worked to force the issue to the top of the political agenda, eventually requiring leaders to take sides. Crucially, by the time the issue came to occupy center stage nationally, the liberals enjoyed a clear majority within the national party, while southern conservatives had become an isolated minority.

Long before Lyndon Johnson and Barry Goldwater took their opposing positions on civil rights, their parties had been remade beneath them. Below the surface a series of developments dating back to the 1930s and 1940s had transformed both parties so that the intraparty pressures in favor of an embrace of racial liberalism were much stronger on the Democratic side, while Republicans increasingly were pushed toward racial conservatism and a concomitant alliance with southern civil rights foes. African Americans and their allies in the CIO had done much of the work in bringing together New Deal liberalism and racial liberalism in the late 1930s and the 1940s. The civil rights movement of the late 1950s and the 1960s provided the catalyst to fulfill the promise of these earlier developments within the parties.

IMPLICATIONS

This reexamination of the civil rights realignment leads to a revised understanding of the New Deal coalition and of New Deal liberalism, which in turn suggests the need to revisit how we think about political parties as institutions. The civil rights case also underscores the ways in which major political transformations can result from the intersection of multiple, partly independent historical trajectories. This understanding of political change puts a premium on a methodological approach that integrates historical and behavioral evidence and draws on diverse data sources for leverage.

Splitting at the Seams: Race, Section, and the New Deal Coalition

The New Deal coalition is often depicted as reflecting a stable bargain in which northern Democrats agreed to avoid addressing civil rights policy in return for southern Democrats' cooperation in building the New Deal welfare state.[19] Such policy decisions as the exclusion of domestic and agricultural labor from the Social Security system have been interpreted as symbolizing a broader détente, facilitated by most northern Democrats' lack of commitment to civil rights.[20] Franklin Roosevelt's refusal to push even for antilynching legislation, for fear of alienating southern Democrats whose votes he needed for his legislative priorities, underscores the extent to which an agreement to ignore civil rights demands seems to have underwritten the New Deal coalition.[21] Although some revisionist accounts have pointed to behind-the-scenes Roosevelt maneuvers to promote racial equality, scholars have generally emphasized the timidity with which the New Deal addressed the problems facing African Americans.[22]

From this standpoint, the pursuit of social democracy in the United States was divorced from the cause of racial equality owing to the peculiar nature of the New Deal coalition. Southern Democrats' pivotal position in Roosevelt's coalition sharply limited the reach of liberal aspirations.[23] It was only in the 1960s, with Johnson's embrace of civil rights, that racial liberalism was brought into the social democratic program. This linkage, however, created a backlash that weakened the cause of economic justice by empowering conservatives who were now able to use appeals to racial resentment to build a new Republican majority.[24]

Rather than viewing the New Deal coalition as a stable equilibrium that was brought down by the disruptions of the 1960s, however, I argue that important actors within the Democratic Party were working to undermine the supposed "bargain" between northern liberals and southern racists starting in the late 1930s. Soon after the entry of the CIO and African Americans into the Democratic coalition in 1936, southern Democrats began to cooperate with Republicans to force antilabor investigations and bills onto the agenda that challenged one key pillar of the national Democratic coalition.[25] Meanwhile, northern Democrats were working to force civil rights bills onto the legislative agenda, thus threatening a second key pillar of that coalition.

In this sense, the New Deal coalition was being torn apart from within by about 1940: while most nationally oriented party leaders preferred to keep both issues off the agenda, southern members of Congress worked aggressively to exacerbate the party's split on labor policy, and northern members pushed civil rights policies that were anathema to their southern colleagues. The version of New Deal liberalism that CIO unions and other urban liberals articulated in the late 1930s—and that was incorporated into the commitments of rank-and-file northern members of Congress and state parties—was unacceptable to the southern wing of the party, and the southerners responded to this threat by seeking to weaken the same labor unions that were essential to electing northern Democrats.

Against the claim that racial liberalism was a belated 1960s addition to economic liberalism, this account suggests that New Deal liberalism—as articulated and developed by its firmest supporters starting in the late 1930s—had racially inclusive elements that ran counter to the well-documented exclusionary aspects of Roosevelt's program. The CIO and its allies fused "class" and "race" in an alignment that was forged amid the vast social and ideological turmoil of the 1930s and early 1940s. Most top party leaders resisted this fusion, but its impact nonetheless was evident in the behavior of rank-and-file members of Congress and state parties. It also was reflected in the southern shift away from the New Deal, and in conservative Republican efforts to demonstrate that their party's antistatism made it the natural home for disaffected southern Democrats. Modern liberalism and conservatism had their roots in these early battles over the future of the New Deal.[26]

The Civil Rights Realignment and Party Theory

The civil rights realignment also speaks directly to recent theories of political parties. In an important series of studies, John Zaller, Kathleen Bawn, and their collaborators have developed a theory of parties as coalitions of intense policy demanders managed by politicians.[27] These intense policy demanders—composed primarily of interest groups and activists—negotiate with one another to forge a "long coalition" to nominate candidates committed to their program. In this view, the candidate nomination process is the key to ensuring that a party's officeholders adhere to a common program: "with only minor local variation, [the] policy-demanding groups" that form the core of a political party "espouse the positions for which their national party stands and require that candidates do so too." As a result, "any candidate who relies on local activists for support is likely to be a credible representative of the national party standard."[28] Ideologies reflect the coalitional bargains struck by these diverse policy demanders and do not necessarily have any intrinsic internal logic. After many elections, these party programs "become accepted as natural manifestations of competing worldviews: a 'conservative' one ... and a 'liberal' one."[29]

Several aspects of the civil rights case nicely fit this understanding of parties. The role of African American voters and the CIO in pushing the Democratic Party to support civil rights exemplifies how group pressure can shape party positions. Similarly, the opposition of one of the GOP's core constituents, the business community, no doubt influenced Republican skepticism toward fair employment legislation.[30]

But other elements of the civil rights case suggest that parties are not simply coalitions of intense policy demanders managed by politicians. The federal nature of American parties means that one cannot take for granted that the "party" is a single coherent entity with the same meaning across regions. The dueling northern and southern wings of the Democratic Party each had a concrete, independent electoral and institutional base that enabled its members to nominate candidates who viewed defeating the other wing of the party as a top priority. The Democratic Party that nominated the racist labor-baiter Howard Smith to represent Virginia from 1931 to 1966 is hardly the same institution (or set of policy demanders) that brought Emanuel Celler, a Jewish prolabor, pro–civil rights Democrat from Brooklyn, to Congress over these same decades.[31] Yet they each occupied important positions of influence in Congress, with Smith the longtime chair of the Rules Committee and Celler leading the Judiciary Committee.

While it is true that presidential candidates and top congressional leaders sought to be acceptable to both northern liberals and southern conservatives, their leadership hardly reflected a long-term bargain that all sides of the party embraced. Smith and Celler may have each agreed to vote for the same presidential candidate and the same candidate for Speaker of the House of Representatives, but they each ultimately hoped to weaken and defeat the other wing of the party, not to coexist with it. The two regionally based camps pursued policy agendas that were deeply opposed to each other. In attacking labor unions, southern conservatives were seeking to undermine a key source of northern Democrats' support; in promoting civil rights legislation and labor rights, northern liberals threatened the core interests of many southern Democrats. Although presidential candidates and other nationally oriented elites sought to act as "party managers," keeping the various elements of the coalition in sync, many other powerful actors within the party maneuvered to disrupt the electoral foundations essential to their regional rivals.[32]

While the divisions among Republicans in the 1940s–1950s were less stark than among Democrats of the era, the conservative "Taft wing"—with its base primarily in the Midwest—saw the potential incorporation of southern Democrats as a way to consolidate conservative control of the party. From the perspective of the northeastern moderate wing, however, this strategy threatened not just its influence within the party but its very survival. Chapter 10 will show that national party leaders' ability to manage the tension between these competing sectionally based interests was limited and that their efforts ultimately failed.

These cases, in which the groups composing a party coalition view one another as adversaries, is a far cry from today's more unified national parties.[33] The contemporary Democratic and Republican parties each nominate candidates who can reasonably be said to reflect a common national brand that resonates with voters and that reflects bargains struck by groups inside the party coalition. But this outcome is a historical product and not an inevitable feature of American parties. Such forces as the nationalization of fundraising networks and of the media landscape, for example, may generate greater pressure to conform to a single national brand.[34] But this pressure has been a variable, not a constant.

There is no single, overriding logic of party politics; instead, parties, like other political institutions, are historical composites shaped by multiple logics.[35] The need to nominate a single candidate for president—along with nationally oriented media coverage and fundraising—introduces an incentive for the groups associated with a party to coordinate on a common strategy and program. But at times groups with sharply opposed interests may end up in the same party coalition. Southern Democrats had been core members of the Democratic Party since its formation in the nineteenth century. The passage of the Wagner Act, which provided expansive collective bargaining rights for workers, brought labor unions into the Democratic coalition.[36] While a few prescient southerners anticipated the threat presented by early New Deal labor policies, most did not foresee the danger posed by incorporating unions into the New Deal coalition until after the rise of the CIO.[37] Southern Democrats and CIO unions entered the party for different reasons and at very different historical moments; once they became important players inside the party, each could draw on an independent institutional base to prosecute their battle for control over its future.

Once one sees that parties may at times encompass deep conflicts, privileging any single type of actor as *the* party becomes problematic. The opposing players will have an incentive to draw on whatever resources are available and to work through a range of power bases—including support from ordinary voters and activists, organized groups, midlevel party officials, and top party leaders. The civil rights case underscores the importance of each of these actors in shaping the partisan transformation. To say that the groups called the shots on their own, or that party leaders successfully managed the groups' demands, or that any other single set of actors defined the parties' position obscures much of the important action, which consisted of the interactions—and battles—across these layers.

In addition to the potential for incoherence introduced by the independent electoral base of state and local parties, the civil rights case also suggests a further limitation of the parties-as-policy-demanders perspective: there does seem to have been a broad, ideological dynamic concerning "what goes with what" that was evident to the actors on the ground early in the realignment process. The entry of the CIO and African Americans into the Democratic Party was widely understood to create a sharp cleavage between the southern wing, which had long been the backbone of the Democratic Party, and this newly ascendant "liberal" (as it was called) wing. This was not simply a dispute between narrow policy demanders: the CIO's drive to remake American political and social institutions represented a threat to the entire southern political economy.[38]

Meanwhile, as Republicans increasingly positioned themselves in opposition to the New Deal on "states' rights" grounds in the mid- to late 1930s, many political actors—including elected officials, intellectuals, and group leaders—saw the basis for an alliance with disaffected southern conservatives.[39] It took several decades to bring that alliance to fruition; it developed gradually, first as congressional Republicans worked with their southern counterparts to sponsor antilabor legislation and investigations and then broadening out to other issues and institutional venues, such as state party organizations and eventually national party conventions.[40]

Strikingly, even ordinary voters appear to have recognized the connections across issues at this early stage. As noted above, economically liberal northern Democrats were especially likely to take the pro–civil rights (and thus antisouthern) view, while economically conservative northern Republicans were especially likely to be skeptical of civil rights. This conservative skepticism was not confined to fair employment legislation, where business organizations' opposition created a coalitional reason for Republicans to oppose civil rights. Indeed, as shown in chapter 5, economically conservative Republican voters provided substantially less support for antilynching legislation than did economically liberal Democrats as early as December 1937. Republican members of Congress also distanced themselves from their earlier civil rights advocacy, not just on fair employment policy but even on issues such as antilynching legislation and the poll tax (see chapter 8). The rise of the CIO, the entry of African Americans into the Democratic coalition, and the growing disaffection of southern conservative Democrats together started to forge a new ideological cleavage that cross-cut the old party lines and constrained the opportunities for both groups and party officials to manage coalitional alignments. The grassroots African American–led civil rights movement repeatedly worked to elevate the prominence of civil rights issues, sharpening this cleavage. As a result of these efforts and battles, liberals from various backgrounds and interests came to identify civil rights as a key element of liberalism, essential both for what it directly represented and for what it said about the place of conservative southerners in the future of the Democratic coalition.

In sum, the civil rights case points both to strengths and to limitations of conceiving of parties as coalitions of intense policy demanders. There is no doubt that group interests and conflicts played a critical role in shaping the development of the parties' positions on civil rights. At the same time, however, the civil rights realignment underscores the extent to which parties encompass conflicting logics and interests. Rather than a coherent brand managed by party leaders, the Democratic Party was at war with itself for decades. Federalism and geographic-based representation, in particular, provided enduring power bases for the contending sides to prosecute their battle for control. Furthermore, the sides in this battle had a clear ideological logic; the political economic vision promoted by the CIO was anathema to the interests of southern Democrats along several dimensions, and southern conservatives, in turn, viewed their survival as dependent on weakening the industrial labor movement. An ideological cleavage in which southern Democrats were identified as a crucial enemy of "liberal" advances across a range of issues—including civil rights—emerged as a product of wide-ranging intense policy battles on the ground in the late 1930s and early 1940s, rather than as a product of some sort of coalitional bargain within the Democratic Party.[41]

Multiple, Intersecting Trajectories and the Realignment

The civil rights realignment exemplifies how political transformations can emerge from the intersection of multiple, initially separate political trajectories. As Karen Orren and Stephen Skowronek demonstrate, political development is often driven by the tensions between political institutions that had their origins in different time periods and that thus incorporated contradictory logics or purposes.[42] A focus on a single institution or political interest is unlikely to help understand major political transformations when much of the "action" occurs at the intersection of multiple institutions and political processes.

Along the first trajectory in the civil rights case, the party system was reshaped starting in the 1930s with little *direct* regard for civil rights politics, as the Democrats embraced New Deal liberalism and new coalition partners in response to the Depression, and Republicans countered with a turn to antistatism. The CIO unionists, African Americans, Jews, and other urban liberals who joined the ranks of the Democratic Party in the 1930s did so because of the Depression and the New Deal's economic programs. With few exceptions, they were not responding to explicit civil rights appeals coming from the Democrats.[43] That is, few if any voters *became* Democrats in the 1930s because of civil rights, nor is it likely that being a Democrat directly led many voters to become pro–civil rights. But the presence of these voters in the New Deal coalition had crucial implications for how the Democratic Party would respond as civil rights reached the top of the national agenda.

Meanwhile, along a second political trajectory, the "long" civil rights movement played a critical role in using protest, litigation, and legislative strategies to force civil rights onto the national agenda.[44] A key initial step occurred during the mobilization for entry into World War II, when A. Philip Randolph's March on Washington Movement pressured Roosevelt into creating a temporary Fair Employment Practices Committee (FEPC) to prevent racial discrimination in defense industries. Although the CIO and other urban liberals had expressed support for civil rights before the FEPC's creation, the intense movement-initiated battles over permanent fair employment legislation in the early to mid-1940s raised the political visibility of racial issues, encouraging liberal leaders and groups to give civil rights a more prominent place in their program. By the end of the war, support for civil rights had become a key marker of one's identity as a liberal.

After the war the violent reaction to a major movement-initiated voter registration drive in the South led to Harry Truman's creation of the President's Committee on Civil Rights. The committee, in turn, issued a set of recommendations that became the basis for Truman's civil rights program and for the ensuing Democratic Party platform fight in 1948 that led to a southern bolt. The far-reaching liberal civil rights coalition that emerged out of these battles reflected the efforts of movement activists to turn civil rights into a defining national issue.

Many of the civil rights movement activists involved in these efforts had ties to the Democratic Party owing to the New Deal's economic programs, but movement strategy had its own, independent logic: civil rights advocates sought to raise the salience of civil rights on the national agenda regardless of whether doing so would help Democrats or economic liberals win elections. Indeed, movement activists capitalized on whatever opportunities were available, even taking advantage of Cold War era concerns about America's international reputation to embarrass national leaders into addressing persistent discrimination.[45]

The key is how these two trajectories intersected: when civil rights activists succeeded in pushing the issue onto the national agenda—despite the resistance of national leaders in both parties but with considerable support from rank-and-file Democrats and midlevel party actors—it was the Democrats who were disposed to embrace the issue because of the changes in the party system along the first trajectory. By remaking the Democratic Party outside of the South to be the representative of CIO unionists, African Americans, Jews, and liberal egalitarianism, New Deal advocates set the stage for the culmination of the civil rights realignment—though this result depended on actors on the second timeline forcing the issue to the decision stage. The changes in the 1930s and early 1940s meant that as civil rights activists moved to push their cause higher on the national political agenda, they would find their main allies within the Democratic coalition. They would also find a less receptive audience for appeals for strong national action among Republicans, who had fashioned a coalition and ideological vision focused on limiting the reach of national governmental authority.

The convergence of two initially distinct political trajectories over time thus shaped the civil rights realignment. It was a gradual process that started in the mid-1930s, gathered momentum in the 1940s as the war mobilization created a window of opportunity for civil rights activists to force fair employment laws onto the agenda, and received a final, decisive push from the reinvigorated civil rights movement of the late 1950s and the 1960s.

One needs to follow each of these trajectories—the remaking of the Democratic Party in the 1930s–1940s and the repeated efforts of grassroots movement activists to push civil rights onto the agenda—to understand the realignment's timing and meaning. While the baseline receptivity to civil rights appeals of northern Democratic members of Congress and partisans was higher than that of Republicans starting in the early 1940s, national Democratic leaders were able to manage the coalitional stresses that resulted from this as long as the grassroots insurgency on behalf of civil rights had not reached overwhelming intensity. Democrats were able to include a relatively pro–civil rights northern wing and a fiercely anti–civil rights southern wing because civil rights was not so high on the political agenda that national leaders were forced to take a clear stand. But once the grassroots insurgency and southern violent response reached a crisis point in the 1960s, this management became impossible.

In the end, national party leaders were compelled to take sides in a context created by the earlier transformation in the party system. They sought to stave off the moment of choice but no longer could. National Democratic leaders, such as Lyndon Johnson, found themselves nominally atop a party in which key coalition partners and core party voters had long ago chosen the pro–civil rights side. National Republicans—men such as Everett Dirksen (R-IL) and Jacob Javits (R-NY) —became the rear guard of a party whose coalition partners had long since stopped caring about civil rights and whose core party voters took a conservative position on civil rights initiatives.

DATA AND METHODOLOGICAL APPROACH

What should one make of an explanation of a broad historical phenomenon—such as a party realignment—that highlights the dynamic interplay of multiple forces over several decades? In recent years political scientists have been rightly focused on improving our ability to make precise, valid causal inferences, drawing heavily on the "potential outcomes" framework developed by Donald Rubin and others.[46] The fundamental problem of causal inference is that one can never observe both the actual value of the dependent variable, given the observed value of the independent variable, and the value that the dependent variable would have been under the alternative scenario in which the independent variable had taken on a different value. Random assignment in an experiment allows us to approximate this counterfactual: in expectation, the treatment and control groups are identical, so on average, the control group's "score" on the dependent variable is what the treatment group would have scored had it not received the treatment. The explosion of interest in experimentation—and in strong research designs that allow one to approximate the advantages of an experiment—has allowed political scientists to make tremendous progress in improving our causal analyses and in rooting out the tendency to move far too quickly from findings of a correlation to claims about causality.

But this important progress leaves open the question of what one should do with political phenomena in which there simply is no adequate counterfactual that allows one to identify causal effects with the precision and confidence made possible by the potential outcomes framework. One option is simply not to study such phenomena. This choice, however, would mean failing to address some of the most important substantive questions about politics. Major political transformations are rarely amenable to identifying a persuasive counterfactual that allows one to assess potential outcomes with confidence.

This book makes the case for drawing on diverse types of evidence and methodological approaches in order to gain insight into a question that is not ideally suited to isolating the causal effect of a single variable. In this substantively important case, tracing the interplay of multiple historical processes over the course of several decades is essential to understanding what happened, why it happened, and what it meant politically. From a methodological standpoint, one goal of the book is to show that even in the absence of a single, decisive test, wide-ranging and systematic data collection and analysis can yield insight into big, complicated questions regarding the sources of political change.

In seeking to understand the civil rights realignment, I draw on three major new data sources. First, I use the earliest available survey data to trace the mass-level relationships among partisanship, economic liberalism, and racial policy views. The analysis uses all the racial policy survey items included in national surveys from January 1937—when the first racial policy item was included—through 1952, along with many additional racial policy questions from the 1950s and 1960s. Starting in 1937 and including a wide range of survey items allow for a more fine-grained understanding of the timing and nature of mass-level change. These early data also provide insight into the timing and dynamics of African Americans' shift toward the Democrats.

Second, the analysis capitalizes on a new database of state party platforms that identify how state Democratic and Republican parties positioned themselves on civil rights from the 1920s through the 1960s. An examination of state platforms again tells a very different story about the timing of partisan change on civil rights from what is evident when one examines national platforms.

Third, I draw on extensive new data concerning congressional action on civil rights. A key limitation of prior studies of congressional decision making on civil rights is that they relied on roll-call votes as their sole measure. This provides an incomplete window into civil rights politics because much of the important action took place off the floor, as advocates struggled to overcome southern-dominated committees that blocked civil rights measures from the chamber floor. In collaborative work with Kathryn Pearson and

Brian Feinstein, I have developed new measures of civil rights views that assess members' support for forcing civil rights measures to the House floor. These new measures tell a much different story about partisan support from that which is evident in the roll-call record.

In addition to these major new data sources, the study employs a range of additional indicators to gain leverage. For example, content analysis of the *New York Times* provides a window into changes in how mainstream political observers viewed the main enemies and friends of New Deal liberalism in the 1930s. Analysis of the *Chicago Defender*—a leading African American newspaper—adds insight into trends in how the African American press viewed the New Deal and labor unions. Systematic examination of liberal publications in the 1930s and 1940s provides evidence of when prominent liberals came to see civil rights as a key element of their program. A survey of convention delegates from 1956 highlights the disjuncture between the position taken by the two parties' national platforms and the views of midlevel party actors.

The results that emerge from these diverse analyses underscore how an integration of historical and behavioral methods allows for progress where experimental approaches are impossible. For historically oriented scholars, this study attempts to demonstrate the value of data on individual-level behavior and attitudes, along with systematic datasets regarding party positioning. For scholars of political behavior, the study aims to illuminate the importance of taking in a long time horizon and focusing on the interplay of multiple institutional venues. For example, the cross-sectional correlation between racial attitudes and partisanship that is evident today is put in much different relief when it is traced back to the late 1930s. Indeed, the relationship of partisanship to many civil rights policy attitudes among white northerners was not consistently stronger in the late 1980s and early 1990s than it had been in the mid-1940s.

Put simply, the inability to construct a satisfactory identification strategy to isolate the effect of a particular causal variable should not lead us to avoid efforts to understand large-scale political developments. Instead, it should be an invitation for broad-reaching efforts to gather the appropriate data needed to gain leverage, however incomplete, toward a fuller understanding of what happened and why it happened.

PLAN OF THE BOOK

This study builds on the work of several scholars who have contributed to a revised understanding of the civil rights realignment. In his important study *The Fifth Freedom*, Anthony Chen shows that Republican opposition to state-level fair employment measures took root in the mid-1940s in the wake of business opposition to these proposals.[47] David Karol finds that northern Democrats emerged as slightly more liberal than Republicans on congressional roll-call votes on civil rights during the 1940s, while also fitting the civil rights case into a broader theory of party-group interactions.[48] Taeku Lee's *Mobilizing Public Opinion* challenges the idea that party elites drove the civil rights shift, instead arguing that a broad-based social movement mobilized mass opinion on civil rights starting in the late 1950s.[49] Most recently, Hans Noel highlights the role of policy intellectuals in bringing racial and economic liberalism together as an ideological package.[50] These works collectively undermine the notion that choices by national party elites in the 1960s were the decisive factor in shaping party alignments and instead suggest that deeper currents in both the Democratic and Republican Parties had a crucial impact on elites' strategic options.[51]

While building explicitly on these works, this book uses a wider empirical base of mass public opinion data, state party platforms, and congressional decision making to develop a new, broader argument about the sources and implications of the civil rights realignment.

The first key question addressed is how racial liberalism became a part of the liberal "project" in American politics. Part 1 takes on this question, charting and explaining the advent of a racially expansive conception of liberalism and the emergence of a new ideological cleavage in which support for civil rights was linked to economic liberalism. Chapter 2 examines the status quo before the start of the civil rights realignment, showing that civil rights was simply not viewed as part of the standard "liberal program" as of the early 1930s. Although African Americans were vocal in attacking Roosevelt's weak civil rights record, they were largely alone. When whites on the left pushed Roosevelt to be a more forthright liberal or progressive, they criticized him for inadequate support for labor, weak business regulation, and insufficient recovery spending—but not for his failure to back civil rights. At this early stage, the "enemies" of a liberal Democratic Party generally were not identified with the South but instead were probusiness Democrats from the Northeast, associated with Al Smith of New York. Economic questions were the key battleground in the eyes of white liberals, and civil rights did not figure in these debates.

Chapter 3 focuses on three developments in the mid- to late 1930s that together helped bring civil rights into mainstream liberals' program. The first is African Americans' emergence as a potential source of votes for northern Democrats. *Pittsburgh Courier* editor Robert Vann and Democratic politician Joseph Guffey worked in tandem to bring African Americans into the Pennsylvania Democratic Party in 1932–34, providing an early example of this potential and in turn inspiring a concerted Democratic effort in 1936 through the Good Neighbor League. The second key change is the rise of the CIO, which pushed for a new interpretation of New Deal liberalism that included civil rights as a component. The third change arose as a response to the first two developments: southern Democrats emerged as key opponents of further extension of the New Deal. These changes brought about a new set of political battle lines, in which a coalition of southern conservatives and Republicans opposed the "ardent New Dealers" of the CIO, African Americans, and other urban liberals.

Chapter 4 documents the deepening and consolidation of these ideological changes as support for civil rights became a defining commitment of a more robust liberal coalition in the 1940s. African American movement activists capitalized on the World War II crisis to force new civil rights issues onto the political agenda—such as fair employment practices and discrimination in the military—and to forge a much broader civil rights coalition. After the war, continued movement activism laid the groundwork for the dramatic fight over the Democratic platform at the convention in 1948. The political work by African American groups, in cooperation with the CIO and other urban liberals, fostered a new understanding of "liberalism" in which support for civil rights was a key marker of one's identity as a liberal.

How did this new liberal coalition—and its expanded conception of liberalism—capture the Democratic Party? The story unfolded in multiple stages and across multiple venues. The first key stage, however, was that racial policy views and attitudes toward New Deal liberalism came into alignment at the mass and midlevels of the party system. Part 2 shows that the civil rights realignment took hold among ordinary voters in the North, northern state parties, and rank-and-file members of the House of Representatives in the late 1930s and 1940s.

Chapters 5 and 6 ask how the mass public fit into the civil rights realignment. Chapter 5 traces the mass-level story among whites. The conventional understanding is that New Deal economic liberalism and racial liberalism were not related among whites until the 1960s or perhaps the late 1950s. According to Carmines and Stimson, the linkage was forged by national elites, while Lee attributes the connection to the actions of movement activists.[52]

Nonetheless, chapter 5 shows that among northern whites, both Democratic partisanship and economic liberalism were linked to support for the major civil rights initiatives on the agenda in the late 1930s and 1940s. Although partisanship was uncorrelated with civil rights views among southern whites, economic conservatism was related to more conservative civil rights views. This connection between economic and racial conservatism in the South provided fertile ground for the GOP's eventual "southern strategy."

The opinion data also suggest that the tie between civil rights liberalism and Democratic partisanship in the North is less clear-cut in terms of racial prejudice and social segregation than on lynching, the poll tax, fair employment practices, and the more general idea of government action to counter discrimination against African Americans and other minorities.[53] Northern white Democrats' views in the 1930s–1950s—more supportive than Republicans' when it comes to many civil rights policies but similar to their Republican counterparts on policies that encourage more intimate social mixing—presage the ambivalence that northern Democrats would exhibit toward busing and related measures in the 1970s and beyond. Still, the general message from the opinion data is clear: economically liberal northern Democrats provided much stronger support for most of the leading civil rights policy initiatives on the agenda than did economically conservative Republicans.

Chapter 6 explores the mass-level changes among African Americans. The entry of African Americans created a new constituency for Democratic politicians; decades of migration from the South magnified these voters' potential importance in northern swing states. It has been difficult for scholars to study the African American realignment because of limited samples of African Americans in most of the early polls. However, the chapter leverages information across a substantial number of polls in order to provide the most comprehensive study of the African American realignment to date.

In addition to assessing the timing of African Americans' shift to the Democrats, the analysis highlights African Americans' distinctive economic liberalism in the late 1930s and 1940s. Perhaps not surprisingly given their socioeconomic situation, these citizens stand out for their liberal views across a range of issues. An important point, not lost on political observers in the 1930s–1950s, was that African Americans' strong economic liberalism left them significantly closer to the Democrats on issues other than civil rights, making it more difficult for Republicans to envision winning back a substantial share of African American voters.

The patterns of mass opinion described in chapters 5 and 6 created a permissive context for northern Democratic Party politicians as they considered incorporating racial liberalism into their interpretation of New Deal liberalism, just as it fostered opportunities for Republican politicians contemplating an alliance with southern white conservatives. However, translating this permissive context into changes in party alignments involved groups and movements working to force civil rights higher on the policy agenda and pushing state parties and individual members of Congress to adapt to these new pressures.

Chapter 7 traces the incorporation of civil rights into the program of state Democratic parties in the North and compares their stance to that of state Republican parties. The main evidence base is a collection of approximately a thousand state party platforms from 1920 to 1968.[54] The platforms show that neither party paid much attention to civil rights prior to the late 1930s, but starting in the 1930s and accelerating in the 1940s, northern state Democratic parties moved to the left on civil rights. Their civil rights positions were generally more liberal than those of their same-state GOP counterparts by 1944–46. Pro–civil rights positions were also more prevalent in states with a substantial African American population, high levels of urbanization, union density, and Jewish population. Thus the same variables that were linked to strong support for New Deal liberalism after 1937 also came to be associated with state parties taking a strongly pro–civil rights position.

Chapter 8 argues that rank-and-file northern Democrats in the House of Representatives also responded to activist and constituent pressure for civil rights by the late 1930s and early 1940s. These locally rooted politicians proved willing to take on southern Democrats and party leaders by signing discharge petitions that extricated civil rights bills from obstructionist committees, forcing the measures to the House floor. Prior to the late 1930s, northern Republicans had outpaced northern Democrats in their civil rights support, and economic liberalism was essentially unrelated to civil rights support among Democrats. Northern Democrats showed increased civil rights support by the end of the 1930s, displacing northern Republicans as the leading advocates of civil rights during World War II. The Democrats most supportive of civil rights came from the highly urban, unionized areas that were most associated with New Deal liberalism, while the smaller number of GOP supporters tended to come from atypical districts for the party. The gap between the parties was substantial from the mid-1940s onward.

If the mass and midlevels of the party system had been transformed by the end of the 1940s, why did it take so long to complete the partisan realignment on race—and what finally brought about the culmination of the realignment? Part 3 takes up these questions, highlighting the tension between national party elites who sought to suppress the civil rights issue and mass- and midlevel party actors who wanted to change their party's position. The civil rights movement ultimately played the pivotal role in overcoming this impasse.

Chapter 9 analyzes the battle for control of the national Democratic Party as the players empowered by the coalitional and ideological changes after 1937 battled not just against southern Democrats but also against national party leaders desperate to hold together the fragile North-South coalition. The bland national platforms that Democrats adopted in the 1940s and 1950s belied the vigorous efforts by the liberal civil rights coalition to push for a strong platform plank, which became a regular focal point of dispute starting in 1944. The national platform fights exemplify both the much stronger push for civil rights on the part of important Democratic constituencies (compared to Republicans) and the efforts of national party leaders to avoid a clear stand. A survey of convention delegates from 1956 shows that despite the two parties' similar national platforms, the distribution of delegate preferences was decidedly more pro–civil rights among Democrats.

As movement activists engaged in direct action to raise the salience of civil rights issues, it became harder for national Democratic elites to limit the impact of these underlying preferences. Where the party's presidential candidates and top congressional leaders in the 1940s and 1950s could generally get away with straddling civil rights, the pressure to take a clear pro–civil rights stand became much more intense starting in the late 1950s. Put simply, by the time Lyndon Johnson entered the White House, it was clear that failure to lead on civil rights would result in serious troubles holding on to the nomination. This shift reflected the intersection of two forces: civil rights activism had sparked a crisis that demanded a response while the earlier changes in the Democratic coalition had created a clear balance of power within the party regarding the appropriate response to that crisis.

Chapter 10 turns to the battle for control of the national GOP and asks how the conservative Goldwater forces triumphed over the moderates who had led the national party for more than two decades. As noted above, the idea of a realignment premised on Republican appeals to disaffected southern conservatives had been a topic of political conversation from 1937 onward. But many national leaders were wary of such a shift, which would tip the balance of power in the party decisively toward its conservative wing, risking a loss of support in urban, liberal states. The chapter analyzes GOP strategy toward civil rights in the 1940s–1950s, as party leaders sought to balance the rank-and-file's (general) lack of interest in pursuing vigorous action with the perceived need to appear at least mildly supportive in order to avoid alienating moderate voters in states like New York and Illinois.

The rough balance of power within the party was broken as Eisenhower's party building in the South created an institutional foothold for conservatives to gain power within the GOP. The Goldwater movement both capitalized on and reinforced these shifts. With most Republican voters critical of Kennedy for pushing too fast on civil rights, and with state parties in the South and West largely under the control of conservatives hostile to civil rights, racial conservatives were well positioned to gain the upper hand.[55] Even as Everett Dirksen and other congressional leaders continued to try to position the party as at least mildly pro–civil rights—providing crucial support for passage of the landmark legislation of 1964 and 1965—the coalitional bases of the party had been gradually transformed from beneath them, creating a party landscape that was now decidedly tilted in favor of the conservatives.

The final chapter turns to the theoretical and methodological implications of the civil rights case, with a focus on party theory and on the challenges of systematically studying major political transformations. The chapter also explores the civil rights realignment's implications for today's politics, considering the politics of backlash and the tensions facing contemporary Democrats' approach to racial issues.

PART 1

Transforming American Liberalism

CHAPTER 2

Race

THE EARLY NEW DEAL'S BLIND SPOT

WHEN FRANKLIN ROOSEVELT was elected president in 1932, civil rights for African Americans was not a part of his agenda. When one considered what it meant to be a New Deal liberal as that concept first took shape in 1933–35, racial policy views were essentially absent as a consideration. By the late 1930s, however, racial liberalism had become tied to New Deal liberalism. The connection was by no means airtight: there were still plenty of southerners who identified as New Dealers but were vigorous defenders of Jim Crow. There also were many northern Democrats who were indifferent or hostile to policies to promote greater racial equality. However, when observers spoke of "100% New Dealers" or "ardent New Dealers," the individuals they were referring to generally had staked out a pro–civil rights position contrary to the southern Democrats who had become the most visible representatives of a more limited understanding of the party's agenda.

In this chapter I show that civil rights was not part of the programmatic liberal vision in the early 1930s. The focus here is on the issue content of liberalism as understood by its main supporters and by political observers, along with the political cleavages and factional conflicts that were seen as crucial to the liberal project's success. In making this argument, I draw on the key liberal and African American publications of the period, as well as early efforts by social scientists to measure political ideology.

It is important to study this early period, before the first stirrings of the civil rights realignment, because any analysis of political change requires a thorough examination of the starting point. The remaining chapters of part 1 will trace the advent of a more racially expansive conception of liberalism and the emergence of a new ideological cleavage and coalition defined, in part, by civil rights. Specifically, the rise of the CIO and the entry of African Americans into the Democratic coalition in the North—coupled with southern Democrats' furious reaction to these developments—transformed New Deal liberalism in the late 1930s, forging a linkage between racial and economic liberalism that would be strengthened in the following decade amid the disruptions of World War II and an important wave of movement activism.

The first part of this chapter shows that the key cleavage in the Democratic Party early in the New Deal was an economic one dividing the "liberal" (as it was understood at the time) South and West against conservative northeastern business interests. It is well-known, of course, that Roosevelt himself avoided taking a clear stand on behalf of civil rights for most of his term. Roosevelt's refusal is often attributed simply to the new president's deference to southern Democrats, whose votes he needed for his recovery program. This explanation is correct insofar as it goes, but the challenges facing civil rights in the early 1930s ran deeper than Roosevelt's personal political calculations.

Among advocates of liberal or progressive policy innovation at the time, the chief enemies were not southern conservatives. Instead, liberals identified the business-friendly, mostly northeastern politicians who, often in alliance with city machines, controlled much of the national party apparatus as the main obstacle preventing the Democratic Party from becoming a force for liberalism. As of 1932 the question of whether Roosevelt would be a genuine "liberal" leader was posed as one pitting the West and the South against the more conservative East. This definition of the political battle lines left civil rights entirely out of the picture. As a result, when white liberals and progressives challenged Roosevelt from the left in the early to mid-1930s—as they often did—his tepid support for civil rights was rarely, if ever, a focus of their complaints. Instead, liberals typically complained that Roosevelt's policies were too conciliatory toward business and insufficiently supportive of organized labor and government regulation. Even as individual liberals at times endorsed civil rights, they treated that concern as separate from the more important battle over economic policy. Statements of the "liberal program" typically left civil rights off the list of priorities. Roosevelt's ambivalent stand reflected *both* southern resistance and the limited pressure from liberals and progressives to incorporate civil rights into the New Deal agenda.

In this political context, southern Democratic leaders were not simply potential veto players who had to be accommodated. Instead, such individuals as Vice President John Nance Garner (D-TX), Senate leader Joseph Robinson (D-AR), and Finance Committee chairman Pat Harrison (D-MS) were widely identified as *the* go-to people responsible for pushing Roosevelt's program through Congress. As the New Deal became more identified with the CIO and labor-oriented liberalism late in the 1930s, Garner would assume leadership of anti–New Deal Democrats and Harrison would be bypassed for Senate leadership owing to Roosevelt's intervention on behalf of the more liberal

Alben Barkley of Kentucky (see chapter 3). But prior to 1937 Garner and his supporters were regarded as loyal lieutenants, allies in the battle against the conservative northeastern wing.

The second part of the chapter considers the obstacles African Americans faced in attempting to gain meaningful inclusion in the New Deal coalition and program in the early 1930s. From the start of the New Deal era, African American leaders sought to take advantage of the ferment in Washington to bring concerns about civil rights into the mainstream of the liberal program. The new administration did reach out to African Americans with a few gestures—such as the formation of the so-called Black Cabinet—but African American leaders quickly learned that their concerns were not a New Deal priority. Within Congress there were a handful of liberal New Dealers who advocated for civil rights, most notably Edward Costigan (D-CO) and Robert Wagner (D-NY), the lead sponsors of the antilynching bill in 1934. But as chapter 8 shows, support for civil rights in Congress was not closely related to standard measures of liberalism in these early New Deal years, and northern Democrats generally fell short of their GOP counterparts in civil rights support. When African Americans looked for political allies in the early 1930s, they sought backing from Republicans and Democrats, without any assumption that liberal Democrats were an especially likely source of support.

While mainstream liberals did not link civil rights to their core economic program, the Communist Party increasingly attempted to appeal to African Americans as a constituency for its revolutionary program. For African American leaders, however, this support was fraught with risks and a source of considerable ambivalence. The rise of the CIO was especially important because it offered a potential ally for African Americans that would be more firmly rooted in the New Deal coalition, rather than a distrusted outsider.[1] But as of the early New Deal years, there was no group within the core New Deal Democratic coalition that African Americans could count on as allies.

The third part of the chapter turns to evidence from social scientists' efforts to assess political ideology. The purpose of this section is to show that those studying political attitudes generally shared the same perspective on ideology as did political elites in this period: "liberalism," as conventionally understood, did not embrace concerns about civil rights. When social psychologists and other scholars sought to identify "liberals," "progressives," and "conservatives," economic issues and civil liberties concerns were front and center, but civil rights were generally absent. Again, civil rights was not seen as part of a broader liberal program. As chapters 3 and 4 make clear, this would soon change. But understanding the nature and significance of this change first requires an examination of the gap separating civil rights from the mainstream liberal program as the New Deal first took shape.

SECTIONAL CLEAVAGES IN THE EARLY NEW DEAL

The story of civil rights in the 1930s is, in part, a story of Franklin Roosevelt repeatedly rebuffing requests from the National Association for the Advancement of Colored People (NAACP) and other civil rights advocates that he publicly endorse mild legislation to punish the most notorious human rights abuse, lynching. As civil rights advocates, led by the NAACP, pushed for antilynching legislation in the Senate in 1934, Roosevelt refused to provide the boost that advocates believed might overcome a southern filibuster. The president reportedly told Walter White of the NAACP that "if I come out for the anti-lynching bill, they [i.e., the southern Democrats in Congress] will block every bill I ask Congress to pass to keep America from collapsing. I just can't take that risk."[2]

The African American press was keenly aware of Roosevelt's silence and, as discussed below, was full of lively debate concerning whether the material benefits provided by the New Deal were sufficient to offset Roosevelt's shortcomings when it came to civil rights. However, white liberals and progressives looked to other policies in assessing whether Roosevelt was one of their own. As shown in chapter 4, by the 1940s a Democratic candidate's stance on civil rights would be taken as a key indicator of the candidate's liberal bona fides; the issue played no such role as most liberals and progressives evaluated Roosevelt in his first term.

The Liberal-Conservative Cleavage in the 1932 Election

Historians have long emphasized that the election contest between Franklin Roosevelt and Herbert Hoover in 1932 was not a sharply ideological affair. The issue with the clearest dividing line between the two major parties was prohibition, with Democrats embracing repeal and Republicans—though edging away from their earlier defense of the Eighteenth Amendment—still clearly identified with prohibition's defenders.[3] Observing the campaign, the philosopher and progressive reformer John Dewey complained that "here we are in the midst of the greatest crisis since the Civil War, and the only thing the two national parties seem to want to debate is booze."[4]

Roosevelt claimed to favor a more vigorous response to the Depression than did Hoover, but the Democrat refused to make the nature of that vigorous response clear to voters. With the election looming, the *New Republic* dismissed the Democratic Party as "a sprawling and disjointed affair combining some of the most reactionary elements in the country with some of the progressive ones" and repeatedly criticized Roosevelt for failing to choose sides among these contending elements.[5] Roosevelt's speeches included appeals to balanced budgets and "economy" in government, calls to save the destitute from starvation, support for expanded public works, and hints about the need for cooperative planning between government and business. Critics on the left charged that Roosevelt's lack of a coherent program was a ploy to appeal to both the liberal and conservative factions of his divided party.[6]

Given how the New Deal and Fair Deal unfolded, one might assume that the "reactionary" forces within the Democratic Party were primarily southerners concerned about maintaining the Jim Crow system. However, when one canvasses liberal publications such as the *New Republic* and the *Nation*, it is clear that in the minds of early 1930s liberals, the most formidable enemies of a progressive Democratic Party were not southerners but northeastern, probusiness conservatives and machine politicians.

The most prominent leaders of this eastern wing included 1928 Democratic nominee Al Smith, along with a coterie of business leaders connected to the former New York governor. The first Catholic major party presidential nominee, Smith is remembered today as an important figure in forging a more urban Democratic coalition drawing heavy support from a range of ethnic groups.[7] As of 1932, however, Smith had positioned himself as the leader of conservative Democrats opposed to a dramatic expansion in the government's role in response to the Depression. Following Roosevelt's "forgotten man" speech—which emphasized the need to help those at the bottom of the economic structure—Smith used a Democratic Jefferson Day dinner as an opportunity to denounce "any candidate who persists in any demagogic appeal to the masses of the working people of this country to destroy themselves by setting class against class and rich against poor."[8]

Smith's public rebuke of the Democratic frontrunner received front-page coverage across the country.[9] Indeed, the Smith-Roosevelt feud was one of the most discussed stories during the 1932 election contest, as it laid bare a deep ideological cleavage within the Democratic Party. Smith's ally, corporate executive John J. Raskob, chaired the Democratic National Committee (DNC) from 1928 to 1932.[10] Liberals charged that the Democrats were a "kept party," drawn to conservative, business-friendly policies by their reliance on Raskob and his allies to fund its campaigns.[11] Other leaders of this conservative group included 1924 presidential nominee John W. Davis and Jouett Shouse, the chairman of the DNC's executive committee and a close ally of Smith. Within a few years these four prominent Democrats would all bolt the party and back the anti–New Deal Liberty League, but in the context of the 1932 campaign, a key question was whether Roosevelt was sufficiently moderate to win over at least some of these conservatives.

As a result, Roosevelt's strategy of ambiguity in the 1932 campaign was largely interpreted as an effort to hold on to the electoral votes of the conservative East. In mid-August 1932 the *New Republic* editorialized that Roosevelt ought to focus his campaign on the progressive West, rather than allowing himself "to be pushed too far toward the conservative side merely as a matter of Eastern political strategy."[12] The editors argued that Roosevelt needed to show the country who he really is, claiming that it would be "far better political strategy than trying to convince the so-called interests of the East that he is a 'safe' man to have in the White House."[13] A few weeks later, when a series of Roosevelt speeches on the railroads continued to straddle questions of government regulation and control, the *New Republic* noted that "it is recognized, however, that the Democratic strategy is to get support from the conservative East, without which the election of their ticket would be hard to obtain."[14] Similarly the *Nation* complained that Roosevelt was showing himself to be "safe and sound for Wall Street"—winning the support of such conservatives as Bernard Baruch—rather than fulfilling the role of "the great reformer, or radical, that he has been sedulously cracked up to be."[15]

For Democrats to become a liberal party, the forces of the West and South would need to triumph over the business interests of the East and thus to "Say Goodbye to Mr. Raskob," as the *New Republic* put it.[16] In looking forward to the 1932 Democratic Party platform, the *Nation* expressed optimism that "there is genuine reason to expect something intelligent and constructive in a platform drafted by such thinking men as Cordell Hull, Tom Walsh, Carter Glass, Tom Connally, Bob Wagner, and Frank Walsh."[17] Hull, Glass, and Connally were prominent southerners; Glass would turn out to be an early critic of the New Deal, while Connally would, by the late 1930s, be a leader of the Southern Caucus in the Senate.[18] Well before the end of the 1930s, it would be inconceivable for liberals to look to men such as Glass and Connally for constructive policy leadership; but as of 1932 their distance from northeastern big business and financial interests meant that they were potential allies, along with western progressives, such as Tom Walsh of Montana, and labor-friendly New Yorkers Wagner and Frank Walsh.[19]

Leading liberals of the time assessed politicians based on their positions on economic issues, and the economic cleavage generally put southern Democrats on the "correct" side. In evaluating newly prominent Democrats who had emerged in the 1932 campaign, the *Nation*'s editorial writers reserved special praise for victorious border state Senate candidate Bennett Clark of Missouri. The *Nation* argued that Clark adopted "a liberal view of economic questions, which is the real test of any candidate." The evidence for Clark's liberalism was clear: he supported federal supervision of public utilities and public power development at Muscle Shoals (which became the original base of the Tennessee Valley Authority); endorsed Robert Wagner's relief and unemployment bills; and backed shorter working hours, lower tariffs, strong antitrust enforcement, and using federal taxes to break up concentrations of wealth.[20] These positions essentially defined what it meant to hold down the left wing of the Democratic Party in 1932.

In the constellation of political forces at work in the early 1930s, the question was whether Roosevelt would be pulled toward the conservative, business interests of the East or instead would advocate a more aggressive liberal program that targeted corporate privilege and was associated with the West, South, and nascent labor movement. Among leading progressives, the "problem" of establishing the Democrats as a liberal party was less about wresting power from conservative southerners than it was a matter of defeating the probusiness eastern leaders associated with Smith and Raskob. Sectionalism, in this context, pitted the progressive West against the conservative East rather than the North versus the South.

Liberal Critiques of the Early New Deal

Once Roosevelt assumed office and the New Deal took shape, the new president fitfully began to resolve the question of where he stood in relation to the old, business-friendly leadership of his party. From the start the administration included conservatives in key positions of influence. Most prominently, Bureau of the Budget director Lewis Douglas, Treasury Secretary William Woodin, and National Recovery Administration (NRA) head General Hugh Johnson were identified as probusiness conservatives.[21] But as Ira Katznelson argues persuasively, the early New Deal also included actors offering a potentially radical vision of remaking the American economic system that easily outstripped the more limited calls for economic regulation that would become a staple of the late New Deal.[22] "Brain Trusters" Rex Tugwell and Adolph Berle, along with Harry Hopkins and Harold Ickes, pushed for aggressive government action that alarmed their conservative counterparts.

Liberals scrutinized every Roosevelt decision for signs of which faction was ascendant. For the first two years of Roosevelt's term, the answer was not entirely clear. Liberal journalist Jonathan Mitchell wrote in November 1933 that the new administration "is essentially a coalition government" with agencies such as the NRA and Agricultural Adjustment Act (AAA) divided between liberals and conservatives and Roosevelt using "stilts of the Right and the Left." Mitchell derided the president's desire to hold on to both business and working-class support, noting that "it is possible that only when Mr. Roosevelt feels he can touch the men of the bonus army with one hand, and Mr. Astor, with the other, can he function at the top of his capacity."[23]

Indeed, Roosevelt faced nearly as much criticism from the left as from the right during his first three years in office.[24] Perhaps most notably, Huey Long's Share Our Wealth program dominated the political news throughout much of 1934 as the Louisiana populist skyrocketed to prominence. Meanwhile, members of Congress pushed farm mortgage forgiveness, currency expansion through the remonetization of silver, and expensive bonus payments to veterans as cures to the Depression, all policies that Roosevelt resisted as irresponsible. The mixed ideological content of the early New Deal was underscored when *Collier's* published a special booklet, *Your Congress-man's Vote on the New Deal*, in 1934. The list of roll calls featured six cases in which the administration, and thus the "New Deal," were clearly identi-fied with the *conservative* position, compared to twelve where it was situated on the "left" of the debate.[25]

This battle over the contours of the early New Deal puts in stark relief the challenge facing civil rights supporters as they sought to have their concerns incorporated into the mainstream liberal program. Put simply, Roosevelt faced considerable criticism from self-identified progressives and liberals for his many compromises with conservative interests, but liberals largely ignored his failure to advocate for civil rights.

There are several indicators of the separation between civil rights and the mainstream liberal program in the early New Deal era. For example, in April 1934 Paul U. Kellogg—a leading social reformer—spearheaded an effort to put together a program for Roosevelt that would greatly expand the scope of the New Deal. The Kellogg group constituted a who's who of liberal reformers, including John Dewey, ACLU cofounder Morris Ernst, *Nation* editor Freda Kirchwey, former *Nation* editor (and continuing con-tributor) Oscar Garrison Villard, the Consumer Union's Lucy Randolph Mason (who later became a leading CIO organizer in the drive for biracial unionism in the South), Senator Edward Costigan (D-CO), the famous an-thropologist Franz Boas, and other prominent New Deal supporters. Several of these individuals were supportive of civil rights for African Americans and involved in the NAACP's efforts to pass antilynching legislation. Indeed, Villard had helped found the NAACP, Costigan sponsored the 1934 anti-lynching bill in the Senate, and Kirchwey, Ernst, and Mason all supported the NAACP's efforts to pass the bill.[26]

However, the bold, detailed plan that the group presented to Roosevelt made no mention of civil rights or the problems facing African Americans.[27] The group's statement began with the observation that "the acid test of the New Deal lies in its effect on the actual distribution of the wealth which our machine age creates but which we have yet to find the way to spread out and use." It proceeds to detail the ways in which an expanded New Deal could meet that test: expanded unionization, strong minimum wage laws, old-age pensions, national health insurance, unemployment insurance, national hous-ing assistance, and greater government planning. The long list of priorities included virtually every idea that would become a staple of urban liberalism as it came to full flower in the late 1930s and the 1940s. Its inclusion of government planning alongside strong unions and social welfare policies suggests that these early liberals were even *more* radical on some dimensions than were the liberals of the 1940s and 1950s.[28]

Yet the plan had one noteworthy omission: civil rights was entirely ab-sent from the program. The Kellogg Papers contain a series of drafts of the document as well as letters discussing what ought to be included.[29] None of these materials even mentions civil rights as a consideration. Roosevelt's view that political prudence militated against a clear stance on civil rights was hardly a stretch for the president when even the boldest versions of the liberal program at the time—put forward by the leading advocates outside the administration—omitted civil rights.

The Kellogg group's statement was by no means an isolated indicator of civil rights' place in the liberal program. Following Democrats' surprising gains in the 1934 midterms, journalist Raymond Gram Swing published an article in the *Nation* detailing the agenda facing Congress.[30] Swing argued that following two years of improvisation, "now begins some permanent construction" for the New Deal. The two fundamental issues that would define the New Deal's meaning would be the NRA and Social Security. Would the NRA provide a strengthened, coequal role for labor and consumers, or would it continue to be dominated by business interests? Would Social Security include medical coverage and a permanent public works jobs program, or would it be a much more limited pension program? Strikingly, the article does not discuss whether domestic or agricultural workers would be included in the new Social Security system. The failure to include these workers initially left out the majority of African American workers. Beyond these two central questions, Swing listed a wide range of other important issues facing Congress, including housing, the bonus, relief spending, monetary expansion, the thirty-hour bill, the Wagner labor bill, amendments to the AAA, banking legislation, the St. Lawrence Seaway, and railroad reconstruction. The extensive summary of liberal priorities for the new Congress omitted the lynching bill that had died in the face of a southern filibuster in 1934, as well as other civil rights issues.

A year later, when a *New Republic* editorial laid out a program for a new party to take the place of Roosevelt's muddled Democrats, civil rights and race were again off the radar screen. The editors argued that Roosevelt's mild regulatory strategy had mostly failed but that the alternative his opponents in the Liberty League offered was even worse. As a result, the United States needed a new party dedicated to extensive redistributive taxation and greater worker control over economic institutions to put it on the right path. Once again, the article outlining the proposed party program—which was radical in many ways—did not mention civil rights.[31]

The liberal press continued to give considerable coverage in 1936 to the idea of forming a new party that would serve as a left-wing alternative to the Democrats. A farmer-labor conference held in June 1936 attracted eighty-five delegates from twenty-three states.[32] The conference adopted a resolution favoring the "formation of a national party of farmers, labor, liberal middle class and professional and unemployed workers' organizations." The group's platform included the abolition of monopoly, public ownership of natural resources, taxes on high incomes to finance an expansive social security program, the thirty-hour workweek, protections for small farmers, legislation to curb the Supreme Court, and opposition to war.[33] Just as was the case with the farmer-labor agitation on behalf of Robert La Follette in 1924, this progressive program once again left civil rights out.[34]

A further indicator of the place of civil rights in the consciousness of prominent liberals comes from a survey conducted by the *New Republic* in the run-up to the 1936 election. The magazine polled well-known "progressives" about their vote intention.[35] The vast majority favored Roosevelt, with a smattering of votes for the Socialist Norman Thomas and Communist candidate Earl Browder. Over the course of a month, the *New Republic* published the explanations offered by forty-seven of these progressives for their vote choice. Even many Roosevelt voters sharply criticized the president's tepid liberalism. Roosevelt's relief policies were inadequate to meet urgent public needs; he favored business interests; he was a slow and reluctant supporter of labor rights.

Not a single letter mentioned Roosevelt's refusal to back civil rights. Only one letter identified southern interests as an obstacle to liberalism: Upton Sinclair noted that "Roosevelt has had a very difficult task—that of turning the Democratic Party from the party of Southern landlords and Northern corruptionists into a party of progress and social justice."[36] The reactionary forces identified in the other letters were financial rather than southern. For example, Stephen Wise noted: "The President has had to face and still faces the challenge of the ruthless tories who demand security for themselves and for the value of their securities, but ... are unconcerned about the life and well-being of the millions of those workers who together with their families constitute our America."[37] Another progressive, Mary Van Kleeck, observed that "compromises with reactionary forces have been all too evident during the Democratic administration," but "these same forces are now massed behind the Republican Party."[38]

Following the election, both the *Nation* and the *New Republic* attempted to push a more ambitious program for the next four years. The *Nation* published a series of short statements by thirteen leading liberals and radicals about the agenda for Roosevelt's second term; only Communist leader Earl Browder's statement discussed race.[39] The *New Republic* ran a series of eleven articles on the "Next Four Years," outlining a progressive program across a range of policy domains. Not a single article mentioned civil rights or the plight of African Americans more generally as a concern. Only one article depicted southern interests as an obstacle to liberalism; in dismissing the prospects for a constitutional amendment to counter the Supreme Court's hostility to labor legislation, Thomas Reed Powell wrote that "southern states and states predominantly agrarian are not enthusiastic supporters of the labor views of the editors of *The New Republic*."[40] But the South was still not high on the radar screen as an obstacle for liberal reformers. Instead, the big question remained whether the defeat of Smith and the Liberty League in the 1936 election meant that Roosevelt would finally lead a genuine liberal movement.

Put simply, while economic liberals were among those who supported limited civil rights initiatives in the early 1930s, the issue was not a core part of the liberal program and was rarely a point of emphasis. A systematic search of coverage in leading liberal publications—such as the *Nation* and *New Republic*—indicates that the publications backed the antilynching bill and sought a fair trial for the Scottsboro defendants. As Hans Noel argues, liberal policy intellectuals had become at least mild advocates for African American interests by the early 1930s.[41] However, the liberal journals' observations on race in these early years were typically passing comments; they did not link civil rights concerns to a broader programmatic vision. Furthermore, I found no examples of the *New Republic* criticizing Roosevelt for his timidity on the lynching bill or the Scottsboro case, and only scant, generally indirect criticism in the *Nation*.[42] Leading liberals found many reasons for attacking Roosevelt during his first term, but his failure to lead on civil rights was rarely one of these grounds. To most white liberals, fulfilling the New Deal's promise was about winning economic policy battles deemed entirely separate from the race question. The rise of the CIO and of southern resistance to expanding the New Deal would soon lead liberals to revise their understanding of what it would take for liberalism to triumph, but the connection between civil rights and economic liberalism remained tenuous, at best, as of 1936.

Southern Democrats: Friends of the Early New Deal

With racial issues so low on the radar screen of prominent liberals, southern Democrats in Congress were widely viewed as key players helping enact the New Deal, rather than as obstacles to liberal policy innovation. When considering the administration's friends and enemies in Congress, southern Democrats were overwhelmingly counted among the friends.

In discussions of the New Deal's prospects, several high-profile southern lawmakers were identified as "administration leaders" or "stalwarts." Joseph Robinson of Arkansas, the majority leader in the Senate, was routinely referred to as an "administration leader" or the "administration's man."[43] A few stories noted that Robinson personally may not have been favorable to specific New Deal policies—particularly as labor began to inch up onto the agenda, with the rise of the Southern Tenant Farmers' Union in 1934–35—but he was nonetheless regarded as a crucial FDR ally.[44] *Time* magazine used the headline "Good Soldier" for an article on Robinson's work for the administration and referred to "the White House orders to Top Sergeant Robinson [which] he will do his dogged best" to carry out. In addition, the story noted that Roosevelt is able "to rely on men like Mississippi's artful Pat Harrison and shrewd Vice President Garner" to push his program.[45]

Time's feature on Finance chair Harrison, published in 1936, refers to Roosevelt depending on him and Robinson as "seasoned stalwarts to direct his battles in the Senate." *Time* credited Harrison with helping pass a range of Roosevelt's initiatives and labeled him "a level headed party regular whose lack of enthusiasm for some New Deal experiments has not abated his zeal helping bring them into being, he has served his President with a loyalty which cannot go unrewarded." Harrison faced the prospect of a challenge from the left in his 1936 reelection bid, with the populist Theodore Bilbo backing Mississippi governor Mike Conner's primary campaign, but *Time* concluded that Mississippi voters "may yet be told that a Democratic President of 1936 cannot do without [Harrison]."[46]

Robinson and Harrison arguably trailed only Vice President John Nance Garner in their importance as Roosevelt intermediaries with Congress. The Texas Democrat had arrived in the House of Representatives in 1903 and was Speaker of the House from 1931 to 1933. Although Garner's status as a wealthy landowner in Uvalde, Texas, hardly predisposed him to liberal policy experimentation, the vice president spent much of Roosevelt's first term on Capitol Hill, working to help pass the president's program and to sidetrack initiatives that Roosevelt viewed as counterproductive. A cover story in *Time* published in June 1935 noted that as a frugal landowner, it is doubtful that Garner believed in "the redistribution of wealth, in Title II of the Banking Bill (government-controlled central bank), in AAA crop restriction." But once the president decides on a policy, Garner works closely with "Leader Robinson, Whip Harrison, and other Administration men of [the] House and Senate" to see that it is enacted. Garner, in particular, was credited with passage of the recent work relief bill in much the same form that the president desired. *Time* concluded that Garner is better at delivering "backstage political licks for the Administration than any Vice President in modern times" and that he had proven "a very useful helper to the New Deal."[47]

Roll-call data reinforce this view that southern Democrats were core New Deal supporters in these early years. When one examines first-dimension DW-NOMINATE scores, the standard measure scholars use to tap economic liberalism, the typical southern Democrat was actually a bit to the left of the typical northern Democrat during the first two New Deal Congresses.[48] Even if one narrows the focus to roll calls that involve social welfare or economic regulation, southern Democrats were just as liberal as northern Democrats during Roosevelt's first two Congresses.[49] As such, roll-call voting by southern members of Congress, along with the behavior of key southern leaders, provided few indications that the South would pose a decisive obstacle to liberals' programmatic goals, as defined during Roosevelt's first term.

The Uncomfortable Fit of African Americans in the New Deal Coalition

While southern Democrats such as Garner, Harrison, and Robinson were considered core administration supporters, African Americans' connections to the New Deal were far more tenuous. As chapter 3 details, there were some signs of outreach by particular Democratic leaders in the early to mid-1930s, which accelerated in 1936 with the rise of Labor's Non-Partisan League (LNPL). But white political observers in the early 1930s tended to view the idea of an African American Democrat as an anachronism. When the first African American Democrat was elected to the House in the 1934 Democratic landslide, Arthur Krock of the *New York Times* commented that "elections, like cyclones, bring freak results. A Democratic Negro, Arthur R. Mitchell, retired the veteran Representative Oscar De Priest, champion of his race, and presents a social 'cloakroom' problem for the Southern Democrats."[50]

More generally, African Americans were not depicted as an important constituency for the Democratic Party or for liberal programmatic innovation as of 1932–34. When progressive advocates of a third party talked of rooting their new party in organized groups of voters, they referred to labor, farmers, and even white-collar workers but not African Americans.[51] Given that more than 70 percent of African Americans lived in the South—where the vast majority were disenfranchised by the poll tax, literacy test, white primary, and other suffrage restrictions—it is perhaps not surprising that most liberals did not view African American voters as an important target. However, the incongruity highlighted by Krock—the idea of an African American Democrat in close proximity to the southern-dominated Democratic Caucus in Congress—underscores the gulf separating the early New Deal from civil rights concerns.

While most white liberals rarely criticized Roosevelt for his failure to lead on civil rights, African American leaders and journalists repeatedly expressed their frustration with the president. Early in Roosevelt's term there were signs that the administration would reach out to African Americans in a meaningful way. Eleanor Roosevelt had close ties to civil rights advocates and interceded to give Walter White and other African American leaders a measure of access to the president. The formation of an informal "Black Cabinet" of racial advisers on staff at New Deal agencies seemed to harbor the potential for closer connections between the administration and African Americans. Also known as the Federal Council on Negro Affairs, the group met regularly and helped gather information about how various New Deal programs were affecting African Americans.[52] Several New Deal administrators also sought to implement policies in ways that were fair to African Americans. Most notably, Harold Ickes, as head of the Public Works Administration (PWA), fought against racial discrimination in hiring and to ensure that construction projects benefited the African American community. Harry Hopkins of the Works Progress Administration (WPA) and the National Youth Administration's Aubrey Williams also sought a fairer distribution of benefits to African Americans despite facing opposition from local officials.[53]

But these hopeful signs gave way to frustration as it became clear that the balance of power within the administration was decidedly tilted away from those pushing racial progress. In contrast to Ickes's PWA, many New Deal agencies, such as the Civilian Conservation Corps and TVA, incorporated segregation and discriminatory job allocations directly into their program implementation.[54] The United States Department of Agriculture (USDA), led by Henry Wallace—who would become a fierce civil rights advocate in the 1940s—allowed rampant discrimination in New Deal farm programs and was one of the most frequent targets of African American complaints.[55]

In this context of disappointment, a conference at Howard University in May 1935, led by left-wing activist John P. Davis and political scientist Ralph Bunche, condemned the New Deal for discriminating against African Americans. Attended by a wide range of African American leaders, the conference "damned every New Deal program as inimical to the black masses."[56] The gathering led to the formation of the National Negro Congress (NNC), which offered a more radical alternative to the NAACP in pushing for civil rights.

Looking ahead to the 1936 election, the *Chicago Defender* editorialized that "New Deal love is not sufficiently brotherly" to extend to the subject of lynching, noting that this verdict is "sustained in no uncertain terms by the deathly silence of the President himself." The *Defender* went on to question whether the administration's gestures toward African Americans reflected genuine progress: the paper argued that it is "noticeable that the 'black cabinet' failed to function in the interest of their Race while the [lynching] bill was pending." The paper concluded that this inactivity suggests that cabinet members "are not there to speak in defense of their own people, but are acting more in the capacity of political shock absorbers for those they are supposed to advise."[57] The NAACP's *Crisis* devoted considerable attention to the question of whether the benefits that New Deal relief programs provided to African Americans were sufficient to warrant support for the administration, given its repeated failure to counter discrimination.[58]

From the vantage point of civil rights advocates themselves, potential supporters included both New Deal advocates and critics. As the NAACP sought to pressure Roosevelt to endorse the antilynching bill in December 1934, the group presented the president with a petition signed by more than two hundred prominent individuals, including nine governors, five of whom were Republicans.[59] The Republican governors included Alf Landon of Kansas, Frank Fitzgerald of Michigan, and C. Douglass Buck of Delaware, none of whom were, to say the least, New Deal supporters. Buck, for example, had the backing of the Liberty League and Du Ponts in his gubernatorial campaign in 1934.[60] The petition was also signed by nearly thirty mayors, again a mix of Democrats and Republicans, with the occasional socialist included. Two of the largest groups of signatories to the petition were church leaders and university professors and presidents.[61] A substantial number of attorneys and writers also signed the petition. Most notably, in light of later developments, not a single signer was identified as a union official or labor leader.[62] Such an omission would be unthinkable following the rise of the CIO.

Where Democrats were not seen as a particularly receptive constituency for civil rights, advocates found a willing partner in the Communist Party, which had come to see African Americans as a potential constituency for revolutionary action in the 1920s. After not mentioning civil rights or African Americans in the Workers' (Communist) Party platform of 1924, the 1928 platform included a detailed plank advocating for "abolition of the whole system of race discrimination. Full racial, political, and social equality for the Negro race." The platform explicitly endorsed an end to African American disfranchisement, repeal of interracial marriage bans, and integrated public accommodations.[63] By the end of the 1920s the party officially embraced the idea that Black Belt African Americans should gain self-determination as an oppressed nationality; although African Americans greeted this call with considerable skepticism, it coincided with a concerted effort to send Communist organizers into the Deep South.[64] The party-sponsored International Labor Defense took the lead in representing the Scottsboro defendants in 1931–32 as part of an effort to persuade African Americans that it, rather than the NAACP, represented their interests.[65] The Communists also reached out by nominating African American James Ford as vice president in 1932, 1936, and 1940, and by once again including detailed civil rights planks in their platform.

These overtures created considerable consternation among NAACP leaders and other African American advocates who worried that their cause would be tainted by its association with radicals harboring ulterior motives. Just as African American newspapers debated how to respond to the New Deal's very mixed record, they featured considerable discussion of whether the Communist Party was a reliable ally. Many disagreed with the NAACP's hostility to the Communists. Thus *Baltimore Afro-American* editor Carl Murphy wrote in the *Crisis* that the Communists "appear to be the only party going our way.... Since the abolitionists passed off the scene, no white group of national prominence has openly advocated the economic, political, and social equality of black folks."[66] Indeed, when the *Crisis* surveyed African American editors about communism, the main argument in favor of an alliance was that the Communists were alone among white-led organizations in aggressively backing civil rights.[67]

But several other editors derided the idea that communism offered a plausible path forward for African Americans. For example, Robert Vann— editor of the *Pittsburgh Courier*, which was one of the top two African

American newspapers in the country—argued that "few intelligent Negroes are to be found in the Communistic movement. Almost all Negroes following Communism are being used chiefly to lend a semblance of democracy to the cause."[68] Critics such as Vann believed that an alliance with the Communist Party would only make it more difficult to force civil rights onto the mainstream political agenda.[69] The problem, however, was finding an alternative set of allies from within the Democratic coalition with both the muscle and the interest in incorporating civil rights as a genuine concern. As described in chapter 3, the CIO—with ties in some cases to the Communists but also close connections to the northern wing of the Democratic Party— would begin to fulfill this role by the late 1930s.

SOCIAL SCIENCE AND THE MEANING OF "LIBERALISM"

The New Deal years constituted a crucial formative period for American liberalism as a political program. As Ronald Rotunda puts it, "for the great majority of Americans, the word 'liberal' was literally born in the early New Deal years."[70] Since the New Deal itself came to represent "liberalism" to many Americans, battles over the scope of the New Deal poured content into liberalism's meaning during these years. The discussion above shows that mainstream New Deal liberals did not see civil rights as part of their program in the early to mid-1930s.

Early social psychologists, sociologists, and survey researchers shared this mainstream conceptualization of liberalism and employed it as a framework for their analysis. During the 1920s and early 1930s several leading scholars developed attitude scales that aimed to classify people into such categories as "reactionary," "conservative," "progressive," "liberal," and "radical." These measures generally focused on economic policy, though the scales often also included civil liberties issues as a component. There were studies that focused specifically on racial prejudice, but these studies were separate from those probing liberal-conservative attitudes.[71] For the most part, civil rights concerns were not included when scholars sought to measure liberalism.

The most commonly used measure of citizens' ideology was the Harper scale, which placed respondents on a radical-liberal-conservative dimension.[72] M. H. Harper's scale asked seventy-one agree-disagree questions about a range of topics, including wealth redistribution, government ownership, taxation, civil liberties, and the role of religion in public life. Civil rights and the status of African Americans were nowhere to be found on the long list of questions. Psychologists and sociologists routinely adopted the Harper scale as their measure for liberalism-conservatism in this era.[73]

Most other studies in this period that claimed to measure liberalism and conservatism also did not incorporate racial policy views. For example, Raymond R. Willoughby's study of college students treated views toward "trial marriage," candidate religion, prohibition, communism, and international involvement (i.e., the League of Nations) as indicators of liberalism-conservatism but included no discussion of racial policy.[74] Percival Symonds developed a list of thirty-two items that were meant to distinguish conservative students from those who are liberal, progressive, or radical. The survey included items about government control of natural resources, stock market regulation, the eight-hour workday, minimum wage laws, and the propriety of inheritance taxes. The questionnaire also included items about the role of religion in public life. There were no questions about civil rights for African Americans; the only question touching on civil rights at all asked about whether Japanese should be permitted naturalization.[75]

The classic Bennington College study of college student attitudes shared in this mainstream conceptualization as well. Launched in 1935 by Theodore Newcomb, the study adopted a "Political and Economic Progressivism" scale to measure the liberalism-conservatism of Bennington students. With the New Deal already underway, the twenty-six-item scale included questions on public relief, attitudes toward strikes and labor unions, government intervention in business, and the role of private and corporate wealth. Racial issues were entirely absent from the survey instrument as Newcomb sought to understand the liberal-conservative orientations of the Bennington students.[76]

The most striking exception is a 1930 study of college students by George Vetter that attempts to connect liberalism-conservatism to respondents' personality traits.[77] Vetter includes two questions on attitudes toward race relations alongside questions probing attitudes toward government ownership of industry, inheritance taxes, labor unions, minimum wage laws, the "socialization of medical care," prohibition, free speech, birth control, no-fault divorce, and abortion. The first race relations question asks about attitudes toward interracial marriage.[78] A second question asks about white supremacy, with the liberal position being that "all the races are of very nearly equal worth ... no race should assume it to be the elect."[79] The inclusion of racial attitudes as a component of liberalism was not the only feature that made the Vetter analysis unusual. For example, his expansive measurement approach also included an item on laws against incest, treating as radical those who favor removing all laws regarding incest, and as liberal those who would allow marriage for relatives more remote than brother-sister or child-parent. Though idiosyncratic, Vetter's analysis is striking in the extent to which it anticipates—however imperfectly—the eventual alignment of economic, racial, and "social" issues along a single dimension.[80] I was unable to find any other studies in the period that treated racial attitudes in this way, however.

In sum, when scholars sought to measure liberalism, progressivism, and conservatism in the 1920s and early 1930s, racial policy views were generally not seen as a defining feature. Again, this is consistent with the more general political environment in which mainstream liberalism and progressivism were widely understood to be defined by economic policy commitments and not linked to concern for civil rights.

CONCLUSION

Looking back on the New Deal, Roosevelt's reputation as a liberal leader has come under well-deserved fire for his refusal to lead on civil rights issues. Critics have rightly taken the president to task for his willingness to partner with racist southern Democrats who were committed to the protection of the Jim Crow system above all else.[81]

Yet when one closely examines the policy debates of the early 1930s, criticism of Roosevelt from the "left" almost never focused on racial issues and instead honed in on his friendliness to business interests and his reluctance to give his full backing to the burgeoning labor movement. The standard "liberal" or progressive program simply did not include civil rights as the New Deal was launched. Far from an enemy of liberalism, southern members of Congress were generally regarded as New Deal backers. The main obstacle to progress came instead from the Northeast, in the guise of probusiness northeastern leaders, such as Al Smith and former DNC chair John Raskob. Building a liberal party would require Roosevelt taking on Wall Street and business, uniting northern labor with western progressives and southern and western agrarians. African Americans were thus on the outside looking in as liberals sought to turn Roosevelt's New Deal in a decidedly reformist direction.

These terms of debate would change dramatically later in the 1930s. As chapter 3 argues, this transformation was rooted in several developments promoting the incorporation of civil rights concerns into a new liberal program. The growing role of African Americans as a potential electoral constituency in the North was an important part of this story, but the rise of the CIO also provided a crucial push. The new labor movement meant that the Communist Party was no longer the only politically consequential white-led group pushing for civil rights legislation; the rise of labor also helped shape a new set of political battle lines in which southern Democrats were increasingly identified as *the* enemy of liberalism. In this context, civil rights became a key marker for who was a true New Deal liberal, something that would have been inconceivable when Roosevelt took the oath of office in 1933.

CHAPTER 3

Transforming Liberalism, 1933–1940

NEW DEAL LIBERALISM, as it was understood by the public and by political elites in the early to mid-1930s, had little to say about civil rights, in terms of both the subjugation of African Americans in the South and the routine discrimination that African Americans in the North faced in employment and other areas of life. Racial discrimination was a concern for several individuals identified with the left, but leaving aside the Communist Party, it was not linked to a broader ideological program. Concerns about racial justice were seen as separate from—and entirely subordinate to—the economic priorities of New Deal liberals. In the late 1930s and early 1940s, however, civil rights support became one of the markers for political figures' status as "genuine" liberals.

This chapter analyzes three interrelated changes that together helped to forge this new connection between New Deal liberalism and civil rights support. The first consists of efforts by political entrepreneurs to bring African American voters into the New Deal coalition. Pennsylvania Democrat Joseph Guffey, working in tandem with *Pittsburgh Courier* editor Robert Vann in 1932–34, offered an early model for incorporating African American voters, which became far more widespread across the North by the 1936 election.

A second change is the rise of industrial labor unions, which took center stage in the northern Democratic coalition in the mid- to late 1930s. The CIO played a lead role in redefining New Deal liberalism to include civil rights. The CIO's stance partly emerged from the organizational imperatives of the unions themselves, which depended on African American workers for their success. However, it also reflected a broader principled commitment on the part of many union leaders and organizers. Crucially, the CIO quickly forged close ties to African American organizations, such as the National Negro Congress, and worked to mobilize African American voters through Labor's Non-Partisan League. The CIO and the league put forward a broad conception of liberalism that included civil rights as a key plank in an aggressive program for both economic and social progress. This program helped to define the aspirations for the urban, northern wing of the Democratic Party.

The third crucial change emerged as a response to the first two developments: many leading southern Democrats began to position themselves as opponents of an expanded New Deal. A handful of southern leaders had opposed the New Deal from the start, but as shown in chapter 2, most southern Democratic elites stuck with Roosevelt. Indeed, southern Democrats in Congress were generally identified as vital Roosevelt lieutenants, while most of the president's conservative critics within the party came from its eastern, Al Smith wing. But prominent southern Democrats viewed the rise of the CIO and the entry of African Americans into their party with alarm.[1]

Starting in 1937, leading southern Democrats in Congress became vocal critics of the CIO, warning their colleagues of the twin dangers posed by labor radicalism and racial change in their region. By 1938 it was evident that conservative southern Democrats were now a formidable enemy of the CIO, seeking not only to block its organizing drives in the South but also to stop its economic policy agenda in Washington. With President Roosevelt's party purge in 1938, the battle lines were drawn clearly: conservative southern Democrats stood in the way of efforts to create a liberal party with the CIO as a major organizational base. In addition to its organizing imperatives and principled commitments, the CIO now had a strong political interest in battling a Jim Crow system that empowered its southern conservative enemies. African Americans were no longer isolated claimants fighting against southern Democrats; their enemies were also the main enemies of labor-oriented urban liberal Democrats, and those same urban liberals came to see the defeat of "poll tax" southerners as the pathway to a liberal national majority.

These interrelated alterations in the New Deal coalition and in the meaning of liberalism in the mid- to late 1930s put constituency changes front and center in understanding the origins of the civil rights realignment. The entry of African American voters into the Democratic Party, the rise of the CIO, and the ensuing southern reaction created a new coalitional alignment in which civil rights was linked to economic liberalism. Rather than narrowly focused policy demanders accommodating one another in a coalitional bargain,[2] the broad policy and political imperatives of building a strong industrial labor movement and of safeguarding the southern economic and racial system were incompatible. As a result, from the late 1930s onward, the Democratic coalition consisted of dueling factions that viewed one another as enemies rather than as partners. This alignment took shape long before national party leaders took a clear stand on civil rights, but as subsequent chapters will show, the new liberal coalition gradually captured the Democratic Party from below.

The evidence base in this chapter draws heavily on news accounts from the 1930s. These sources—which are analyzed both qualitatively and through simple quantitative content analyses—trace the changes in who is identified as a New Deal supporter and opponent in the 1930s. The coverage also underscores the increasingly important role of the CIO both as a supporter of New Deal liberalism after 1936 and as an ally of African Americans. Through canvassing the mainstream press, the labor press, and African American news coverage—and seeing the issues that the CIO and its allies emphasize—one can trace the process through which civil rights concerns first enter into the liberal program. Chapter 4 will show how the early civil rights movement capitalized on World War II to tighten this connection, making support for civil rights legislation a basic marker for liberalism.

THE SEEDS OF AFRICAN AMERICANS' REALIGNMENT

African Americans entered the electorate during Reconstruction as Republicans. Following the Civil War, Republican hopes to compete in the South hinged on enfranchising and appealing to the freed slaves. But northern Republicans failed to make the substantial economic, military, and political investments required to secure a genuine reconstruction of the South.[3] Instead, southern white Democrats gradually disenfranchised African Americans and instituted Jim Crow. Although Republican efforts to ensure African Americans' civil rights had weakened by 1876 and virtually ended by the 1890s, most African Americans continued to view the GOP as more welcoming than the southern-dominated Democratic Party. The small African American population in the North thus generally continued to vote Republican in the 1910s and 1920s.

The rewards for African Americans' loyalty were scant. Republicans were the main backers of the antilynching bill in 1922–23—sponsored by a St. Louis Republican, Leonidas Dyer, who had a substantial African American constituency—but GOP leaders made only a tepid effort to overcome a southern filibuster.[4] While African American leaders received access to patronage through the GOP, even this began to fade in the late 1920s. The Democrats' nomination of Catholic Al Smith created an opening for the GOP in the heavily Protestant white South, and Herbert Hoover sought to capitalize by encouraging "lily-white" Republican Party organizations in the region. Southern GOP campaign literature depicted Smith as a friend of the pope and even of African Americans.[5] These attacks allowed Hoover to make real inroads in the South, winning outright in Florida, North Carolina, Texas, Tennessee, and Virginia, and coming close in Alabama. The vast majority of African American voters stuck with Hoover in the election despite these overtures to white southerners, but several African American newspapers and elites backed Smith, including the *Chicago Defender* and *Baltimore Afro-American*.[6] Hoover's subsequent failed Supreme Court nomination of North Carolina Republican John J. Parker—who had disavowed efforts to win African American votes when he campaigned for governor in 1920—served as a further signal of the president's utter lack of concern for African Americans' votes and interests.

The question remained whether Democratic politicians and liberal leaders would seek to capitalize on the opportunity created by Hoover and the Republicans. Most northern Democratic politicians had paid little attention to their African American constituents in the 1920s. Furthermore, when progressive reformers talked about building a constituency for liberalism in the late 1920s and early 1930s, they would typically highlight workers, farmers, and even middle-class professionals but not African Americans as likely backers for their movement.[7]

But the economic and political upheaval created by the Great Depression widened the opening for ambitious Democratic politicians and African American leaders to foster new alliances. One of the earliest developments occurred in Pennsylvania. Democrats had long been a powerless minority in the state and were in need of new coalition partners to have a realistic shot at winning a statewide majority. Democratic leader Joseph Guffey aspired to be a "big time machine politician," but the Democrats' lack of competitiveness had frustrated this ambition.[8] As a result, Guffey was quick to seize on an opportunity to expand the party's reach in 1932 when *Pittsburgh Courier* editor Robert Vann approached him.

Vann had become alienated by Hoover's lily-white strategy in the South; his newspaper had reported in August 1928 that "it is no secret that Lily White Republicans and Democratic bolters in the South have formed an alliance with the hope of carrying Dixie for Hoover by completely eliminating the Negro."[9] Vann even approached New York State Democratic chairman James Farley in 1928, offering his support in exchange for patronage. The Smith campaign informed Vann in late August that no such deal would be accepted; Vann stuck with the GOP despite his qualms, not being "ready to change parties unless assured of a warm reception."[10] Following the election, however, Vann did not receive the federal appointment he had expected in return for his support for Hoover. Continued slights from Hoover and state Republican leaders over the next few years, combined with the desperate economic conditions amid the Depression, left Vann more ready than ever to abandon the GOP.

In the lead-up to the 1932 election, Vann passed along a message to Guffey's sister—through her African American beautician—that he was eager to talk with her brother.[11] At the ensuing meeting, Vann presented Guffey with an indictment of the Republicans' mistreatment of African Americans and with the message that he could help swing African American voters to the Democrats. Writing about the episode a few years later, reporters Joseph Alsop and Robert Kintner noted that Guffey's "horizon, always elastic, suddenly broadened; at the end of a bright vista he saw millions of Negro voters, Republicans no longer, Democrats all."[12]

Guffey immediately set up a meeting between Vann and Roosevelt in Hyde Park.[13] He also persuaded Roosevelt's campaign managers, Farley and Louis Howe, to establish an active Negro division during the campaign, and they named Vann as one of four in charge of it. Vann gave several high-profile speeches, including one in Cleveland in which he advised African American voters that it was time to "turn the picture of Lincoln to the wall."[14] The *Courier* published an August 1932 editorial, "The Parting of the Ways," calling on African Americans to vote Democratic: "the intelligent Negroes of this country feel it no disgrace to abandon the Republican party, after supporting it without suitable reward for over a half century."[15]

Notwithstanding Vann's efforts, Hoover still won both the African American vote and Pennsylvania in 1932. But Roosevelt evidently did win a majority in the black wards of Pittsburgh, where the *Courier* was published.[16] After the election, Guffey persuaded Roosevelt to reward Vann with a position in the Justice Department. The job—as a special assistant to the attorney general—did not require Senate confirmation and thus avoided the potential to raise the ire of southerners suspicious of efforts to reach out to African Americans.[17]

The 1932 campaign was a prelude to Vann and Guffey's elaborate efforts two years later to sway African Americans to support Guffey's campaign for Senate and Democratic gubernatorial nominee George Earle. Vann's *Courier* backed the Democrats strongly, even running a special supplement listing the African Americans appointed to government jobs with Guffey's help. The African American wards in Pittsburgh voted big for the Democrats, and Earle even won 41 percent of the vote in Philadelphia's African American wards, despite the continued strength of the GOP machine in the city. Five African Americans were also elected to the state legislature as Democrats. Guffey and Earle's statewide triumphs "removed any doubts Democratic leaders may have had about capturing the Negro vote." Farley was sufficiently impressed that he provided well-paying jobs to 150 African Americans in ten northern cities with substantial black populations.[18]

As governor, Earle pressed successfully for adoption of a Little New Deal in Pennsylvania, including a state version of the Wagner Act on labor relations. He also signed a civil rights bill providing for nondiscrimination in public accommodations. Vann had pushed the proposal for two decades; though it passed on a bipartisan vote, Guffey and his Democratic allies were credited with securing its adoption.[19] A Republican newspaper commented, "Obviously, the legislation was designed to increase Democratic Party enrollment in Pennsylvania. We shall not be surprised, however, if the Earle Administration has merely succeeded in throwing its political machinery into reverse."[20] But Democrats continued their gains among Pennsylvania African Americans in 1936, winning the African American wards even in Philadelphia.[21]

By the mid- to late 1930s Guffey had emerged as a very public representative of a reshaped Democratic Party in the North. Conservative commentator Frank Kent wrote in 1938 that "it was Guffey who, in 1934, inaugurated the New Deal national campaign to take the Negro voters away from the Republicans."[22] As Kent noted, Guffey was also closely linked to CIO leader John L. Lewis and to the emergent CIO in Pennsylvania; Kent argued that as much as anyone else, Guffey "brought about the Roosevelt-C.I.O. political accord." Indeed, Guffey was known to make speeches praising Roosevelt and Lewis as the two best leaders in world history.[23] Writing in the *Saturday Evening Post*, Alsop and Kintner argued that Guffey was a new kind of political boss, "the first of the liberal bosses, liberal in platform and enjoying tremendous support from the left wing."[24] They again attributed Guffey's distinctive appeal to his linking together the CIO, African American voters, and support for Roosevelt.

Guffey's outreach to African Americans was by no means an isolated phenomenon. His success encouraged a broader shift within the party. The presidential campaign of 1936 witnessed an unprecedented effort to persuade African Americans to vote Democratic. Roosevelt's team formed the Good Neighbor League as an auxiliary organization to the Democratic National Committee. The league was designed to help woo groups that had not traditionally been Democratic but who were seen as potentially supportive of the president. Led by Stanley High, formerly of the National Broadcasting Corporation, the Good Neighbor League created specialized committees targeting particular groups, including a "Colored Committee" that sought to win over African American voters. The committee emphasized the benefits that the New Deal had provided to African Americans, publishing widely distributed pamphlets with such titles as *Has the New Deal Helped the Colored Citizen?*[25]

The Good Neighbor League's efforts to reach out to African Americans culminated in September 1936 with an "Emancipation Day" rally at Madison Square Garden in New York that was broadcast over a national radio hookup and linked to twenty-five similar meetings in other northern cities.[26] The Madison Square Garden event drew over fourteen thousand African Americans to listen to Robert Wagner, Roosevelt aide Donald Richberg, and others extol the New Deal and attack Roosevelt's enemies, such as the Liberty League.[27] The crowd at the rally adopted by voice a resolution—drafted by Colored Committee chairman Bishop R. R. Wright—urging African Americans to "emancipate ourselves from mere party names and party shibboleths, even though this may shatter tradition and ancient loyalties," and to "carry forward the real spirit of Abraham Lincoln by supporting the social and economic programs of the great President, Franklin D. Roosevelt." Wagner received a standing ovation when he predicted Congress would finally pass the antilynching bill. Richberg's speech condemned the Liberty League for "preserving the liberty of a few men to wring their bread from the sweat of other men's faces" and defended the New Deal's programs to help the unemployed and poor.[28]

Frank Kent highlighted the rallies as an example of how this campaign "was unlike any other that can be recalled.... Whoever heard of the Democratic Party celebrating 'Emancipation Day'?... What could be more absurd than for the Democratic party, so large a section of which still believes that emancipation of the Negro was a great mistake, to regard that day as one upon which to hurrah?"[29] Harold Ickes's diary also took note of the change represented by African American turnout for Democratic rallies, observing that Wagner had remarked to him that "in former times, Negroes would not turn out to see any Democratic candidate. There were thousands of them, and they displayed great enthusiasm" for Roosevelt.[30]

The Good Neighbor League's efforts coincided with other signs that party leaders hoped to reach out to African American voters for the first time. The most famous episode occurred in June, when the virulently racist "Cotton" Ed Smith (D-SC) stormed out of the Democratic National Convention in objection to an African American minister giving the invocation and the prominent speaking role afforded to African American Democratic congressman Arthur Mitchell. The African American press highlighted the changed tone at the convention—and Smith's and other southerners' anger. The *Defender* emphasized the inclusion of African American delegates from northern states, commenting that "the old time Southerners are dying by degrees in seeing how the Democratic party is being colored up; but the white Democratic North is getting independent, and telling right out in meetin': 'We want votes and don't give a damn.'"[31]

At the same time, Republicans also took note of the transformation taking place among their foes. Republican newspaper editor and Landon supporter William Allen White wrote that at the 1936 Democratic convention "it was decided that for the decade, and possibly for a generation to come, the Democratic Party would be regenerated as the urban party of the United States.... Then and there the great cities of the nation took charge of the Democratic Party—chiefly the cities of the two coasts and the Great Lakes." White highlighted the divisions that this shift portended: "The new party has no flowery path before it. Franklin Roosevelt may, probably will, be able to hold it together while he commands its fortunes. But the seeds of death are in it." In particular, the South will increasingly find "white supremacy" under threat as "both the farmer-labor group and the Tammany group will be vastly more insistent on treating the Negro as a worker and not as a serf."[32]

Reflecting Roosevelt's general popularity and northern Democrats' outreach efforts, African Americans voted decisively to reelect the president in 1936. Writing just a few years later, Ralph Bunche observed that "the spell of the Lincoln legend over the Negro has been broken ... the working class, the unionized and the underprivileged Negro gives enthusiastic support to the Democratic party." Bunche added that this support had resulted in only limited gains in national policy for African Americans, but the group's potentially pivotal role in municipal elections was already starting to yield real gains at the local level.[33]

Chapter 6 uses quantitative data to trace, in detail, the dynamics of the African American realignment from the late 1930s through the 1960s, but for understanding the changing meaning of liberalism in the 1930s and early 1940s the crucial point is that African American voters were finally viewed as a potentially important constituency, and their demands for action on civil rights now had political appeal.[34] Guffey cemented this new alliance in Pennsylvania without driving away white voters, demonstrating the viability of the strategy within northern states. A northern Democratic Party that could win elections by appealing to industrial workers, urban ethnic voters, and African Americans had begun to take shape, with important long-term implications for the party's imagery and program.

The CIO: A Linchpin of the Emerging Linkage

More than any other organized group, the CIO was the lead player in cementing the Democrats' identity as an urban, liberal party and, alongside this transformation, in broadening the liberal program to include civil rights. In elbowing its way into the Democratic coalition, the CIO sought to make northern politicians dependent on its support and thereby reshape the party's commitments. The message—often stated by John L. Lewis and other labor leaders—was that if the Democratic Party did not become a *true* liberal party, labor would forge a new party that was not burdened by the Democrats' conservative elements. Where Roosevelt had initially sought to define the New Deal as a centrist force, steering between the radicalism of the left and the complacency of the Al Smith wing of the party, the CIO pushed for a bolder vision that would reorder social, economic, and political institutions. Roosevelt never fully embraced this vision, but it specified the outer reaches of New Deal liberalism and became a standard against which true, ardent New Deal liberals would be judged.

In late 1930s America, the CIO far surpassed other white-led organizations in its support for civil rights. Before the CIO entered the scene, the labor movement was by no means identified with civil rights; indeed, AFL unions were notorious for countenancing routine discrimination (and continued to have at best a mixed record long after the CIO became a competitor). It was no accident that the names of labor leaders were absent from the NAACP's lynching bill petition in 1934 (see chapter 2); most prominent labor leaders in the United States had evidenced little or no interest in civil rights legislation.

But from early on, the CIO made a point of including civil rights as part of its agenda. The CIO's liberal policy pronouncements on the issue can be partly traced to the organizational imperatives of unionizing an industrial workforce, in which African Americans constituted a potential group of strikebreakers. The craft-based AFL unions could generally rely on their control of entry into the skilled labor force to reduce the risk of strikebreaking. But exclusion was not a viable strategy for industrial unions seeking to organize unskilled workers. In his definitive history of the CIO, Robert Zieger writes that "the circumstances of mass production industry, in which increasing numbers of blacks were integral to production processes, made obvious the need for color-blind unionism.... African Americans comprised 15 percent of steel workers, 25 percent of Chicago packinghouse workers, 4 percent of automobile workers, and significant proportions" in the other main CIO targets.[35] These numbers were not lost on the CIO's leaders: "to the men who launched the CIO, the *importance* of black workers in industrial America was clear."[36]

The United Mine Workers (UMW), which formed the nucleus of the early CIO, had already learned this lesson as it sought to organize the coal mines. Lewis's mineworkers union "had long enjoyed a reputation for relative racial equality. Black and white mine workers could be found in the same local unions and the dynamics of coal mining dictated that segregation and discrimination at the job site translated into weakness in confrontations with coal operators. Almost alone among AFL affiliates, the mine workers' union could boast of a tradition of egalitarianism."[37] CIO organizers and leaders thus understood from experience that organizing African Americans would be crucial to the movement's success.

This strategic imperative was reinforced by the genuine commitment to racial equality that was especially strong among CIO activists who emerged from the Communist and Socialist Parties.[38] From this perspective, the goal of fostering unified working-class consciousness was incompatible with racial exclusion.[39] The Reuther brothers in Detroit, for example, came from a socialist (but noncommunist) political tradition. They organized their first picket lines to protest racial discrimination at Detroit City College and to fight the ban on African Americans at a local pool; they rushed to join the United Automobile Workers (UAW) union soon after it formed.[40] Noting the contributions of both the organizing imperatives and left-wing commitments to solidarity, Zieger concludes that "before long the CIO's identification with the rights of black workers—and black citizens—went beyond the

relatively practical egalitarianism that characterized the UMW tradition—
and far beyond the often-discriminatory practices of AFL unions."[41] Appealing to African American workers not only required a policy of biracial
organizing and nondiscrimination within the union, it also meant backing
legislation to secure African Americans' civil rights.[42] Through its internal
organizing approach, along with its external lobbying and electoral mobilization strategies, the CIO forged important connections between New Deal
liberalism and racial liberalism.

Understanding the CIO's significance to the politics of civil rights requires
first tracing its role as the leading organizational force behind New Deal
liberalism. I then discuss its approach to racial issues and the African American response to this outreach. By the late 1930s both whites and African
Americans viewed the CIO as an aggressive advocate for economic liberalism and civil rights. The final section of the chapter addresses the southern
response to this emergent linkage.

Labor's Non-Partisan League and the Changing Place of Organized Labor

The first signs that the CIO might play a role in transforming both American
politics and African Americans' place in the Democratic Party came with the
formation and early activities of Labor's Non-Partisan League, a voter mobilization and lobbying group that aimed to represent a cross-section of the
labor movement. Founded in April 1936, the LNPL was the brainchild of CIO
leaders Sidney Hillman and John L. Lewis, though the group initially also included New Deal backers from several AFL unions.[43] Funded primarily by
Lewis's mineworkers union, the LNPL organized extensively for the 1936
campaign. The league staged hundreds of rallies across key states, such as
Illinois, Ohio, and Pennsylvania.[44] By spring 1936 it had enrolled over thirty-
four thousand active precinct, county, and state workers and formed special
committees "of women, youth, Negroes [and] foreign language groups."[45]

The LNPL spent considerable resources seeking to persuade African
American voters to go to the polls and cast their vote for Roosevelt. The
Nation credited the LNPL and CIO with playing an important role in bringing African Americans to the Democrats, while from the opposite end of the
political spectrum, Frank Kent also saw the CIO as a key force behind African Americans' shift to the Democrats, which he referred to as "the really
sensational political fact" of the 1936 election.[46]

The league's activism represented a dramatic shift in labor's role in American elections. Where the AFL had generally shunned electoral politics, the
CIO and LNPL embraced the idea that labor could achieve its goals through
helping sympathetic candidates. Organized labor spent nearly $800,000 on
the 1936 campaign, with the CIO (and LNPL) responsible for the vast ma-

jority of the funds, which represented about 10 percent of the Democrats' spending.[47] With business interests increasingly worried about the New Deal's direction, "the DNC became increasingly dependent on organized labor as its largest single source of campaign contributions."[48]

In assessing whether a second Roosevelt term would be more liberal than the first, the *New Republic* commented in September 1936 that "more significant than anything Mr. Roosevelt may say is the support he is receiving from the Labor's Non-Partisan League."[49] Although many on the left continued to be skeptical of Roosevelt's commitment, members of Congress from the industrial East who had received help from the league may "feel that their first allegiance should be to the labor unions rather than to the administration."[50]

Following Roosevelt's landslide victory, the *Nation* argued that the result was more than a personal victory for Roosevelt and instead represented "a triumph also for labor, which now emerges from this election with greater political prestige than it has ever before had in American history." The editors thus interpreted the election as a clear mandate to move left, "toward progress in social legislation, the protection of labor's rights, [and] the curbing of big enterprise."[51] Writing in the *New York Times*, Louis Stark observed that "the organization of the labor vote for President Roosevelt by the league ... is credited with being a major factor in rolling up the large Roosevelt vote" and has sparked talk of a "realignment of political forces which would bring a third or labor party into existence" for 1940 if Roosevelt and the Democrats failed to live up to expectations.[52] Roosevelt himself told state labor officials that the election constituted a "mandate in unmistakable terms to its legislators and executives" to better workers' conditions and wages.[53]

Crucially, the LNPL's goals extended beyond helping Roosevelt win. Its convention in August 1936 adopted two main resolutions: the first urged Roosevelt's reelection, while the second called for the group to continue after the election "as an instrumentality for the furtherance of liberalism in the United States."[54] Speaking at the convention, Hillman boldly proclaimed that "in the great realignment which will mean liberal forces on one side opposed to the forces of reaction, labor should take its place in an organized manner."[55] The LNPL's chairman, George Berry, declared that "there will be a new political alignment before the 1940 election. I conceive it important that we who are opposed to the return of reaction [should] ... participate in a feast that has to do with the permanent establishment of a liberal party, if necessary, in the United States in 1940."[56]

Immediately after Roosevelt's win, Lewis told the CIO executive board that "we must capitalize on the election."[57] The LNPL soon announced it would set up legislative committees on the national and state levels. Despite the participation of several AFL affiliates in 1936, it became apparent that the LNPL was the "political arm" of the CIO, which quickly became a key force defining the leading edge of New Deal liberalism.[58]

Rather than just focusing on shop floor concerns or benefits for union members, the CIO developed a broad program that pushed for dramatic expansions of the New Deal state, including national health care, expanding Social Security to cover farm and domestic workers, and civil rights protections for African Americans. The LNPL's second convention, held in March 1937, declared that its purpose was not merely to fight for labor but to represent "every progressive group whose purpose is to secure the enactment of liberal and humanitarian legislation."[59]

The breadth of the CIO's agenda and the boldness of its tactics quickly turned it into a crucial symbol. It became a lightning rod for conservatives fearful of the threat that the New Deal seemed to pose to the existing social order and a hero to many on the left who viewed it as the culmination of the New Deal's promise.

The wave of sit-down strikes that shot into the headlines in December 1936 through February 1937 were an especially important moment. These strikes resulted in major successes, such as when the UAW won recognition at both General Motors and Chrysler in early 1937. They also garnered immense national publicity: between December 29, 1936, and February 28, 1937, over 150 front-page stories in the *Chicago Tribune, Washington Post, New York Times,* and *Los Angeles Times* discussed the sit-down strikes.[60] Historians Melvyn Dubofsky and Warren Van Tine note that "the UAW victory over General Motors legitimized the CIO as a national trade union center competitive with the A.F. of L. and magnified Lewis's role and influence as a labor leader."[61] Polls taken during and after the strike wave revealed considerable public anger at the CIO's tactics.[62] But it was notable that Roosevelt and other liberal leaders did not condemn the strikes; indeed, critics charged that the administration's pro-CIO stance tacitly encouraged its "lawlessness."

The CIO followed up the sit-down strikes by strongly endorsing Roosevelt's court-packing plan. Acting through the LNPL, it became the most vocal outside advocate for the bill, spending thousands of dollars to purchase radio time and to pressure members of Congress through letter-writing campaigns and petitions.[63] Within days of Roosevelt's announcement of the plan, league chairman Berry declared that the LNPL would "put all of its resources into a national campaign to secure passage of the bills embodying President Roosevelt's plan for judicial reform.... Only by judicial reform can the way be opened to social and labor progress." Berry added that "American labor is behind the President today, as it was during his election campaign, in his program for progressive social and labor legislation"[64]

A few weeks later the second LNPL national convention focused heavily on the court issue. Senator Robert La Follette Jr. headlined the event with a speech declaring that when a majority of the Supreme Court "stubbornly cling to an outmoded philosophy which the people of the country have emphatically renounced, it is a threat to a functioning democracy."[65] The thousand delegates present approved a resolution endorsing the court plan. CIO leaders kept up a steady drumbeat of pro-court-packing appeals, with Hillman going on a CBS radio network broadcast to proclaim the necessity of tackling "judicial dictatorship."[66] The LNPL sought to rally the public through pamphlets with such titles as *Packing the Court or Petting the Sweatshop*, which attacked the Court for its hostility to labor rights. Throughout the Court battle, the CIO and the LNPL stood out as the main liberal groups supporting Roosevelt's controversial efforts, even as many more established New Deal supporters balked at the proposal.[67]

In addition to its lobbying efforts, the CIO undertook mass mobilizations to support liberal candidates and oppose conservatives in both primaries and general elections. As J. David Greenstone argues, the CIO made labor unions into a major electoral organization of the Democratic Party, taking on many functions ordinarily performed by a party.[68] The insider and outsider strategies proved mutually reinforcing. When Roosevelt considered which groups had the muscle to push congressional Democrats to back his proposals, he counted heavily on the CIO.[69] Writing in 1937, Stanley High emphasized the CIO's growing organizational strength and concluded that "for its long-time importance, the Roosevelt program stands in greater need of the kind of support that [CIO president] Mr. Lewis can rally than of the apparently more significant backing of the party's conservatives."[70] In this way, the CIO helped reshape the Democratic Party in the North, creating the infrastructure for a more ideological, ambitious party agenda.

By 1938 the CIO was a lead backer of Roosevelt's party purge targeting conservative Democrats. The purge is correctly remembered as a political failure as nearly all the targeted Democrats held on to their seats. However, it signaled a deepening of the rift between liberal advocates of pushing forward with New Deal initiatives and more conservative party members who believed that the reform wave had gone too far already. In several states the CIO led the charge against conservative Democrats, not just attacking such southern stalwarts as "Cotton" Ed Smith and Walter George (D-GA) but even going after northern conservatives, such as the antilabor governor of Ohio, Democrat Martin Davey, whom Roosevelt had left off his purge list.[71] Where the ideological content of New Deal liberalism had remained diffuse early in Roosevelt's term, when the president was attacked from both the left and the right, the controversies and setbacks of 1937–38 fostered a clearer sense of what it meant to be an "ardent" or true 100% New Dealer.[72] One's stance toward the CIO constituted a critical marker of that identity.

One indicator for the changing imagery of the New Deal is that organized labor in general and the CIO in particular became much more prominent in front-page coverage of the New Deal legislative agenda. Just three of the front-page *New York Times* stories in 1935–36 discussing New Deal initiatives treated labor—either specific unions or their leaders—as New Deal supporters.[73] By contrast, nineteen stories did so in 1937, as did twenty-eight stories in 1938 and sixteen in 1939.[74] No other outside group was discussed nearly as often as a supporter of Roosevelt or his policies. The labor movement was explicitly and repeatedly linked to the New Deal side in coverage of Roosevelt's court-packing plan, strike controversies, WPA funding battles, the purge, and other election contests. As Roosevelt's agenda became associated with more ideologically charged policy controversies, the CIO stood squarely beside the president, prodding him to make good on the New Deal's reconstructive potential.

The CIO and Racial Liberalism

In this context in which the CIO came to represent the New Deal's boldest ambitions, it is especially important that the union placed civil rights alongside more traditional, economic concerns on the agenda for New Deal liberalism. Where mainstream liberals had generally not included civil rights legislation on lists of priority legislation in the past, the LNPL's first scorecard of key votes, issued in 1938, included the lynching bill alongside antistrike legislation, the wage and hours bill, and a farm tenants bill on its list of twelve tests to rate members of Congress.[75] The LNPL, in promising its "full support" for the lynching bill, stated that the "voting records of Senators and Congressmen were being clearly watched for their action on this and all similar progressive labor legislation."[76] The LNPL listed the lynching bill and poll tax as priorities in the following Congress, with the roll call on the lynching bill used as one of ten test votes to evaluate House members.[77] While the LNPL disbanded in 1942, the CIO continued to include civil rights measures as priority legislation used to judge the liberalism of members of Congress. For example, of twelve key votes the CIO used to rate senators in the Seventy-Ninth Congress (1945–46), two related to civil rights: the failed cloture votes on the poll tax and FEPC bills.[78]

More generally, in his study of the CIO's participation in politics, William H. Riker observes that while labor issues were always the top priority, the group lobbied on a range of other issues, "often with almost as much enthusiasm." The issues Riker identifies can be read as a catalog of conventional New Deal priorities—including expanding Social Security, medical services, housing, and the WPA—along with such civil rights initiatives as abolition of the poll tax and the FEPC.[79] Where racial policies were not treated as a yardstick of New Deal support or liberalism in 1933–34, the CIO and its allies began to make civil rights a part of the standard program of liberal aspirations against which potential supporters were evaluated.

The CIO's support for civil rights legislation was not simply an insider game of lobbying in Washington. The *CIO News*, the official weekly distributed to CIO households across the United States, printed many articles promoting civil rights initiatives soon after it began publishing in December 1937. For example, the January 29, 1938, issue included an article headlined "CIO Attacks Filibuster on Lynching Bill."[80] The paper repeatedly highlighted the poll tax, lynching bill, and, starting in the early 1940s, the FEPC, as major issues.[81] It also included numerous stories about Hillman, Lewis, and other top CIO leaders giving speeches to African American groups, which typically emphasized the shared political and policy goals of the CIO and African American community.[82] As Harvard Sitkoff notes, "never before had the proponents of the black struggle reached so broad an audience."[83] These efforts helped the CIO appeal to African American workers, while also signaling to its white members and other audiences that it viewed combating racial discrimination as part of its mission.

From the start, the *CIO News* sought to link the issues of labor rights with policies against racial discrimination under the common rubric of "civil rights." Thus many stories referred to the right to strike as a "civil right," just as other stories referred to African Americans' struggles in similar terms. CIO leader John Brophy declared in one speech that lynching is "a weapon in the arsenal of anti-union terror" and that "behind every lynching is the figure of the labor exploiter, the man or the corporation who would deny labor its fundamental rights."[84] In the CIO vocabulary, the enemies of African American rights and of labor rights were the same: southern "Tories," business interests that sought to weaken labor by dividing workers on the basis of race, and even fascists from abroad.

Indeed, the CIO and allied left-wing groups repeatedly pointed to Hitler and the Nazis as a threat both to labor and to racial and religious minorities, juxtaposing fascism to liberal New Deal principles. In a November 1938 cartoon (fig. 3.1), the *CIO News* depicted Roosevelt and the CIO defending "American democracy" from the Nazi "wolf," which had victimized both "labor unions" and "racial and religious minorities" in Europe.

The CIO also issued pamphlets highlighting the group's commitment to civil rights, including *The CIO and the Negro Worker* and *Equal Opportunity*, which were published in 1940.[85] The latter featured a reprint of John L. Lewis's 1940 speech to the National Negro Congress, in which Lewis denounced "the iniquities of the poll tax" that empowers "men who are in the forefront of the fight to strike down the rights of labor and the common people … men who would not be here in Washington if the citizens whom they are supposed to represent could cast a vote."[86] The CIO head called for the passage of "anti-lynching legislation, so long delayed by the cowardly tactics of those who would knife it behind the scenes." He also invited the NNC to join in an alliance with the CIO, arguing that "no group in the

Figure 3.1. The *CIO News* takes on Nazi threat to labor unions and racial minorities, 1938. © AFL-CIO, used with permission.

population feels more heavily the burden of unemployment and insecurity than the Negro citizens.... The denial of civil liberties lie with heavy discrimination upon Negroes. Only when these economic and political evils are wiped out will the Negro people be free of them."[87]

Mainstream news coverage of the CIO also regularly highlighted its civil rights support. Thus the *New York Times* report on the group's first constitutional convention noted that "there was considerable cheering and the delegates rose to their feet when a resolution was adopted entitled 'Unity of Negro and White Workers' and which pledged the C.I.O. to 'uncompromising opposition to any form of discrimination, whether political or economic, based upon race, color, creed or nationality.' "[88] Subsequent CIO conventions would recapitulate this message, with resolutions condemning Jim Crow and endorsing civil rights legislation.[89] A systematic search of the *Times* reveals a big increase in the number of articles that associate the CIO and labor movement more generally with African Americans and the civil rights cause: after just five stories on the topic in 1936, there were twenty-seven stories in 1937 and twenty-nine the following year.[90] This linkage was drawn both by liberals celebrating the CIO's role—such as Stanley High—and by conservative critics, such as syndicated columnist Frank Kent, who noted that the CIO, the communists, and the New Deal administration were "three separate but sympathetically linked forces [working] to swing the negroes away from the Republicans and over to the Democrats."[91]

The African American Response

Decades of discrimination on the part of AFL unions had fostered deep skepticism among African American workers and leaders about the labor movement. A key question is when and how the CIO managed to overcome this well-founded skepticism. In his excellent analysis of the CIO-NAACP relationship, Christopher Baylor attributes the critical decisions to the NAACP's leaders, who in the early 1940s chose to embrace an alliance with the CIO.[92] While I agree that the CIO's relationship with African Americans tightened in the period identified by Baylor, I argue that the CIO–African American alliance was in evidence several years earlier. More important, I see the alliance as less a matter of a strategic choice by the NAACP and more a product of a broad-based shift in African Americans' views of unions that took shape soon after the rise of the CIO.

Winning African American support would require demonstrating that the CIO's promises were not just empty rhetoric but instead reflected a genuine change in policy. Writing in 1936, the Urban League's Lester Granger praised the CIO, arguing that "it is not hard to see the advantages for black workers in the spread of the industrial union idea with its traditions of inclusiveness instead of exclusiveness because of race." At the same time, Granger noted that there is no guarantee that industrial unions will treat African Americans fairly, warning that "by the manner in which unions of textile, tobacco, oil and petroleum workers, and similar bodies of industrially organized labor face this race question, Negroes in industry will judge the effectiveness and good faith of the industrial union movement."[93]

The CIO's actions in its organizing campaigns in 1936–38 persuaded many of these African American leaders that the union was, indeed, sincere. The communist-influenced National Negro Congress was one of the first African American organizations to sign on. The CIO contributed money to the NNC, which in turn backed the Steel Workers Organizing Committee (SWOC) drive to unionize the steel industry in 1936–37.[94] There were an estimated seventeen to twenty thousand African American steelworkers; the

NNC assigned its own organizers to help win over African American workers to the steel drive.[95] At the same time, the NNC sponsored a "campaign among Race organizations to secure resolutions endorsing the program and campaign of the CIO" and to create "sentiment among the masses of the Race favorable to the program and campaign of the CIO."[96] As part of this effort, the NNC distributed a quarter million pro-CIO leaflets to African Americans. It also worked closely with the CIO and LNPL in fighting for the court-packing plan. NNC conventions routinely included CIO leaders as speakers; in 1940 the group even honored John L. Lewis for his distinguished service to African Americans.[97]

Although not involved in labor organizing, the more moderate, business-oriented National Urban League also showed support for the CIO by 1937.[98] Less than two years after Granger had cautioned African Americans to wait to judge the CIO's sincerity, he published an article in the *Chicago Defender* arguing that "for the first time in history, the trade union movement shows signs of coming close enough to Negroes for them to join it and receive its support."[99] The Chicago Urban League was especially active in working with the CIO, sponsoring a major interracial conference in 1937 that drew representatives from the CIO, NAACP, and NNC.[100] The executive secretary of the Chicago chapter, A. L. Foster, declared in April of that year that the CIO has "the full support of the Race because the organization recognizes the black man's value to American industry."[101]

The NAACP also proved responsive to the CIO's outreach, though winning over the organization as a whole required overcoming significant crosscurrents. Four days after John L. Lewis resigned from the AFL in 1935, NAACP executive secretary Walter White wrote him that "Negro workers feel confident that the new movement will be guided by the same policy of freedom from racial discrimination which has characterized the United Mine Workers under your leadership."[102] Even so, White had long resisted the calls of more radical NAACP leaders—such as W.E.B. DuBois—that the organization ought to adopt a more mass-based approach focused on economic issues. As a result, White and his allies initially resisted a full-fledged alliance with the CIO.[103]

White, however, found himself under pressure from a growing faction of younger, more militant members who believed that changes in the labor movement required a shift in the NAACP's approach. Thomas Sugrue observes that "militant activists led insurgencies throughout the North, pushing local branches to organize blue-collar workers, stage visible protests, and support industrial unionism…. The NAACP's grassroots insurgency paid off. NAACP membership doubled between 1935 and 1940."[104] As Raymond Wolters put it, the CIO's rise meant that NAACP officials "at last felt that they could, in good conscience, implement the program for working class solidarity which DuBois had advocated."[105] In 1935 the NAACP board endorsed a recommendation from a committee led by one of the young militants—Howard University professor Abram Harris—that called on the group to support the "building of a labor movement, industrial in character, which will unite all labor, black and white."[106] The NAACP's annual conference in 1936 went a step further, adopting a resolution that endorsed the CIO: "We urge support and active participation in the effort for organization of industrial unions in the American labor movement without regard to race or color."[107]

The NAACP's *Crisis* quickly became a vocal proponent of the African American–CIO alliance. A September 1936 editorial concluded that if the CIO "follows the pattern of the United Mine Workers of America—and there seems no reason to doubt that it will—in the matter of the color line in labor, then Negro workers ought to flock to the C.I.O. unhesitatingly, for the U.M.W. are known far and wide for their absolute equality, regardless of color."[108] A July 1937 article observed that African American workers have "nothing to lose and everything to gain by affiliation with the C.I.O."[109] A few months later the *Crisis* reported that "not in fifty years has America witnessed such interracial solidarity" as put forward by the CIO.[110] In 1939, when the Ku Klux Klan attacked the CIO's Textile Workers Organizing Committee for its interracial organizing program, the *Crisis* noted that "it has often been said that you can tell a man by the kind of enemies he makes. If this is true of organizations also, then the C.I.O. is certainly an unparalleled blessing in our land."[111]

Despite this support, not all NAACP chapters or leaders were enthused about the developing alliance between African Americans and the CIO. The Detroit chapter, in particular, was dominated by African American business and religious elites who believed that Henry Ford's relatively good treatment of African American workers meant that labor unions had little to offer.[112] When the NAACP annual conference was held in Detroit in 1937, antiunion delegates succeeded in greatly watering down the prounion language adopted the previous year. The NAACP's Roy Wilkins—no radical himself—penned an editorial in the *Crisis* denouncing the "very small clique of Detroiters" who had defended "the billionaire manufacturer" Ford, who, Wilkins noted, does little for African American workers in his plants in other cities. Wilkins claimed it "would have been a farce" for the NAACP, as the representative of "12,000,000 Negroes, ninety-five percent of whom work with their hands, to have held a national conference and ignored a discussion of the biggest labor movement in a quarter century."[113]

Though winning over Detroit African American leaders (and workers) would be a more gradual process, the connections between the CIO and NAACP were tightening elsewhere in the late 1930s.[114] CIO leaders were invited to address local NAACP meetings, where they highlighted the group's advocacy for equality.[115] In 1938 NAACP officials and the CIO worked together to force the New York subway system to promote African American workers, to fight discrimination in the TVA, and to defend sharecroppers arrested in Alabama for unionizing.[116] The following year NAACP representatives and CIO officials joined in fighting cuts to the WPA and in lobbying for antilynching legislation.[117] Locally, the NAACP and CIO cooperated in campaigning for an African American candidate for the St. Louis School Board, in a Pennsylvania Committee for the Defense of Negro Rights that formed in response to a wave of police terror against African Americans, and in a drive to pass a New Jersey antidiscrimination law.[118] When Stockton, California, police "deported" forty African American agricultural workers from the county for joining a union, the NAACP worked with the CIO's United Cannery, Agricultural, Packing and Allied Workers of America to fight back.[119]

An alliance between prominent African Americans and the CIO had thus been forged on the ground in 1936–39 and had important implications for both the labor movement and the civil rights struggle. Even as individual NAACP leaders such as White and Wilkins blanched at the radicalism of some in the CIO, they were keenly aware that their organization needed to appeal to the grassroots, working-class sentiment and the young militants attracted by the National Negro Congress and CIO. As Sugrue notes, the NNC had "forced established groups to become more militant as a matter of survival."[120] In other words, the alliance between African Americans and the CIO was less the product of the choices of elite decision makers in the NAACP than it was a broadly based response to the opportunities for cooperation presented by the CIO's stance.

African Americans' gravitation toward the CIO in the late 1930s was also evident in the African American press. The *Pittsburgh Courier* and the *Chicago Defender* were the two most prominent African American newspapers; each published a national edition with a wide circulation. The two papers provided considerable positive coverage of the CIO.[121] The *Courier*'s editor, Robert Vann, participated in the SWOC drive in Pennsylvania, writing in 1937 that "to advise [that] Negro labor avoid the responsibility and opportunity which is now in its grasp is little short of criminal."[122] A *Courier* reporter, George Schuyler, undertook a long tour of cities where labor strife was occurring in 1937–38, filing sympathetic stories that were echoed in pro-CIO editorials. In one such editorial, the *Courier* argued that "[the CIO] has done more than any single agency in the history of the country's labor movement to eliminate the biracialism which has so slowed the emancipation of the workers from industrial feudalism.... The wisdom of the Negro workers who joined this stand for better working conditions and industrial democracy is to be commended."[123]

The *Chicago Defender* also expressed support for the CIO, citing the union's extensive efforts to win over African American workers.[124] For example, the *Defender* described how the Maryland-Washington, DC, CIO's 1937 decision to move its conference out of a hotel that had Jim Crow restrictions, election of three African American vice presidents, and support for a wide range of civil rights causes had "further cemented" the "relationships between white and black workers."[125] The *Defender* also covered the UAW's push for antilynching legislation, the CIO's repeated attacks on racial discrimination by New York City corporations, and the CIO's bid—in the face of violent repression—to organize African American and white workers together in the South.[126]

After publishing no stories linking the CIO or its affiliates to support for African Americans in 1935, the *Defender* published twenty-three such stories over the next two years, another twenty-six in 1938 alone, followed by over one hundred stories in 1939–40 (see fig. 3.2 for the trend).[127] None of these stories was critical of the CIO's treatment of African Americans, though several noted the AFL's continued mixed record on racial issues. For example, a 1938 editorial compared the CIO favorably to the AFL, stating that "the C.I.O., opposed for the most part by many of the 'economic royalists' has been more liberal in its attitude. Regardless of what may be said of C.I.O. general policies, it has proved that doors of opportunity can be opened regardless of color."[128] While the *Defender*'s coverage of the CIO in 1936 had linked it most often to the communist-backed NNC, by 1939 the NAACP was the African American group most often linked to the CIO.[129]

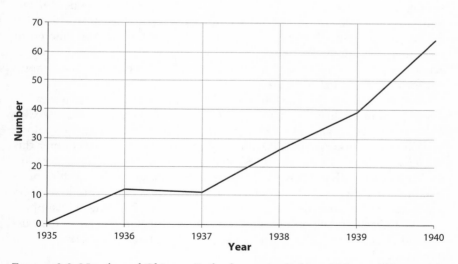

FIGURE 3.2. Number of *Chicago Defender* stories linking CIO or affiliates with African Americans

Other African American newspapers, such as the *Los Angeles Sentinel* and the *Baltimore Afro-American*, also provided expansive coverage of the CIO's efforts on behalf of African Americans in the mid- to late 1930s.[130] The *Afro-American* even criticized the NAACP after its 1937 Detroit conference refused to endorse the CIO: the newspaper accused the NAACP of "sidestepping" its "direct responsibility" by failing to acknowledge that the CIO "offers the colored workers the best opportunity they have ever had to participate in the industry of this country on an equal basis with white workers."[131]

This support from African American organizations and newspapers reflected and reinforced the behavior of ordinary workers. The steel drive was one of the earliest successes. Horace R. Cayton and George S. Mitchell's detailed study estimated that African Americans joined the union at a rate comparable to that of native-born whites (though below that of foreign born whites). They noted that "organizers in Chicago and Pittsburgh reported that in some cases Negroes joined the S.W.O.C. in even greater proportion than did white workers," while providing exhaustive interview evidence that African American workers saw the new union movement as much more inclusive than the old AFL.[132] Similar success was also evident in the meatpacking industry, where African American workers voted repeatedly to join the CIO.[133] Although other CIO unions had a tougher struggle in winning over African American workers—for example, it was not until 1941 that African American workers at Ford decisively sided with the UAW—the general trend was clear. William Riker observed that "so general is the feeling among negroes the CIO is the place for them that an independent negro railroad union [the Transport Service Employees] joined the CIO in 1939."[134] Public opinion polls also suggest that African Americans were distinctive in the late 1930s and 1940s in their prolabor views. Where many whites reacted negatively to the CIO's perceived radicalism, African Americans stood out for their prolabor views (see chapter 6).

This is not to say that the CIO–African American relationship was without important challenges. In particular, the racial liberalism of most CIO leaders and many organizers coexisted with persistent racial prejudice among rank-and-file workers. The CIO and its publications sought to counter this prejudice by appealing to workers' shared class interests. While these appeals were evidently at least partly successful, there was considerable variation in the degree to which individual CIO unions and rank-and-file workers practiced genuine inclusion.[135] The tension between CIO leadership support for civil rights and rank-and-file ambivalence—particularly on issues of housing and close interracial contact—was genuine and had long-term political importance.[136]

Even granting these caveats, political observers in the 1930s and 1940s were virtually unanimous in viewing the CIO as the most significant white-led organization advocating for civil rights in the United States.[137] Within the context of American politics in the late 1930s and the 1940s, both friends and enemies of the CIO viewed it as a leading voice for civil rights. Those CIO unions with a strong African American presence were often among the most aggressive in their advocacy both for civil rights and for a bold liberal program, reinforcing the connection between civil rights and economic liberalism.[138] In an era in which discrimination and segregation were rampant in both the North and the South, the CIO's policies of inclusion and nondiscrimination set it apart from other groups. Indeed, Sugrue notes that "even if many CIO unions were white-dominated, no institution in wartime America was as racially diverse as the CIO."[139] Given the CIO's role as the leading organized group promoting New Deal liberalism, its prominent association with civil rights helped bring these issue constellations into alignment.

Indeed, starting in 1938 every major umbrella group promoting civil rights featured the CIO as a prominent participant. The Southern Conference on Human Welfare (SCHW), which was formed in 1938, immediately sparked controversy when it organized an integrated meeting in Birmingham, Alabama. The group—which included Eleanor Roosevelt as an early supporter—consistently put forward a program that backed both progress on civil rights and expansion of the economic programs of the New Deal. Throughout its turbulent existence, the SCHW depended almost entirely on the CIO for funding, and its conventions included many CIO delegates.[140]

A few years later, when the National Committee to Abolish the Poll Tax was formed in 1941–42, the CIO was once again there as a founding member.[141] Indeed, historian Thomas Krueger credits John L. Lewis's February 1940 speech condemning the poll tax with inspiring numerous other groups to join the anti–poll tax crusade, leading to creation of the National Committee.[142] Similarly, the CIO was a founding member in September 1943 of the National Council for a Permanent FEPC. The council's "strategy board" included the NAACP's White, CIO president Philip Murray, and representatives of various religious groups.[143] In his classic account of the FEPC, Louis Kesselman credits the CIO with being an early, aggressive backer; indeed, pressure to match the CIO led the more conservative AFL to endorse the initiative.[144] The CIO's Murray was also on the executive committee of the Committee Against Mob Violence, which mobilized alongside the NAACP for antilynching legislation in 1946.[145]

After the rise of the CIO, the concerns of African Americans were understood to be a part of liberals' program. Before the CIO had entered the scene, those few liberals who were concerned about racial issues viewed civil rights as subordinate to and separate from their core interest in progressive economic reform. The CIO's leaders, however, saw a deeper connection between racial issues and economic policy goals. Not only did the CIO need African Americans for its internal organizational goals; the success of its broad policy agenda depended on a more general reconstruction of American politics in which African American voters would need to play an active role. Indeed, the reaction of southern Democrats to the rise of the CIO underscored the centrality of struggles over African Americans' rights to the future of the emergent rendition of American liberalism.

THE CONSERVATIVE RESPONSE

Political observers immediately took notice of the CIO's disruptive potential for the existing Democratic coalition. Writing just weeks after the 1936 election about his expectations for Roosevelt's second term, the economist Alvin Johnson argued that "if Roosevelt tries to move forward in the field of the industrial struggle he will necessarily produce a cleavage between the old Southern wing of the party and the new labor wing. If he sidesteps the issue, labor will turn against him."[146] Up to this point, southerners had generally been loyal backers of Roosevelt's New Deal program. But as Johnson anticipated, the entry of the CIO into the coalition as a full-fledged partner threatened that loyalty.

Southern Democrats had voted for the Wagner Act in 1935, which provided collective bargaining rights for workers and created the National Labor Relations Board (NLRB), but even then several key southern conservatives were skeptical of what expanded labor rights portended for their region's racial and economic orders.[147] In his history of the Wagner Act's passage, Irving Bernstein notes that Senate leaders Joseph Robinson (D-AR) and Pat Harrison (D-MS) "were cool to the bill in its entirety. They tried to defer consideration in hope that the session would terminate before it came to a vote."[148] But Robinson and Harrison relented after Roosevelt sided with Wagner. On the House side, future conservative coalition leaders Eugene Cox (D-GA) and Howard Smith (D-VA) both attacked the bill on the floor, charging that it was unconstitutional. In Cox's words, the bill "carries upon its face the most terrible threat ... to our dual form of government that has thus far arisen ... it is intended by this measure through the use of the commerce clause of the Constitution to sap and undermine that great document to the extent of ultimately striking down and destroying completely all State sovereignty."[149]

The Wagner Act eventually passed on a voice vote, but this was not reflective of a consensus on behalf of the initiative. Several amendments that aimed to weaken the bill were decided by closely fought, nonrecorded votes. Another southern critic of the bill, Malcolm Tarver of Georgia, complained about the "concerted effort about which we read in the press to avoid a roll call on this bill."[150] He attributed this effort to members' reluctance to publicly oppose workers despite their personal disapproval of the bill. Bernstein concludes that many opponents decided it was better to let the Supreme Court kill the measure by ruling it unconstitutional than to be recorded in opposition to the growing labor movement.[151]

Two years later the sit-down strikes spurred more Democrats to push back against the administration's growing ties to the CIO. In April 1937 southern Democrat James (Jimmy) Byrnes (D-SC) introduced a proposal to force striking workers off of company property, seeking to attach it as an amendment to Guffey's bill to help the coal industry.[152] The *New York Times* noted that opposition to Byrnes's amendment "included practically all of the New Dealers"—a group that comprised such northern liberals as Wagner and Guffey but also such prominent southern Senate leaders as Robinson and Harrison, along with Kenneth McKellar of Tennessee.[153] Indeed, it is striking that most southerners stuck with the administration on the amendment, voting 16–8 against Byrnes's proposal, as did 28 of 45 northern Democrats.[154]

Where Byrnes focused on a legislative remedy for the sit-down strikes, another southerner, Representative Martin Dies (D-TX), proposed an investigation. Republicans and "anti–New Deal Democrats" quickly "shoved it through [the Rules] committee and to the floor before the administration spokesmen knew what was happening." The resolution was subject to an "uproarious" debate in which Dies charged that an investigation was needed to highlight the "nation-wide proportions which this form of lawlessness has assumed."[155] Ohio Democrat Byron Harlan spoke against the investigation in terms that anticipated the regional split that would soon come to dominate the Democratic Party, noting that many Democrats can count on being reelected "term after term regardless of the success or failure of a national Democratic administration. But most of us who make up most of this great majority come from States where this is a vital issue, and we do not want it stirred up unnecessarily." Harlan suggested that the true beneficiaries of the investigation would be the Republican Party, colorfully arguing that "you don't have to look far into that rat-hole to discover the poison."[156] Enough party members in the overwhelmingly Democratic House—including 49 of 101 voting southerners—stayed loyal to the administration and thus defeated the Dies resolution.[157] Even so, it is noteworthy that a slim majority of southerners backed the attack on the CIO, along with its implicit rebuke to the Roosevelt administration.

By summer 1937, following biracial efforts to organize the southern textile industry, along with tobacco factories in North Carolina and ironworks in Alabama, southern Democrats explicitly began to highlight the threat the CIO posed to white supremacy in their region.[158] Conservative leader Cox took to the House floor on June 30, 1937, to denounce the CIO in a long speech that tied the organization to communism and civil rights: "It is the declared intention of John Lewis, Sidney Hillman, and other Committee for

Industrial Organization officials to invade the South and to organize both the white and the Negro labor.... they have preached social and political equality.... if minions of the Committee for Industrial Organization attempt to carry through the South their lawless plan of organization, if they attempt to demoralize our industry, to corrupt our colored citizens, to incite race hatreds and race warfare, I warn them here and now that they will be met by the flower of southern manhood and they will reap the bitter fruits of their own."[159]

Commentators noted from the start that southern concerns about race, labor, and the changing Democratic Party were interwoven. Thus Frank Kent observed in early August 1937 that "it is in the South that resentment toward the President's alliance with Mr. Lewis' CIO and his acquiescence in the sit-down strike has been most deeply resented." Southern Democrats had come to view the NLRB as "destructive of southern industry and so dominated by the CIO as to be completely partisan." This southern anger, however, was closely tied to concerns about the changing racial composition of the Democratic coalition: as Kent noted, "it, of course, is in the South that real apprehension is engendered by the potentialities involved in the wooing away from the Republican party of some two million negro voters" through "patronage, relief money, and the social equality legislation promoted by such New Deal spokesmen as Governor Earle of Pennsylvania."[160]

Indeed, when several northern Democrats pushed the antilynching bill in Congress in fall 1937, southern opponents returned repeatedly to the bill supporters' ties to labor unions and their bid for African American votes. Tom Connally (D-TX) characterized the bill's lead supporter, Wagner, as "our outstanding labor agitator. They talk about John L. Lewis. Why John is just one of the pupils of the junior Senator from New York."[161] Connally highlighted the bill's exemption of labor violence from its coverage, arguing that "the Senator from New York provides that if you want to mob anybody, join the union and picket and it is all right; you can mob them."[162] Josiah Bailey of North Carolina also highlighted the alleged inconsistency between support for the lynching bill and northern liberals' refusal to condemn the sit-down strikes: "I have no patience with politicians who cater to the men who maintain that policy [of the sit-down strikes]. I am perfectly willing to go to grips with the institution called the C.I.O. It either has to obey the law or fight with me. Talk about lynch law; let us apply your principle right there."[163]

According to Connally, Bailey, and other southerners, these CIO-aligned Democrats were forsaking the South in order to win over African American voters. Connally argued that "the bill ought to be entitled 'A bill for the purpose of insulting the South.... A bill to catch the colored votes in New York.' "[164] Bailey charged that "whenever the Republican Party or the Democratic Party or the New Deal party or any other party begins to cater to the

Negro vote, it is going to elect to office common fellows of the baser sort, and destroy the party."[165] Connally also derided the foreign roots of those backing the lynching bill, claiming that while white southerners had been fighting for the United States since the revolution, those "who will vote for the bill to shackle the South were somewhere over in Europe, God knows whether in Russia or in Germany or some other place, associating with elements that were alien to everything American."[166]

The twin dangers of racial change and CIO radicalism again figured prominently in conservative southern Democrats' efforts to fight off Roosevelt's 1938 purge campaign. Purge target "Cotton" Ed Smith argued that white supremacy was being threatened "because Negroes were being welcomed into the Northern Democratic party and into the C.I.O."[167] The *New York Times* observed that Smith has "apparently made it stick with his constituents that the inside managers of the 'purge' are for [the lynching bill]."[168]

Similarly, in a speech carried by a statewide radio hookup, Walter George claimed he wore as a "shining emblem the condemnation I have received from James Ford, the Negro Vice Presidential nominee of the communist party. Another badge I proudly wear is the condemnation of ... Labor's Non-partisan League, the Communist group of John L. Lewis." George repeatedly emphasized his opposition to the antilynching bill, claiming, "I am a liberal, but a liberal within the limits of the Constitution." George concluded his speech with unintentional irony by declaring that "I am persuaded that this generation of white Democrats will not let democracy down in our beloved state."[169]

Southerners were not the only ones to link CIO "radicalism" to racial change: in an article highlighting the CIO's ties to communism, the Republican-allied *Chicago Tribune* noted portentously that "another activity in which the communists and C.I.O. are cooperating is organization of the Negroes."[170] A year later a Detroit law enforcement official testified to the Dies Committee on Un-American Activities that the Communist Party's strategy was to boost the CIO and organize blacks.[171] But where northern conservatives generally focused on the CIO's communist ties, southern critics were far more likely to bring up its racial program.

By the late 1930s southern Democrats and Republicans regularly joined forces in Congress to pursue legislation and investigations targeting the labor movement and the CIO in particular. Howard Smith (D-VA), a leader of the conservative coalition, spearheaded a high-profile investigation of the National Labor Relations Board that targeted the agency for its alleged ties both to the communists and the CIO. Smith drew on the investigation's findings to propose legislation revamping the Wagner Act. Liberal journalist Russ Stone argued that Smith was seeking to "wipe out the New Deal" by bringing down the labor movement. The committee had become a "propaganda agency aimed at convincing the middle class groups and the great numbers of still unorganized workers that the [National Labor Relations] Board is an agency for radical unionism." According to Stone, Smith was motivated by both economic and racial considerations: "He is resolved that Southern competitive advantages obtained by cheap labor shall not be lessened by the Washington radicals." At the same time, Smith's move against the New Deal started when "he began to see that the New Deal was designed to extend economic security even to the po' white trash—that economic freedom was incompatible with keeping the Negro in his place." For southerners such as Smith, the NLRB was dangerous precisely because it bolstered the political and economic muscle of the CIO: "The conservatives are not worried over the administrative techniques of the NLRB, its personnel or its decisions. They are worried over the Board as a major factor in contemporary politics."[172]

While the conservative coalition started on labor issues, it soon came to encompass a broader set policies. With the rise of the CIO and the entry of African Americans into the Democratic coalition and the labor movement, southern politicians increasingly came to see labor-sponsored extensions of the New Deal as a threat to their core interests and became far more skeptical of liberal proposals to expand the welfare state and the reach of government regulation.[173]

Southern Democrats and the New Deal Coalition

The political contours of the New Deal coalition had been hard to pin down prior to the rise of the CIO and the subsequent southern reaction. Roosevelt had been reelected in 1936 with 62.5 percent of the two-party vote, drawing extensive support across classes, regions, and ideological groups. Polling by Gallup indicates that Roosevelt won over 60 percent of the two-party vote in farm areas, small towns, and cities, with a gap of only 4–5 points separating his support in cities from farms and small towns.[174] Roosevelt polled over 40 percent even among self-identified conservatives (compared to winning nearly 80 percent of liberals) and won approximately 40 percent among those with the highest socioeconomic status.[175] Even a majority of voters who supported cutting relief expenditures in their home community claimed to have voted to reelect Roosevelt.[176] In this context, what it meant to be a New Dealer or a Roosevelt supporter was far from precisely defined.

The events of 1937–38, with the sit-down strikes, court packing, and the party purge, sharpened what it meant to be a New Dealer and clarified who stood in the way of further expansion of the New Deal agenda. In place of the diffuse coalition that cast ballots for Roosevelt in 1932 and 1936, ardent New Dealers were increasingly identified with the northern, labor-oriented, urban wing of the party. The association of the New Deal with agrarian, rural voters faded, and southern Democrats were now identified as critics of proposals to expand the New Deal's reach.

If, in 1933–36, one asked a politically engaged, self-described New Dealer who, inside his or her party, was an enemy of New Deal liberalism, the answer likely would have been Al Smith and his allies; by the end of the 1930s, it would have been Vice President John Nance Garner and his fellow southern "reactionaries." Thus *Time*, which had depicted Garner as "a very useful helper to the New Deal" in its 1935 profile (see chapter 2), declared in 1939 that the vice president was engaged in an "undeclared war" with the president.[177] According to the magazine, Roosevelt's refusal to condemn the sitdown strikes, coupled with the court fight and purge, had led to an irreparable breach. The "rebellion which John Nance Garner now leads is ... the biggest political struggle now going on in Washington.... Garner has become to arch New Dealers a symbol of sabotage." The same story noted that Finance chairman Pat Harrison of Mississippi—who not long before had been seen as a key New Deal supporter—was acting as Garner's "field marshal" in fighting Roosevelt.[178] From 1933 to 1936 just eight stories in the *New York Times* or *Washington Post* used the word "conservative" within fifteen words of Garner's name; from 1937 to 1940 a total of ninety-three stories did so.[179] Stanley High put the emergent cleavage in vivid terms when he noted that "no political and economic gulf is wider than that which separates John L. Lewis from John N. Garner."[180]

As maneuvering began for the 1940 Democratic nomination, the big fear of liberals was that the strong norm against presidents serving more than two terms would provide an opening for a conservative such as Garner to replace Roosevelt. Speaking at a convention of Young Democratic Clubs of America, Senate Democratic leader Alben Barkley (D-KY) argued that Americans have "as much to fear next year from reactionary members of the Democratic party as from openly hostile Republicans." His speech was taken as a clear shot against the idea of Garner replacing Roosevelt as the Democratic nominee in 1940.[181]

This regionally based ideological cleavage became a staple of political discussion, even finding its way into early opinion polls. Thus when Gallup started polling in advance of the next presidential election, it asked Democrats who they would prefer if Roosevelt did not run, "a conservative type of candidate like Garner, Clark, or Byrd, or a New Dealer like Hopkins, Wallace, or Barkley?" Two of the three "conservatives" were southerners—Garner and Virginia's Byrd, while the third was border-state senator Champ Clark of Missouri.[182] Later in the year Gallup asked respondents who they would support in a three-cornered race for president between "Garner running on a conservative-Democratic ticket, Roosevelt on a liberal-Democratic ticket," or a Republican.[183]

Voters also generally identified Roosevelt as a liberal and Garner as a conservative. When Gallup asked about Garner's ideology in June 1939, 56 percent viewed him as conservative and 28 percent as liberal. In that poll, just 7 percent viewed Roosevelt as conservative, compared to 59 percent who labeled him liberal and another 34 percent who viewed him as radical.[184] The terms "liberal" and "New Dealer" now clearly did not include such southerners as Garner and his allies; instead, these labels had become identified with the labor-oriented, urban, ethnically and racially diverse party taking shape in the North.[185]

As one window into the changing imagery of the New Deal, I undertook a systematic search of front-page coverage in the *New York Times*. I identified all stories that used such terms as "New Dealer," "100 percent New Deal," "anti-New Deal," and "anti-administration," along with mentioning Congress.[186] Each story was coded to identify which individuals and groups were depicted as pro– and anti–New Deal, along with the more general topic of the stories. Table 3.1 provides the simple counts of members of Congress on each side by party and region, while figure 3.3 summarizes the proportion of members identified as critical of the New Deal among northern and southern Democrats over time.

A first pattern to note is that these terms were not used heavily in 1933–36, but to the extent that they were used, both northern and southern Democrats were generally identified as New Deal supporters. (The total for 1933 is especially low because while the term "New Deal" often appeared in the

TABLE 3.1. Count of members of Congress identified with pro– or anti–New Deal cause (front-page stories, *New York Times*)

	Northern Democrats		Southern Democrats		Republicans	
	Pro	Anti	Pro	Anti	Pro	Anti
1933	2	5	7	2	0	6
1934	8	1	8	3	1	21
1935	12	4	24	5	0	17
1936	7	5	17	2	0	21
1937	17	26	13	19	0	23
1938	124	98	42	66	1	20
1939	78	27	44	75	7	54

Note: The search terms used were ("anti-New Deal*" OR "anti-administration*" OR "New Dealer*" OR "New Deal Democrat*" OR "100 per cent New Deal*" OR "100 percent New Deal*" OR "100% New Deal*") AND (Congress OR House OR Senate OR representative OR senator), with a limitation to front-page stories. Each story was hand-coded; a member was coded as "pro" if he or she was identified as supporting the position or goals of the administration and/or New Deal. The member was coded as "anti" if he or she was identified as critical of the position or goals of the administration and/or New Deal.

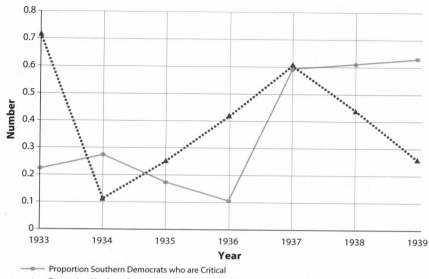

FIGURE 3.3. Proportion of southern and northern Democrats depicted as critical of Roosevelt administration or New Deal (front-page coverage, *New York Times*)

news coverage, the term "New Dealer" was rarely used initially; even if one does loosen the search to include "New Deal," however, the number of references in 1933 is well below later years).[187] From 1933 to 1935 northern Democratic members are associated with the pro–New Deal side by a 22–10 margin, while southern Democrats are associated with the pro–New Deal side by a more decisive 39–10. Republicans, of course, are overwhelmingly anti–New Deal (44–1). Ten of the stories focus on attacks on Roosevelt that come from the left; twenty highlight attacks from the right. The stories on attacks from the left often emphasize the role of Huey Long and focus on such issues as the administration's opposition to paying the prevailing wage on relief projects (angering organized labor, along with populist Democrats), Roosevelt's bonus bill veto, and the administration's stance against publicizing high-earners' tax returns.

By 1936 the attacks from the left essentially disappear as the second New Deal defused the charge that was Roosevelt was a closet conservative. Many more stories emphasize criticism from the right: thirty-six front-page stories in the *Times* highlight attacks from conservatives, while just four focus on attacks from the left.[188] Among members of Congress, southern Democrats remain quite unified in support for the administration; southern Democratic members are labeled as antiadministration on just two occasions—both in reference to longtime New Deal skeptic Carter Glass of Virginia—while seventeen are associated with support for the New Deal. By contrast, northern Democratic members are associated with the pro–New Deal side on seven occasions and with anti–New Deal positions five times. As before, Republican members of Congress are unified in taking an anti–New Deal stance (21 to 0).[189]

While only a handful of congressional Democrats are mentioned as New Deal opponents in the front-page stories during Roosevelt's first term, several Democrats outside Congress are identified with opposition to the administration. Strikingly, most of these opponents are northerners prominent in the party before the rise of the New Deal. The Liberty League is a frequent focus of discussion,[190] with former presidential nominees Al Smith (1928) and John W. Davis (1924) spearheading the group's attack on Roosevelt's alleged radicalism. In 1936 alone, twenty-one front-page stories in the *Times* pointed to Smith as a New Deal critic. Roosevelt's first budget director, Lewis Douglas, former Massachusetts governor Joseph Ely, former DNC chairman and business leader John Raskob, former Missouri senator James Reed, and former Michigan governor William Comstock are also each identified as anti–New Deal Democrats.[191]

The leading southern Roosevelt critic in 1936 was Georgia governor Eugene Talmadge, who called a special convention ahead of the 1936 election to denounce the New Deal for its alleged communism and for its growing ties to African Americans.[192] Talmadge's movement was greeted with unanimous condemnation by Georgia's congressional delegation and found little support elsewhere in the South.[193] Instead, with the notable exception of Talmadge, Democratic opposition to the New Deal was—at the public level—most associated with northern Democratic holdovers from the pre-Roosevelt era, rather than southerners.[194]

This began to change in 1937 and had been reversed completely by 1939. Where both northern and southern Democrats in Congress were generally depicted as administration supporters in 1935–36, the more difficult political context in 1937 generated many stories highlighting Democratic divisions. As a result, seventeen northern congressional Democrats are identified with administration support, compared to twenty-six identified as critical. The proportions are similar among southern Democrats: thirteen are identified as supporters, nineteen as critics. Court packing and the sit-down strikes were the two main topics of the stories featuring this Democratic disaffection with the administration. Importantly, however, southern leaders in Congress continued to be labeled as "New Dealers" despite their underlying conservatism. Thus in *New York Times* coverage of the Senate debate over the southerner Byrnes's bid to force sit-down strikers off of company property, Joseph Robinson and Pat Harrison were both referred to as "New Dealers" fighting on behalf of the administration and against Byrnes. Such an identification, however, would become far less common for mainstream southern Democrats of their ilk.[195]

Democratic criticism of the administration broadened to a larger, but more disproportionately southern, set of legislators in 1938. Amid Roosevelt's purge campaign, the sheer number of front-page stories framed as a battle between New Deal and anti–New Deal forces expanded considerably.[196] Over the course of the year, northern Democratic members of Congress are characterized as taking the pro–New Deal side by a 124–98 margin. By contrast, the southerners are characterized as anti–New Deal by a 66–42 margin.

Southerners kept up their criticism of the administration in 1939, while the remaining northerners increasingly coalesced under the New Deal banner. Thus northern Democrats are depicted as siding with the administration by a 78–27 margin, while southerners are opposed by 75–44. Notably, more than half of the positive southern Democratic mentions are in reference to party leaders backing the administration. If one drops formal party leaders who were repeatedly identified as administration supporters—namely, Senate Democratic leader Barkley of Kentucky, House majority leader Sam Rayburn (D-TX), and Speaker William Bankhead (D-AL)—there are seventy-five mentions of southern Democrats in opposition to the administration or New Deal and just twenty in favor. By comparison, seventy-seven Republicans are noted as administration opponents, while seven Republicans are associated with administration support.

Southern members of Congress encompassed substantial diversity in the late 1930s (and the 1940s); several southern representatives continued to support most New Deal programs.[197] But southern members of Congress were unified in their opposition to civil rights, nearly as unified in their hostility to organized labor, and increasingly provided the main opposition within the Democratic Party to a range of other New Deal programs.[198]

Therefore a major shift in the enemies of the New Deal—as depicted in front-page coverage in the *New York Times*—occurred between 1935 and 1939. An opposition that came from both the left and the right in 1935 was replaced by an opposition that came almost entirely from the right. Furthermore, an opposition within the Democratic Party that was not regionally based in 1935–36 became much more clearly a "southern" phenomenon by 1938–39.

The changing meaning of the term "New Dealer" was not confined to the news coverage of the *Times*. By 1937–39 the liberal and labor press explicitly framed domestic politics as a battle between progressive New Dealers and reactionary southerners. Where the *New Republic* and the *Nation* had treated Roosevelt's alleged timidity as a major obstacle to progress during his first term, they now portrayed the president as pushing hard to turn his party and American politics more generally in a liberal direction. Stories in both magazines now highlighted the role of conservative southern Democrats in blocking liberal advances, rather than focusing on probusiness eastern conservatives. Looking ahead to the 1938 midterms, Heywood Broun commented in the *New Republic* about "demagogic reactionaries in the Southland" and concluded that "only a long battle of education will convince many Southern voters that the Civil War is not an issue and that it is silly to send men to Washington to fight economic betterment."[199] More generally, political coverage in both liberal magazines routinely lambasted conservative southerners for stalling progress and for pushing initiatives to undermine the New Deal in the late 1930s.[200]

Labor publications depicted the political battle lines in similar—if often more colorful—terms. Throughout the late 1930s and early 1940s the *CIO News* is full of stories describing the clash between southern "Tories," on the one hand—such as Smith and Cox—and the New Deal and labor unions, on the other. In this way, southern reactionaries were the most important enemy of liberal advances, not just on civil rights but across a range of policy domains. Indeed, the CIO drew attention to the connection between civil rights and labor rights by repeatedly labeling these southern conservatives as the "poll tax representatives," highlighting the belief that free and fair southern elections would lead to more prolabor members of Congress.[201] Following the 1940 election the *CIO News* noted that "the usual crop of southern reactionaries, aided by the disfranchising poll tax, were returned to Congress." A separate story in the same issue featured pictures of Howard Smith and Eugene Cox, along with a discussion of how the poll tax keeps these "reactionaries" in office.[202]

The African American press also came to see a sharp distinction between the New Deal Democratic Party and the old southern-dominated party. As early as August 1938 the *Chicago Defender* argued that years of GOP abandonment had led to a "drastic change of feeling, and consequent casting of ballots. The New Dealers, rather than the Democratic party with its iniquitous record of southern disfranchisement, made an appeal for a change of front, and their message was listened to with hopeful anticipations."[203] The following year the *Defender* published an article again setting the New Deal in opposition to the old Democratic Party of the South: "If the New Deal ultimately won't work, it will be because the philosophy of the new deal is one thing, the old line democracy of the solid south is another, and these two diametrically opposed concepts have been artificially held together to keep the electoral vote safe for the Democratic party."[204] Looking ahead to the 1940 election, the *Defender* editorialized that "the people demand a return to a strengthened 'New Deal' program," noting that John L. Lewis's call for a platform satisfactory to labor and the common people was "a direction with which Negro America can certainly find no fault." The same editorial also joined Lewis in warning Democrats that they could not take labor and

African American support for granted.[205] More generally, the *Defender*'s coverage of the "New Deal" became markedly more positive in 1938–40: from 1933 to 1936, *Defender* front-page stories or editorials mentioning the New Deal were about equally positive and negative in tone (42% positive, 36% negative, 22% mixed). From 1938 to 1940, 79 percent of the stories were positive in tone and 6 percent were negative.[206]

This shift in the political line-up of New Deal opponents and supporters corresponded to a change in how liberal opinion magazines treated civil rights issues in the late 1930s. As Hans Noel shows, liberal policy intellectuals had begun to express support for African American rights as early as 1930.[207] Even so, as noted in chapter 2, discussions of civil rights were generally kept separate from and subordinate to economic issues, which were seen as the defining battle for liberalism. But as southern Democrats became identified as key New Deal opponents in 1937–39, the liberal journals "made hesitating steps toward developing racism as an issue to use against conservative Southerners in support of the efforts to purge them from power."[208] A new coalition had started to form on the ground, in which CIO unions and African American voters were becoming a critical constituency for northern liberal Democrats advocating an expanded New Deal. With southern Democrats increasingly identified as opponents of that new coalition and its broad policy agenda, civil rights went from being a side interest of liberal magazines to a vital front in a battle to control the ideological direction of the Democratic Party. The political muscle and coalitional logic brought about by the CIO's entry as a key player were likely necessary preconditions for liberal intellectuals' ideas to be folded into the broader program of urban-oriented New Deal liberalism in the late 1930s.

Conclusion

When Franklin Roosevelt launched his New Deal in 1933, the standard liberal program did not include civil rights as an element. Roosevelt's failure to lead on civil rights in this period reflected not just his reluctance to avoid alienating his southern allies in Congress but also the conventional understanding of the progressive or liberal program. By the start of Roosevelt's second term, however, constituency changes in the Democratic coalition established crucial initial connections between economic liberalism and racial liberalism. The dramatic entry of African American voters into the Democratic Party in 1934–36 created a constituency within the party for progress on racial issues. Votes could now be plausibly won by pushing for civil rights. But with the prewar African American population heavily concentrated in the South and a handful of northern cities, most northern Democratic politicians could still steer clear of civil rights support with few electoral consequences.

However, the rise of the CIO in 1935–39 played a crucial role in forcing African American concerns into the mainstream liberal Democratic program. The union quickly became the most significant source of outside campaign support for northern Democratic candidates, simultaneously incorporating civil rights into its own, ambitious policy program.

The southern reaction against these constituency changes in the Democratic coalition cemented the new alliance between the CIO and African Americans. From African Americans' perspective, the same individuals fighting against their rights were also condemning the CIO for its political and economic agenda. From the CIO's perspective, it became clear that the group's mortal enemies within the Democratic Party were also the die-hard foes of extending civil rights to African Americans. Dislodging the power of conservative southern Democrats was essential for the CIO's long-term ambitions; this meant allying with African Americans to end the poll tax, halt violent intimidation, and create a more democratic South in which a working-class coalition might succeed. Within the North, electing liberal, prolabor politicians would depend on constructing a coalition, based primarily in big industrial cities, that incorporated the growing African American population.

Indeed, changes in intraparty politics in the North were critical to the development of a sharply defined regional cleavage with race and labor as focal points. During the late 1930s and early 1940s, the leading anti–New Deal northern Democrats in Congress either were defeated for reelection, retired, or died in office.[209] Roosevelt's northern opponents outside Congress—such as Smith, Davis, Douglas, and Raskob—made considerable noise in the 1936 campaign but soon became political nonentities. The political challenge facing northern liberals would have been much different had the Smith-Raskob wing of the party remained to fight Roosevelt alongside the southern conservatives, but they lacked any sort of electoral base in the region. As a result, their choices were to abandon the party, abandon politics, or both. In contrast, southern conservatives, with their secure hold on the electoral apparatus in their region, held on and grew in numbers, clarifying the regional (and racial policy) line of cleavage within the party. Federalism and the geographic decentralization of the American party system therefore afforded secure power bases for the contending wings of the Democratic Party to fight it out, rather than forcing a single unified brand on the party.

As a result of these developments, by the end of the 1930s, New Deal liberalism, as articulated by its fiercest advocates, was now connected to civil rights progress in a way that had not been true as late as 1936. Chapter 4 traces how the cleavage between urban, liberal northern Democrats and conservative southerners expanded in scope and came to occupy a central place in American politics in the 1940s.

CHAPTER 4

Liberalism Transformed

THE EARLY CIVIL RIGHTS MOVEMENT AND

THE "LIBERAL LOBBY"

As WE HAVE seen, by the end of the 1930s the cause of African American civil rights had a foothold in the mainstream liberal program that it had lacked during Roosevelt's first term. This foothold, however, did not necessarily imply that civil rights would become a defining component of New Deal liberalism. This chapter traces the development of the liberal civil rights coalition in the 1940s and early 1950s, as it broadened out from the initial CIO–African American alliance forged in the late 1930s. I first trace the role of African American activists in capitalizing on the disruptions stemming from World War II in order to raise the visibility of civil rights on the political agenda. I then show how the fairly narrow CIO–African American alliance widened to include a larger array of actors as racial issues became more salient, transforming civil rights groups into core members of the liberal coalition by the end of the 1940s.

World War II transformed the politics of civil rights in two ways. First, it generated social transformations that rendered northern African Americans a far more potent electoral constituency than they had ever been before. Second, the war provided a crucial window of opportunity for civil rights movement activists to raise the visibility of civil rights issues and thus to encourage liberal leaders and groups to give civil rights a more prominent place in their program. African American leaders and activists highlighted the glaring contradiction between the ideals ostensibly motivating U.S. participation in the war and the reality of American racial practices. Starting with the March on Washington Movement launched by A. Philip Randolph in 1941 and continuing throughout the war, African Americans highlighted discrimination in the military and in war industries, along with the long-standing indignities of life under Jim Crow.

Fueled by these wartime forces, civil rights became a crucial marker of liberal identity, and civil rights organizations became full-fledged members of the liberal coalition. Liberal groups such as the CIO Political Action Committee (CIO-PAC) and Americans for Democratic Action embraced civil rights as central components of their agenda. They took leading roles alongside African American groups in emerging civil rights umbrella organizations such as the National Council for a Permanent FEPC and the National Emergency Committee Against Mob Violence. These groups brought together the most prominent actors associated with urban liberalism in the 1940s. Meanwhile, African American organizations actively promoted the economic agenda of their liberal allies alongside their civil rights concerns. Economic liberalism and racial liberalism thus became inextricably, programmatically linked.

As argued in chapter 1, thinking about the civil rights realignment in terms of the intersection of multiple political trajectories helps to understand the significance of the early civil rights movement. The changes in the composition of the New Deal coalition in the mid- to late 1930s had important implications for how political actors would respond when African American activists began to push civil rights higher onto the national agenda. Critically, these activists—such as A. Philip Randolph—were not concerned with helping the Democratic Party or the CIO. They were seeking to force national political leaders in both parties to make civil rights a priority. Their tactics—such as the threatened March on Washington—were opposed by national Democratic leaders. But in the new coalitional context that had developed in the late 1930s, the pressure from civil rights activists provided an organizing focus for developing a more robust liberal coalition that put civil rights at or near the top of its agenda.

The expansion and deepening of the liberal civil rights coalition in the 1940s also speaks to theories of parties. Liberal groups agreed with one another that most southern Democrats' economic and racial conservatism made them critical enemies of progress. At the same time, southerners fought back by working with Republicans to attack the foundations of union power. In doing so, southern Democrats undermined a central pillar necessary for electing northern Democrats. The intense battle to control the Democratic Party was not simply a contest among coalition partners to see who would have the greatest influence over nominations for office. A more apt description is that it was a long-term struggle for survival, in which conservative southern Democrats were willing to weaken their party's electoral foundation in the North to protect their own vital interests. Civil rights had become a key differentiating issue along a broad, liberal-conservative ideological dimension, in which the contending sides *within* the Democratic Party had come to view one another as enemies occupying opposing poles of the political spectrum.

WORLD WAR II AND AFRICAN AMERICAN MOBILIZATION

African American leaders and activists seized on the mobilization to fight World War II to further the developing effort to incorporate civil rights into the liberal program. Although there are several relevant dimensions along which World War II influenced civil rights politics, two main areas warrant emphasis for exploring the war's implications for the civil rights realignment.[1]

First, the war effort generated dramatic social changes that made African Americans an important constituency for northern politicians. The First Great Migration of 1910 to 1930 had boosted the African American population in several northern states, but the vast majority of African Americans continued to be stuck in the rural South, where disfranchisement and Jim Crow left them with little political leverage. As late as 1940, 77 percent of African Americans lived in the South, where they constituted 24 percent of the overall population; by contrast, African Americans constituted less than 4 percent of the population in the rest of the country.

Wartime migration changed this picture dramatically, with the bulk of the population movement concentrated in several northern cities that were war production hubs. Government data indicate that Detroit gained sixty-five thousand African American residents during the war; Chicago gained fifty thousand from just the four southern states of Mississippi, Georgia, Alabama, and Tennessee; and Los Angeles gained nearly sixty thousand from 1940 to 1944.[2] The wartime migration was reinforced by returning African American soldiers, who settled disproportionately in the North. Soon after the war ended, the census found that the nonwhite population in the Northeast and North Central states had increased from 2.9 million in 1940 to 4.6 million in 1947.

Although continuing to face deeply entrenched discrimination in both the workplace and housing, northern African Americans did have the vote. These voters tended to be concentrated in urban areas, where they could be incorporated into political machines and help elect mayors.[3] Indeed, an early literature highlighted the extent to which urban politics provided an initial point of entry for African American politicians and voters.[4] Many African Americans also worked in war industries where they were able to join unions and earn a decent wage for the first time. The growth in the African American working and middle class helped the NAACP gain new members. The organization had just 355 branches with 50,556 members in 1940; six years later it boasted 1,073 branches with nearly 400,000 members.[5] Sugrue notes that the NAACP "made its biggest inroads in cities where it was closely associated with organized labor," as it became more of a "mass membership organization with a populist orientation."[6]

These demographic and social changes increased the number of northern politicians who viewed winning African American votes as a strategic imperative. Migration also made African American voters a potentially pivotal group in the electoral college. African American writer and activist Henry Lee Moon's book *Balance of Power* was written ahead of the 1948 election with a clear message to both parties: success in northern swing states such as New York, Illinois, and Michigan depended on a genuine commitment to civil rights.[7] Just twenty years earlier, both the Al Smith and Herbert Hoover campaigns showed little or no interest in appealing to African American voters; by contrast, the contest for African American support was a major topic of discussion in presidential elections in the 1940s.[8]

A second, related aspect of the war is that it provided a window of opportunity for African American leaders and activists to raise the visibility of civil rights issues on the political agenda. While liberal Democrats had been increasingly supportive of civil rights in the late 1930s, they still faced a national party leadership fearful of the explosive potential of civil rights for their party's coalition. As a result, it was crucial for civil rights activists to find ways to force their way into the political conversation.

Demands to include African Americans in war employment became a defining issue early on. Randolph formally launched the March on Washington Movement in January 1941 after Roosevelt had shunted aside earlier pleas from African American leaders to act against the rampant discrimination in war industries and the military.[9] Grassroots activists, at times working with NAACP and Urban League branches, organized demonstrations in numerous northern cities. The *Pittsburgh Courier* and other African American newspapers pressed the issue hard, encouraging African Americans to join Randolph's protest drive.[10]

The threat of a massive protest march in Washington, DC, led the reluctant Roosevelt to issue Executive Order 8802 creating the Fair Employment Practices Committee to enforce nondiscrimination in defense industries. Randolph declared the executive order the "Second Emancipation Proclamation"; the order was also widely praised in the African American press.[11] Most white northern politicians initially paid little attention to the executive order, but Guffey—who had worked with Robert Vann to bring African Americans into the Pennsylvania Democratic Party—praised the president for "insisting upon a fair racial and creed policy in employment in Government service" and inserted the text of the order into the *Congressional Record*.[12]

Although the FEPC's record proved mixed, its creation represented the president's first clear step on behalf of civil rights.[13] Perhaps even more important, the FEPC itself became an organizing point for civil rights advocates for more than a decade, displacing antilynching legislation and the poll tax as the major civil rights issue on the legislative agenda. While the white press largely ignored the FEPC's formation, African American newspapers highlighted cases of discrimination and urged the agency to act. Over time, liberal journals such as the *New Republic* and the *Nation* paid increasing attention to the FEPC's efforts and became forceful advocates of making the committee permanent. Meanwhile, labor activists—such as the Reuther brothers—worked with the NAACP to pressure the FEPC to act decisively.[14]

As Sugrue concludes, "the committee gave black activists, particularly in the trade union movement, a focal point.... The battle for a stronger, permanent fair employment practices law led to the creation of an interracial alliance that spanned the left flank of the Democratic Party, various religious groups, many CIO unions, and various Socialist and Communist organizations."[15]

African American activists and newspapers couched concerns about discrimination in war industries within a broader critique of the hypocrisy inherent in fighting a war against fascism abroad while oppressing African Americans at home. Although disaffection with discrimination led some African Americans to refuse to support the war effort altogether, the *Pittsburgh Courier* advocated for a "Double V" campaign, seeking "victory over our enemies at home and victory over our enemies on the battlefields abroad."[16]

Discrimination in the military became one of the main targets for movement activists, with a long, hard campaign forcing gradual concessions that finally culminated with Harry Truman's desegregation order in 1948.[17] Civil rights advocates also joined the drive to ensure that the government provide a "federal ballot" that would make it easier for all soldiers to vote; this well-publicized battle furthered the growing belief that Republicans—who feared soldiers would side with Roosevelt and thus sought legislation making it harder to vote—were allied with southern Democrats in the battle against civil rights.[18]

Conflicts over wartime housing—where African American migrants to northern cities often faced numerous obstacles to finding decent living conditions—became yet another flashpoint demonstrating that America's racial problems were entrenched in the North as well as South. The Detroit race riot of 1943, which was one of several cases of major racial violence in centers of African American migration in 1942–43, was perhaps the most egregious indicator of endemic racism in the North.

Nonetheless, the reaction to the riot also hinted at signs of change. African Americans were no longer entirely alone in identifying white racism and insufficient government action on behalf of African Americans as the underlying source of trouble. In the aftermath of the riot, the "UAW stood out" as one of very few predominantly white institutions "to defend the black community and denounce police brutality."[19] UAW leaders spoke out against the whites who had targeted African Americans seeking fair housing. Liberal publications such as the *New Republic* and the *Nation* also forcefully denounced the white racism that was the root of the conflict. The *New Republic* noted that "it is the Negroes who do the suffering and the dying in American riots.... They don't start riots. They are the victims."[20] The *Nation* editorialized that the Detroit riots demonstrated that "we cannot fight fascism abroad while turning a blind eye to fascism at home. We cannot inscribe on our banners: 'For Democracy and a caste system.' We cannot liberate oppressed peoples while maintaining the right to oppress our own minorities."[21]

More broadly, it is telling that white liberals were finally willing to criticize Roosevelt directly for his failure to act against racism. A few months before the Detroit riots, Thomas Sancton argued in the *New Republic* that Roosevelt had been wrong to rein in the FEPC's investigations of discrimination in transportation industries. Sancton charged that Roosevelt "should have never given his ear to the group of Southerners in Washington" who urged him to call off the hearings.[22] Similarly, I. F. Stone warned readers of the *Nation* that the "White House has passed the word along to soft-pedal the fight against the poll tax. The Fair Employment Practices Committee and the fight against racial discrimination are being elbowed to one side.... This is another of those cases in which progressives must lead the President if he is unwilling or unable to lead them."[23]

This progressive criticism intensified following the Detroit riots. Writing in the *New Republic*, Sancton was unsparing in his criticism of Roosevelt: "The President has shown greatness as a military leader.... Yet, if he continues to lose his grip on domestic issues, his failure as a President may in the end be even greater. If it happens, history must render a merciless verdict against the little group of yes-men and intriguers who are his immediate advisers."[24] Sancton argued that when racial tensions began to increase earlier in the war, Roosevelt "should have come to this nation and talked to us.... Why, in these months when the peril of open race war hung upon the air, hasn't Mr. Roosevelt come to us with one of his greatest speeches, speaking to us as the great mongrel nation; immigrants (and the descendants of immigrants) all of us; none of us the master race." The article concluded with the demand that Roosevelt must speak to the nation now: "Whether Mr. Roosevelt will be able to measure the necessity against the political cost we shall see; he has failed miserably to do so in the past."[25]

The social disruptions of the war years, combined with African American activists' efforts to highlight civil rights abuses and to link these abuses to the problem of developing a unified front in the fight against fascism, had begun to change the place of civil rights in American politics. In the 1930s white liberals had criticized Roosevelt when he seemed reluctant to take on business interests but not when he failed to attack Jim Crow.[26] But now his failure to confront discrimination was identified as a key shortcoming, one that united African Americans, CIO unions, and white New Deal liberals against enemies of democracy that included southern reactionaries, Republican conservatives, and fascist governments abroad. The earlier shift among liberals in the late 1930s made them more receptive than conservative Republicans to calls to fight racial injustice, but it was up to African American activists to capitalize on the war effort to raise the visibility of civil rights abuses and thus turn this baseline receptivity into concrete political action.

The New Liberal Coalition

When liberals made general programmatic statements about their goals in the early 1930s, civil rights was typically absent from the list. Even in 1936, after the Roosevelt campaign and the CIO began their outreach to African American voters, election coverage in the *New Republic* and the *Nation* made little mention of civil rights. When liberal and left-wing leaders were asked about the campaign's stakes, few drew any connection between Roosevelt's reelection and civil rights progress (see chapter 2). This began to change with the CIO's and LNPL's activities in the mid- to late 1930s, and by the end of World War II civil rights had become one of the mainstays of liberal Democrats' programmatic statements.

As noted in chapter 3, the LNPL included civil rights proposals on its lists of legislative priorities from 1937 onward, while the *CIO News* and individual CIO leaders publicly advocated for these measures as part of their program. The war mobilization had a major impact on the labor movement as well as the African American civil rights movement. The boom in defense employment provided a big boost to the CIO's membership and finances. Furthermore, the politicization of labor relations that occurred in the context of wartime price and wage controls contributed to the labor movement's power.[27] Although the LNPL disbanded in the wake of divisions over U.S. entry into World War II, it was soon superseded by the CIO-PAC, which proved even more aggressive in promoting racial liberalism and even more central to the electoral interests of northern Democrats.

The CIO-PAC

Formed in 1943, the PAC had one overriding goal: to elect supportive candidates for office. With an antiunion coalition of southern conservatives and Republicans in firm control of Congress following the 1942 midterms, the shared enemies of African American activists and the CIO came into even sharper focus. African Americans played an important role in the PAC organization from the start; for example, Henry Lee Moon served as an assistant director and southern field organizer for the group.

The first widely distributed pamphlet issued by the PAC, *This Is Your America*, embraced civil rights alongside a broad liberal program. Speaking in plain terms to American workers, the pamphlet argued that the essence of being an American is the "belief that all men are created equal—regardless of race, religion, or nationality." The pamphlet listed five duties of an American, one of which was to "support (and fight for, if necessary) our ideals of freedom for all our people, the Negro as well as the white, the foreign-born as well as the native-born." It noted that many fail to live up to American ideals by hating people based on their religion or race, adding that "the worst sufferers of this un-American feeling are the Negroes." Finally, in discussing the need for better education, improved health care, and housing, the CIO-PAC declared that "most important of all, we must destroy prejudice against the foreign-born and the hatred of Negroes and other peoples."[28]

The PAC's *People's Program for 1944* provided a more detailed policy blueprint while elaborating on the themes in the earlier pamphlet. The program called for expanded access to medical care, housing, education, and unemployment insurance, while noting that each American ought to have the right to earn a decent living, regardless of race, creed, or occupation. It included a prominent section on civil rights that attacked racially discriminatory policies and called for a well-funded, permanent FEPC with enforcement power.[29] More generally, historian James Foster writes that the CIO-PAC's 1944 campaign revolved around four issues: inflation, civil rights, postwar reconversion, and the historic failures of the GOP.[30] A PAC pamphlet targeting African American voters not only endorsed a wide range of specific civil rights initiatives, it fit these plans into a broader ideological framework, arguing that "he who hates Negroes and wishes to curtail their rights also hates labor and wishes to curtail its rights. *Your enemies are our enemies: and your friends are our friends.*"[31] A year later, when the PAC announced that it would poll members of Congress to assess their support for American workers, the FEPC was listed among the key tests.[32]

The CIO-PAC's significance, however, extended beyond the particular set of issues that it chose to emphasize. The PAC became a major source of campaign funds for Democratic candidates. Writing in 1945, Louise Overacker identified the group's spending as one of the "most controversial issues of the [1944] campaign."[33] Through the PAC and its sister organization, the National Citizens Political Action Committee (NCPAC), the CIO spent over $1.3 million in the 1944 presidential campaign.[34] This was by far the single biggest source of spending on behalf of the Democrats, representing roughly 20 percent of the total spending for the party.[35]

In addition to its financial power, the CIO-PAC became a key mobilizing instrument for liberalism across much of the country. Riker estimates that by the mid-1940s the CIO and its lobby dominated the Democratic Party organization in about twenty-five congressional districts and constituted a "strong voice" in another seventy-five districts. As Patricia Sullivan argues, the PAC "sought to build party realignment from the ground up by organizing labor and the diverse constituency of New Deal liberalism into an articulate political movement capable of countering the powerful bipartisan coalition in Congress at the ballot box."[36] This meant undertaking voter registration drives in both the South and the North, along with efforts to help pay the poll taxes of southern African Americans.

The disruptive potential of this mission was not lost on political observers at the time. The election of 1944 was widely interpreted as a sign of the

PAC's vote-winning prowess, persuading DNC chairman Robert Hannegan that "future party successes depend on attracting labor and independent voters by a record of liberal accomplishment." The DNC chair worried that "Conservative Southern Democrats in Congress, in combination with like-minded Republicans, have virtually stalled" such a program.[37] Hannegan's determination to "tie an unmistakably liberal tag on the Democratic Party" led him to work with the PAC, a development that especially "vexed" the southerners.[38]

When a DNC-sponsored publication seemed to criticize southerners for their antilabor votes, a furious reaction ensued, with Eugene Cox declaring in a Jackson Day dinner that "the Democratic party needs to be purged ... but it needs to be purged of alien plotters, of alien thinkers, of alien ideologies, and of alien doctrines.... Throw out these alien interlopers and these native exploiters who have no use whatever for the Democratic party except for what they can get out of wrecking it."[39] The confrontation between conservative southerners and Hannegan resulted in a stalemate: Hannegan defended his support for FEPC and his work with the PAC while denying any effort to purge southern reactionaries. The *New Republic* concluded that the basic intraparty conflict remained, but at least the conservatives had "failed to break the Democratic-PAC alliance, which was their real objective."[40]

The Union for Democratic Action/Americans for Democratic Action

During World War II the CIO was joined by other groups putting forward a rendition of liberalism committed to an expansive welfare state, strong labor rights, and civil rights. One of the most notable such groups was Americans for Democratic Action (ADA), which began as the Union for Democratic Action (UDA) in 1941. The UDA's founders included Reinhold Niebuhr, important labor leaders such as James Carey and Walter Reuther of the CIO, A. Philip Randolph, and the editors of both the *New Republic* and the *Nation*. The group's original purpose was to unite liberals on behalf of the war against fascism abroad. But from the start, the UDA included fighting racial discrimination among its top priorities.

The UDA's "Program for Americans," issued in May 1941, linked the fight against fascism with the drive for greater economic and racial equality in the United States. The group argued that "for thousands of Americans the freedom of the individual is even now a mockery ... in the case of Negroes the freedom to compete without chance of success against fellow-Americans who happen to be white." It claimed that the defeat of fascism abroad would not save democracy at home unless there were "basic economic changes and new social relations."[41]

The UDA took an active role in working with African American activists and the CIO to fight discrimination during the war. A few months after its formation, the organization sent representatives to meet with the U.S. Navy to protest the exclusion of African American sailors.[42] In 1942 it formally launched a campaign—headlined by Mayor Fiorello La Guardia of New York—to end all discrimination in the armed forces.[43] UDA president Frank Kingdon expressed the belief that "in a war for democracy we should begin by exemplifying democracy in our own country. The outstanding aspect of our undemocratic practice is discrimination against Negroes."[44] Following the Detroit race riots, the UDA joined the CIO, NAACP, and other liberal groups in urging Roosevelt to "ferret out the real causes of recent racial clashes and to adopt measures preventing their recurrence," such as passing legislation preventing violence against war workers because of their minority status.[45]

In May 1944 the UDA worked in cooperation with the *New Republic* to publish a special supplement, "A Congress to Win the War." The issue included a "Platform for Progressives" that listed "an end to discrimination" as a priority, urging "the most vigilant activity, official and unofficial, to fight race prejudice and all other types of discrimination."[46] The supplement rated each member of Congress based on their roll-call voting on a series of policies; three of the eighteen Senate votes pertained to civil rights (FEPC, the poll tax, and soldier voting) as did two of the eighteen key House roll calls (the poll tax and soldier vote bill). It followed the vote analysis with an article titled "The Unholy Alliance" that emphasized the role of Democrats from the "Poll-tax South" in helping Republicans stymie progress.[47] Liberal New Dealer Joseph Guffey (D-PA) had coined the term "Unholy Alliance" when he lambasted southern Democrats for cooperating with Republicans during the fight over soldier voting in December 1943. Echoing Guffey, the *New Republic* decried "a fusion of the Tory Democrats with the Republicans, an unholy alliance" that has blocked needed legislation.[48]

After the war the UDA faced rising divisions between left-leaning activists who embraced Henry Wallace's opposition to the Truman administration's Cold War policies and mainstream liberals who identified as anticommunists. While the left-leaning members joined Wallace's Progressive Citizens of America (PCA), Americans for Democratic Action succeeded the UDA to bring together anticommunist liberals in 1947. The ADA's founding meeting was attended by a mix of AFL and CIO leaders, an array of New Dealers, Eleanor Roosevelt, and rising young liberal politicians, such as Hubert Humphrey.[49] Most of the funding for the group came from organized labor.

Much like its predecessor, the ADA identified civil rights as a core commitment from the outset. Its founding principles included the idea that civil liberties "must be extended to all Americans regardless of race, color, creed, or sex."[50] Indeed, civil rights served as a defining issue for ADA liberals, offering a rebuttal to the left-wingers of the PCA and other radical groups who charged ADA liberals with being conservative opportunists. Humphrey, for example, spent much of his early career battling with communist-leaning activists in Minnesota's Democratic-Farmer-Labor Party. In her book on liberals' triumph in Minnesota, Jennifer Delton argues that racial liberalism offered a bold position that anticommunist liberals like Humphrey could use to confer moral legitimacy and signal their liberal bona fides to progressive voters.[51] Even with few African American voters in Minnesota, taking a liberal position on civil rights offered an opportunity for Humphrey to show that his anticommunism did not mark him as a conservative. Similarly, when the PCA challenged Paul Douglas's liberalism during his 1948 Senate run, the University of Chicago economist responded in the *New Republic* with a statement of his priorities, which prominently featured "the protection of racial and religious minorities from being discriminated against in employment, in the courts and at the polls."[52]

On the national level, Peter John Kellogg notes that the ADA sought ways to develop a strong liberal program to compete with Wallace's appeal. Thus, Humphrey wrote in early 1948 to fellow ADA leader Chester Bowles that the organization needed to find ways to gain a reputation for progressive thought to compete with Wallace. By March, amid the legislative battles over the civil rights program introduced by Truman in the wake of his commission's report, the ADA executive committee agreed that civil rights would be the centerpiece for this effort to seize the liberal mantle from Wallace.[53]

At the same time, civil rights was a crucial weapon in the ADA's battle to take over the Democratic Party from centrists and conservatives, turning it into a genuine liberal party. Delton argues that Humphrey saw civil rights as a means to identify and isolate those elements that stood in the way of a genuine, liberal Democratic party.[54] Southern racists provided a new evil for liberals to battle as World War II came to an end. In a speech to an ADA group in 1947, Chester Bowles claimed that "it is entrenched reactionarism that we have most to fear—the monopolists who strive to stifle production in the hope of higher prices, the destroyers of our national resources, the embittered opponents of all economic and social reform, the devotees of poll taxes and the Jim Crow laws."[55] Kellogg concludes that civil rights "was the issue which struck hardest at the liberals' greatest enemies, reactionary southerners."[56]

From this perspective, focusing the 1948 convention battle on forcing a strong civil rights plank perfectly fit the liberals' broader mission of redefining the Democratic Party. The ADA had 110 delegates at the convention, and its leadership provided the "headquarters for the forces that were to turn [the civil rights] plank into a rallying cry for progressives, perhaps save the great Northern cities for the Democrats, and either drive the mint-julep faction out of the party or put an end to its blackmail once and for all."[57] In a letter to Humphrey following the convention victory, Bowles noted that before the southern bolt the "Democratic Party has been more or less of a hodgepodge of big city organizations, southern reactionaries, and northern liberals, held together by the leadership of a Wilson or a Roosevelt. At Philadelphia, it seems to me, we laid the groundwork for a Democratic Party based on liberal principles." Humphrey responded that "the civil rights issue was but a means of clearly identifying certain elements in our Party for what they are."[58]

While the ADA never had a massive membership, it attracted the participation of many of the acknowledged leaders of American liberalism in the 1940s and 1950s.[59] Its board included such prominent liberals as Bowles, Humphrey, Walter Reuther, Joseph Rauh, and Leon Henderson. It also played an active role in encouraging promising liberals to run for office; for example, it was credited with helping recruit Douglas to run for Senate.[60]

Following Truman's victory in 1948, the ADA sought to hold the Democratic Party to its word. The ADA sponsored a conference of "national liberal and labor leaders" in January 1949, which issued a manifesto declaring that "the liberal-labor coalition expects results in this session on labor legislation, which includes repeal of Taft-Hartley and restoration of the Wagner Act; a substantial civil rights program; aid to education; a health program which includes an insurance scheme; and aid to the family-sized farm."[61] The organization's must-pass list of seven legislative priorities for the new Congress included civil rights as a prominent item. Its recurrent push for filibuster reform, which began in 1949, emphasized that Senate obstruction was a crucial obstacle to civil rights progress.[62] Later in 1949 the ADA's legislative director, Violet Gunther, issued an action memorandum to all chapters across the country focused on the FEPC, urging that "the time for liberals to organize for this battle is now. The ADA is actively cooperating with the National Association for the Advancement of Colored People in a Nationwide drive to dramatize civil rights, particularly FEPC."[63] The memorandum called on each chapter to contact the local NAACP group to coordinate their efforts on behalf of the FEPC. A December 28, 1949, ADA memorandum urging congressional action on the "most significant pending legislation" put the FEPC at the top of its list of must-pass bills.[64]

As it became evident that the new Congress was not going to act on civil rights, the ADA complained bitterly about the failure. In the lead-up to the 1950 election, the ADA National Board issued a statement on civil rights, featuring the "demand that this vital issue be brought to a vote so the people will know where there representatives stand on this.... In judging the records of our national legislators, we cannot but regard silence or equivocation on this issue as a vote against it." The statement continued by calling on "liberals in both parties to insist that FEPC be the first matter" on the Senate agenda and insisting that the bill "must not be weakened as a sop to the Republican-Dixiecrat coalition."[65]

News coverage often treated the ADA as representing the aspirations of American liberalism. Following the 1948 election the *New Republic* declared that the organization could "now speak with ... authority for the country's liberals and independents."[66] Arthur Krock, in commenting on efforts to unify liberal forces, observed in July 1949 that "ADA has become a very important ally of the President and his Fair Deal," while the *Los Angeles Times* characterized the ADA as "by all odds the strongest and best-organized political pressure group in America."[67] The *Chicago Defender* referred to the ADA as "the strongest organization of liberals in the country" while underscoring its support for civil rights.[68] For conservative Republicans, the ADA joined the CIO in symbolizing the dangers posed by liberalism: just days before the 1950 midterm election, Republican Congressional Campaign Committee chairman Leonard Hall complained to the press that the "Democratic-CIO-ADA" alliance had far more money to spend than the Republicans.[69]

The ADA's roll-call measure tracking the liberalism of members of Congress became arguably the most frequently cited yardstick for assessing members' ideological location in the late 1940s and 1950s.[70] In those years when Congress voted on civil rights proposals, the ADA generally included civil rights as one of its test votes, just as the *New Republic* and UDA had done during World War II. In this concrete way, support for civil rights came to be identified as one of the markers for liberalism.[71]

The "Liberal Lobby"

Where the NAACP, the National Negro Congress, and other African American organizations were largely on their own as they sought to push New Dealers to embrace civil rights as a priority in 1936, African American–led civil rights groups were now spearheading a much broader and more potent coalition that drew on a wide range of liberal supporters. This shift was first evident with the National Committee to Abolish the Poll Tax, which formed in 1941–42 and included the CIO, AFL, American Civil Liberties Union (ACLU), and Southern Conference for Human Welfare, alongside the NAACP, NNC, and Urban League.[72] When the National Council for a Permanent FEPC was created in September 1943, it included the CIO, UDA, ACLU, NAACP, and several Jewish groups.[73]

Soon after the war ended, African American activists launched a southern voter registration drive in the wake of the Supreme Court's *Smith v. Allwright* (1944) decision outlawing the white primary. These efforts provoked a violent reaction, which in turn led to the creation of the National Emergency Committee Against Mob Violence, an umbrella organization consisting of the NAACP, Urban League, CIO, AFL, UDA, SCHW, and Jewish groups. The committee played a crucial role in pressuring Truman to create his Civil Rights Commission in December 1946; its proposals then set the stage for the liberal mobilization on civil rights at the Democratic convention of 1948.

These same liberal groups continued to form the backbone of the civil rights coalition in subsequent years. In January 1950 the National Emergency Civil Rights Mobilization held a mass meeting in Washington, DC, drawing over four thousand delegates. The organization's sponsors included the NAACP, CIO, AFL, ACLU, American Jewish Committee, Anti-Defamation League, and ADA.[74] A majority of the delegates were from the NAACP, but there were 383 from the CIO, 350 from the Anti-Defamation League, 184 from the American Jewish Committee, and 119 from the AFL.[75] Hubert Humphrey headlined the event, with a speech demanding that Congress deliver on the Democratic Party platform promises of "equal treatment in the armed forces; legislation to abolish the poll tax; a meaningful and effective anti-lynching bill, and fair employment practices legislation."[76] In covering the event, the *Washington Post* noted that the organization was "described by members as 'liberal in the Americans for Democratic Action sense.' "[77] The Emergency Mobilization soon turned into the Leadership Conference on Civil Rights (LCCR), which played a central role in civil rights politics for more than a generation and linked together a wide range of African American, labor, Jewish, and other liberal groups.[78]

The close connection between civil rights groups and other liberal groups is evident in patterns of testimony and position taking before Congress. A search of the *Congressional Quarterly Almanac* revealed forty-two cases in which the NAACP took a clear position either in favor of or opposed to pending legislation from 1946 to 1955.[79] The *Congressional Quarterly* identified the CIO as taking the same position in thirty-eight of the cases (90.5%); it is never identified as taking a position opposed by the NAACP.[80] The ADA is identified with the NAACP's position in 67 percent of the cases following its formation and also is never identified as an opponent.[81] Jewish groups are included on the same side as the NAACP in just over half the cases (twenty-two) and are listed as taking an opposed position in just one case.[82]

It is important to note that while the NAACP most often spoke in favor of civil rights legislation, it also lobbied in favor of Truman's national health insurance program, public housing legislation, rent control extension, the Marshall Plan, liberalized immigration laws, expanded Social Security benefits, and repeal of Taft-Hartley.[83] Liberal groups were not simply helping the NAACP out on its priority legislation; the NAACP and other African American–led civil rights groups were part of a coalition with expansive aspirations.[84] Indeed, the ADA's national chairman, Francis Biddle, testified in 1950 before the House Select Committee on Lobbying Activities that the "ADA is proud to be a part of what might be called the liberal lobby here in the Nation's capital."[85] The junior counsel for the committee later asked the ADA's executive secretary, James Loeb Jr., whether the National Council for a Permanent FEPC was also part of this liberal lobby. Loeb responded that "I think it should be so construed.... It is the kind of organization we like to be associated with."[86]

LIBERALISM TRANSFORMED

Working alongside and in tandem with the burgeoning African American civil rights movement during and immediately following World War II, the CIO, UDA/ADA, and other prominent liberal groups helped to make civil rights a defining commitment of liberalism.[87] Writing about civil rights politics in the 1940s, Kellogg observes that FEPC and the poll tax ban "had become planks of the liberals' platform, part of the yardstick of liberalism."[88] The labor historian Nelson Lichtenstein traces UAW leader Walter Reuther's close involvement in civil rights politics from the 1940s onward and concludes that "Reuther understood that by the early 1950s civil rights was one of the central questions by which liberalism defined its meaning and measured its progress."[89]

In a telling early case, border-state senator and vice presidential nominee Harry Truman defended his record in a way that explicitly tied liberalism to civil rights support: "I am a liberal, as proved time and again by my record in the Senate, and I dare anyone to challenge these facts. I am for a permanent FEPC. I am for a Federal law abolishing the poll tax. I am for a Federal anti-lynching law."[90] A few years later, when Truman found himself in the White House, the new president's endorsement of a permanent FEPC provided an opportunity to show that liberalism had not died with Roosevelt. Truman's open letter to Rules Committee chairman Adolph Sabath (D-IL) backing the FEPC generated about four thousand letters to the White House; analysts in the mail room concluded the letter had "established him as a liberal in the eyes of liberals."[91]

Despite these liberal overtures, Truman was a national party leader seeking to hold together a coalition that was essentially at war with itself. Throughout 1946–48, the president continued to send mixed signals about the degree of his commitment to civil rights. But the urban, liberal wing of his party staked out a clear position of its own independent of top party leaders. When Truman sought a weak, compromise platform plank on civil rights in 1948—in the hope of holding on to the southern wing of the party—the liberal journalist Robert Bendiner noted that the president believed that the vague statements from the 1944 civil rights plank should be "good enough for the Negroes of the party today and for the survivors of the New Deal, concentrated in the C.I.O. caucus and the A.D.A." In Bendiner's view, had the compromisers succeeded in avoiding a clear stand on civil rights, "the last shreds of liberal support would have fallen away." Instead, the result was a historic rout of the "Confederate" faction that has "long been a millstone around [the party's] neck."[92]

In short, civil rights had come to occupy an important place in a broad-scale, ideological battle for control of the national Democratic Party. Rather than a coalition of policy demanders seeking to accommodate one another, northern liberals and southern conservatives sought to undermine one another's very survival. It was not lost on the northern liberals that southerners had worked with Republican conservatives to undercut the same labor movement that was a cornerstone of their own electoral coalition: the Smith-Connally Act of 1943 sought (unsuccessfully) to restrict unions' ability to contribute funds to candidates, while the Taft-Hartley Act of 1947 struck a harsh blow against union organizing. At the same time, southerners viewed liberals' civil rights drive as the ultimate betrayal.

The liberals' convention triumph in 1948 turned out to be insufficient to take over the Democratic Party. The vibrant civil rights movement of the war years faded in the late 1940s. As Doug McAdam and Karina Kloos demonstrate in their book on the rise of contemporary party polarization, the number and visibility of civil rights movement actions in the late 1940s and early 1950s were relatively low, amid a more general downturn in mobilized grassroots activism in the United States.[93] The early civil rights movement and its liberal allies had proven strong enough to place civil rights onto the political agenda, but it would require the intense, disruptive protest of the late 1950s and 1960s to force national party leaders to take a decisive stand. In the meantime, national Democrats continued to vacillate between the competing goals of holding onto the South's electoral votes and of consolidating the new coalition that had formed in the North. Below the presidential level, however, individual northern politicians and state parties had strong incentives to embrace civil rights in response to the new liberal coalition. Gradually, they redefined the party's stance, notwithstanding the reluctance of national party elites (see chapters 7 and 8).

Part 1 of this book has shown how the confluence of two distinct political trajectories—the coalitional reshuffling of the mid- to late 1930s and the civil rights movement activism of the war years—transformed the meaning of liberalism in American politics. When the New Deal was launched in the early 1930s, few political observers identified civil rights with the liberal agenda. The entry of African American voters into the Roosevelt coalition in the mid-1930s, the rise of the CIO as a leading exponent of an aggressive version of New Deal liberalism, and the ensuing bitter southern reaction against the emergent changes in the Democratic Party began to forge a connection between support for New Deal economic liberalism and racial liberalism. This connection deepened in the 1940s as movement activists took advantage of the war mobilization to force civil rights issues onto the political agenda. A broad liberal coalition that upheld civil rights support as a central tenet took shape during these years, long before national party elites took a decisive stand. In 1936 no prominent political observer doubted that Roosevelt was a "liberal" despite his steadfast refusal to talk about civil rights. By the time Harry Truman assumed the presidency, support for civil rights had become a litmus test for liberalism.

PART 2

Realignment from Below:
Voters and Midlevel Party Actors

CHAPTER 5

Civil Rights and New Deal Liberalism
in the Mass Public

THE PRECEDING CHAPTERS traced how the coalitional and ideological changes unleashed by the New Deal and by the early civil rights movement's activism during World War II forged a redefinition of liberalism that incorporated concerns about civil rights. Part 2 will demonstrate that these connections came to pervade the party system at the mass and middle levels starting in the late 1930s.

Economic liberalism, Democratic partisanship, and civil rights support became aligned in the mass public just as these connections were being made at the coalitional level in the late 1930s and early 1940s. During the same period, state Democratic parties gradually came to advocate for civil rights as part of their platforms, outpacing their same-state GOP counterparts. Similarly, rank-and-file northern Democrats in Congress surpassed Republicans in support for civil rights, working with civil rights organizations to put the issue higher on the legislative agenda. The data also reveal that urban residence, union membership, and Jewish self-identification were each associated with civil rights support among white voters, and that midlevel party actors were most supportive of civil rights when they represented urban areas with unions, African Americans, and Jews. The political line-up of enemies and friends of civil rights had thus come into a rough alignment as economically liberal northern Democrats confronted economically conservative southerners and Republicans in the late 1930s and the 1940s, decades before national elites took a decisive stand.

This chapter focuses on the partisan and ideological dynamics of civil rights support among whites in the mass public; chapter 6 takes up the critical role of African American partisan change. Both chapters rely on the earliest available mass survey data. Starting in the mid-1930s, polling companies surveyed the public on a regular basis. Questions on civil rights are spotty in these early polls, but there are useful items assessing civil rights policy attitudes that go back to 1937.

While opinion polls conducted in the 1930s and 1940s have numerous problems that have limited their use by scholars, the National Science Foundation has funded an extensive collaborative effort to make the data suitable for analysis. Our team recoded the datasets and put together a series of poststratification weights that partially address the problems introduced by the quota-sampling techniques used in the 1930s and 1940s.[1]

The civil rights realignment is often interpreted as evidence that mass partisans divide on issues only after their respective party leaders provide clear cues.[2] In contrast, I show that economic liberalism and Democratic partisanship became linked with northern whites' support for the major civil rights initiatives on the agenda by the late 1930s and early 1940s, before national party elites began to provide distinct signals to their partisans. In the South, though partisanship was unrelated to civil rights support, economic conservatives were more strongly anti–civil rights than were economic liberals.

These mass-level connections had important implications for politicians: the views of white economic liberals and African American Democrats made it harder for Democratic politicians to ignore civil rights. Instead, the wind would be at the back of pro–civil rights liberal Democrats—such as Hubert Humphrey (D-MN) and Paul Douglas (D-IL), both elected to the Senate in 1948—who supported the cause of racial equality. More broadly, when the African American–led civil rights movement mobilized sufficiently to force civil rights to the top of the agenda, northern Democratic voters (and politicians) were the most likely to be responsive. At the same time, conservative Republican voters' greater skepticism toward government policies promoting civil rights provided a permissive backdrop for entrepreneurial conservative politicians as they sought to build a coalition with southern whites by distancing their party from its earlier support for civil rights.

When one shifts the focus to aggregate-level opinion, states that were, on average, economically liberal also tended to be more racially liberal. Thus not only were individual economically liberal Democratic voters more racially liberal than their GOP counterparts, representatives of economically liberal constituencies also faced constituencies that tended to be more racially liberal.

There were, however, important limitations to the alignment of civil rights and partisanship: the tie between racial liberalism and Democratic partisanship in the North is less clear when it comes to racial prejudice and policies touching on social segregation than when it comes to lynching, the poll tax, fair employment practices, and the more general idea of government action to counter discrimination against African Americans and other minorities.[3] Northern Democrats' views in the 1930s–1950s—more supportive than Republicans when it comes to many civil rights policies but not when it comes to policies that encourage more intimate social mixing—presage the ambivalence that northern Democrats would exhibit toward busing and related measures in the 1970s and beyond. Rather than viewing these later troubles as a backlash against new civil rights demands, they reflected enduring tensions in the Democratic Party with respect to elements of the civil rights agenda.[4]

The chapter also considers the sources of the mass-level alignment among partisanship, economic views, and racial policy liberalism. The early emergence of these linkages clearly goes against a simple top-down story in which national elites drive mass partisan change.[5] Ordinary voters evidently participated in the partisan realignment on race at an earlier stage than commonly understood. In addition, the breadth of the relationship among economic liberalism, Democratic partisanship, and racial liberalism—which holds up across a wide range of class, education, and religious groups—indicates that the mass-level alignment was also not a simple product of changes in the demographic group composition of the parties.

While data limitations require caution in putting forward a strong alternative causal argument, the results show that the mass-level connection first became strong as the new urban liberal coalition in the North began to take shape in the late 1930s, with the rise of the CIO and the entry of African Americans into the northern Democratic Party. The sharpening of the cleavage between the CIO's aggressive rendition of New Deal liberalism and southern Democrats' conservative alternative may have helped clarify the place of racial politics in the New Deal. Ardent New Dealers were now identified with historically oppressed groups, such as the ethnically diverse industrial labor force, and were placed in opposition to the most blatant oppressors of African Americans. Voters, as well as group leaders and activists, may have been able to situate themselves in relation to these contending symbolic poles.

This interpretation has important implications for thinking about the relationships among parties, ideologies, and ordinary voters. Where Kathleen Bawn and her colleagues suggest that "bargaining among policy demanders constructs not only the party system, but also the ideological space," this account views the ideological landscape as the product of an intense battle in which the CIO articulated a wide-ranging policy vision—rather than a narrow set of particular demands—and southern conservative Democrats and Republicans countered with a sharp critique of the CIO's alleged radicalism.[6] Political actors at multiple levels—including ordinary voters—evidently saw the connections across multiple issues early on, suggesting a broad ideological dynamic to the civil rights realignment.

PARTISANSHIP, ECONOMIC LIBERALISM, AND THE
EARLY CIVIL RIGHTS POLICY AGENDA

As discussed in chapters 3 and 4, civil rights advocates focused most of their legislative efforts in the 1930s and 1940s on four issues: federal action to protect African Americans from the continued threat of lynching in the South; a ban on the poll tax; efforts to fight discrimination in the military; and enactment of fair employment practices legislation to prevent racial discrimination in hiring. The major survey houses—especially Gallup—asked about each of these topics as they became prominent on the political agenda.

For each survey item, I compare the level of support for the pro–civil rights position among northern white Democrats to that of northern white Republicans. The earliest surveys generally do not include party identification; as a result, I classify partisans using a dummy variable for Democratic vote choice in the last presidential election.[7] The online appendix tables present the full question wording for the civil rights items, marginal totals for each question, and responses broken down by party and region for each item.[8]

In addition, for both southern and northern respondents, I compare the level of civil rights support among economically liberal and economically conservative respondents. In coding economic liberalism, I identified all questions that asked about the government's role in the economy (e.g., business regulation, government ownership of industry, government spending on relief and other social programs, and labor policy).[9] Respondents are coded as economically liberal if they provide the liberal response more often than the conservative response to the set of economic policy items in the survey. To facilitate comparisons with the partisanship measure, the economic liberalism measure also ranges from 0 to 1, with conservatives scored 0, moderates scored 0.5, and liberals scored 1.

The results for economic liberalism need to be interpreted with caution, as the items used to construct the measure change across the surveys; therefore, one cannot assume that the variable taps the exact same concept in the same way across each data point. However, close inspection does not suggest an overall trend in the measure's quality; as a result, the consistency of the results over time is likely a meaningful indicator of a significant and relatively stable relationship.

In addition to cross-tabulations, I estimate the same bivariate regression model separately for each civil rights item in each survey, with support for the pro–civil rights position (scored from 0 to 1) as the dependent variable and either partisanship (scored 1 for Democratic voters and 0 for Republicans) or economic liberalism (scaled from 0 to 1, with moderates scored 0.5) as the independent variable. To facilitate presentation of the results across so many different indicators, I rely mainly on time series plots of the coefficient estimates and 95 percent confidence intervals from this simple model.[10] This strategy makes it easier to assess whether the magnitude of the relationships changes over time.[11] As discussed below, adding a series of demographic controls to the baseline model does not change the results, indicating that the relationships are not a simple product of the changing demographic composition of the parties.

The findings are remarkably robust across the four issues: from early on, northern white Democrats are more supportive of the pro–civil rights position on each issue. Similarly, economic liberals in both the North and the South are more likely to take the pro–civil rights position.[12] While the size of the association varies across indicators, there is little evidence of a trend in the magnitude over time. Indeed, such watershed events as President Truman's endorsement of a broad civil rights program early in 1948 leave little evident trace in the relationship between partisanship and civil rights views among whites at the mass level.[13] As discussed in greater detail below, these results suggest that cues from national party elites did not drive patterns in mass opinion on civil rights.

Antilynching Legislation

The NAACP made antilynching legislation its top priority in the 1920s and 1930s, believing that the gross injustices involved would make possible a momentum-building victory in Congress.[14] As a result of the NAACP's efforts, legislation requiring the national government to step in when local authorities failed to act against a lynching became the main item on the congressional civil rights agenda in the 1930s. Congress wrestled with antilynching bills several times, with legislation passing the House in 1922, 1937, and 1940, but in each case the NAACP's hopes were dashed by Senate filibusters.

The first poll with a civil rights attitude item was conducted in January 1937, as Congress considered the antilynching bill. Gallup asked about this legislation on six surveys from 1937 to 1940; an additional six Gallup surveys in 1947–50 asked more generally about whether the federal government should have the right to "step in and deal with the crime" when a lynching takes place, or whether this should "be left entirely to the state and local governments." The earliest surveys—conducted from January through November 1937—showed roughly a 60–25 percent majority in favor of the lynching bill. However, when the question wording was changed in December 1937 and January 1940 to include specific information about the punishment for counties that countenance a lynching, the respondents leaned only slightly in favor of the legislation (44%–40% in 1937 and 49%–42% in 1940). The 1947–50 items on the federal government's role also generally revealed a closely divided national public.[15]

The surveys conducted from January to November 1937 show little or no relationship between Democratic vote choice and support for the lynching bill among northern whites. Indeed, in the first survey, white Landon voters in the North reported being slightly more in favor of the bill than were Roosevelt voters.[16] Starting in December 1937, however, there is a clear relationship: northern white Democratic voters were about 10 points more supportive than their Republican counterparts. Northern Democrats backed the lynching bill by a 50–33 percent margin in the December 1937 survey, while northern Republican voters were evenly split, 43–43 percent. Three years later Democratic voters favored the bill 52–39 percent while Republicans opposed it by a 50–42 percent margin.

Figure 5.1A presents the results of separate bivariate regression models run for each survey, with vote choice in the last presidential election used to predict support for federal action against lynching. The results suggest that the party gap opened up in December 1937 and remained about the same over the next thirteen years. The point estimates indicate that a change from Republican to Democratic vote choice is associated with a 10–15 percentage point shift in the likelihood of supporting action against lynching. While Harry Truman was the first Democratic president to embrace racial liberalism explicitly—particularly in his 1948 campaign—the interparty gap appears about the same before and after this transition.

Figures 5.1B and 5.1C show the results when economic liberalism is used to predict views on lynching among northern and southern whites, respectively. In both regions there is a consistent positive association between economic liberalism and support for action against lynching by late 1937.[17] While the magnitude of the point estimates varies across surveys, a shift from economic conservatism to liberalism is typically associated with a shift of 10–20 percentage points in lynching views in both the North and the South.

It is important to emphasize that economic items that seem unlikely to have even remote racial implications—for example, government ownership of the railroads—are as closely tied to views on lynching as are items on issues that potentially have racial implications (such as government help for the unemployed). For example, in the December 1937 survey in which a strong liberalism–civil rights connection is first evident, white northern supporters of government ownership of the railroads back the lynching bill by a 57–31 percent margin, while opponents of government ownership are evenly divided on the lynching bill (favoring it by just 44%–43%). In contrast to this gap of 12–13 points, the same survey shows that backers of government help for the unemployed are only 7 points more supportive of the lynching bill than are opponents of government help. The relationship between economic views and support for action against lynching also holds up when demographic controls are added, including accounting for differences within the South (for example, Rim South vs. Deep South; level of urbanization).[18]

One question these results raise is whether economic liberalism or partisanship is more relevant to racial attitudes. The evidence suggests that both

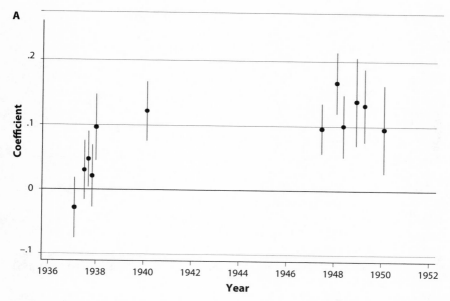

FIGURE 5.1A. Relationship between Democratic vote choice and support for federal intervention against lynching, 1937–50, northern whites

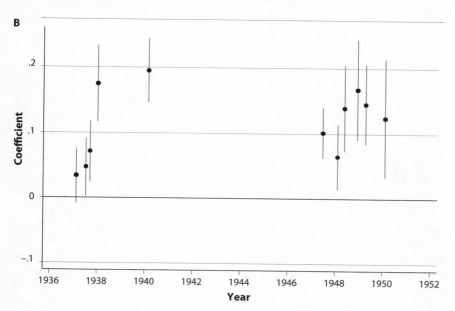

FIGURE 5.1B. Relationship between economic liberalism and support for federal intervention against lynching, 1937–50, northern whites

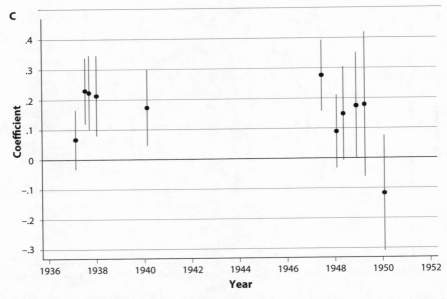

FIGURE 5.1C. Relationship between economic liberalism and support for federal intervention against lynching, 1937–50, southern whites. Dependent variable is scored 0, 1; independent variable ranges from 0 to 1; point estimate and 95% confidence interval presented for each survey. From Schickler, Eric, "New Deal Liberalism and Racial Liberalism in the Mass Public, 1937–1968." *Perspectives on Politics,* 2013; 11:75–98.

matter. When one estimates a model predicting northern whites' support for the lynching bill—pooling the data for all the post–December 1937 surveys and including a separate intercept for each survey—both economic views and partisanship are associated with support for the bill. The point estimate for presidential vote is 0.09 (SE = 0.01)—suggesting a 9-point gap in support by party—in the model accounting for economic liberalism (compared to 0.12 without controlling for economic views), while the point estimate for economic views is 0.11 (SE = 0.01).

An alternative approach is to classify individuals based on both their vote choice and ideology. This allows a closer examination of potential interactions between these traits. Paul Sniderman and Edward Stiglitz highlight the concept of "sorted partisans"—individuals for whom ideology and partisanship are in alignment—arguing that such individuals will behave in distinctive ways compared to partisans with views that are out of sync with their party.[19] Indeed, the gap between economically liberal Democrats and economically conservative Republicans is especially large. In the December 1937 Gallup survey, economically liberal Roosevelt voters favored the lynching bill by a lopsided 60–28 percent margin, while economically conservative

Alf Landon voters opposed it, 53–33 percent.[20] Across all the post–December 1937 surveys, the gap between economically liberal Democratic voters and economically conservative Republicans averages 20–25 points (see online appendix fig. 5.1).[21]

In sum, support for federal action against lynching was higher among northern Democratic voters and economic liberals starting in late 1937. As of 1937, however, Roosevelt continued to keep his studied distance from civil rights supporters, refusing to offer any help to advocates of the lynching bill. Meanwhile, northern Democrats in the House of Representatives were less clear in their support for lynching legislation than were northern Republicans: they were less likely to sign the discharge petition promoting the legislation, and they were more likely to support a watered-down alternative to the NAACP's favored version of the bill (see chapter 8).[22]

The Poll Tax

The poll tax became a prominent issue by 1940 as civil rights advocates focused attention on barriers to African American voting in the South.[23] The CIO and other liberal activists also backed the effort because they believed that the poll tax contributed to the disproportionate power of southern conservatives by disenfranchising both African Americans and poor whites. The failure of Roosevelt's purge of southern conservative members of Congress in 1938 made reforms of southern election laws more urgent, with legislation to ban the poll tax repeatedly introduced in Congress starting in 1939.

Gallup asked a national sample about banning the poll tax on six occasions from December 1940 through February 1953. Respondents in several southern states were asked about eliminating the poll tax "in this state" on two additional occasions in 1941. A substantial majority of the national population favored banning the poll tax throughout this period: the smallest margin was 63–26 percent in 1940; the most lopsided was 72–21 percent in 1953 (see appendix table 5.2). From the start in 1940, northern white Democratic voters were more supportive of banning the poll tax than were northern white Republicans.

A bivariate regression model predicting support for the poll tax ban among northern whites, estimated separately for each survey, suggests that Democratic vote choice is associated with support for the ban across each survey from 1940 to 1953, with little variation in the size of the association (see fig. 5.2A). The point estimates are generally a bit smaller than in the lynching case. With such a lopsided margin in favor of banning the poll tax, the item fails to separate weak from strong civil rights supporters. Indeed, even southern whites leaned in favor of the poll tax ban, though less decisively than did northerners (see appendix table 5.2). The results for economic liberalism are somewhat more variable—perhaps due to the varying quality of the liberalism measures—but nonetheless suggest that there was a significant

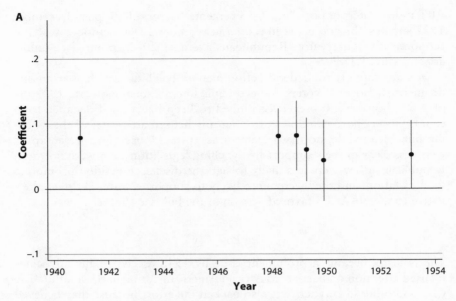

FIGURE 5.2A. Relationship between Democratic vote choice and support for poll tax ban, 1940–53, northern whites

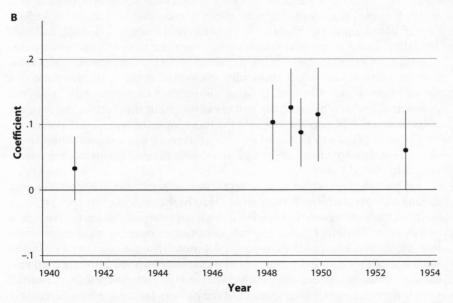

FIGURE 5.2B. Relationship between economic liberalism and support for poll tax ban, 1940–53, northern whites

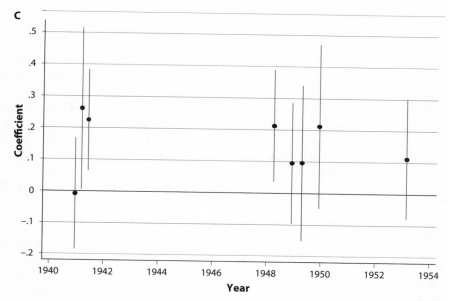

FIGURE 5.2C. Relationship between economic liberalism and support for poll tax ban, 1940–53, southern whites. Dependent variable is scored 0, 1; independent variable ranges from 0 to 1. From Schickler, Eric, "New Deal Liberalism and Racial Liberalism in the Mass Public, 1937–1968." *Perspectives on Politics*, 2013; 11:75–98.

association between economic liberalism and support for an end to the poll tax among whites in both the North and the South (see figs. 5.2B and 5.2C).

As with the lynching items, views on the poll tax continue to be associated with partisanship and economic views when both variables are included in the same model. In a model pooling data from each time the poll tax question is asked—with a separate intercept for each survey—both economic liberalism and Democratic partisanship are associated with greater support for banning the poll tax, though the size of association is smaller than for the lynching items.[24]

When one examines interactions between partisanship and economic views, "sorted partisans" are also once again particularly far apart. Economically liberal Democrats are a full 12 points more in favor of the poll tax ban than are conservative Republicans (see appendix fig. 5.2). By contrast, moderate Democrats are just over 7 points more favorable than conservative Republicans, and economically conservative Democrats and liberal Republicans are both about 4 points more favorable than are economically conservative Republicans.

Military Integration

While lynching and the poll tax were the main items on the sparse congres-sional civil rights agenda in the late 1930s and early 1940s, discrimination in the U.S. military became more salient with the onset of World War II. As discussed in chapter 4, the NAACP and other civil rights advocates began a drive for improved treatment of African American troops in 1940 and the issue gained prominence over the course of the decade.[25]

A June 1942 Gallup survey asked respondents about integrating the U.S. military.[26] Northern white Roosevelt voters were just 6 to 7 points more supportive than northern white Wendell Willkie voters: Willkie voters op-posed integration by a 53–38 percent margin; Roosevelt voters opposed it by 47–45 percent.[27] But when one isolates economic liberals who voted for Roosevelt and compares them to economic conservatives who voted for Willkie, there is a much bigger gap, with economically liberal Democrats backing military integration by a 56–40 percent margin and conservative Republicans opposing it 58–35 percent. Thus six years before Truman's executive order desegregating the military, economically liberal northern white Democrats backed military integration at the mass level, while eco-nomically conservative Republicans opposed it. It is worth emphasizing that the integration question—like the earlier poll tax and lynching questions—made no mention of the position of any Democratic or Republican elites. When Gallup asked again about military integration in May 1948—amid Truman's civil rights initiatives (though before his executive order desegre-gating the military)—the gap between Democratic and Republican voters was about 10 points—so a bit larger than in 1942, but not by much (see appen-dix table 5.2).

Fair Employment Policy

Job discrimination became the single most prominent civil rights issue in the mid-1940s.[28] Following Roosevelt's reluctant creation of a Fair Employment Practices Committee during the war, there were repeated efforts to enact FEPC legislation at the national and state level. More so than lynching, the poll tax, and military integration, fair employment practices continued to occupy a top place on the political agenda for several decades, allowing comparisons of public opinion over a long time span.

Gallup first asked about fair employment practices in 1945, one year after Republicans adopted a national platform endorsing the legislation while the Democratic platform remained conspicuously silent. The Gallup item focused on state laws, rather than federal legislation, which is a potential advantage since it separates out concerns about federalism.[29] Gallup worded the question in two ways on the survey: half the respondents were asked about a state law barring discrimination by employers; the other half were instead asked about a state law requiring "employees to work alongside persons of any race or color."[30] Respondents split evenly (44%–44%) on the ban on employer discrimination, while opposing requiring employees to work alongside people of other races by a 57–34 percent margin (see appendix table 5.3). But in both cases, Roosevelt voters were substantially more supportive than were Dewey voters. Northern white Roosevelt voters supported a state ban on employer discrimination by a 52–31 percent margin, while Dewey voters opposed the ban, 51–39 percent. Although Roosevelt supporters were much less supportive when the wording focused on integrated workplaces, they still were significantly more likely to back the proposal than were GOP voters. Dewey voters opposed requiring integrated workplaces by a decisive 61–32 percent margin, while FDR voters opposed it by a more modest 48–41 percent margin.

Economic liberalism is also strongly related to support for state fair employment practices. For example, white northerners who favored government ownership of the railroads backed a ban on employer discrimination by a 58–30 percent margin, while opponents of government ownership opposed a discrimination ban, 45–43 percent.[31] When one isolates economically liberal Roosevelt voters and compares them to economically conservative Dewey voters, the gap is even bigger: economically liberal Roosevelt voters back a ban on employer discrimination by a 59–26 percent margin, while economically conservative Dewey voters oppose it 59–31 percent.[32] Given that Dewey himself signed a state FEPC law in New York in 1945, it is telling that Republican voters were so much more opposed than Democratic voters at this early stage in the drive against job discrimination.[33]

Southern whites overwhelmingly opposed fair employment practices in the 1945 survey, regardless of party. Nonetheless, southern economic liberals were about 10 points more likely to back a ban on discrimination than were southern economic conservatives: 24 percent of the liberals backed the ban on employer discrimination, compared to 14 percent of moderates and 13 percent of conservatives.[34] While this degree of support among southern economic liberals is far from impressive, it reinforces the more general message that economic views were related to racial attitudes, even among white southerners in the Jim Crow era. The same questions regarding state fair employment laws were asked again in July 1947, eliciting a similar pattern of responses (see appendix table 5.3).

Gallup continued to ask about fair employment laws in the late 1940s and 1950s but with the focus now on federal rather than state legislation. The results tell the same story as the polls from the mid-1940s: there is a substantial gap between northern Democrats and Republicans in their support for government intervention against employment discrimination. The gap varies in size across surveys but without an evident trend. For example, a

March 1948 Gallup survey asked how far the federal government ought to go "in requiring employers to hire people without regard to their race, religion, color, or nationality" (appendix table 5.3, item 4). The survey was taken shortly after Truman announced his civil rights program and thus is more vulnerable to the concern that elite cues were driving the responses. But the 1948 results are much the same as the earlier surveys: white northern Dewey voters overwhelmingly opposed the federal government requiring nondiscrimination (59%–27%), while white northern Roosevelt voters narrowly backed it (41%–39%).[35]

Figure 5.3A presents the same bivariate regression model estimated separately for each poll with a fair employment question from 1945 to 1972, using presidential vote choice to predict northern whites' support for action to prevent job discrimination. While the early items are entirely from Gallup, the National Election Studies and Roper began to ask about job discrimination policy in 1952. In each case, the dependent variable is recoded to range from 0 to 1 (see appendix 5.1 for detailed coding). With few exceptions, the results suggest a strong, consistent relationship between voting Democratic and support for action against job discrimination. Democratic vote choice is typically associated with a 0.1 to 0.2 increase on the 0 to 1 scale in support for policies to combat racial discrimination in employment. Although changes in question wording require some caution, it is striking that the magnitude of the relationship in the late 1940s is evidently not any smaller than the relationship in 1964–72.

When economic liberalism is substituted for presidential vote choice, the results are similar in the North, with a consistent relationship evident in nearly every poll (see fig. 5.3B). For southern whites, economic views also appear to be tied to views on action against job discrimination; although the relationship falls short of statistical significance in several of the polls, it is positive in all but one case (see fig. 5.3C). On balance, the evidence thus suggests that economic conservatism and racial conservatism were connected at the mass level in the South by the 1940s.

When one pools the data across multiple surveys and allows for interactions between partisanship and economic views, the results are similar to the lynching and poll tax cases. Owing to the differences in the kinds of questions asked by the different survey houses, the pooled analysis focuses on the Gallup polls, which span 1945–53. Regression models with a series of indicator variables for each partisan/ideological group reveal that economically liberal Democratic voters are 0.25 more supportive of government action "to combat job discrimination than are economically conservative Republican voters on the 0 to 1 scale (see appendix fig. 5.3).[36] For each party, economic liberals are more supportive of the FEPC. At the same time, for each ideology level, Democrats are more likely to back the FEPC than are Republicans.

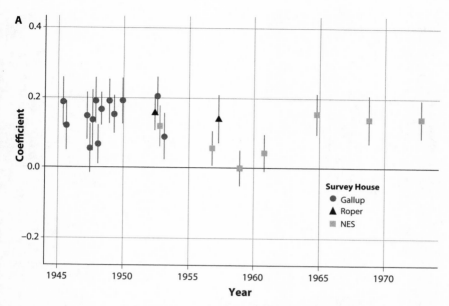

FIGURE 5.3A. Relationship between Democratic vote choice and support for fair employment policies, northern whites

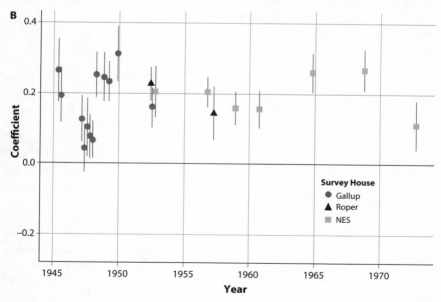

FIGURE 5.3B. Relationship between economic liberalism and support for fair employment policies, northern whites

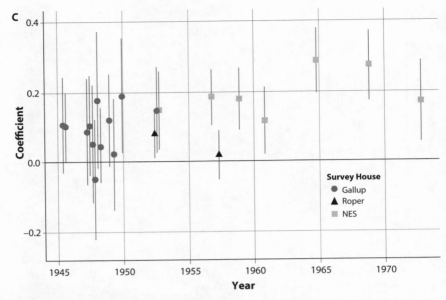

FIGURE 5.3C. Relationship between economic liberalism and support for fair employment policies, southern whites. Dependent and independent variables range from 0 to 1; NES 1956–60 items refer to "jobs and housing." From Schickler, Eric, "New Deal Liberalism and Racial Liberalism in the Mass Public, 1937–1968." *Perspectives on Politics*, 2013; 11:75–98.

Aggregate Opinion: State-Level Liberalism and Civil Rights Support

One might ask how the individual-level relationship between economic liberalism and civil rights support translated to patterns of constituency support at the aggregate level. Was the relationship strong enough so that politicians facing a racially liberal constituency would also likely face an economically liberal constituency? To help answer this question, Caughey, Dougal, and Schickler draw on approximately 650 survey items from 1936 to 1952 to develop estimates of state-level liberalism in three domains: racial policy, labor policy, and nonlabor economic issues.[37]

Figure 5.4 presents the correlation between racial liberalism and both labor and nonlabor economic liberalism across a range of years (the analysis is limited to nonsouthern states; it includes both white and African American respondents).[38] Consistent with the individual-level evidence, there is only a weak relationship between state-level racial liberalism and both labor and nonlabor liberalism at the very start of the series in 1937. As of 1937, northern states that were more prolabor were only modestly more pro–civil rights than other northern states. While the low correlations owe in part to

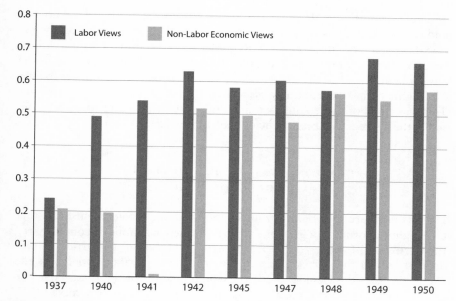

FIGURE 5.4. Correlation between racial liberalism and liberalism on labor and nonlabor economic issues, 1937–50, northern states. Analysis restricted to years with civil rights policy survey items.

measurement error in the aggregate measure—which was somewhat higher at the start of the series for the racial policy item—when one corrects for the reliability of the measures, the correlations are still lower than in later years: 0.47 between racial and labor liberalism and 0.41 between racial and economic liberalism on nonlabor issues.

But both the raw and corrected correlation between racial and labor liberalism pick up substantially by 1940 (raw correlation of 0.49, corrected correlation of 0.84), and the raw correlations are consistently in the 0.5–0.7 range after 1940, with corrected correlations generally above 0.75. For non-labor economic liberalism, the raw and corrected correlations first become substantial in 1942 and remain high after that: raw correlations generally are in the 0.48–0.58 range, with corrected correlations above 0.7. These results indicate that prolabor, economically liberal constituencies were much more likely to be pro–civil rights by the early 1940s.[39] It is intriguing that the relationship between labor liberalism and racial liberalism tightened first—by 1940—while economic liberalism on other issues followed a few years later. This is consistent with the qualitative evidence in chapter 3 that the CIO played an important role in bringing together racial and economic liberalism.[40]

The bottom line is that starting in the late 1930s, northern Democrats and economic liberals supported the leading civil rights policies on the national agenda more than northern Republicans and economic conservatives. Several years before Harry Truman's well-publicized civil rights push—let alone the upheaval of the 1960s—New Deal liberalism and support for key civil rights policies were clearly associated with each other at the mass level. This was true both when one examines individual voters and when one considers the aggregated constituencies confronting elected officials.

SEGREGATION, PREJUDICE, AND THE PARTISAN
GAP ON CIVIL RIGHTS

Even as northern Democratic voters supported fair employment and other civil rights reforms to a greater extent than their Republican counterparts, the partisan differences did not hold across the board. In particular, two areas in which the partisan gap in the North was weaker underscore the challenges that the Democratic Party would face down the road. First, the evidence with respect to racial *prejudice* among whites is more mixed than is the evidence concerning the main racial *policy* issues on the political agenda in the 1930s and 1940s. That is, white northern Democrats were not consistently less prejudiced than were white northern Republicans during this period, even as they were more likely to endorse legislation to bar employment discrimination, to fight lynching, and to ban the poll tax.[41] For example, a 1944 NORC survey showed that white FDR voters were 7 points *less* likely than Republicans to agree that "Negro blood" is the same as "white blood." While Roosevelt voters evidenced a bit less prejudice than Republicans on some other items,[42] the party gap on prejudice questions is generally small. This finding is consistent with Sniderman and Carmines' research on racial attitudes, which shows only a modest correlation between racial prejudice and partisanship in the 1990s.[43]

The similar (high) level of prejudice among white Democrats and Republicans helps to understand a second important limitation to Democratic support for civil rights: the partisan gap on civil rights policy in the 1940s–1950s—as well as later—is smaller and less consistent when it comes to issues that involve close social contact between the races. This is evident in early surveys that ask about eating at integrated restaurants or having an African American nurse.[44] It also persists in the late 1940s when Gallup asked about integrating bus and rail travel: there is generally only a small relationship with partisanship among northern whites.[45] Similarly, evaluations of the *Brown v. Board of Education* (1954) decision on school segregation show little, if any, tie to partisanship. While some items relating to social segregation do show a significant partisan gap—such as the soldier integration items in 1942 and 1948—for the most part the tie between partisanship and civil rights views is small and inconsistent on this set of issues.

This difference may also explain one wrinkle worth noting in the fair employment analysis presented above: when questions about job discrimination also refer to housing—as in the National Election Studies 1956–60 surveys, which ask about "jobs and housing" (unlike the 1952 and 1964–72 NES)—the partisan gap in support for government action is smaller than in the other surveys (see fig. 5.3A). While it is possible that the relatively small partisan gap in 1956–60 is due to the muddled national party messages on civil rights in the late 1950s, the Roper item on fair employment from 1957, which asks about jobs but not housing, generates the same substantial interparty gap as the 1952 NES (and earlier and later surveys that also focus on jobs).[46] As a result, it is at least plausible that "housing" signified something very different for respondents from "jobs," generating the different results.

Interestingly, when one turns to surveys conducted in the years following the 1964 election, the difference between questions focused on job discrimination and interracial social contact persists. For example, in the 1972 National Election Study, white northern Democratic identifiers are more supportive of federal action to ensure equal job opportunities for blacks than are white northern Republicans (39%–36% in favor among Democrats, compared to 40%–32% opposed among Republicans). By contrast, Democratic and Republican identifiers are very similar in their general views on segregation (40% of Democrats favor desegregation over "strict segregation" or "something in between," compared to 39% of Republicans).[47]

Despite the persistent similarities between northern Democrats and Republicans on issues relating to segregation in the 1940s–1970s, economic liberalism was, with few exceptions, clearly tied to support for policies to promote integration. For example, while partisanship was less related to views on the NES item referring to "jobs and housing" than to items focusing solely on jobs, economic liberalism had a strong relationship to both sets of items (see fig. 5.3B). Similarly, when the NES asked about whether the federal government should stay out of the issue of school integration in 1956–60, economic liberalism was strongly tied to respondent attitudes even as partisanship bore only a weak, inconsistent relationship. For example, in the 1956 NES, economic conservatives sided with the idea that the federal government should stay out of school segregation by a 49–34 percent margin, while the proportions were reversed among economic liberals. The relationship between economic liberalism and support for school desegregation and other forms of integration held up in later surveys as well.

In sum, the linkage between partisanship and views on prejudice and segregation among northern whites is weaker and less consistent than is the linkage on such civil rights issues as lynching, the poll tax, and job discrimination. To the extent that battles over open housing and busing would reveal the limits of many northern Democrats' commitment to civil rights, these limitations reflected enduring features of the party–civil rights alignment rather than a post-1964 backlash.

At the same time, economic liberalism was tied to northern whites' views across the full range of civil rights issues throughout the time period examined here. It is not obvious why both partisanship and economic views appear to be related to support for some civil rights policies, while only ideology is strongly tied to others. But even as one recognizes northern white Democrats' ambivalence on questions of integration, northern Republicans appear to have entered the 1960s primed to be receptive to racially conservative appeals. GOP voters had long taken the more racially conservative stance across a range of civil rights issues than their northern Democratic counterparts. Thus it should be no surprise that when Gallup began asking about the Kennedy administration's civil rights policies in 1962, Republicans were far more eager to criticize the administration from the right ("pushing too fast") than the left ("pushing too slow") (see chapter 10).[48]

Explaining the Linkages

The great question that emerges from the evidence presented thus far is: what explains the alignment between Democratic partisanship, economic liberalism, and racial liberalism among northern whites that was already evident by the late 1930s? Unfortunately, there are many obstacles standing in the way of a definitive answer, including the absence of racial policy survey questions prior to 1937, the lack of panel data, and the limited number of potential explanatory variables that are included on a consistent basis in the early surveys.

Although it is clear that civil rights support was tied to Democratic partisanship and economic liberalism in the late 1930s, the evidence that these connections were *new* is suggestive but not definitive. The Gallup surveys conducted prior to December 1937 show little indication that Democrats were more supportive of action against lynching than were Republicans; while this may be attributable to the lopsided response distribution for the question used in those surveys, the poll tax items in the 1940s had a similar lopsided distribution and yet showed Democrats to be more supportive than Republicans. The surveys from 1940 also indicate that new Roosevelt voters were more supportive of action against lynching and the poll tax than were voters who had backed the president in 1936. For example, in a January 1940 survey northern whites who had not voted for Roosevelt in 1936 but identified him as their current choice favored the lynching bill by a 70–30 percent margin, compared to the 58–42 percent margin for 1936 Roosevelt voters.[49] Similarly, the December 1940 Gallup survey showed that 1940 vote choice was more strongly related to support for the poll tax ban than was 1936 vote choice.[50] These findings suggest that the relationship between support for civil rights and vote choice tightened between 1936 and 1940 and thus that it makes sense to look, at least in part, to this period in seeking to understand the connection between partisanship and civil rights views.[51]

At a minimum, one can reject several seemingly plausible explanations that have important theoretical implications. A fierce scholarly debate focuses on whether racial prejudice explains the contemporary linkage between civil rights policy views and partisanship.[52] However, it is unlikely that a simple prejudice story accounts for the early emergence of a linkage between partisanship and civil rights views. The gap between northern white Democrats and Republicans in racial prejudice is small and inconsistent in these early surveys. While racial prejudice has a powerful impact on civil rights attitudes, that relationship cannot account for the association between partisanship and racial policy views evident in the 1940s.[53]

Second, it is difficult to argue that cues from national party elites generated the mass-level connections discussed here. Several leading accounts of the civil rights realignment—and of the dynamics of mass opinion more generally—have emphasized how cues from top party leaders are crucial drivers of mass-level change. In their classic studies, both Carmines and Stimson and Zaller depict top party leaders as sending signals about where their parties stand to voters, who recognize these cues and adjust their policy views—or, under certain circumstances, their partisanship—accordingly.[54] As described in chapters 2–4, the most visible national Democratic leader before 1945, Franklin Roosevelt, kept quiet on civil rights for fear of alienating southern Democrats in Congress. There were, of course, several prominent Democrats who did advocate for civil rights early on, including Eleanor Roosevelt and Robert Wagner (D-NY). The First Lady was friends with several African American leaders throughout the 1930s and increasingly was publicly identified as a civil rights advocate. However, her most visible pro–civil rights actions—such as her stand against segregation at the first convention of the Southern Conference on Human Welfare in 1938 and her resignation the following year from the Daughters of the American Revolution in response to the group's refusal to allow African American singer Marian Anderson to perform at Constitution Hall—occurred *after* the mass-level linkages between civil rights and partisanship first became evident. Similarly, Wagner, along with Edward Costigan (D-CO) and Joseph Gavagan (D-NY), were lead sponsors of the lynching legislation pending in Congress in the mid- to late 1930s. However, Democratic leaders in the House and Senate provided no support for the bill, and House Republicans backed the legislation more strongly than did northern Democrats in 1937. Furthermore, in the 1936–44 presidential elections, the Republican national platform said more about civil rights and advocated a more liberal position than did the Democratic platform.[55] In sum, the inconsistent cues emanating from top party leaders in the late 1930s are not a likely explanation for the early linkage between civil rights policy views and partisanship in the North.

National Democrats did eventually send clear signals of their civil rights liberalism, particularly during the 1948 campaign. The elite cues perspective would thus lead us to expect a much sharper tie between partisanship and civil rights views in 1948. But the interparty gap was about as big before 1948 as it was during and following the campaign (see figs. 5.1–5.3).[56] Indeed, on all twelve survey items asking about lynching, the poll tax, soldier integration, and fair employment practices from December 1937 to December 1947, there is a clear gap separating northern white Democrats and Republicans, with Democrats taking the more liberal position. Lest one is concerned that these findings are artifacts of the particular issues under consideration, when Roper asked more generally in June 1947 how certain "racial and religious" groups are treated in this country, 37 percent of northern white Democrats agreed that "strong measures" are needed to help these groups, compared to 24 percent of Republicans.[57] Furthermore, 41 percent of economically liberal white Democrats favored strong measures, compared to just 21 percent of economically conservative Republicans. Again, this was *before* Truman unveiled his civil rights program.

It simply does not appear that the relationship between civil rights views and partisanship among whites in the North tightened amid the 1948 campaign or in its immediate aftermath. There are well-documented instances in which party elite cues on issues precede—and encourage—mass partisan polarization.[58] But in this case mass partisan and ideological cleavages formed *before* clear signals from national party elites.[59]

Third, changes in the demographic group composition of the parties fail to account fully for the relationship between racial liberalism, Democratic partisanship, and economic liberalism. It is true that several of the groups associated with the Democratic Party and economic liberalism in the late 1930s and 1940s were more racially liberal than the groups associated with the GOP. Figure 5.5 presents the results when support for antilynching legislation and for the FEPC are related to a wide range of demographic characteristics. The coefficient estimates and 95 percent confidence intervals are from a series of pooled models in which support for antilynching legislation or the FEPC is the dependent variable and the independent variable is a specific demographic characteristic.[60] On the whole, these bivariate results indicate that several of the groups associated with the Democratic Party and New Deal in the North—particularly unions, Jews, and urban voters— provided more support for civil rights than did groups associated with the GOP, such as rural voters.[61]

Nonetheless, across the vast majority of civil rights items, controlling for a wide range of demographic variables does not eliminate—and generally

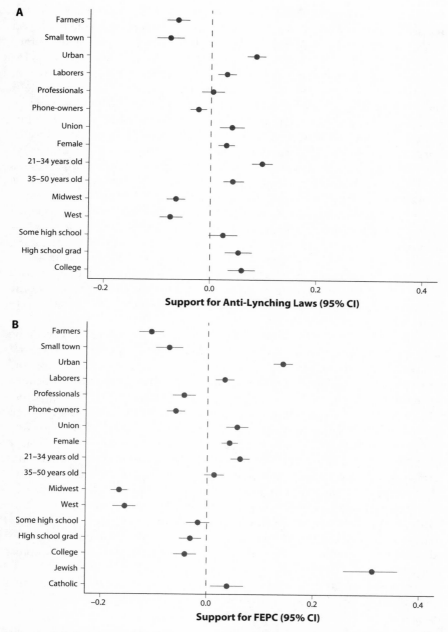

FIGURE 5.5. Demographic characteristics and support for issues. *A*, Antilynching legislation. *B*, FEPC. Dependent and independent variables range from 0 to 1.

barely changes—the estimated relationships among the key variables of interest. For example, the estimated coefficient for Democratic vote choice on FEPC support in 1945–53 is 0.15 (SE = 0.01) when no controls for demographics are included, compared to 0.125 (SE = 0.01) when one controls for education, gender, occupation, poverty, age, urban residence, farm residence, and region (West, Midwest, Northeast).[62] The estimate does not budge if one also adds a control for union membership, though this does require dropping a handful of surveys that do not include the union item. The same pattern is evident when one examines the relationship between economic liberalism and civil rights support.[63] Put simply, controlling for the demographic group composition of the parties (or of liberals as a group) accounts for only a small portion of the observed relationship between civil rights support and Democratic partisanship (or economic liberalism).

This still leaves open the possibility that the partisan differences on civil rights are particularly sharp among certain subgroups in the electorate—and such subgroup differences could provide clues about the origins of the partisan differences. I again estimated a series of models pooling data across surveys, analyzing northern whites' support for each set of policies as a function of Democratic presidential vote. This time, however, the models are estimated *separately* for a variety of demographic groups (again with a separate intercept included for each survey).

Figure 5.6 presents the results when support for action against lynching and support for fair employment legislation are the dependent variables.[64] The results are remarkably consistent across groups: for both lynching and fair employment, Democratic presidential vote was significantly associated with the pro–civil rights position across class groups (laborers, professionals, phone owners, non–phone owners, union members, nonunion), regions (Northeast, Midwest, West), age-groups, gender categories, religious groups, and education levels. The sole estimate to fall short of statistical significance is for farmers on fair employment policy. The association between Democratic voting and support for civil rights is strongest among urban residents; it is also somewhat higher for professionals and college graduates. But the relationship is still strong and statistically significant even for those with only a grade school education, suggesting that the connection between partisanship and civil rights views was by no means restricted to a narrow slice of the electorate and reached even those with lower socioeconomic status.[65]

These results cast doubt on the idea that the partisanship–ideology–civil rights linkage emerged as a straightforward product of group-membership-based politics. This is not simply a story of Democratic CIO members supporting the civil rights agenda promoted by their leaders. It also does not appear simply to be a story of educated Democrats responding to subtle cues emanating from party leaders.[66]

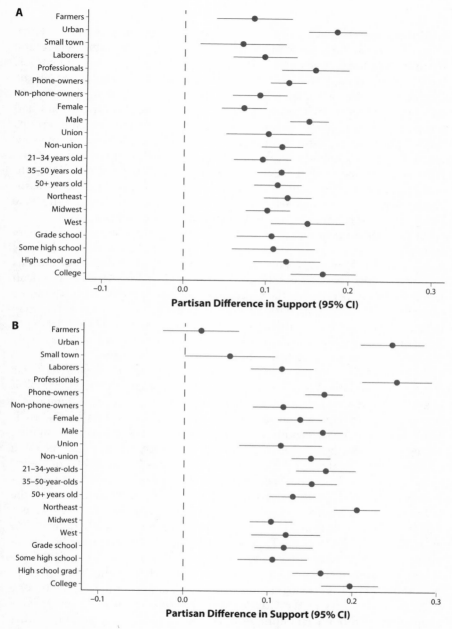

FIGURE 5.6. Presidential vote and views on issues, by demographic group. *A*, Antilynching bill. *B*, FEPC. Dependent and independent variables range from 0 to 1. From Schickler, Eric, "New Deal Liberalism and Racial Liberalism in the Mass Public, 1937–1968." *Perspectives on Politics*, 2013; 11:75–98.

Nonetheless, changes in the group composition of the Democratic Party in the 1930s likely promoted linkages among racial liberalism, Democratic partisanship, and economic liberalism. With the 1936 elections, CIO unions, African Americans, Jews, and urban liberals emerged as core voters in the Democratic coalition outside the South. News coverage at the time repeatedly made reference to these new Democratic constituents and how they had the potential to redefine the party (see chapters 3–4). These same groups were prominent civil rights supporters.[67] Thus, even as Roosevelt kept silent on civil rights, the incorporation of new groups held the potential to transform how the mass public viewed the Democratic Party and New Deal liberalism. These groups' support for civil rights and their simultaneous association with the New Deal may have sent the message to voters that the New Deal Democrat brand included—or ought to include—civil rights.

These cues need not have been limited to group members. Some voters were likely repulsed by these new groups' ties to the New Deal, while other voters viewed them more favorably. Indeed, southern Democrats' furious response to the rise of the CIO and entry of northern African American voters likely contributed to the perception that being opposed to expanding the New Deal went along with opposition to civil rights. Urban voters may have been particularly aware of the changing composition of the party coalition and thus were quicker to respond to it, with conservatives increasingly repelled by the new associations and liberals more receptive.

In this way, the alignment among whites at the mass level evident in this chapter can be linked to the changes at the constituency level discussed in chapters 3 and 4—as African American voters first entered the Democratic Party, and as activists and group leaders associated with the CIO, NAACP, UDA/ADA, and Jewish groups teamed up to forge a civil rights coalition with strong ties to the liberal wing of the Democratic Party. The popular meaning of New Deal liberalism shifted as these new groups connected labor rights, civil rights, and the New Deal, and as southern Democrats responded by cooperating with Republicans to counter liberal ambitions. In this sense, the CIO's significance is not primarily a matter of its immediate, direct role as a cue-giver. Instead, it rests in how the inclusion of the seemingly radical CIO as a prominent force in the Democratic coalition changed how both supporters and opponents perceived the parties.

How did members of the mass public decide whether they supported or opposed the civil rights agenda that they saw taking root in the Democratic Party with the entry of the CIO, African Americans, and other civil rights supporters? Although data limitations require caution, one possibility is that some of the same mechanisms were at work at the mass and group levels. CIO leaders and activists, for example, were evidently motivated by a combination of instrumental organizing imperatives and a general commitment to egalitarianism. As conservative southern Democrats emerged as foes of

New Deal liberalism in the late 1930s, it is at least plausible that individual liberal voters came to see enfranchising African Americans and providing them with basic civil rights protections as tied—in an instrumental sense—to the success of the broader New Deal program. But a general commitment to egalitarianism also may have played a role for ordinary voters, just as it evidently did for the CIO. As the New Deal became more closely identified with the industrial labor movement—and as the opposition of conservative, antilabor forces came into clearer focus—voters with a commitment to egalitarianism may have been more likely both to remain comfortable under the New Deal banner and to support the growing civil rights agenda.

The aggregate-level evidence presented above—which suggests that labor liberalism in particular became closely linked to civil rights liberalism by about 1940—is consistent with each of these mechanisms. It provides further support for the idea that the rise of an aggressive industrial labor movement committed to civil rights contributed to a new ideological landscape in which civil rights support was part of a constellation of ideas that set "liberalism" apart from "reaction." In other words, the much broader conception of liberalism unleashed by the New Deal and the rise of the CIO—and later reinforced by World War II—may have been difficult to square with racial oppression, at the level of both group activists and individual voters.

This account suggests that ideological formations and party coalition alignments do not merely reflect the bargaining among contending policy demanders. While Bawn and colleagues are right in highlighting the role of group interests as one important part of the story, the civil rights case suggests that issues also may become connected to one another through other processes.[68] The CIO put forward a bold, expansive program and social vision that fused concerns about race and labor and that threatened the core interests of southern conservatives. The two sides engaged in a battle for control of the Democratic Party that extended across multiple issues and that forged an ideological space that evidently resonated even with many ordinary voters.

CONCLUSIONS

The mass-level connection among civil rights liberalism, Democratic partisanship, and economic liberalism had important implications for political elites. Put simply, Democratic politicians in the North faced a very different constituent balance of pressure on these issues from that faced by their Republican counterparts. Northern Democratic representatives' core constituents tended to include the voters most interested in civil rights, while GOP representatives generally faced constituencies that were either indifferent or opposed to much of the key civil rights legislation on the agenda. For African

American activists working to raise the political visibility of civil rights issues, this meant that northern Democratic representatives and state parties
were more likely to prove to be responsive partners than were Republicans.
At the same time, the enduring racism of many northern white Democrats—
and their resulting resistance to full integration—meant that this alliance
would be at least somewhat fraught.

The mass-level tie in the South between economic conservatism and racial conservatism would also prove important for elite incentives. Starting
in the late 1930s, dissident southern Democrats and ambitious northern
conservatives talked about the possibility of creating a formal alliance that
would be rooted in a common commitment to states' rights and opposition
to civil rights (see chapter 10). The relationship between economic conservatism and racial conservatism among white voters in the South provided a
promising context for this alliance. As shown in chapter 10, when Republicans began to invest in an indigenous party organization in the South, racial
conservatives were well positioned to capture this apparatus and deploy it
to help burnish the cause of the most economically (and racially) conservative wing of the national GOP.

Following chapter 6, which focuses on the African American realignment
to the Democrats, the remainder of part 2 traces the gradual incorporation
of civil rights issues into state party politics and congressional coalitions—as
it emerged from the changing group constellation of the parties and from
the mass-based pressures analyzed in this chapter and chapter 6. State Democratic parties in the North and rank-and-file Democratic representatives
incorporated civil rights into their programs by the 1940s, helping the issue
gain a foothold in the mainstream liberal Democratic agenda, notwithstanding the resistance of the many national leaders desperate to hold the fragile
North-South coalition together.

CHAPTER 6

The African American Realignment
and New Deal Liberalism

ALTHOUGH NORTHERN WHITE Democrats and economic liberals provided greater support for civil rights initiatives than did Republicans and economic conservatives starting in the late 1930s, white voters rarely treated civil rights as a top priority. The civil rights views of economically liberal white Democrats provided a supportive context for northern Democratic politicians to back civil rights but were by no means the main source of energy behind this push.

The entry of millions of African American voters into the Democratic coalition was a different story, providing many Democratic politicians and state parties with a direct, mass-based incentive to support civil rights actively. At the same time, Republican politicians had to decide whether the party was better off attempting to win back African Americans or instead should turn to new targets, such as southern white conservatives. The skepticism toward civil rights that economically conservative Republican voters expressed made the latter choice an easier one.

Chapter 3 briefly discussed the important shift in African Americans' voting behavior in the 1930s, as Pennsylvania's Joe Guffey and other New Deal Democrats capitalized on African Americans' growing alienation from the Republican Party. The mobilization efforts of the Good Neighbor League and CIO-backed Labor's Non-Partisan League in the 1936 campaign signaled that national Democrats and their allies in the labor movement were paying increased attention to African American voters. African Americans matched whites in their overwhelming support for Franklin Roosevelt in his 1936 landslide, and, unlike many white northerners, they stuck with the president for the remainder of his time in office rather than drifting back to the Republican column.[1]

Yet the question remained whether African Americans were Roosevelt voters or Democratic *partisans*. At the same time as African Americans voted for Roosevelt by a nearly two-to-one margin, their party identification remained evenly split between the parties.[2] Writing soon after the 1936 election, the Good Neighbor League's Stanley High argued that "the northern Negro did not demonstrate, in the last election, that he was a Democrat. He demonstrated that he was a free lance." African Americans would stick with the Democrats "as long as the Democrats continue to talk his language and support his kind of legislation."[3] Roosevelt and the Democrats had shaken African Americans loose from their long-standing ties to the GOP, but they were now swing voters, with the potential to tilt toward either party.

There is little doubt that most African Americans were hardly committed Democratic partisans in the 1930s. A key question, though, is when and how African Americans became more firmly tied to the Democrats—and more permanently estranged from the GOP.

A prominent perspective is that African American voters remained swing voters for several decades, not finally siding definitively with the Democrats until the 1964 election, when Lyndon Johnson and Barry Goldwater firmly aligned their parties on opposite sides of the civil rights divide.[4] One can find signs of this continuing "freelance" status throughout the 1940s and 1950s. The famous James Rowe/Clark Clifford 1947 memo to Harry Truman arguing that the president needed to back civil rights in order to appeal to the growing African American population in crucial northern battleground states was premised on the idea that African Americans were swing voters.[5] Similarly, Henry Lee Moon entitled his 1948 book *Balance of Power* to underscore his view that African Americans were not committed to either party. Moon argued that "the vote of Negro citizens in 1948 will certainly not be a bloc vote ... where the majority of this vote will go will depend primarily upon what the parties have to offer the Negro by way of meeting his demands."[6] Four years later Alexander Heard claimed that African Americans were keeping their options open, willing to vote for Republicans when they offered a better alternative than the Democrats.[7] Adam Clayton Powell's (D-NY) endorsement of Dwight Eisenhower in 1956—and the Republican president's improved showing among African American voters that year— reinforced the argument that African Americans were by no means firmly tied to the Democrats.

This chapter takes a different view. Two claims are central. First, African Americans' economic liberalism gave Democrats a critical advantage in winning their support from the 1930s onward. Second, most African Americans had clearly realigned to the Democrats by the late 1940s; Democrats made further gains in the late 1950s and early 1960s, but the Democratic partisan advantage had become substantial more than a decade earlier.

The first section of the chapter focuses on African Americans' economic views. African Americans were much closer to the Democratic Party than to the GOP on the array of economic issues relating to social insurance, welfare state expansion, labor rights, and the role of government that set the two parties apart with the arrival of the New Deal. In particular, many African American voters saw themselves as beneficiaries of the New Deal's welfare state and labor policies and as a result opposed Republican efforts to retrench these policies. African Americans were sharply critical of the discrimination prevalent in New Deal programs, but their response was to work to make these programs more universalistic; GOP calls to give the states greater control over implementation threatened to move in the opposite direction.

From the perspective of theories of parties as coalitions of policy demanders and of ideologies as elite constructions with little intrinsic logic, one might expect that the GOP could have easily found a way to appeal African American voters, given the continued presence of racist southern Democrats in Roosevelt's coalition and the persistent discrimination in many New Deal policies. But, as shown below, when African American Republicans put forward programs that they believed could win more African American support, these proposals gained no traction because GOP leaders saw them as undercutting their party's main lines of attack on the New Deal. Winning back African American votes would have required a dramatic reshuffling of Republican Party priorities.

African Americans' distinctive economic liberalism meant that even if national Democrats only matched Republicans on civil rights, most African Americans were predisposed to vote Democratic. With the CIO inside the Democratic coalition, eager to work with African American activists to push northern Democratic politicians to go well beyond matching the GOP on civil rights, the path to entering the Democratic Party was that much wider. The movement of African Americans into the Democratic Party was not simply a matter of party managers aiming to satisfy narrow, group-based demands. Rather, it stemmed from a broad-ranging programmatic battle in which African Americans' interests and views made them a far better fit with the remade Democratic Party as it emerged during the New Deal years.

The second section of the chapter focuses on changes in party identification. Partisanship, of course, is understood to change more slowly than voter behavior. The African American realignment was no exception. In particular, older African Americans, who came of political age long before the New Deal, often held on to their Republican partisanship even as they tended to vote Democratic. Still, the Democratic edge among younger African Americans—who of course would have more to say about the future—was consistently strong from the 1930s onward. Interestingly, national Democrats' clear (but brief) embrace of civil rights during the 1948 campaign sparked a noticeable jump in African Americans' allegiance to the Democrats, while reducing the differences across age and social class groups. Democrats enjoyed a substantial advantage in African American partisanship throughout the late 1940s and 1950s. This advantage went from substantial to overwhelming soon after civil rights liberals Democrats finally gained decisive control of the national party in the late 1950s and early 1960s; notably, however, the shift in partisanship was evident a few years *before* the 1964 Johnson-Goldwater showdown.

The concluding section of the chapter briefly assesses how the combination of growing Democratic partisanship among African Americans in response to the New Deal and the massive migration of African Americans to the North influenced the composition of the Democratic electorate in key northern states. African Americans thus became an important constituency for northern Democratic politicians in the 1940s and 1950s. As shown in subsequent chapters, civil rights organizations leveraged this newfound electoral clout, working with allied groups—such as organized labor and the ADA—to push northern Democrats to embrace racial issues as a legislative priority. The confluence of two initially distinct political trajectories was critical to the transformation: the initial African American shift to the Democrats was not attributable to the party's stance on civil rights and instead was primarily rooted in economic issues and interests. But once African Americans became a part of the Democratic coalition, this shift had critical implications for how Democratic politicians would respond when the emerging civil rights movement, acting largely independently of the national Democratic Party, raised the prominence of civil rights issues on the political agenda.

African Americans and New Deal Liberalism

At the most basic level, New Deal Democrats' embrace of an expansive welfare state and prolabor policies meant that most African American voters were substantially closer to national Democrats than to Republicans when it came to the core issues that were the focus of interparty competition starting in the New Deal era. Indeed, as shown below, even African Americans who continued to vote Republican in the late 1930s and 1940s were distant from white Republican voters on economic issues, suggesting the long-term tensions facing GOP efforts to hold on to African American voters.

Scholars have rightly emphasized the myriad ways in which New Deal programs accommodated and perpetuated racial discrimination.[8] African American observers were keenly aware of these inequities, authoring critiques of New Deal policy and sponsoring conferences to highlight discriminatory treatment.[9] African American newspapers and magazines published numerous articles focusing on the ways in which Social Security, relief, housing, and farm programs failed to deliver a fair share of benefits to African Americans. African American leaders also testified before Congress against the exclusion of agricultural and domestic workers from several New Deal programs and the discriminatory implementation practiced throughout the South.[10]

Notwithstanding these severe limitations, African American leaders and ordinary voters believed that the New Deal, on balance, provided important benefits. In his masterful report *The Political Status of the Negro in the Age of FDR*, Ralph Bunche noted both the prevalence of discrimination and the concrete material gains achieved by African Americans under the New Deal.[11] Bunche observed that "the New Deal for the first time gave broad recognition to the existence of the Negro as a national problem and undertook to give specific consideration to this fact in many ways." He reported that African Americans constituted a sizable share of work relief beneficiaries and Civilian Conservation Corps participants and gave particular praise to the National Youth Administration, which "as a result of sympathetic and effective administration" has "probably been more successful than any other governmental agency in promoting full integration and participation of minority groups in all phases of its program."[12] Bunche also highlighted the role played by African American administration officials, such as Mary Bethune and Robert Weaver, in pushing for better treatment of African Americans in New Deal programs.

The dogged efforts of these officials (and their handful of white allies, such as Harold Ickes, Harry Hopkins, and Aubrey Williams)—combined with the pressure brought by African American critics on the outside—ensured that even with its many limitations, the New Deal provided meaningful benefits for many African Americans.[13] African Americans received about 31 percent of the total wages paid by PWA construction projects in 1936, even as southern states often ignored nondiscrimination directives.[14] The federal government estimated that 21.5 percent of African American families were on relief in 1935, compared to 12.8 percent of white families. Indeed, the percentage of African American families on relief was above 40 percent throughout much of the North, though it was much lower in the rural South.[15] African Americans constituted 14 percent of WPA employees in 1939, which meant that they were overrepresented relative to their population share (11%) but underrepresented (and typically underpaid) relative to their need.[16] The following year, the census showed that 13.5 percent of emergency workers were African American, with a huge urban-rural disparity as 18 percent of emergency workers in (mostly northern) urban areas were African American, while just 7.4 percent in (largely southern) farm areas were African American.[17]

Still, even with the rampant discrimination in the South (and parts of the North), the New Deal represented a vast improvement over past treatment for the more than one million African Americans receiving government help. Thus Moon commented that "at no time since the curtain had dropped on the Reconstruction drama had government focused as much attention upon the Negro's basic needs as did the New Deal."[18]

Given the prevalence of poverty and unemployment among African Americans, their critiques of New Deal social welfare programs had a distinctive cast: rather than backing Republican pleas to scale back the New Deal or turn programs over to the states, African American leaders sought fair implementation of the existing programs and their expansion to be more universalistic. Writing about African American leaders' stance in the 1936 election, James Harrell observed that "Negro critics directed harsh words and a call for congressional investigation at the administration of relief" while at the same time "affirming the necessity and validity of New Deal relief measures." Similarly, the NAACP condemned the exclusion of agricultural and domestic labor from the recently passed Social Security legislation, "but despite the sharp attack, NAACP leaders immediately undertook to lobby for an extension of the coverage," which was finally enacted in 1950. More generally, "the NAACP weighted its judgment in favor of Roosevelt. It noted that he had attempted to make relief administration just, whereas Landon's plan for state administration of relief was fated in advance to be extremely discriminatory."[19]

Beyond welfare state policies, Democrats' alliance with the labor movement—and Republicans' opposition to the CIO—encouraged African Americans to turn away from the GOP. Writing in the Urban League's *Opportunity*, C. William McKinney highlighted how African Americans' socioeconomic status predisposed them to back the New Deal: "Like most of America's laboring population, the Negro had faith in the democratic principles of the New Deal."[20] Similarly, Harrell observes that as early as 1936, "the need felt by the NAACP and most Negro leaders for assimilation of Negro labor into the mainstream of the labor movement also made the President appear in a better light than his opponent."[21]

Indeed, the CIO's efforts to link the labor movement to civil rights advances provided a strong incentive for African American leaders and voters to back prounion policies. Even as the Wagner Act countenanced discrimination in unions, African Americans witnessed the concrete gains made through the CIO.[22] At the same time, Republicans' fervent opposition to the CIO—the white-led organization most closely associated with civil rights—accentuated the divide between African Americans and the GOP.

The Republican Policy Alternative?

As African Americans turned to Roosevelt in the 1930s, a key question was whether the Republican Party would offer a credible policy response that might win back African American support. The GOP created a program committee in 1937 that was charged with drawing up a report on how the party could win back majority status nationally. As part of that effort, the committee asked Bunche to write about African Americans' problems and concerns. Bunche offered a 130-page analysis that chided the GOP for ignoring the plight of African Americans and that called on the party to undertake a major antidiscrimination drive and to build on the New Deal's economic programs to help the dispossessed. Bunche argued that African Americans needed "employment, land, housing, relief, health protection, unemployment and old-age insurance, enjoyment of civil rights, all that a twentieth century American citizen is entitled to." To Bunche, the New Deal "had improved the situation, but it still fell a long way short of the 'minimal needs' of African Americans."[23]

The program committee ignored Bunche's recommendations, viewing them as too "impractical" and "revolutionary."[24] Instead, it decried the New Deal "shunting of Negroes out of the normal productive enterprise into a kind of separate relief economy, leaving them as it were, on permanent 'reservations' of public relief."[25] Indeed, the program committee called for lump-sum grants to the states for relief, a policy that likely would have exacerbated racial discrimination.[26]

The treatment of the Bunche report captured an essential aspect of the GOP's relationship with African American voters from the 1930s onward. With the exception of a relatively small number of liberals who were outside the mainstream of the party, there was a substantial gap between the economic policy demands of African Americans and the party's officeholders and candidates.

This gap is evident even when one examines the demands made by those African Americans who remained active in the GOP. In August 1945 the Republican American Committee—a group of African American Republicans led by Memphis businessman Robert Church—issued a declaration to the party, charging that it would continue to lose African American support unless it returned "to the hallowed principles of the founding fathers." The committee argued that the party had moved away from African Americans and that "its entire attitude and strategy must be completely changed as it affects colored citizens," who had left the party due to the "growing convictions that the Republican Party is increasingly deserting the cause of equal rights." The committee called on party leaders not only to fight for the "immediate passage" of FEPC but also to "give their full support of legislation for full employment."[27] The goal was not to scale back or reverse the New Deal; indeed, the group urged Republicans to carry Roosevelt's Four Freedoms both to smaller nations and to African Americans.[28] These pleas came during the same Congress in which Republicans were working with southerners to water down proposed full employment legislation and to turn the United States Employment Service over to the states.

The African American Republicans' policy demands were similar to those put forward by African American Democrats and to a "Declaration of Negro Voters" issued by twenty-seven African American leaders from the NAACP and several other organizations.[29] A November 1942 letter from Walter White to Republican House leader Joe Martin summed up the growing distance between African American voters and the Republican Party, not just on civil rights but on all issues where the GOP sided with southern conservatives to sidetrack the New Deal: "On too many fundamental issues, economic, military, and social, there has been an unholy alliance in Congress between Negro-hating Southern Democrats and reactionary Republicans who think of the Negro only when he is forced to around election time."[30] Republicans' collaboration with southern Democrats to scale back relief spending in the late 1930s, and their successful efforts a few years later to kill the National Youth Administration—an agency noted for its relatively fair treatment of African Americans—were hardly likely to win back the support of African American leaders or voters.[31]

The disconnect between African Americans and mainstream Republican economic (and racial) policies did not automatically translate into a warm embrace of national Democrats, who after all still had to address the problem of their conservative southern wing. But it meant that disaffection with Democrats might translate into support for left-wing third-party challenges rather than necessarily generating GOP gains. Writing in 1937, Stanley High cited the National Negro Congress, along with such African American leaders as A. Philip Randolph and John Davis, as crucial allies should the CIO and other true New Deal liberals be forced to bolt the Democrats in response to the South's continued influence.[32] In fact, the National Negro Congress was closely allied with John L. Lewis in 1940 as he threatened to form a liberal third party if Democrats failed to back the CIO's agenda.[33]

A few years later African Americans strongly backed keeping Henry Wallace on the Democratic ticket for the 1944 election, reflecting the prevailing view among many African Americans that "progressive government social and economic planning ... was linked to the cause of racial justice."[34] Early polls also revealed considerable African American interest in Wallace's third-party bid in 1948.[35] In the end, Truman and the Democrats' strong civil rights stand in the 1948 election dissuaded the vast majority of African Americans from voting for Wallace. Still, the lesson remained that African Americans' economic liberalism meant that Democratic failures to deliver on civil rights could just as easily lead to staying home at election time or third-party support as it could translate into Republican votes—unless the GOP adopted a substantially more liberal policy agenda.

African American Economic Liberalism: Evidence from Public Opinion Polls

The evidence presented above emphasizes the economic liberalism of many African American leaders and organizations and highlights the economic interest of African American voters in the continuation and expansion of the

New Deal. But systematic survey data are required to determine the extent to which ordinary African American citizens' economic policy views aligned with each party.

Assessing African American opinion in the 1930s–1940s is challenging because Gallup, the leading survey organization, systematically excluded southern African Americans from most of its samples. Given that approximately 70 percent of African Americans lived in the South, this exclusion poses a deep problem. Even when southern African Americans were included in surveys, one cannot necessarily take their stated opinions at face value, particularly if white interviewers were used to interview them. For example, a 1942 NORC study demonstrated that African Americans in Memphis gave less liberal responses—particularly on racial policy questions—when they were interviewed by whites rather than by African Americans.[36]

Still, the existing poll data allow us to make some inferences about African American opinion. Fortunately, Gallup was not the only pollster in the field. Roper's surveys generally included a healthy sample of southern African Americans, as did polls by NORC. Examination of a wide range of policy questions in these surveys during the late 1930s and early to mid-1940s—the period when Gallup excluded southern African Americans—reveals that northern and southern African Americans shared a broadly similar outlook on economic issues. Southern African Americans were more likely to provide "don't know" as a response to survey items than were their northern counterparts. But among those expressing an opinion, the percentage liberal was remarkably similar across the two regions.[37]

Figure 6.1A displays the difference in the percentage of northern and southern African Americans providing a liberal response (of those with an opinion) to eighty policy items included in Roper and NORC surveys with reasonably large samples of southern African Americans conducted between 1939 and 1945. Positive values indicate that northern African Americans were more liberal. In general, the two groups look quite similar, particularly when contrasted with whites in their own region. Across the eighty items, southern African Americans take the more liberal position forty-seven times, while northern African Americans are more liberal on thirty-three occasions. But across all the items, the average difference in liberalism is less than 1 percentage point.

By contrast, northern African Americans are more liberal than their white counterparts on seventy-eight of eighty items; the average difference between the groups is 22 percentage points (see fig. 6.1B). The same holds true in the South: southern African Americans are to the left of whites on seventy-eight of eighty items, with an average gap of 18 points (see fig. 6.1C).[38] The bottom line is that the exclusion of southern respondents from the Gallup surveys does not lead one to systematically overstate the extent of African Americans' liberal leanings. Across both the North and the South, African Americans appear far more liberal than whites.

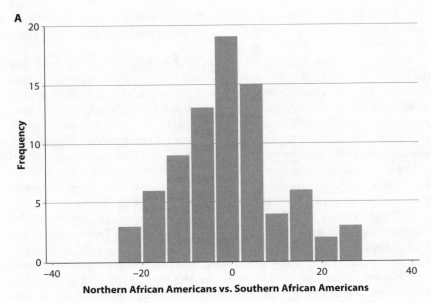

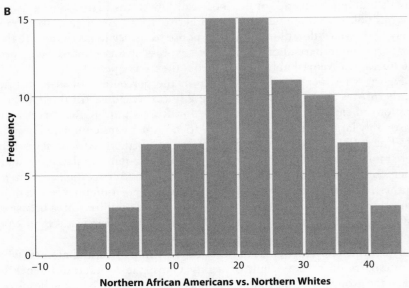

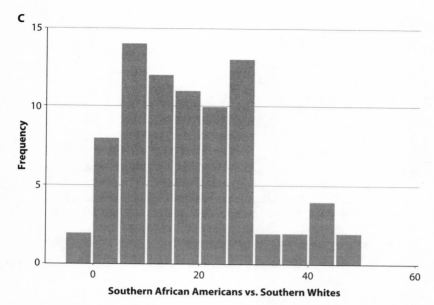

FIGURE 6.1. Comparison of economic liberalism of different groups. *A*, Northern African Americans vs. southern African Americans. Positive values indicate northern African Americans are more liberal. *B*, Northern African Americans vs. northern whites. Positive values indicate African Americans are more liberal. *C*, Southern African Americans vs. southern whites. Positive values indicate African Americans are more liberal.

An alternative approach is to use a group-level item-response model to estimate aggregate liberalism scores for African Americans and other groups. Following the approach in chapter 5, the scores are based on scaling approximately 650 survey items that ask about a wide range of economic policy questions; the model allows one to estimate group-level mean liberalism scores, by year, along with a measure for the uncertainty of the estimates.[39] Figure 6.2 presents the estimated mean level of economic liberalism for northern African Americans, along with whites in both regions.[40] The results tell a consistent story: African Americans are, on average, well to the left of both southern and northern whites on economic policy.

When one considers the intersection of race and voting behavior, the challenge facing Republicans in winning back African American voters comes into even sharper relief. First, northern African Americans who vote Democratic are even more liberal on economic issues than are other northern Democratic voters. (Though the differences are not always statistically

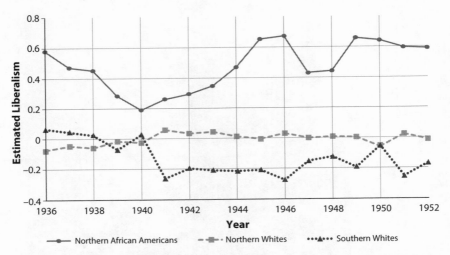

FIGURE 6.2. Estimated economic liberalism of northern African Americans, northern whites, and southern whites. The standard error for each annual estimate is approximately 0.05 for African Americans, 0.02 for northern whites, and 0.05 for southern whites.

significant, the point estimates indicate that the mean liberalism for African American Democratic voters in the North is higher than for white Democrats in all seventeen years from 1936 to 1952).[41] Second, African American nonvoters and third-party voters in the North (and South) tend to be quite liberal on economic issues. Indeed, in all but two years from 1936 to 1952, African American nonvoters and third-party voters are estimated to be *more liberal* than the typical white northern Democratic voter.[42] Finally, African American GOP voters are far more liberal than other Republican voters but are only modestly less liberal than the typical white Democratic voter, at least after 1940. From 1941 onward, the typical African American Republican is twice as far from the typical northern GOP voter (in estimated liberalism) as he or she is from the typical northern white Democrat.[43]

Earlier chapters have emphasized the importance of labor unions in the changing politics of civil rights. As described in chapter 3, the CIO played a key role early on in bringing concerns about race and class together in articulating an aggressive version of New Deal liberalism. Given the history of union racism, however, one could easily imagine that African Americans were hesitant to embrace labor. Christopher Baylor, for example, highlights the challenges facing the CIO as it sought to woo African Americans to its ranks and argues that the NAACP played a key role in the early 1940s in forging an alliance between African Americans and organized labor.[44] I argued in chapter 3 that the roots of this alliance were broader, and that the NAACP itself was responding to grassroots pressure from militants and ordinary workers.

Figure 6.3 focuses in on liberalism on labor-related issues to provide a further window into African Americans' views at the mass level.[45] These data clearly indicate that northern African Americans were distinctive in their prolabor orientation from the late 1930s onward. African Americans were consistently well to the left of both northern and southern whites on labor policy.[46] Again, this situated African Americans much closer to the Democratic Party on arguably the critical front in partisan policy battles of the era.

The survey evidence reinforces the conclusion from qualitative studies that have argued that the economic conservatism put forward by the GOP constituted an important obstacle to winning back African American voters. Simon Topping, for example, argues that "the economic conservatism of the Republicans alienated them from African Americans.... In fact, the African American presence, as the poorest section of American society, was incongruous in a party of businessmen and conservative middle-class whites. The Republicans simply did not and could not espouse the liberal economic policies needed to improve the position of African Americans."[47]

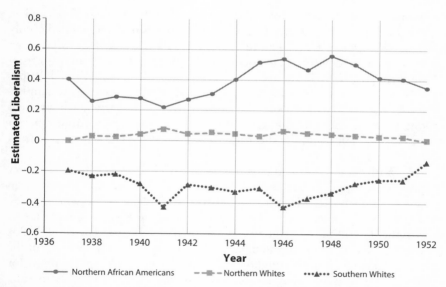

FIGURE 6.3. Estimated labor liberalism of northern African Americans, northern whites, and southern whites, 1937–52. The standard error for each annual estimate is approximately 0.07 for African Americans, 0.02 for northern whites, and 0.05 for southern whites.

This dynamic played out in concrete form in election contests at various levels of government. An early example came in Pennsylvania, where Republicans made a major bid to win back African American voters in 1938. The GOP attacked discrimination in New Deal agencies and the failure to pass antilynching legislation in Congress.[48] Republicans nominated an African American candidate for a congressional seat and, for the first time in years, campaigned aggressively for African American votes. But African Americans stuck with the Democrats by a lopsided margin, even as Republicans captured the governor's office. As Andrew Buni writes, African Americans were "not about to desert the party that represented relief, job-giving agencies like the WPA and the CCC, significant state and federal appointments, and social legislation." Indeed, the victorious Republicans' "retrenchment policies" offered little for African Americans.[49] Rather than acting as narrow policy demanders, African Americans—much like the CIO—sought progress on a whole range of economic and social issues that they believed were connected with one another.

THE CHANGING DYNAMICS OF AFRICAN AMERICAN PARTISANSHIP

Even as African Americans voted Democratic at the national level and in many state and local contests, their underlying partisanship remained evenly divided for several years. Figure 6.4 presents the percentage of African Americans who identify as Democrats and the percentage Republican from 1937 through 1969. The data source is primarily Gallup polls, though Roper and NORC surveys are included when available. It is important to emphasize that the quality of the samples in the early years (particularly prior to about 1948) is suspect. Southern African Americans are few in number in these early samples, and the sheer number of African American respondents per survey is often quite low.

Still, with these caveats, the data tell a fairly clear story. The two parties appear to be roughly equal in their share of African American identifiers in 1939–44, with a slight Democratic advantage evident as the war ended.[50] This margin expands noticeably in 1948, amid the first clear embrace of civil rights liberalism by Truman and national Democrats. The roughly 25-point Democratic advantage in partisanship that emerged in the wake of the 1948 campaign held up throughout the 1950s, despite the tepid support for civil rights offered by many national Democratic leaders. The Democratic edge in 1959—when 53 percent of African Americans identified as Democrats and just 24 percent as Republicans—was hardly indicative of a group that might swing to either party. With Kennedy's election on a clear pro–civil rights platform in 1960, this advantage expanded even further. African

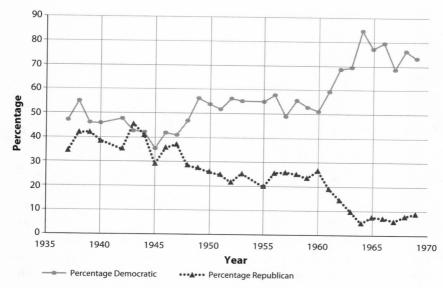

FIGURE 6.4. African American partisanship, 1937–69

Americans identified with the Democrats by an overwhelming 59–19 percent margin in 1961 and by 69–14.5 percent in 1962. Thus before Goldwater launched his campaign for the GOP nomination in 1963–64, African Americans had already decisively shifted not just in their vote choice but in their partisanship.[51]

One might view figure 6.4 as suggesting that Republicans still had a strong opportunity to win back African American voters as late as 1947–48, given the close balance between the two parties prior to the 1948 election. However, Republican strength in those years was partly a result of the enduring GOP leanings of older voters who came of age well before the New Deal. Figure 6.5 compares the partisanship of African Americans born before and after 1905. Notice that Republicans generally maintain a slight advantage among the older cohort up through 1947. By contrast, the younger cohort shows a clear—roughly 20-point—Democratic advantage throughout the late 1930s and 1940s. Both groups show signs of moving more toward the Democrats amid the 1948 campaign. The age-based differences become quite muted by about 1953, as both age cohorts give Democrats a sizable advantage, 25–40 points. Both groups again move further to the Democrats in the early 1960s. When one models African American partisanship as a function of age, younger voters are clearly more Democratic up to the early 1950s, but the differences become much smaller after about 1952.[52]

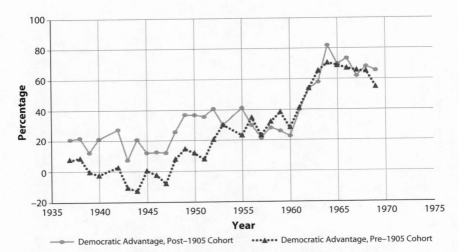

FIGURE 6.5. Comparison of Democratic partisanship advantage among African American age cohorts. Democratic advantage = % Democrat – % Republican for each cohort.

A similar story is evident when one compares African American partisanship across social class groups. Data limitations loom especially large in this case: consistent indicators of social class are in short supply in the 1930s–1950s surveys. Historical accounts suggest that African Americans of higher socioeconomic status in the North were more resistant to the CIO's entreaties in the late 1930s than were the greater number of working-class and poor African Americans.[53] Consistent with this qualitative evidence, the survey results show that early on, northern African Americans with lower socioeconomic status were especially likely to identify with the Democrats, but that these class differences largely gave way by the 1950s as partisanship and racial identification came into closer alignment.[54]

If one combines all the polls prior to 1948, northern African Americans with no telephone in their household identified with the Democrats by a 45–36 percent margin, while those with a phone identified with the GOP by a 44–32 percent margin. From 1948 to 1952, however, the gap between phone owners and those without a phone is much smaller: northern African Americans without a phone identify with the Democrats by a 51–26 percent margin, while those with a phone lean Democratic by 48–28 percent.[55]

Similar patterns are evident when it comes to alternative measures of social class. Among northern African Americans who are judged to be "average" or above in social class, Republicans enjoyed a 40–31 percent partisanship advantage prior 1948.[56] By contrast, among northern African Americans who were "poor" or on relief, Democrats had a 43–37 percent edge. If one isolates African Americans who were on relief or unemployed, Democrats had a more decisive 51–33 percent advantage prior to 1948.

These class differences again dissipated starting in the late 1940s. From 1948 to 1952 the "average or above" African Americans identified as Democrats over Republicans, 49–25 percent, while those who were poor or on relief sided with the Democrats by a similar 51–27 percent margin. Again, this suggests that Democratic partisanship was less tied to low socioeconomic status among northern African Americans by the late 1940s.[57]

The socioeconomic status indicator that is available across the longest time span is education. Once again, the small number of African Americans with the highest status—those who attended at least some college—were less Democratic than other northern African Americans prior 1948. These African Americans leaned Republican by a 35–25 percent margin (N = 338). By contrast, African Americans who did not graduate from high school identified with the Democrats by a 42–37 percent margin. From 1948 to 1952 the gap narrowed, as those with at least some college now leaned Democratic by a 40–24 percent margin, while those with no high school degree identified with the Democrats, 53–27 percent.[58] By the mid- to late 1950s the education gap was even smaller, with college-educated African Americans identifying with the Democrats by a 47–23 percent margin, and those without a high school degree identifying Democratic by 54–25 percent.[59] In sum, class cleavages in partisanship among northern African Americans were fairly strong in the late 1930s through the mid-1940s but became much less noticeable after 1948 as Democratic identification became common across class groups.

Strikingly, the very small southern African American samples in the early years tell a different story: the handful of African Americans with higher socioeconomic status appear *more* Democratic than their lower-status counterparts. While the limited southern samples require considerable caution, it is plausible that southern African Americans who were better educated or in professional occupations may have more directly experienced the social and political changes brought about by the New Deal and the rise of the CIO and so were more likely to shift to the Democrats early on. By the 1950s, however, these class differences in the South largely disappeared: both very poor and higher-status African Americans identified with the Democrats by a wide margin.

This pattern is also consistent across indicators. For example, prior to 1948 the small number of southern African Americans with a phone identified with the Democrats by a 53–30 percent margin, while non–phone owners were only narrowly Democratic (41–37 percent). From 1948 to 1952, however, both groups were heavily Democratic (57%–25% for phone owners, 59%–24% for those without a phone). Prior to 1948, southern African

Americans who were "average" or above in social status, identified with the Democrats by a 50–31 percent margin.[60] By contrast, those who were poor or on relief were only narrowly Democratic (41%–37%). From 1948 to 1952 both groups were heavily Democratic: 59–23 percent for the average or above respondents and 51–27 percent for the poor and on-relief respondents.

Finally, the best-educated southern African Americans were more heavily Democratic than were less-educated African Americans before 1948. The small number with some college education leaned Democratic by a 53–25 percent margin, while those with no high school degree gave Democrats just a 39–33 percent edge.[61] From 1948 to 1952 those with some college sided with the Democrats by a 66–13 percent margin, but those who never finished high school were not that far behind, giving Democrats a 59–25 percent advantage.[62] By the latter part of the 1950s less-educated southern African Americans were as Democratic as their better-educated counterparts.

These results are broadly consistent with a social identity perspective on partisan change.[63] African Americans' realignment initially was most pronounced among younger voters who came of age during the New Deal and, at least in the North, among voters with low socioeconomic status who experienced firsthand the benefits of New Deal social welfare and labor policies. However, as the social imagery of the parties changed so that the Democrats became more closely associated with African Americans as a social group, even older African Americans shifted to the Democrats, and social class was only weakly related to partisanship. That is, one's social identity as a "Republican" and as an African American were not in conflict in the 1930s and early 1940s. But northern Democrats' growing association with racial liberalism and Republican officeholders' burgeoning alliance with anti–New Deal southerners made it clear to more African Americans that identifying with the GOP was in tension with their racial group identity. For those Republicans who continued to believe that the party could win back a substantial share of African Americans, the economic liberalism and growing Democratic partisanship of African American voters in the 1950s and early 1960s stood as potent obstacles (see chapter 10 for a detailed discussion of GOP strategy).

CONCLUSION

It made sense to regard African Americans as swing voters who might opt for either party in the mid-1930s and early 1940s. The historical ties between African Americans and the GOP led many, particularly older African Americans, to stick with the "party of Lincoln." Furthermore, with most national Democrats unwilling to back civil rights initiatives and northern state Democratic parties only beginning to embrace civil rights liberalism, it should not be surprising that African American partisanship remained closely divided between Democrats and Republicans.

Nonetheless, African Americans' strong economic liberalism predisposed them to join the Democrats, sacrificing this "swing voter" status but gradually becoming an important constituency within the Democratic Party. African Americans were far more distant from the GOP than from the Democrats across a range of issues that largely defined the political battle lines in the 1940s and 1950s. This meant that as long as Democrats roughly matched the Republicans on civil rights, it would be very difficult for Republicans to win many African American votes without dramatically changing their economic policy stance.

The coalitional logic that pulled African Americans increasingly into the Democratic camp was not something easily under the control of party elites seeking to woo particular groups. Instead, it had important roots in the wide-ranging economic programs put forward by the New Deal and was reinforced by the even broader inclusive vision articulated by the CIO and other ascendant liberal forces in the late 1930s. The GOP's broad alternative—a more limited welfare state that returned power to the states—promised little in comparison.

As a result, Democrats enjoyed a substantial advantage in partisanship among young African Americans and low socioeconomic status northern African Americans by the late 1930s and early 1940s. Once prominent Democrats did begin to signal even a mild interest in civil rights in the late 1940s, African Americans of all ages and backgrounds evidently responded by tilting more decisively to the Democrats. African American partisanship remained strongly in the Democrats' favor throughout the 1950s and moved even further to the party in 1961–62 as it became even clearer that northern liberals had won control of the national party.

By the 1950s, however, African Americans already stood out relative to virtually all other demographic groups in their support for Democratic candidates. In 1952 Gallup estimates that 79 percent of African Americans voted for Adlai Stevenson, compared to 43 percent of whites, 55 percent of manual workers, 51 percent of southerners, 56 percent of Catholics, and 61 percent of labor union families. Four years later, even as Stevenson's vote share among African Americans evidently declined to 61 percent, the gap with whites was still 20 points (41% of whom voted for Stevenson), and the Democrat fared better among African Americans than among manual workers (50%), Catholics (51%), southerners (49%), or union families (57%).[64] In 1960 John F. Kennedy won African Americans by a 68–32 percent margin, which outpaced his standing among whites (49%), manual workers (60%), southerners (46%), and union families (65%).[65]

Massive population changes magnified the political importance of African Americans' Democratic identification. The African American population remained concentrated in the South as late as 1940. The 1940 census—more than twenty years after the Great Migration had started—revealed that while nearly a quarter of southerners were African American, only 3.8 percent of the Northeast was African American, along with 3.5 percent of the Midwest, and 1.2 percent of the West. The African American population was a bit higher in some key northern states but still constituted a fairly small proportion of the total: it ranged from 4 percent to 5 percent in Michigan, Illinois, New York, Ohio, and Pennsylvania, while standing at 5.5 percent in New Jersey and a mere 1.8 percent in California.

Wartime and post–World War II migration changed this picture dramatically, particularly in northern cities. By 1960 the African American population had doubled (or more) in California (5.6%), Illinois (10.3%), Michigan (9.2%), and New York (8.4%), while increasing by at least a factor of one-half in New Jersey (8.5%), Ohio (8.1%), and Pennsylvania (7.5%). The major population shift, along with African Americans' increased tendency to vote Democratic, combined to make African Americans a key building block for Democratic majorities in these northern states. With whites either evenly divided or leaning slightly to the GOP in each of these states in the 1960 election, African American votes proved critical to the Democrats' chances. Based on turnout and polling data on vote choice, it appears that African Americans constituted roughly 10–15 percent of the Democratic votes cast in each of these key states in 1960, with the exception of California.[66]

For northern Democratic state parties and rank-and-file members of Congress in the 1940s–1960s, the entry of a substantial number of African Americans into their party coalition had important implications for both their positioning on civil rights and the priority that they would accord the issue. African Americans were an increasingly significant element of their electoral coalition, and, as shown in chapters 3 and 4, they were now allied with other key groups that were at the forefront of defining the scope and meaning of New Deal liberalism. Chapters 7 and 8 trace how these state parties and members of Congress responded to—and reinforced—this new constellation of forces, and chapter 9 analyzes how these ascendant groups eventually captured the national party. Critically, voters who initially entered the party for reasons not directly connected to civil rights ultimately had an important impact on party officials' behavior as activists worked to raise the place of civil rights on the national agenda. In this way, understanding the civil rights realignment requires attention to the intersection among multiple political trajectories, rather than a focus on a single logic or set of actors.

For Republicans, African Americans' shift into the Democratic column gradually strengthened the hand of conservative party members advocating that the party downplay its historic advocacy of civil rights and instead make common cause with southern white conservatives. Below the surface, one finds rank-and-file Republican members of Congress showing less commitment to civil rights than northern Democrats from the mid-1940s onward (see chapter 8). Chapter 10 details the struggle between moderates and conservatives for control of the national GOP, arguing that conservatives' ultimate victory had deep roots in the transformations unleashed by the New Deal.

CHAPTER 7

State Parties and the Civil Rights Realignment

PREVIOUS CHAPTERS HAVE shown that economic liberalism, Democratic partisanship, and support for civil rights became linked together in the late 1930s and early 1940s. These connections were evident both in the set of groups battling over the future of the New Deal in Washington (see chapters 3 and 4), and in the views of ordinary voters (see chapters 5 and 6).

But how were these new linkages incorporated into a party system that had long been premised on suppressing civil rights issues from the agenda? National Democratic leaders faced a difficult trade-off in deciding how to respond to the push to act on civil rights. Southern states continued to represent an important bloc of electoral votes in presidential contests, and Democratic majorities in Congress depended heavily on the Solid South. Mindful of these considerations, Democratic presidential nominees and senior congressional leaders treaded carefully. As far as Franklin Roosevelt, Adlai Stevenson, John F. Kennedy, Senate leader and vice president Lyndon Johnson, or Speaker of the House Sam Rayburn were concerned, political strategy would have been much simpler if civil rights disappeared as an issue (see chapter 9 on national party leaders).

State party politics, however, tell a much different story. Advocates for moving the Democratic Party in the liberal direction on civil rights found some of their earliest success at the state level in the North, where locally rooted politicians had much less reason to worry about placating southern Democrats.

A small but important literature has shown that Democratic legislators were more supportive of state fair employment practices laws than were Republicans. In his authoritative book *The Fifth Freedom*, Anthony Chen offers systematic evidence from the 1940s–1950s demonstrating that Democratic control of state government was associated with a substantially higher chance of FEPC enactment and that Democratic legislators were generally more supportive than Republicans of the underlying legislation.[1]

Political observers at the time noted this disproportionate Democratic support. In an article in the *Crisis* in 1949, Arnold Aronson and Samuel Spiegler ask provocatively, "Does the Republican Party Want the Negro

Vote?"[2] The authors review developments across a wide range of states, highlighting the common pattern of Democratic support for strong fair employment practices legislation and GOP opposition. In Illinois, for example, the Democratic-controlled House passed an FEPC bill in a highly partisan vote, only to see it rejected in the GOP-controlled Senate. The Senate Republican Caucus in Illinois publicly signaled its neutrality, but the party's leaders privately urged members to vote it down. The final vote rejecting the bill was 25–24, with twenty-four out of thirty-one Republicans voting nay, and all but one Democrat recorded in favor.[3] Aronson and Spiegler also attribute the failure of state-level FEPC legislation in California, Minnesota, Michigan, Colorado, Pennsylvania, Ohio, and Indiana to opposition from Republican legislators.

Duane Lockard's study of FEPC and fair housing bills in state legislatures tells a similar story. Not only were Republicans less supportive than Democrats on the key roll-call votes in the 1944–63 period, the roll-call record likely *overstates* the true level of GOP support. On several occasions when Republican leaders unsuccessfully sought to prevent civil rights initiatives from reaching the floor, they turned around and urged members to vote in favor at the roll-call stage to safeguard the party's reputation.[4]

This chapter builds on these analyses of state fair employment practices laws, presenting further evidence that the civil rights realignment was well underway at the state level in the 1940s and 1950s and that it spanned a wide range of issues, not just FEPC laws. I rely primarily on a new data source, state party platforms. Platforms offer a rare opportunity for a state party to speak as an institution with a single voice. The platform allows each state party to outline the vision that it seeks to present to the electorate, and in this way to express what it stands for and whom it stands with in political battles. The argument here is not that the state platforms *caused* the Democrats to become the party of civil rights. Instead, the platforms are a *measure* of how the state parties chose to position themselves on the issue. These positions reflected genuine political battles on the ground in which state-level Democrats fought for civil rights; these fights did have causal purchase, cementing a liberal pro–civil rights coalition at the midlevel of the Democratic Party that ultimately acted as a progressive influence on national party leaders as they responded to the civil rights movement.

A content analysis of approximately a thousand state party platforms from 1920 to 1968 shows that northern Democratic and Republican state parties were roughly equal in their very limited civil rights support in the 1920s and early to mid-1930s. The parties paid increasing attention to civil rights from 1936 to 1945, with Democrats generally exhibiting greater support than Republicans. By the mid- to late 1940s the vast majority of northern state Democratic parties were clearly to the left of their GOP counterparts on civil rights.

When one examines *which* state parties adopted civil rights liberalism earliest and most extensively, the results offer interesting parallels to the mass-level analyses presented in chapters 5 and 6. As one might expect, both parties appear to be more liberal on civil rights in northern states with substantial African American populations than in states with smaller African American populations.[5] Furthermore, urbanization, unionization, and the size of the Jewish population are each associated with state parties taking a pro–civil rights position, particularly starting in the late 1930s. These findings suggest that the same constellation of groups that came to be associated with ardent New Deal liberalism—African Americans, unions, Jews, and urban residents—also came to be associated with state parties taking a strongly pro–civil rights position.[6]

The party platform evidence reinforces my broader argument that the partisan realignment on civil rights took root long before the 1960s and that national party elites followed, rather than led, officials and activists at the state and local levels. Analysis of state-level change also provides insight into *how* the realignment succeeded. State parties provided an institutional mechanism through which civil rights advocates were able to gain a foothold in the Democratic Party. Rather than having to capture the national Democratic Party as a whole, pro–civil rights forces capitalized on the decentralized, fragmented party system in which state parties and candidates were able to adopt their own positions on issues. State parties and politicians drew on a different calculus from top party leaders, showing less concern for national coalitional imperatives and greater responsiveness to the emergent demands from the new groups that were becoming the backbone of their electoral support.

The reaction of northern state parties is consistent with the idea that parties seek to accommodate the demands of coalition group members.[7] But the independent electoral base of state parties cuts against the idea that "the party" is a single, unified entity. Instead, the federal nature of the American party system allows intraparty divisions to be institutionalized: northern state parties accommodated one set of groups and interests, while southern parties provided a home for a sharply opposed set of interests.

After describing the primary data source and the approach to coding, the chapter tracks Democratic and Republican state party liberalism on civil rights from 1920 to 1968. I then estimate a series of simple models that identify which state-level factors are associated with greater civil rights liberalism in the platforms. A brief examination of civil rights politics in New York, Michigan, and California complements the quantitative evidence indicating that African Americans, unions, Jews, and other urban liberals provided the political muscle pushing for action on civil rights, with Democratic Party officials proving far more responsive to these demands than were Republicans.

DATA AND METHODS

State Party Platforms as Data

To assess how politicians at the state level positioned themselves and their parties on civil rights, this chapter utilizes a new data source that offers several important advantages. Working with Brian Feinstein, I attempted to compile a comprehensive database of state party platforms covering 1920 to 1968, coding each platform for the state party's position on a range of civil rights issues, as well as the prominence given to civil rights. Finding platforms proved to be a difficult challenge. Nevertheless, we collected and coded 1,021 platforms.

By allowing one to locate the position of each state party across a long period of time, the platforms—which in many states were published biennially—provide a fine-grained ability to trace the development of party positioning on civil rights at the state level. Comparing the position of Democrats and Republicans from the same state is particularly useful, as it holds geographic constituencies constant. Furthermore, variation across states and over time provides leverage for understanding the sources of the realignment.

Before proceeding to the analysis, however, key questions include who wrote the platforms and how we should interpret their meaning. State platforms were typically written neither by ordinary citizens nor by national elites. Rather, platform writers tend to come from the middle level of the parties: state and county party chairmen and executive committee members, state legislators, mayors, amateur activists, and, in some cases, rank-and-file members of Congress.[8]

To gain further insight into who was involved in drafting and approving these documents, we examined a sample of 117 newspaper articles published in 1942 and 1950 that mention state party platforms and are included in the ProQuest Historical Newspapers database.[9] While the available newspapers were limited geographically, there was a considerable amount of information on the process in several states. Typically, the state party chair or executive committee appointed a platform committee consisting of twenty or more members. Often, a subset of the committee, which in the states examined usually included state legislators and party officials, would draft a preliminary version of the platform. The full committee then considered and the party convention approved the document. The members of the full committee mentioned in the newspaper coverage included a mix of party officials, state legislators, and amateur activists.[10] In several cases the platform writers solicited input from interest groups, through either public hearings or informal consultation.[11] For example, New York Democrats held a series of formal platform hearings in both 1942 and 1950 at which numerous interest groups—including civil rights groups and unions—testified. While the newspapers only occasionally reported the full text of the platforms, they provided extensive coverage of the maneuvering over key platform planks, which often reflected factional battles within the parties.[12]

The state platforms thus reflect the thinking of state and local party officials, state-level officeholders, state legislators, and amateur activists. In writing these platforms, the authors were no doubt attentive to what the party convention would accept, and to the need to appeal to voters and key constituency groups. While the sincerity of the individual platform writers cannot be assessed, that is arguably beside the point. Instead, the platforms indicate how each party chose to position itself on major issues.[13] If northern Democrats consistently chose to position themselves as the party of civil rights liberalism—long before the "critical period" of the early 1960s—that is evidence that the party realignment was rooted in factors that were in place by the 1940s.

How Representative Are These Paired Platforms?

To evaluate differences between the parties within a given state over time, one must possess a sufficient number of platforms from both parties across many different years. The platform collection was obtained by searching through state government registers, newspapers, and pamphlets distributed by the state parties themselves.[14] It provides good coverage of twenty-two nonsouthern states, in addition to Texas and North Carolina, and represents approximately 57 percent of all platforms written by northern state parties during the period.[15]

Figure 7.1 illustrates the number of platforms obtained for each year in the period under study, while figure 7.2 displays the coverage by state. Since a complete collection of platforms from one state party is less useful without the other party's platforms in that state, the figures show only the number of "paired" Democratic and Republican platforms, with a pair defined as same-state Democratic and Republican platforms in the same year. As figure 7.2 illustrates, during this forty-eight-year period, there is excellent coverage for the upper Midwest; acceptable coverage of New England, the Mid-Atlantic, and the mountain West; and poor coverage for the Northwest, South, and border South.[16] Fortunately, it turns out that the interparty differences are substantively similar in the Midwest, Northeast, Mid-Atlantic, and West, suggesting that uneven coverage across regions does not distort the overall story (see discussion below).

Coding the Platforms

Three distinct content analyses were undertaken to determine the extent to which state party platforms favor or oppose civil rights measures. The first is

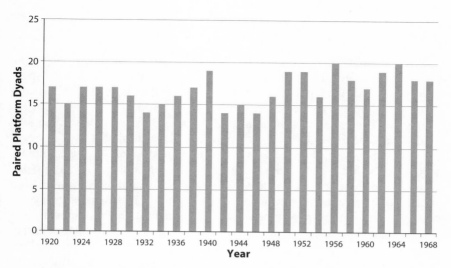

FIGURE 7.1. Paired platform coverage, by year. From Brian D. Feinstein and Eric Schickler, "Platforms and Partners: The Civil Rights Realignment Reconsidered," *Studies in American Political Development* 22, 1 (2008): 1–31.

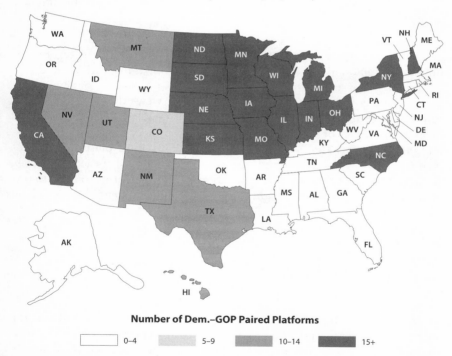

Number of Dem.–GOP Paired Platforms

0–4	5–9	10–14	15+

FIGURE 7.2. Paired platform coverage, by state. From Brian D. Feinstein and Eric Schickler, "Platforms and Partners: The Civil Rights Realignment Reconsidered," *Studies in American Political Development* 22, 1 (2008): 1–31.

a tally of the number of paragraphs devoted to civil rights in each platform. Carmines and Stimson conduct a similar analysis of the amount of space devoted to civil rights issues in national party platforms, noting that it constitutes a "simple measure of the importance of a topic."[17]

A second measure is a 10-point (–4 to 5) ordinal scale assessing each platform's general outlook on civil rights. A platform that makes no mention of civil rights policy receives a 0. The highest value on this summary score signals that a platform advocates government policies to outlaw discrimination broadly across at least two different issue dimensions, in what appears to be an enforceable manner. For example, a platform that supports both a state fair employment practices commission with enforcement powers and a fair housing practices law would be coded as a 5. A platform that endorses the concept of equal treatment but does not include any call for concrete governmental action receives a score of 1. Platforms that are critical of governmental civil rights initiatives receive negative scores. The lowest score, –4, is reserved for those platforms that most explicitly oppose civil rights legislation; many of these platforms predict "chaos" or a "breakdown in civic society" if civil rights proposals become law. Appendix table 7.1 (available online) provides a summary of the coding criteria.

Third, each platform's attention to five specific civil rights issue areas was assessed: fair employment practices, fair housing practices, desegregation of public accommodations, desegregation of educational institutions, and voting rights.[18] The scale for these measures ranges from –1 ("condemns past or proposed government action on this issue, or views the issue as best left to the private sphere") to 3 ("claims credit for new law or commission, or proposes new law or commission that aims to protect minorities from discrimination in this area"). In the 1920s and 1930s, most platforms did not mention any of these issues and thus received a score of 0 each. However, starting in the 1940s, it became more common for platforms to refer to one or more of the specific civil rights issues (see online appendix table 7.2 on the coding).[19]

PARTISAN PLATFORM DIFFERENCES

Attention to Civil Rights Issues

Perhaps the most basic indicator of a party's attention to civil rights is the amount of space that it devotes to these issues in its platforms. In most presidential election years prior to the 1960s, the Republicans devoted slightly more space in their *national* platforms to civil rights than did Democrats.[20] While exceptions exist (e.g., the 1948 Democratic platform edges out that year's GOP platform), this general tendency holds until 1964, when Demo-

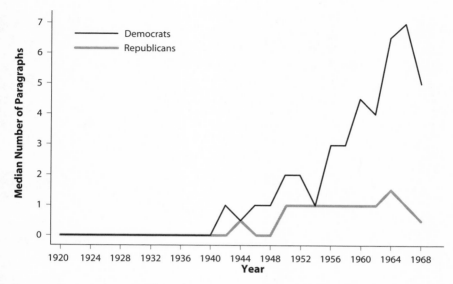

FIGURE 7.3. Median number of paragraphs devoted to civil rights in northern state platforms

crats suddenly surpass Republicans in attention paid to civil rights (see chapters 9 and 10 for a discussion of national platform politics).

State party platforms tell a much different story. Figure 7.3 presents the median number of paragraphs devoted to civil rights in state platforms in each election year from 1920 to 1968. The figure includes only cases for which both state parties' platforms were obtained in the same year, though the results look much the same if all available platforms are included.[21]

Neither party paid much attention to civil rights in the 1920s or 1930s. But from at least the mid-1940s Democrats devote more attention to civil rights than Republicans. In addition, there is no abrupt and permanent change in 1964. Concerning differences in attention between the two party's platforms on civil rights, the story is one of gradual change, with Democrats surpassing Republicans by the mid-1940s.

Summary Measure of Party Position

The number of paragraphs devoted to civil rights is, of course, a very rough measure of party positioning. A more fine-grained approach is to use the ordinal scale described above to summarize each party's stance. The main data source again is the 423 sets of "paired platforms"—Democratic and Republican platforms from the same state and same year (a total of 846).

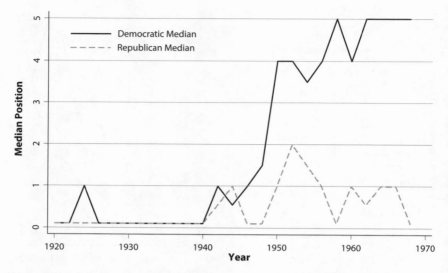

FIGURE 7.4. Median position of state Democratic and Republican parties on civil rights, 1920–68, northern states. States are included only when there is an available platform for both parties in the same year. Two-year election cycles are used—e.g., the data point for 1940 includes platforms for 1939 and 1940.

Figure 7.4 presents the median score for state Democratic and state Republican platforms in each even-numbered year from 1920 to 1968.[22] Throughout the 1920s and 1930s the typical Democratic and GOP state platforms took no position at all on civil rights. But the parties began to address civil rights from the 1940s onward. Democratic state parties became steadily more liberal from 1940 through 1964, with the biggest jump in the median state party position from the end of World War II through 1950. By contrast, the Republicans took their most progressive stance on civil rights—which was still clearly to the right of their northern Democratic counterparts—during the early to mid-1950s and gradually became more racially conservative thereafter.

From 1946 on, the median Democratic summary score outpaced the median Republican score in each election cycle. The gap in the median positions was just under 1 point in 1946, reached 1.4 points two years later, and remained at least 2 points on the 10-point scale in each election cycle from 1950 onward. In contrast to national party platforms, 1964 does not appear to be a "critical moment" when it comes to state party positions. Instead, that year saw the continuation of a trend that began many years before. The state party platforms support the view that, outside the South, the realignment of the parties on civil rights had essentially already been completed well before the 1960s.

The gap of 2 to 3 points evident in the party medians by 1950 reflects a substantial difference in what the parties were saying about civil rights policy. For example, Illinois's 1952 Democratic platform, which scored a 4 on the scale, condemned GOP opposition to the FEPC bill pending in the state legislature, promising that "we will not relent in our effort to eliminate discrimination between our citizens.... We will persist in our efforts to give to Illinois an enforceable Fair Employment Practices Law." The state's Republican platform, which scored a 1, avoided endorsing any legislative or administrative action and instead included only a vague promise to "continue to zealously guard the civil rights of every citizen without regard to race, creed, or color, to explore discrimination and to vigorously oppose racial and religious prejudice in whatever form it may arise." Republican platforms of the period that mentioned civil rights often included similar generic calls for equal treatment but steered clear of support for binding legislation to achieve that end. Thus Indiana Republicans called in 1954 to preserve "equal protection of the law and equal opportunity to work, without regard to sex, race, color or religion." The state's Democrats, by comparison, called for adoption of a compulsory Fair Employment Practices Act and for an end to segregation.[23]

One might wonder whether the use of party medians obscures important variation in the relationship between party and civil rights support. An alternative measure that demands less of the ordinal scale is to simply code which party was more liberal than its same-state counterpart in a given year. Figure 7.5 presents the results. Through 1936 the two parties are equal in the vast majority of cases (79%), but the number of times in which the Democrats are to the left of their same-state GOP counterparts (seventeen, or 12%) is roughly equal to the number of times in which the Republicans are more liberal (fourteen, or 10%).[24] During the transitional period from 1937 to 1944, Democrats are to the left of the Republicans in sixteen cases (25%), while Republicans are more liberal just eight times (12.5%), with the parties equal (generally in their inattention to civil rights) most of the time (62.5%). The picture changes dramatically over the next decade, from 1945 to 1954, when Democrats are to the left of their same-state Republican counterparts fifty-three times (62.4%), while Republicans are to the left just nine times (10.6%). From 1955 to 1963 Democrats are to the left of Republicans 82.4 percent of the time, with Republicans more liberal in just 4 percent of the cases.[25] In the final period examined, 1964 to 1968, Democrats are to the left of Republicans 91 percent of the time (with the parties tied in the remaining cases). These results reinforce the conclusion that state-level northern Democratic parties had moved decisively to the left of the Republicans

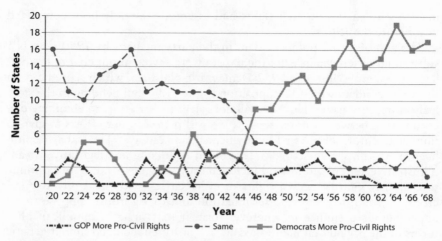

FIGURE 7.5. Relative state party support for civil rights, northern states. States are included only when there is an available platform for both parties in the same year. Two-year election cycles are used—e.g., the data point for 1940 includes platforms for 1939 and 1940.

by the mid-1940s, with a gradual increase in the interparty gap over the following two decades.

As noted in the introduction, one limitation of the state platform data is uneven coverage across states. This could lead to misleading inferences if the relative placement of the parties varied substantially across regions in ways that correlate with the available platform data. A closer look at the data, however, underscores the robustness of the finding that northern Democratic state parties outpaced Republicans in their civil rights advocacy well before the 1960s. Figure 7.6 presents the share of cases in which each party is more liberal than the other from 1945 to 1954 for the three census regions outside the South. In each case the state Democratic parties are more pro–civil rights by a substantial margin.[26] The same results hold if one extends the time frame into the late 1950s or early 1960s.

Issue-Specific Measures

While the summary measure suggests that state Democratic parties generally outpaced their GOP counterparts in civil rights liberalism by the mid- to late 1940s, this still leaves open the question of whether the party gap was confined to one or two issues—such as fair employment practices—or instead pervaded the entire civil rights agenda. Therefore the platforms were also coded for their position on five specific issues areas, each of which was

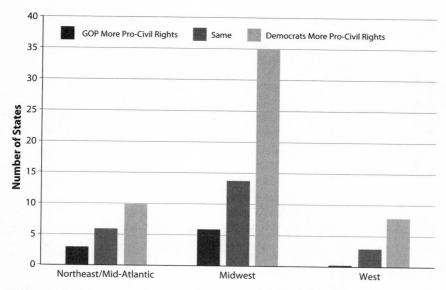

FIGURE 7.6. Relative state party support for civil rights, 1945–54, by region

the subject of major legislative and legal battles: fair employment practices, fair housing, desegregated public accommodations, desegregated educational institutions, and voting rights.

Figure 7.7 displays the percentage of states in which the Democratic platform was to the left of the GOP platform on a particular issue, compared to the percentage of times the state Republican Party took the more liberal position on the issue.[27] The results tell a consistent story with only minor variations.

Issues emerged onto the agenda at different times, with fair employment practices the first to engage the parties in a serious way. When it came to job discrimination, northern state Democratic parties were far ahead of state Republican parties by the mid-1940s. Thus while Connecticut Republicans were silent on fair employment practices in their 1942 platform, the state's Democrats announced that they "stand for equality of opportunity in employment in all fields of endeavor irrespective of race, creed or color. We favor the appointment of a commission on Fair Employment Practice with the power to act in such instances." Similarly, Minnesota's Democratic-Farmer-Labor Party called in 1946 for "fair employment practices legislation on the national, state, and local levels to protect all who want to work from discrimination on account of race, religion, creed, nationality, or ancestry." By contrast, the state's Republican platform did not endorse fair employment protections. As figure 7.7A suggests, the gap in party positioning on

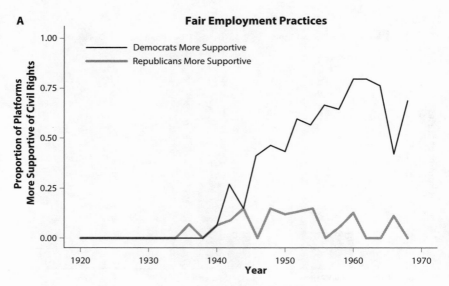

A **Fair Employment Practices**

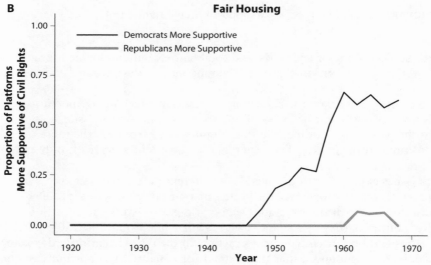

B **Fair Housing**

fair employment practices gradually increased over time until it peaked in the early 1960s.

Education, by contrast, did not emerge onto the agenda until later—with the *Brown* decision clearly evident in the spike in attention after 1954—but state Democratic parties again outpaced state Republicans in taking the pro–civil rights side when they did engage with the issue in the mid-1950s.[28]

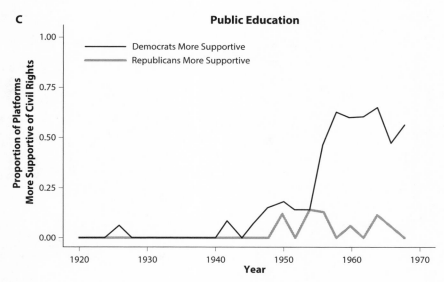

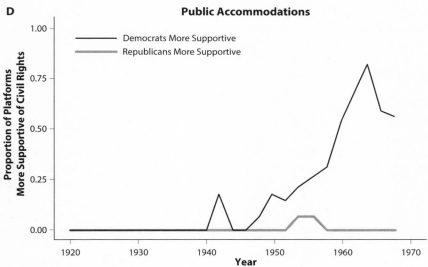

Public accommodations and fair housing tell a broadly similar story: they received less attention in the 1940s than did fair employment practices, but once the parties began to take a stance on the issues in the early 1950s, Democrats clearly took the more pro–civil rights side. For example, Wisconsin Democrats' 1950 platform urged that state law "make unlawful the discrimination in places of public accommodation or amusement" based on

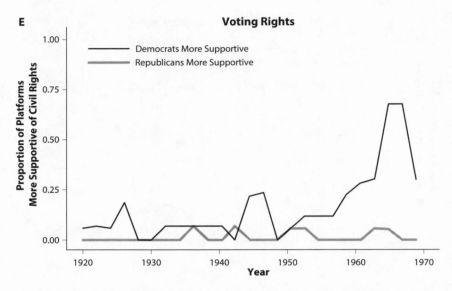

FIGURE 7.7. Relative position of state parties across specific issues. *A*, Fair employment practices. *B*, Fair housing. *C*, Public education. *D*, Public accommodations. *E*, Voting rights. From Brian D. Feinstein and Eric Schickler, "Platforms and Partners: The Civil Rights Realignment Reconsidered," *Studies in American Political Development* 22, 1 (2008): 1–31.

race, color, creed, or national origin. Again, state Republicans were silent on the issue.

Even on voting rights, the one issue that arguably was easiest for Republicans to embrace—since ending the poll tax and other restrictions on the franchise would directly affect only the South—state Democratic parties took the more liberal position well before the 1960s (see fig. 7.7*E*). The Democrats tended to take slightly more progressive stances on voting rights in the 1930s and 1940s, with more substantial differences emerging in the 1950s.

The issue-specific measures suggest one important difference between the mass-level dynamics on civil rights and the positions adopted by midlevel actors, such as state parties. Among rank-and-file white voters in the North, Democratic partisanship was associated with greater support for the key civil rights policies on the national agenda in the late 1930s and the 1940s, such as fair employment practices, antilynching legislation, military integration, and the poll tax, but the party gap was smaller and less consistent when it came to prejudice and several issues related to close social contact between the races (such as fair housing and education, which would become prominent in the 1950s–1960s). By contrast, key actors in the liberal coalition—

such as the NAACP, CIO, and ADA—did take the pro–civil rights position on these issues as well (as did economically liberal voters more generally). As is the case with the liberal groups, state Democratic parties evidently also were more consistent in their support for the range of civil rights initiatives than were rank-and-file partisans.

STATE CHARACTERISTICS AND CIVIL RIGHTS SUPPORT

The descriptive data demonstrate that northern state Democratic parties came to embrace civil rights to a greater extent than did northern Republican parties by the mid- to late 1940s. Again, as in earlier chapters, it is clear that the state parties were not following cues from national party elites. Indeed, the state Democratic parties' liberalism emerges a few years before the one early case in which national Democrats do explicitly embrace civil rights, the 1948 election campaign. But to what extent are specific state-level characteristics associated with greater civil rights support?

In earlier chapters I argued that a liberal, pro–civil rights coalition took shape in the late 1930s and early 1940s that consisted of African Americans, CIO unions, Jewish groups, and other urban liberals. African Americans' migration northward and movement into the Democratic Party provided an incentive for northern Democratic politicians to support civil rights. Among white voters, economic liberals, union members, Jews, and urban residents were also more likely to back civil rights. To what extent are similar factors associated with state parties' positioning on civil rights?

As a first cut at this question, figure 7.8A presents the bivariate relationship between state-level demographic characteristics and the civil rights position taken in northern state party platforms by period.[29] Through 1936, when only a handful of Democratic state parties were taking a pro–civil rights position, the relationship between state demographics and civil rights support is generally weak.[30] Urbanization and state-level unionization are unrelated to civil rights support, while the state-level Jewish population has a weak, inconsistent relationship.[31] The one exception is that the size of the African American population is a significant predictor of Democratic platform support for civil rights. This suggests that early on, state Democrats were at least somewhat responsive to the promise of African American electoral support, but—given the low African American population share across most of the North—this incentive was generally insufficient to generate much attention to civil rights.

After 1936 a broader set of state demographic characteristics are associated with Democrats' civil rights support. The estimate for African American population continues to be reasonably large.[32] In addition, urbanization, unionization, and the percentage of the population that is Jewish are each significantly associated with Democratic platforms' support for civil rights.[33]

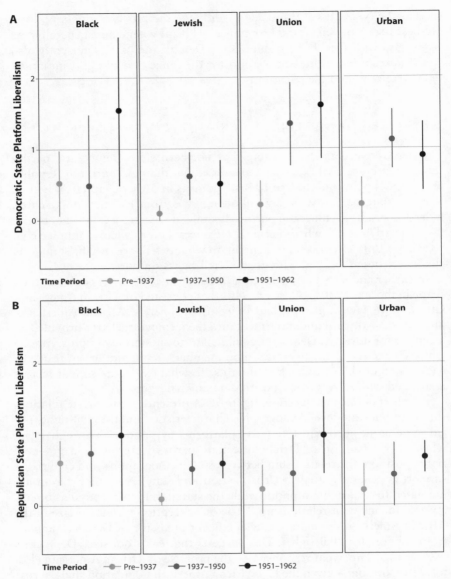

FIGURE 7.8. State demographic predictors of party platform liberalism. *A*, Democratic platform. *B*, Republican platform. The figures show the estimated change and 95% confidence interval in the platform liberalism score, which ranges from –4 to +5, when the independent variable in a regression changes from the 20th to 80th percentile among northern states. Each regression includes just one demographic variable and dummy variables for year.

With respect to unionization, both a measure of the state's CIO membership (as of 1939 and 1953) and total union membership are generally statistically significant predictors of platform liberalism. The sparseness of the data militates against drawing a sharp dichotomy across periods, but it is evident that as state Democratic parties became more likely to support civil rights in the late 1930s and 1940s, the correlates of that support broadened beyond the African American population to also include other key elements of the developing liberal coalition.[34]

One might also ask how the results are affected when one controls for a range of potentially competing demographic predictors of civil rights support. One challenge confronting a multivariate model is that the various predictors are closely related to one another, and the causal ordering among the variables is not entirely clear. For example, urbanization may contribute to union success, making it misleading to simply control for both variables in a regression (since one would underestimate the total effects of urbanization). Nonetheless, a few observations are worth noting with respect to state Democratic platforms. First, when one controls for both African American population and state-level unionization, the former is significant prior to 1937 while unionization has no effect. After 1936, however, state-level unionization holds up as a predictor, while the state-level African American population is insignificant (though the estimates are positive and the large standard errors mean that any inferences need to be tentative). Second, if one controls for all four major demographic predictors of civil rights support (African American population, unionization, urbanization, and Jewish population), the estimate for African American population again is strong in the pre-1937 period while the other variables are generally insignificant.[35] After 1936 the unionization variable holds up fairly well, as does the Jewish population, but the results are more mixed than in the bivariate case, and the remaining variables are insignificant.[36]

Among Republican state parties, the share of the population that is African American has a strong, significant impact on civil rights support across each period.[37] The same holds true for the Jewish population (see fig. 7.8B). Urbanization and unionization each appear associated with civil rights support after 1936, though the estimates are not always statistically significant.[38]

The broadly similar results for state Democratic and Republican parties raise the question of whether the *relative* position of the parties was also related to state-level demographic characteristics. Prior to 1936 the only demographic variable that predicts relative state liberalism is African American population, but the results indicate a high African American population was associated with the *Republicans* being more pro–civil rights than Democrats in this early period.[39] After 1936 the size of the African American population is not associated with the relative liberalism of the state parties.

However, urbanization, state-level unionization, and, to a somewhat lesser extent, state Jewish population are each associated with the Democrats taking the more liberal position after 1936. For example, in states with an above-average level of urbanization, Democrats took the more liberal position than Republicans 54 percent of the time from 1937 to 1950, while Republicans took the more liberal position just 10 percent of the time. In states with below average urbanization, the parties are more closely matched, with Democrats outpacing Republicans by just a 26–11 percent margin. Similarly, from 1937 to 1950 Democrats edged Republicans in their civil rights advocacy in 50 percent of the states with above-average unionization, while falling short just 8 percent of the time. The margin was a much closer 31–13 percent in states with below-average unionization.[40]

On the whole, these results are consistent with the idea that as civil rights liberalism became associated with the urban liberal coalition in the late 1930s, Democrats were especially attuned to demands emanating from these core constituent groups. While state Republicans continued to show some support for civil rights in the 1940s and 1950s, particularly where the African American population was high, this support was substantially less than that provided by same-state Democratic parties.

THE CIVIL RIGHTS COALITION IN ACTION AT THE STATE LEVEL

The quantitative evidence suggesting that state Democrats' support for civil rights was linked to the presence of African Americans, unions, Jews, and urban residents is reinforced by case studies drawn from the Northeast, Midwest, and West. These brief case studies also underscore the argument that Democratic legislators proved more supportive of civil rights than did Republicans. Indeed, qualitative evidence from the states suggests that the level of GOP civil rights support in the platforms actually outstripped what rank-and-file state legislators were willing to countenance when it came to policy making.

Michigan

Michigan is a particularly interesting case highlighting the role of liberal activists and labor in spurring Democrats to embrace civil rights. The state Democratic organization was quite weak in the 1930s and early 1940s and did not reflect national New Deal Democratic priorities. In his study of Michigan civil rights politics, Sidney Fine writes that the "all but moribund and leaderless" state Democratic apparatus was "controlled at the time by old-guard, conservative elements more concerned about patronage than issues."[41] In that initial period, the state platform did not even mention civil rights, let alone take a strong position.[42]

Starting in the mid-1940s, a coalition of liberals mobilized in a bid to take over the party. The Michigan Democratic Club, which Fay Calkins describes as "an issue-oriented group of depression-bred New Dealers," reached out to the recently formed state CIO-PAC to forge an alliance.[43] It took about a year for the PAC to persuade local CIO leaders that their best strategy was to work within the state party, but the PAC assured skeptics that "we are not accepting the Democratic Party in Michigan as it now is. Our purpose in going into it is to line up with its liberal elements and remold the Party into a progressive force"[44] The Club and the PAC reached out to liberal AFL unions, African American groups, the ADA, and "liberal church groups" for support. According to Calkins, a "common bond" uniting the coalition "was agreement on a liberal legislative program, including progressive taxation, civil rights, public housing, improved social security, and workmen's compensation."[45] The coalition recruited candidates—many of them union stewards and officers—to run for precinct delegate positions to gain control of the party apparatus.

The old guard barely held on to control of the 1948 platform-writing process, which produced only a very mild civil rights plank. However, the liberal coalition did succeed in nominating G. Mennen Williams, a New Deal liberal who was an aggressive civil rights advocate, for governor. Furthermore, the liberals gained control of the entire party apparatus by 1949, and the state platform in 1950 had an extensive civil rights plank, which called for "a continued fight for workable fair employment legislation to end job discrimination for reasons of race, creed or color." The platform also backed Governor Williams's bid to eliminate discrimination in the state National Guard and pledged to "to continue the fight to make the Bill of Rights and the Constitution of Michigan apply equally to all citizens."[46] After 1950 the state Democratic platform consistently included one of the strongest civil rights planks of any state party.[47]

The liberals' bid to control the state Democratic Party was paralleled by efforts to push civil rights initiatives in the state legislature. The Metropolitan Detroit Council on Fair Employment Practice (MDFEPC), which formed in March 1942, was an "interfaith, interracial federation of some seventy civic organizations and labor unions."[48] It lobbied the legislature for an enforceable state FEPC law and drafted the bill that was introduced in the state Senate in 1943 and 1945. The companion bill in the House was modeled explicitly on a CIO bill and dealt not only with job discrimination but also with discrimination in "housing, education, recreation, health, and social welfare." The Michigan Republican convention had pledged support for FEPC in its 1944 platform, but the Republican legislature stymied the legislation and the GOP governor, Harry Kelly, refused to lobby on its behalf.[49]

After the war ended, the MDFEPC worked with the leftist-aligned Civil Rights Congress to sponsor a petition drive to force a referendum on state FEPC legislation. The UAW's Walter Reuther and Jewish groups joined African American activists in pushing the referendum, and the Wayne County CIO collected nearly one-third of the signatures.[50] Concerns about the Civil Rights Congress's communist ties led Reuther to join the NAACP, Detroit Urban League, and religious groups in forming still another organization, the Michigan Council for Fair Employment Legislation (MCFEPL) in January 1947. Business groups financed the opposition to the referendum and ultimately succeeded in having it removed from the ballot on a technicality.[51]

Following this setback, the MCFEPL changed its name to the Michigan Committee on Civil Rights (MCCR) and broadened its agenda to include additional issues beyond FEPC. The MCCR brought together African Americans and religious, labor, civic, and women's organizations in attempting to pressure Republican governor Kimber Sigler to act on civil rights.[52] While Sigler proved unresponsive, his successor, liberal Democrat Williams, worked closely with the UAW and African American groups to implement much of the MCCR's agenda. Williams also became one of the key advocates at the national level for Democrats to embrace a strong position on civil rights. In this way, a drive by liberal New Dealers to take over the state Democratic Party gained its greatest support from groups that backed civil rights as part of a broad liberal program. The liberal Democrats then delivered concrete civil rights changes once they took over the state party and state government.

New York

In New York, the first state to adopt strong fair employment legislation, Martha Biondi credits a grassroots mobilization involving fifty civic, religious, political, labor, and civil rights groups for the measure's enactment.[53] Similarly, Anthony Chen finds that CIO unions, the NAACP, Urban League, American Jewish Congress, and "dozens of other liberal groups" provided the main support for the legislation.[54] But the business community rallied against the measure, making its passage in the GOP-controlled legislature far from assured.

New York's Republican governor, Thomas Dewey—harboring national aspirations and mindful of African Americans' importance in statewide elections—eventually gave prominent backing to the FEPC legislation. But notwithstanding the condemnations of discrimination in previous state Republican platforms, the rural, upstate party members who dominated the GOP's state legislative caucus proved a major obstacle.[55] As Chen writes, "Republican legislators, working closely with the business lobby, wasted no time setting out to undermine the bill in the legislature."[56]

A key moment in the battle came in a series of public hearings that Republican conservatives had hoped would help rally popular opposition. Instead, however, the hearings showcased the "willingness and ability of liberal groups to mobilize a massive and unprecedented show of support," including powerful testimony from representatives of the NAACP, American Jewish Congress, and labor movement.[57] The hearings led one political observer to note that "legislators were not insensitive to the fact that the proponents represented forces which could ruin a political career," citing labor, Jews, and African Americans in particular.[58] While upstate conservatives continued their efforts to weaken the bill behind the scenes, they could read the writing on the wall and mostly dropped their public opposition. The bill was approved by the assembly in a 109–32 vote and by the Senate 49–6. Not a single Democrat was recorded in opposition; although most Republicans voted in favor, the margin "greatly understated the extent of Republican opposition."[59]

Beyond the FEPC case, the Negro Labor Victory Committee (NLVC) exemplified the labor–civil rights alliance in New York City politics. It cosponsored annual mass rallies starting in the early 1940s that brought together African Americans, labor representatives, and other left-wing activists. When Adam Clayton Powell was elected to Congress in 1944, the NLVC sponsored an inaugural ball in Harlem attended by three thousand activists, including the leaders from forty-five AFL and CIO unions.[60] A few years later the NAACP, CIO, Union of Lady Garment Workers of New York, American Jewish Congress, and other religious groups formed the New York State Committee Against Discrimination in Education, which pushed successfully for a ban on discrimination that was enacted in 1948. In sum, Biondi argues that a "black-liberal-left alliance" was the main advocate for civil rights in New York throughout the 1940s; this alliance found a much friendlier reception in the state Democratic Party than in the GOP.[61]

California

On the opposite coast, in California, liberal Democrats who put forward an expansive view of the New Deal also worked closely with unions and African Americans to push for civil rights legislation. The 1938 convention of Labor's Non-Partisan League of California endorsed "equal civil service, political and economic rights for all racial minorities."[62] In 1941 the LNPL sponsored a resolution supporting abolition of the poll tax.[63] The following year, under the leadership of liberal Democratic governor Culbert Olson and his "band of union labor politicians," the state party adopted an extremely liberal platform that took strong prolabor and pro–civil rights stands.[64] The platform included a section, "Home Front for Victory," that began with the declaration that "Racial Discrimination Impedes Our War Effort." It called for a Fair Employment Practices Act and insisted that schools be kept open "for all on a basis of complete equality regardless of race, color, or creed."

Although Olson lost reelection in 1942, the drive for the FEPC continued in the state. Mark Brilliant credits African Americans and organized labor as the strongest supporters of the movement for a statewide FEPC, which gained steam in the mid- to late 1940s.[65] Liberal Democrat August Hawkins was the lead sponsor in the State Assembly, but a GOP-dominated committee killed the bill in 1945. After hearing from advisers concerned about Democratic gains among the state's African American voters, Republican governor Earl Warren endorsed FEPC legislation the following year. Several Republican legislators refused Warren's request to introduce the legislation; while he finally won over Raup Miller (R-Santa Clara), the legislation nonetheless met an ignominious end, defeated 10–6 in the GOP-controlled Ways and Means Committee. A similar fate met Democratic-sponsored FEPC legislation in the same session.[66]

After falling short in the state legislature—primarily owing to GOP opposition—liberals mobilized to adopt the legislation through a ballot proposition. The NAACP, the CIO, and religious groups were among the most active supporters of the ballot initiative. Amid business opposition—and Warren's "studied silence"—the proposition failed by a wide margin at the polls, with Republican voters evidently providing far more opposition than Democrats.[67]

The civil rights coalition tried again in the state legislature in 1949. The 1948 state GOP platform had asserted that "equal opportunity" must be "guaranteed all individuals regardless of race, religion, color or country of origin, and we urge favorable enactment of state legislation in that interest." But when Democratic state legislators sought to force FEPC legislation to the floor in the GOP legislature, a clear majority of Republicans voted against considering the measure, defeating the near-unanimous Democratic delegation in favor.[68]

Advocates regrouped from these failures by forming the Committee for a California FEPC (CCFEP) in January 1953; the NAACP led the charge to create the CCFEP but was joined by the CIO, Jewish Labor Committee, and ACLU. Most of the CCFEP's funding came from labor and the NAACP, with Jewish groups and the California Democratic Committee also providing funds.[69] According to Brilliant, "under the CCFEP's leadership, fair employment practices inched closer to passage" in the mid-1950s.[70] Democratic state platforms included a strong, direct endorsement of a state FEPC throughout the 1950s. The party was finally in a position to act on this endorsement when liberal Democrat Pat Brown took office in 1959, alongside a Democratic legislature. Brown made a state FEPC a top priority and gained speedy enactment during his first year as governor.

Lessons from the Case Studies

The Michigan, New York, and California case studies suggest that the aggregate-level correlation between state Democratic platform liberalism and the presence of African Americans, Jews, and union members accurately reflected the political dynamics on the ground. In each state, these groups were part of a broad coalition that claimed to represent the promise of New Deal liberalism. When the state party was controlled by a faction that was not seen as committed to liberalism—as in Michigan in the late 1930s—this liberal coalition fought to take over the party. Thus liberals working on the state level put forward a broad agenda that paralleled the far-reaching program advanced by ardent New Dealers at the national level starting in these same years. Strikingly, civil rights was repeatedly seen as a key part of that program, across a range of states.

The case studies also help to understand why there was something of a time lag between the initial crystallization of the liberal civil rights coalition in the late 1930s and early 1940s and the adoption of pro–civil rights platforms in several states. Liberals often had to contend for power with more conservative, old-guard leaders that had control of the state party apparatus. Liberal New Dealers drew on a coalition of unions, African Americans, and Jews in prosecuting this battle for control, which in cases such as Michigan took several years to win.

Moving beyond these three states, Duane Lockard credits African American activists as the most important and consistent players promoting civil rights across the range of northern states in the 1940s and 1950s but emphasizes that this work typically occurred in close alliance with CIO unions.[71] Lockard finds that CIO unions provided crucial backing for fair employment legislation in Massachusetts, Connecticut, Pennsylvania, and Ohio. In Massachusetts, the CIO proved so active in the FEPC fight that one Republican legislator complained that "unless you're for [fair employment legislation], the CIO will get you."[72] Similarly, in Pennsylvania, the state CIO endorsed fair employment legislation as far back as 1945 and provided much of the leadership and funding for the campaign that finally led to its enactment in 1955. Moreover, although the CIO focused much of its attention on fair employment practices, its role extended further. In Connecticut, for example, labor representatives spoke out in favor of fair housing legislation in hearings and other venues.[73]

In sum, the common story that emerged across the North is that Democratic legislators and state party officials provided far more support than did Republicans for civil rights from the mid-1940s onward. Furthermore, the groups most active in lobbying for legislative action on civil rights were the same groups associated with support for New Deal liberalism more generally.

CONCLUSION

Earlier chapters traced the development of a civil rights coalition that brought together African Americans, CIO unions, Jews, and urban liberals in seeking to transform the Democratic Party, in opposition to the entrenched conservative southern wing. Most top national party leaders had a stake in muting this intraparty conflict, which meant finding ways to straddle or avoid civil rights issues. The national platform that Democrats adopted in the 1940s and 1950s typically reflected the views of these nationally oriented leaders (see chapter 9).

But below the surface, civil rights advocates—most prominently featuring African American activists, often joined by CIO unions, Jewish groups, and other urban liberals—were gradually capturing much of the party apparatus. State parties offered a mechanism for these groups to gradually transform the Democratic program from within, rather than directly confronting the national party leadership. Starting in the early to mid-1940s, civil rights advocates reshaped state Democratic platforms and won over Democratic state legislators. This not only helped move civil rights onto the political agenda but was also a sign that national party leaders would have to find ways to manage rank-and-file convention delegates who personally supported greater action on civil rights.

Republicans, by contrast, had a more ambivalent relationship to civil rights at the state level: where there was a substantial African American population, candidates for statewide office at times had an incentive to support civil rights. But they generally found it far more difficult to persuade rank-and-file legislators—who often hailed from conservative, rural districts—to go along with these initiatives. GOP state convention delegates, reflecting the broadly based party view, generally were wary of dramatic action on civil rights.

Rather than a top-down story of national party elites moving their party at a critical moment in the 1960s, the state platform evidence reveals how the liberal civil rights coalition gradually took control of the Democratic Party from below starting in the late 1930s. These state-level dynamics were important because they underscore that the bottom-up drive for national Democrats to embrace civil rights liberalism was much greater than the corresponding pressure for Republicans. This pressure built over time and became difficult to suppress as grassroots civil rights activists forced the issue to the top of the nation's political agenda.

The next chapter turns from the state level to the House of Representatives, where one sees a similar pattern at work: rank-and-file liberal Democratic members came to embrace civil rights by the mid-1940s, while Republicans provided less support. Crucially, these House Democrats supported efforts to force civil rights legislation to the House floor, thereby contributing to the public visibility of civil rights on the national agenda. The local, geographically concentrated power base of both state party officials and rank-and-file House members meant that they were freer to respond to growing constituency interest in civil rights, without needing to persuade nationally oriented Democrats who often were more sensitive to the coalitional incentive to keep southern segregationists inside the party tent.

CHAPTER 8

Beyond the Roll Call

THE CONGRESSIONAL REALIGNMENT

CONGRESS IS THE core representative institution in the American political system. As such, one might expect the legislative branch to be among the first to respond when groups in society mobilize to redress entrenched inequalities. Yet Congress is also a complex obstacle course where those who benefit from existing inequalities are often well positioned to exercise a veto.

In accounts of the legislative drama surrounding civil rights, scholars and political observers have emphasized the central role of the Senate filibuster and House Rules Committee in frustrating advocates of equality. Southern senators repeatedly capitalized on the right of extended debate to block civil rights bills. While the House had much stricter debate limitations, the seniority system allowed southern committee chairs to stand in the way of action. For legislation to reach the House floor through the ordinary legislative process, it had to pass through the Rules Committee, which for many years was chaired by southern civil rights foe Howard Smith of Virginia.[1] The determined Smith even disappeared from Washington to block a committee meeting to report the 1957 civil rights bill to the floor. Smith claimed the barn on his dairy farm had burned down, leading Speaker Sam Rayburn to comment ruefully that "I knew [Smith] would do anything to block a civil rights bill, but I never suspected he would resort to arson."[2]

In addition to these institutional obstacles, several authors have pointed to the personal and political motivations of congressional party leaders as a barrier to the passage of civil rights legislation.[3] With few exceptions, the top Democratic and GOP leaders in Congress were tepid, at best, in their support for vigorous action on civil rights in the 1930s–1950s and thus were generally content to allow major initiatives to die at the hands of obstructionist committee chairs and filibustering senators. Some would go even further and argue that many of the northern members who claimed to support civil rights in this period cared little about the issue and privately did not mind seeing the legislation die, so long as they were not blamed.[4] Since all Democrats shared the goal of maintaining their majority coalition, they all benefited from institutions that allowed action only when both factions agreed while submerging initiatives that divided the party.[5] While this system frustrated the few genuine civil rights liberals, it could be sustained because it met the critical needs of most majority-party Democrats.

The narrative above is partly correct: congressional institutions gave crucial leverage to civil rights opponents. Furthermore, the nationally oriented party leaders who had the greatest stake in maintaining the Democrats' North-South coalition often made only a token effort to overcome civil rights filibusters and committee obstruction. Democratic leaders in Congress, such as Speaker Rayburn, Majority Leader John McCormack (D-MA), and Senate majority leaders Alben Barkley (D-KY), Scott Lucas (D-IL), and Lyndon Johnson (D-TX) saw the danger posed by civil rights to the national party coalition and were, at best, slow to respond when politicians and activists attempted to graft civil rights onto New Deal liberalism. In much the same way, the many Democratic presidential aspirants in the Senate had to keep one eye on their local constituents and another trained on their viability in both the North and the South.[6]

But this conventional account underestimates the important changes that took place among rank-and-file members of Congress with the rise of the liberal, pro–civil rights coalition in the late 1930s and 1940s. A reexamination of civil rights politics in Congress supports key elements of the argument presented in chapter 1 regarding the timing and dynamics of the partisan realignment on civil rights.

First, a substantial partisan gap in civil rights support emerged among northern members of the House of Representatives in the early to mid-1940s, before top party leaders took a clear stand. Rank-and-file northern Democratic members pushed to force civil rights onto the legislative agenda, angering southern Democrats and complicating party leaders' efforts to submerge the issue. Northern Democrats' shift began in the late 1930s, just as CIO unions, African American voters, and other urban liberals were making major inroads into the Democratic Party.

Second, consistent with the idea that the expansive version of liberalism pushed by these groups played a key role in the partisan realignment, many of the same factors that were associated with civil rights support at the mass level and in state parties were also related to Democratic representatives' behavior. Economic liberalism, which did not predict northern Democrats' civil rights support in the mid-1930s, became a significant predictor in the late 1930s. Votes on labor-related issues were an especially strong predictor of civil rights support among northern Democrats at this early stage. Urbanization and, to a lesser extent, state-level unionization and African American population are also significant predictors of northern Democrats' support for civil rights. Interestingly, economically liberal Republicans from urban areas—and especially from districts that vote Democratic for president—were also more pro–civil rights than were other northern Republicans.

The evidence thus suggests that members of Congress were acting consistently with the *relative* levels of civil rights support prevalent in their constituencies: urban, economically liberal northern Democrats were the most likely to back civil rights initiatives both at the mass level and in the House.[7] Republicans from liberal-leaning districts—as measured by presidential vote—were more supportive of civil rights initiatives than were other Republicans, but the overall level of GOP support was lower than that of northern Democrats. Where the Republicans who provided the strongest support for civil rights were decidedly outside the GOP mainstream, representing districts that were atypical for the party, the northern Democrats who backed civil rights reflected the urban, labor-oriented liberalism that was increasingly becoming the hallmark of the party in the 1930s and 1940s.

Third, rank-and-file members' behavior reinforces the argument that the fragmented American electoral system provided a mechanism for pro–civil rights forces to capture the Democratic Party from below despite national elites' interest in submerging the issue. The decentralized system of electing individual members of Congress through separate geographic districts created the space for locally based politicians to respond to activist and constituent pressure for civil rights, without requiring an immediate showdown with national party leaders. These locally rooted politicians then contributed to civil rights activists' efforts to raise the salience of the issue.[8] In doing so, they proved willing to challenge southern Democrats' core interests in a bid to remake the national Democratic Party in a more liberal image.

Finally, the dynamics in Congress contributed to the gradual unraveling of the Democratic coalition. Many standard accounts of the New Deal coalition in Congress have downplayed the extent to which the party's northern and southern wings actively sought to bring each other down during the 1930s–1950s.[9] This characterization fits the idea that parties can be understood as coalitions of intense policy demanders that work together as a team to enact the policies that each group cares about most.[10] I argue, however, that rank-and-file northerners' push for civil rights legislation was not a mere symbolic stance intended to position-take for the voters at home while the two regional factions cooperated behind the scenes to build the New Deal state. Instead, northern Democrats' actions had real consequences: by working with civil rights movement activists to push civil rights onto the House floor, they raised the political visibility of civil rights as a national issue. This, in turn, made it harder for Democratic leaders to focus debate on issues that did not split the party.

The southern reaction to this threat was also noteworthy. Many southern Democrats genuinely feared that these legislative actions had a significant likelihood of succeeding. Southern conservatives accused their northern counterparts of disloyalty and came to view them more as adversaries than as allies. Just as northern liberals in Congress worked to force civil rights measures to the floor that threatened the core interests of their southern copartisans, these southern Democrats sought to take down the labor unions that were crucial to electing northern Democrats to Congress.[11] The Democratic Party in this era did not resemble an alliance of policy demanders cooperating with one another to achieve shared ends.[12] Instead, rank-and-file members of the Democratic Party's dueling factions actively sought to undermine one another's core interests.

This chapter briefly reviews the evidence, based on roll-call voting, which appears to show that Democrats and Republicans in Congress provided similar levels of support for civil rights prior to the mid-1960s, when the two parties finally diverged. Most of the chapter is devoted to analyzing new, more refined measures of legislators' support for civil rights, which demonstrate that northern Democrats in the House were far more legislatively active than Republicans by the mid-1940s. The primary measure used here to assess civil rights support is members' willingness to sign discharge petitions, which were the main pathway through which these initiatives reached the House floor. But the results are robust to considering alternative indicators, such as bill sponsorships and floor speeches. The chapter then examines *which* Democrats and Republicans were the most pro–civil rights, showing that economically liberal members from urban districts were especially supportive.

The last part of the chapter considers the political implications of the civil rights legislative drives of the 1940s and 1950s. Although civil rights initiatives repeatedly fell short of enactment, it is wrong to dismiss their political significance. As discussed below, these were important political battles that received considerable press attention for much of the mid-1930s and the 1940s. I draw on southerners' private correspondence to show that they took the threat posed by this civil rights legislation very seriously.

In this way, Congress was the site of genuine responsiveness to the mass- and group-level changes and the movement activism traced in earlier chapters. Rank-and-file members contributed to an emergent public debate even as they fell short in their struggle to enact legislation.[13] Liberal civil rights advocates in Congress were working to cement a growing alliance with northern African American voters, CIO unions, and urban liberals that increasingly came to define both the Democratic Party brand and liberalism as a political program. The change in House members' behavior thus emerges as part of a broader transformation of the mass and middle levels of the Democratic Party, setting the stage for the confrontation between rank-and-file partisans and the national leadership that is the focus of part 3.

Toward a Better Assessment of Support for Civil Rights

Scholars have generally relied on roll-call votes to track members of Congress' civil rights support; it is this reliance that has led many to conclude that northern Democrats and Republicans were similar in their degree of civil rights advocacy prior to the mid-1960s.[14] Along these lines, figure 8.1 provides a simple assessment of the likelihood of northern Democrats and northern Republicans taking the pro–civil rights position on each House roll call from 1937 through 1966.[15]

Starting in the mid-1940s, northern Democrats are a bit more likely to cast votes in support of civil rights than are northern Republicans, but the point estimates are quite small, indicating that the gap in the probability of a pro–civil rights vote between the two groups is typically in the 0.05 to 0.10 range. These results differ only marginally from Carmines and Stimson's, and they are consistent with Karol's civil rights support scales.[16] Based on the small gap between the parties evident in the roll-call record, Car-

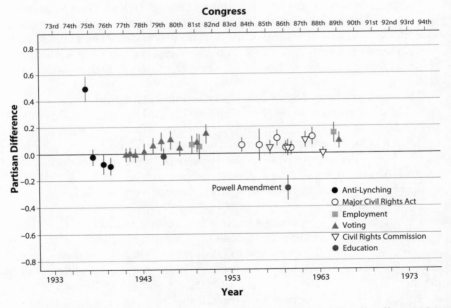

FIGURE 8.1. Partisan difference in support for civil rights on roll calls, 1930s–1960s, northern members. Positive values indicate northern Democrats are more supportive than northern Republicans. From Eric Schickler, Kathryn Pearson, and Brian Feinstein, "Shifting Partisan Coalitions: Support for Civil Rights in Congress from 1933–1972," *Journal of Politics* 72, 3 (2010): 672–89.

mines and Stimson's argument that either party could have embraced civil rights liberalism in the mid-1960s seems reasonable.[17]

Roll-call votes tell us how members choose to position themselves publicly on issues that make it to the floor stage for a decision. But they do not tell us whether members actually want to see these issues reach the floor or would prefer to see them buried in committee. Nor do roll calls tell us how members would vote on the vast majority of proposed bills that never escape committee.[18] Roll-call measures thus provide some information about members' public preferences, but they can also be misleading.

The limited roll-call record is a particular problem when it comes to civil rights because southern Democrats were able to use their disproportionate influence over key committees—such as the Rules Committee—to bottle up civil rights proposals. Indeed, despite the nearly 250 civil rights bills introduced between 1933 and 1948, there were only 19 civil rights roll-call votes on the House floor during that period, and a handful of those votes incorporated other issues.

Civil rights legislation typically reached the House floor for a vote only when members were able to circumvent the Rules Committee through a successful discharge petition drive. A member of Congress may file a discharge petition once a bill or resolution has been stuck in a legislative committee for twenty days or in the Rules Committee for seven days.[19] Once the petition has 218 signatures, the signatories' names are entered into the *Congressional Record,* and after a motion to discharge passes on the floor, the committee under question is discharged. Under ordinary circumstances, the names on petitions that fail to reach the 218 threshold are not public but are accessible to fellow members of Congress.[20]

Discharge petitions reveal that a group of members care enough about an issue to mount a drive to bypass the usual legislative process. As such, signatures on discharge petitions have important advantages as a preference measure. A member's ability to sign a petition is not constrained by negative agenda control; any member can sign a discharge petition kept at the clerk's desk on the House floor. Furthermore, signing a discharge petition is not costless for members of Congress. Many members view signing a discharge petition as a violation of congressional norms and an intrusion on committee authority, potentially aggravating chairs and other influential members of Congress.[21] Members' varying willingness to incur the costs involved in signing a discharge petition thus provides information about their preferences and priorities.

From 1933 to 1946 there were nineteen discharge petitions filed on pro–civil rights bills; another twelve were filed from 1947 to 1960, with three more during the 1960s. Seven of the discharge petitions reached the signature threshold of 218 needed to discharge the bill from committee; all these cases occurred in the 1930s and 1940s. In a handful of important later cases, bills were brought to the floor in response to a petition nearing 218 signatures. Most of the earliest petitions focused on proposals to combat lynching and ban the poll tax—the main civil rights items on the legislative agenda in the 1930s and early 1940s. Fair employment practices bills became prominent in the 1940s, and a handful of other topics—such as fair housing—also were subjects of discharge petition drives.

Despite their promise as a preference indicator, research on discharge petitions has been limited. Until 1993 the names of the members who signed the petitions were made public only in the cases in which the petition reached the threshold number of signatures and was printed in the *Congressional Record*.[22] However, recently discovered, heretofore unexamined discharge petitions filed from the Seventy-First through the Ninety-Fourth Congress at the National Archives have made the analysis of all discharge petitions during this time period possible.[23] This new data source makes possible a much more fine-grained analysis of support by members of Congress for civil rights.

In addition to a measure of civil rights support based on discharge petition signatures, I draw on two additional indicators: bill sponsorships and floor speeches. Each indicator reflects members' active participation in the legislative process, which, as Richard Hall demonstrates, offers important insight into the intensity of member preferences.[24] While discharge petition signatures have the important advantage of reflecting members' behind-the-scenes activity on behalf of legislation, bill sponsorships and floor speeches are still useful for identifying the members who are most publicly active on behalf of civil rights.

FINDINGS: SUPPORT FOR CIVIL RIGHTS USING NEW MEASURES

Partisanship and Civil Rights Support

A first, simple question is which party's members provided greater support for civil rights discharge petitions. Figure 8.2 displays the percentage of northern Democrats and of northern Republicans who signed each civil rights discharge petition that gained at least fifty signatures from 1933 to 1970.[25] The results are clear. After initially providing less support than northern Republicans, northern Democrats soon surpassed their GOP counterparts by a substantial margin.

Republicans signed the petitions at a high rate in the 1930s, with roughly 70 percent of party members signing each petition, while northern Democratic support was more variable and generally lower. By the mid-1940s (Seventy-Eighth and Seventy-Ninth Congresses), however, roughly 70–80 percent of northern Democrats were signing the petitions, with Republicans

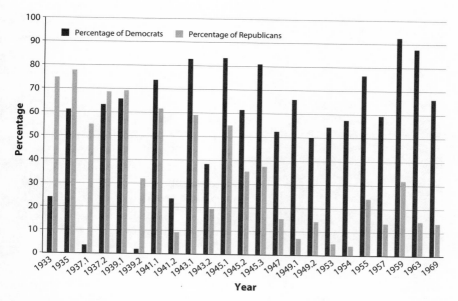

FIGURE 8.2. Percentage of northern Democrats and northern Republicans sign-ing civil rights discharge petitions. Key to petition topics: year of petition, with .1, .2 added if multiple petitions in a given year—House restaurant desegrega-tion, 1933; lynching, 1935, 1937.1, 1937.2, 1939.1, 1939.2, 1941.2, 1943.2, 1945.2, 1947; poll tax, 1941.1, 1943.1, 1945.1; FEPC, 1945.3, 1949.1, 1949.2, 1954, 1969; public accommodations in DC, 1953; omnibus civil rights bill, 1955, 1957, 1959, 1963.

signing at just a 30–60 percent rate. Starting with the Eightieth Congress (1947–48), not a single pro–civil rights petition garnered support from even one-third of Republicans.[26]

It is important to emphasize that agenda change—in particular, the rise of the FEPC as an issue, which Republicans' probusiness leanings predisposed them to oppose—accounts for only a portion of the party gap. For example, in the Seventy-Ninth Congress (1945–46), the gulf between northern Dem-ocrats and Republicans was 44 points on the FEPC petition but was a still-sizable 25–30 points on the poll tax and lynching petitions. Indeed, where Republicans had outpaced northern Democrats in signing the lynching bill petitions throughout the 1930s, the pattern was reversed in the 1940s. While not all northern Democrats signed each petition after the mid-1940s, a solid majority of northern Democrats took part in the major petition drives.

When one estimates a model predicting members' propensity to sign the petitions—either a simple bivariate model or a multivariate model controlling for seniority and committee memberships—the results tell the same story.

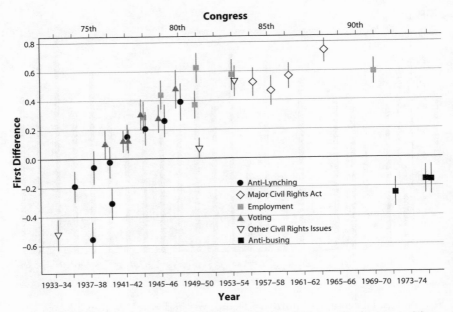

FIGURE 8.3. Partisan difference in support for civil rights discharge petitions, northern members. Positive values indicate northern Democrats are more supportive than northern Republicans. Figure presents the estimated change in the probability of signing each petition as one moves from a northern Republican to a northern Democrat. Member seniority and the percentage of other petitions targeting one's committee are set at their means; the remaining controls are set at their modal values: no exclusive committee membership, no committee leadership position, and no membership on the committee targeted by the petition. From Eric Schickler, Kathryn Pearson, and Brian Feinstein, "Shifting Partisan Coalitions: Support for Civil Rights in Congress from 1933–1972," *Journal of Politics* 72, 3 (2010): 672–89.

Republicans were more likely to sign the discharge petitions in the mid-1930s, but the partisan gap closed by about 1940 and Democrats were substantially more likely to sign than Republicans by about 1943 (see fig. 8.3).[27] For the typical petition, the predicted probability of a northern Democrat signing was about 0.40 higher than the probability for a northern Republican.[28] This gap remained relatively stable over the next two decades.

Where the roll-call record suggests northern Democrats and Republicans differed only modestly in their civil rights views prior to the 1960s, the discharge petitions thus provide a more fine-grained measure and reveal a very different pattern of support. A likely reason for the discrepancy is that roll-call votes were generally obtained only in the case of bills that had sufficiently wide support among both northern Democrats and Republicans to overcome committee gatekeeping. The discharge petitions, however, include a wider array of proposals, which do a better job of separating stronger from weaker civil rights supporters. In addition, as the qualitative evidence below suggests, it is possible that Republicans' position-taking concerns led them to vote more liberally on the floor than one would expect based on their behind-the-scenes behavior.

It is worth noting that the partisan gap in civil rights support is not simply a function of differences in the districts electing Democrats and Republicans. First, the Democratic edge in support for civil rights discharge petitions remains robust when one controls for a range of constituency characteristics, such as urbanization, African American population, unionization, and district presidential vote.[29] Second, if one compares Democrats who won their most recent election by a very narrow margin to Republicans who won by a narrow margin—so that the districts are very closely balanced between the two parties—the Democratic advantage in support emerges in the mid-1940s and remains substantial over the ensuing decades.[30]

The sequence in which members sign the petitions provides a further indicator of the intensity of their support. Early signers are likely more vigorous, proactive supporters of civil rights. In addition, early signers likely incur greater risks from acting against members of the committee targeted by the discharge petition and others invested in preserving committee autonomy than do members who sign after it is already clear that a petition has wide support.

At the start of the period, from the Seventy-Third through the Seventy-Fifth Congresses (1933–38), Republicans were not only more likely to sign the petitions than Democrats, but among the signatories, they were more likely to sign early, revealing that intense support was more concentrated among Republicans. Between the Seventy-Ninth and Ninety-First Congresses (1945–70), however, northern Democrats tended to sign petitions before the Republicans. The petition to discharge legislation to ban the poll tax in the Seventy-Ninth Congress (1945–46) exemplifies the shift. Northern Democrats accounted for forty-two of the first fifty signatories, while Republicans accounted for just six, with one minor party member and one southern Democrat also signing. By contrast, Republicans accounted for thirty-nine of the last fifty signatories. More generally, from the Seventy-Ninth to the Ninety-First Congress, the median Democratic signature occurred earlier in the signature sequence than the median Republican signature in twelve of the fourteen civil rights discharge petitions; this difference was greater than would be expected from chance (i.e., if the signatories' order had been random) in eleven of the fourteen cases.[31]

Other indicators of member activism on civil rights reveal a similar story. Figure 8.4 compares the proportion of northern Democrats and northern Republicans who delivered at least one pro–civil rights speech on the floor of the House in each Congress from 1919 to 1968.[32] A partisan difference in

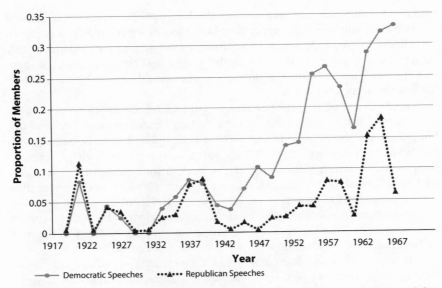

FIGURE 8.4. Proportion of northern Democrats and northern Republicans delivering pro–civil rights speeches on House floor

members' delivery of pro–civil rights speeches emerged by the early to mid-1940s, when northern Democrats were slightly more likely to deliver civil rights speeches than were Republicans.[33] The gap between the parties is substantial by the early 1950s and remains robust even as both parties show increased attention to civil rights in later years.

Bill sponsorship data provide a final measure of civil rights support.[34] Members may sponsor legislation for a variety of reasons, but regardless of their motives, bill sponsorship is a necessary precondition for legislative action and a public sign of support for a particular policy.[35] Only a modest number of civil rights bills—never more than ten and typically about five—were introduced from 1919 to 1934 (Sixty-Sixth to Seventy-Third Congresses). The number of bills jumped to thirty-four in the Seventy-Fourth Congress and averaged twenty-eight over the next two decades. There is another increase in the volume of civil rights bills starting with the Eighty-Fifth Congress (1957–58), with an average of fifty bills introduced in each Congress from 1957 to 1966.

When one compares bill sponsorship by northern Democrats and northern Republicans, the pattern resembles that for discharge petition signatures. Figure 8.5 displays the number of Democratic-sponsored bills and number of Republican-sponsored bills, in relation to the size of each partisan group. Prior to the mid-1930s neither group sponsored many bills, but

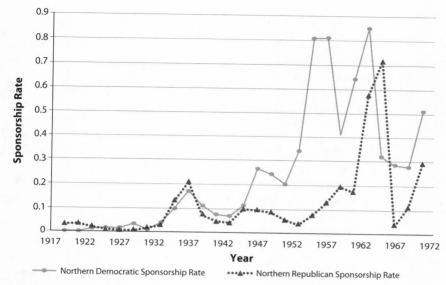

FIGURE 8.5. Civil rights bill sponsorship by party, 1919–72. Figure presents the number of civil rights bills sponsored by northern Democrats and northern Republicans in relation to the size of each partisan group, by Congress.

northern Republicans were at least as likely to sponsor the legislation as northern Democrats. Starting with the Seventy-Sixth Congress (1939–40), however, northern Democrats sponsor the bills at a higher rate than northern Republicans in each Congress for the next twenty-five years. The gap is very small at first but is substantial by the end of the 1940s and remains large throughout the 1950s and into the early 1960s.[36]

In sum, an examination of three distinct indicators of member support for civil rights—discharge petitions, floor speeches, and bill sponsorships—reveals a story that parallels the findings at the mass level and from the state party platforms: northern Democrats outpaced northern Republicans as civil rights supporters by the late 1930s or early 1940s, with a substantial gap in place well before national party leaders took a clear stand on the issue.

But these findings still leave open the question of *which* northern Democrats and Republicans were particularly likely to back civil rights initiatives. A closer analysis of the member and district characteristics associated with support for forcing civil rights bills to the House floor provides additional hints about the process through which Democratic partisanship and liberalism became tied to civil rights support.

Economic Liberalism and Civil Rights Support

A key initial question is: when did general member "liberalism" become tied to support for civil rights? To begin to answer this question, I estimated a series of models evaluating the relationship between first-dimension NOMINATE scores and the willingness to sign discharge petitions for civil rights measures. The models focus on first-dimension scores because these are supposed to reflect members' more general stance toward the government's role in the economy, rather than the regional cleavages over race and related issues tapped by the second NOMINATE dimension. Since NOMINATE scores may reflect partisanship in addition to ideology, I estimate the models separately for northern Democrats and northern Republicans. The question then becomes: within each partisan group, are members with more liberal NOMINATE scores more likely to support civil rights initiatives?

Figure 8.6 presents the results when an identical model is estimated for each Congress from the 1930s through the early 1970s. The dependent variable is a dummy variable for whether each member signed a given civil rights discharge petition; for Congresses with multiple petitions, a separate intercept is included for each petition to allow for different baseline levels of support.[37] The model controls for seniority and for membership on the committee targeted by the discharge petition since both of those characteristics have been found to be deterrents to signing discharge petitions, regardless of the issue content.[38] The graph presents the change in the predicted proportion of members signing the petitions as one moves from the 20th percentile of liberalism to the 80th percentile of liberalism for the relevant partisan group (e.g., from a relatively moderate Democrat to a liberal Democrat, or from a conservative Republican to a moderate Republican).[39]

Among northern Democrats, the results suggest that early on, liberalism as measured by NOMINATE scores was only weakly, if at all, related to the willingness to back civil rights initiatives (see fig. 8.6A). In the Seventy-Third and Seventy-Fourth Congresses (1933–36), no relationship is evident. The gap between more conservative and more liberal Democrats in the Seventy-Fifth Congress (1937–38) is statistically significant but small in magnitude (moving from the 20th to the 80th percentile of liberalism is associated with a 0.08 shift on the 0 to 1 scale, with a 95 percent confidence interval of 0.02 to 0.13). However, the relationship strengthens in the late 1930s and early 1940s. From the Seventy-Sixth Congress (1939–40) through the Eighty-Fifth Congress (1957–58), a shift from the 20th to 80th percentile of liberalism is associated with roughly a 0.15–0.25 shift along the 0 to 1 scale of support for civil rights discharge petitions. There continues to be a statistically significant relationship between liberalism and support for the initiatives among northern Democrats in the late 1950s and 1960s. These findings parallel the results in chapter 5, which indicated that civil rights became

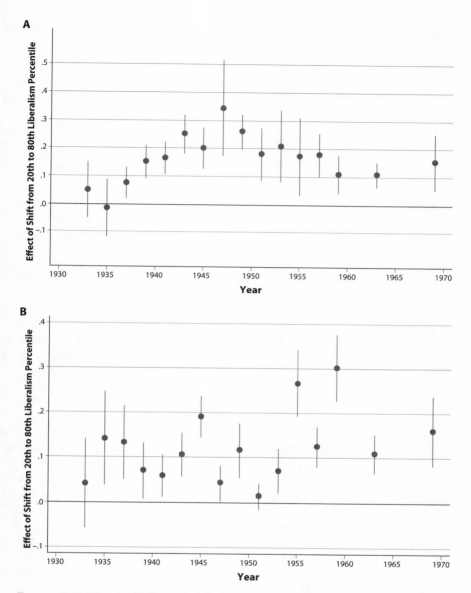

FIGURE 8.6. Marginal effect of shift from 20th to 80th percentile of economic liberalism on civil rights support. *A*, Northern Democrats. *B*, Northern Republicans. Dependent variable is an indicator for whether each member signed each civil rights discharge petition in a given Congress; for each Congress with multiple petitions, a separate intercept is included for each petition. Dependent variable ranges from 0 to 1. First differences and 95% confidence intervals, controlling for seniority and membership on the targeted committee. OLS with robust standard errors, clustered by member when multiple petitions per Congress. Economic liberalism is measured with first-dimension NOMINATE scores.

associated with both economic liberalism and Democratic partisanship at the mass level in the late 1930s.

Among Republicans, economic liberalism generally has a moderately sized relationship with support for civil rights discharge petitions (see fig. 8.6*B*). The point estimate for economic liberalism is correctly signed in every Congress and is statistically significant in all but two Congresses. A shift from the 20th to 80th percentile in liberalism is associated with roughly a 0.08 to 0.20 increase in civil rights support, though the point estimates bounce around across years.

What generated the relationship between liberal NOMINATE scores and Democrats' civil rights support in the mid- to late 1930s? In chapter 3 I argued that the rise of the CIO played a crucial role in changing the political meaning of New Deal liberalism to incorporate civil rights concerns. One piece of evidence that views toward labor were a bridge between economic and racial liberalism is that roll-call voting on labor policy seems to have had a stronger early connection to civil rights support than did first-dimension NOMINATE scores.

The Seventy-Fifth Congress (1937–38) was the first in which there were roll calls related to the CIO. The House voted on a proposal to investigate the CIO-led sit-down strikes and had a handful of roll calls on the Wage and Hour bill (which became the Fair Labor Standards Act), for which the CIO was a leading advocate.[40] As noted above, first-dimension NOMINATE scores are only a weak predictor of northern Democrats' willingness to sign civil rights discharge petitions in this Congress. But votes on the labor-related roll calls are much more strongly tied to civil rights support. If one runs a simple model predicting northern Democrats' support for the civil rights discharge petitions as a function of both first-dimension NOMINATE scores and members' position on the sit-down strikes, NOMINATE scores are a weak, insignificant predictor (a shift from the 20th to 80th percentile of liberalism is associated with a 0.05 change, with a 95 percent confidence interval of –0.01 to 0.11). By contrast, a vote against the sit-down strike investigation is associated with a 0.17 increase in support for civil rights discharge petitions (with a 95 percent confidence interval of 0.07 to 0.27).[41] The same pattern holds when one examines the December 1937 votes on the Wage and Hour bill or when one constructs a summary scale for the three labor-related votes.[42]

These results are striking when one considers that a single roll call or small number of votes are likely to have far more error in measuring latent policy views than would NOMINATE scores.[43] They are consistent with the argument presented in chapters 3–4 that views toward the CIO and the rising labor movement were coming to define a new rendition of New Deal liberalism and that this ideological formation was, from the start, associated with racial policy views. Indeed, as early as February 1938 the CIO-backed

Labor's Non-Partisan League identified support for the lynching bill as one of twelve key tests in its member scorecards.[44] Southern Democrats also lashed out at CIO unions for pushing civil rights bills to the House floor.[45]

Over time, economic liberalism as tracked by NOMINATE scores incorporated this version of labor-based liberalism.[46] Indeed, while labor votes continue to outperform NOMINATE scores in predicting northern Democrats' civil rights support in the Seventy-Sixth Congress (1939–40), the gap narrows by the Seventy-Seventh Congress (1941–42).[47] After that, northern Democrats are so unified on the union-related roll calls that there simply is no variation to exploit in explaining their civil rights support. But by that time, economic liberalism as a whole is strongly related to civil rights support among northern Democrats (see fig. 8.6A), and these same Democrats clearly outpaced northern Republicans in their support for civil rights discharge petitions.[48]

District Demographics and Democrats' Civil Rights Support

When one considers the relationship between district-level demographic characteristics and civil rights support, the results are similar to the findings for state party platforms and mass opinion, reinforcing the message that urban, labor-oriented liberalism became associated with civil rights by the 1940s. In analyzing district-level predictors of support for civil rights, I primarily rely on data that Scott Adler has compiled starting with the Seventy-Eighth Congress (1943–44). The data are constructed based on county-level information, which works well when district lines match county boundaries. But where multiple urban districts are carved out of a single county, the dataset generally gives each of the districts the same constituency characteristics.[49] For example, the nine Chicago districts in the Seventy-Eighth Congress are each estimated to be 7 percent African American even though the black population was actually concentrated in the district of William Dawson (D-IL). Fortunately, Thomas Ogorzalek has recently drawn on more fine-grained maps to compile district-level estimates for the African American population from 1943 to 1962.[50] In the Ogorzalek data, Dawson's district is estimated to be 61 percent African American in the Seventy-Eighth Congress.[51]

Following the approach described above, I estimate the same model for each Congress with civil rights discharge petitions from 1943 through 1970. The dependent variable is an indicator variable for whether each member signed a given civil rights discharge petition; the model is estimated separately for each party, and, for Congresses with multiple petitions, an intercept is included for each petition.[52] I focus on the association between support for civil rights and three constituency characteristics: urban population, unionization, and percentage African American.

Among northern Democrats, urbanization stands out as a consistent predictor. It is significantly related to the willingness to sign discharge petitions in every Congress from the Seventy-Eighth through the Ninety-First (1943–70). Figure 8.7A presents the change in the predicted proportion of northern Democrats and northern Republicans signing the petitions when there is a two-standard-deviation increase in district urbanization (again, measured on a 0 to 1 scale; 95 percent confidence intervals included in the figure).[53] The point estimates generally suggest that moving from a low to high urbanization district is related to a 0.15 to 0.40 increase in the willingness of northern Democrats to sign civil rights discharge petitions.[54] Indeed, support for the major petition drives was nearly universal among urban northern Democrats in the mid-1940s. A full 93 percent of northerners from districts above the mean level of urbanization (for northern Democrats) signed the FEPC petition in the Seventy-Ninth Congress (1945–46), compared to 59 percent of northern Democrats from districts below the mean level of urbanization. Again, this result is consistent with findings at the mass level, where urban residence was strongly associated with civil rights support (see chapter 5).

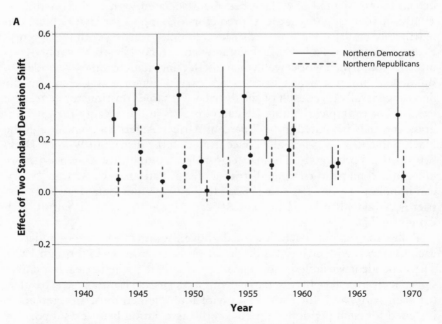

FIGURE 8.7A. Marginal effect of a two-standard-deviation change in district urbanization on civil rights support, northern Democrats and northern Republicans

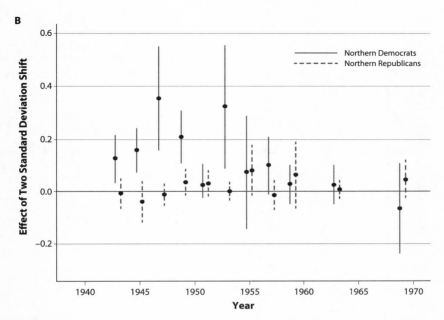

FIGURE 8.7*B*. Marginal effect of a two-standard-deviation change in state-level unionization on civil rights support, northern Democrats and northern Republicans

The association between urbanization and support for civil rights holds up when one includes first-dimension NOMINATE scores as a predictor, which is also strong and significant during this period. These results suggest that civil rights support was related both to economic liberalism, as measured by NOMINATE, and to having an urban constituency.

A similar, though somewhat weaker, story is evident when one considers state-level unionization as a predictor of northern Democrats' civil rights support. Union density is a significant predictor of support for civil rights discharge petitions in most Congresses in the 1940s and 1950s, with positive point estimates in each Congress during those years (see fig. 8.7*B*).[55] A two-standard-deviation increase in union density is associated with roughly a 0.10–0.30 boost in civil rights support. The relationship weakens, however, by the late-1950s and is insignificant in the remaining Congresses.[56]

One would certainly expect the share of the population that is African American to influence Democrats' willingness to back civil rights initiatives. However, using district-level African American population to predict Democrats' willingness to sign civil rights discharge petitions yields null results in most Congresses (see fig. 8.7*C*). Even when one drops the controls for

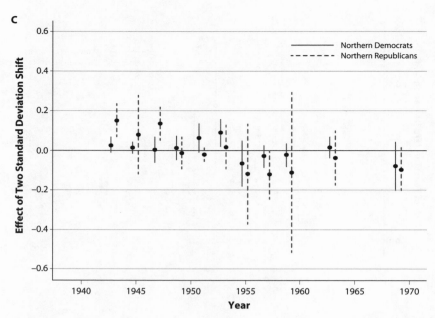

FIGURE 8.7C. Marginal effect of a two-standard-deviation change in district African American population on civil rights support, northern Democrats and northern Republicans. Dependent variable is an indicator for whether each member signed each civil rights discharge petition in a given Congress; for each Congress with multiple petitions, a separate intercept is included for each petition. Dependent variable ranges from 0 to 1. First differences and 95% confidence intervals, controlling for seniority and membership on the targeted committee. The standard deviation is computed based on all northern members of the House in that Congress. All three demographic variables—urbanization, unionization, and African American population—are included in each model. OLS with robust standard errors, clustered by member when multiple petitions per Congress.

urbanization and unionization, district African American population is significant only in the Eighty-Third Congress (1953–54), though it is positive in each Congress.

Nonetheless, there are indications that district African American population is associated with civil rights support if one uses a "tougher" measure of civil rights liberalism—such as bill sponsorships—that better distinguishes the most ardent advocates from ordinary supporters. Going back to the 1920s, the lead antilynching bill sponsor, Leonidas Dyer (R-MO), hailed from a St. Louis district with a substantial African American population.[57] The lead House sponsor in the 1930s, Joseph Gavagan (D-NY), was an Irish American representing a district that included the growing African American population in Harlem. In reflecting back on his career, Gavagan noted that in the early 1930s "the eastern end of my district was becoming very race conscious and they were demanding that something be done for them— especially for their brothers and sisters and families in the South." Following a series of high-profile southern lynchings in 1934, "the people in my district were beginning to scream." Gavagan met repeatedly with Walter White of the NAACP and soon introduced the antilynching bill.[58]

Indeed, when one predicts northern Democrats' civil rights bill sponsorships with the African American population share, there is a significant bivariate relationship throughout 1943–62.[59] Even when one controls for urbanization and unionization, the relationship between African American population and bill sponsorship is significant in eight of ten Congresses and is positive in all ten cases.[60] In sum, while it appears that simply being a mainstream urban northern Democrat was sufficient to induce discharge petition signatures by the mid-1940s, the presence of African American constituents provided an important boost to members' willingness to take on the more visible public role of sponsoring civil rights legislation.[61]

There also is considerable qualitative evidence that northern Democrats became mindful of the need to appeal to African American constituents in the late 1930s. For example, in the run-up to the 1938 elections, a series of letters asked the NAACP's Walter White to attest to the active role that Democrats Edward O'Neill (D-NJ), Edward Curley (D-NY), Elmere Wene (D-NJ), and Ray McKeough (D-IL) had played in promoting the antilynching bill. White responded with letters that praised each Democrat for his support, citing such evidence as signatures on the lynching bill discharge petition, floor speeches, and roll-call votes.[62] On the whole, it seems reasonable to conclude that the presence of African American voters played a significant role in promoting Democrats' activism on civil rights by the late 1930s, even though the quantitative evidence with respect to discharge petitions is weaker than expected.[63]

District Characteristics and Republican Support for Civil Rights

The results for Republicans suggest that district demographics are generally less tied to their civil rights support than was the case for Democrats. Urban population is significant in roughly half of the Congresses, but its impact is generally smaller in magnitude than is the case for Democrats (see fig. 8.7A).[64] State-level unionization is unrelated to Republican support for civil rights throughout the period (see fig. 8.7B).[65]

Interestingly, at the start of the period examined, district-level African American population was related to support for civil rights among Republicans. In the Seventy-Eighth to Eightieth Congresses (1943–48), a two-standard-deviation increase in the African American population was associated with roughly a 0.10–0.15 increase in Republican support, though the estimate falls short of statistical significance in the Seventy-Ninth Congress (see fig. 8.7C).[66] But this relationship faded entirely after the 1948 election. One possibility is that Truman's victory and Democrats' congressional comeback led rank-and-file House Republicans to give up on the notion that there were substantial gains to be had from appealing to African American constituents.[67]

When one adds members' first-dimension NOMINATE scores to the district demographics, the results indicate that Republicans' ideology had a substantial impact on their support for civil rights throughout the 1943–70 period. Where district demographics generally have weak and insignificant estimates, the NOMINATE variable is strong and significant in each Congress.[68] Republicans who were more economically liberal were consistently more pro–civil rights.

One further wrinkle highlights the extent to which Republicans' civil rights stance reflected pressure to appeal to more liberal-leaning voters than the GOP generally attracted. When one uses district presidential vote share to predict civil rights discharge petition signatures for Republicans, one observes a clear relationship in most Congresses from the Seventy-Fourth Congress (1935–36) onward (see fig. 8.8A). That is, Republicans from districts in which the Democratic presidential candidate fared well were more likely to support civil rights initiatives than were other Republicans. The magnitude of the relationship was quite strong in 1935–39, with a shift from the 20th to 80th percentile in district Democratic presidential vote associated with roughly a 0.20 increase in the proportion of members expected to sign civil rights discharge petitions. The estimated effects are generally in the 0.10 range over the next several Congresses, though with a fair bit of variability in magnitude. This relationship holds up when one controls for district urban and African American population and for state-level unionization.[69]

When presidential vote share is used to predict northern Democrats' civil rights support, the results are much different. In the first two Congresses (1933–36), the variable is actually wrongly signed and significant, indicating that Democrats from districts where Roosevelt did better were *less* likely to back civil rights (see fig. 8.8B). In later years the point estimates are of the correct sign but tend to be relatively small and are often statistically insignificant.

Taken together, the results suggest that Republican support for civil rights depended on coming from a district that was somewhat out of tune with the party as a whole. Republicans from Democratic-leaning districts were more

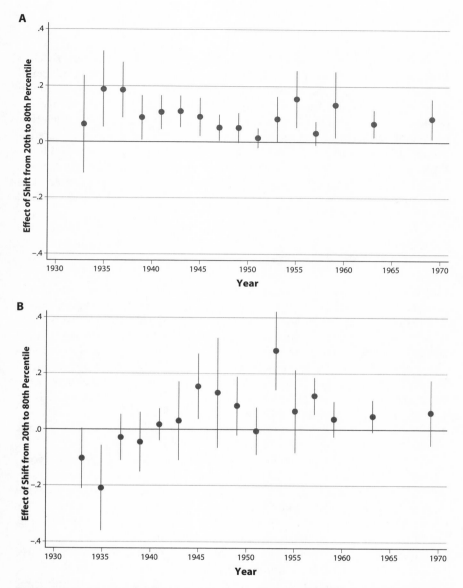

FIGURE 8.8. Marginal effect of shift from 20th to 80th percentile in district Democratic presidential vote share on civil rights support. *A*, Northern Republicans. *B*, Northern Democrats. Dependent variable is an indicator for whether each member signed each civil rights discharge petition in a given Congress; for Congresses with multiple petitions, a separate intercept is included for each petition. Dependent variable ranges from 0 to 1. First differences and 95% confidence intervals, controlling for seniority and membership on the targeted committee. OLS with robust standard errors, clustered by member when multiple petitions per Congress.

likely to back civil rights initiatives than were other party members. By contrast, by the late 1930s Democratic support for civil rights was bolstered by district characteristics—such as high urbanization and state-level union density—that made the districts better fit the prototype of a northern Democratic constituency in the New Deal era. This is consistent with the idea that civil rights support had become a broadly based, core identifying feature for northern Democrats, while such support was more of a marker for House Republicans who were at least somewhat out of sync with their colleagues and party base. Indeed, as noted above, no discharge petition gained even one-third of House Republicans' signatures from 1947 onward (see fig. 8.2).

BEYOND THE QUANTITATIVE EVIDENCE: RANK-AND-FILE VIEWS OF CIVIL RIGHTS INITIATIVES

One might reasonably ask whether the roll-call evidence—which suggested only a modest gap between northern Democrats and northern Republicans—or the discharge petition data revealing a much bigger partisan gap offers a more accurate characterization of party members' civil rights views. I argued above that discharge petitions offer important benefits as a preference measure since they are not subject to agenda control, and they reflect members' willingness to push legislation to the decision stage. The case that the discharge petitions offer the more accurate assessment is bolstered by a qualitative examination of civil rights legislative drives in the 1940s and 1950s. This examination reinforces the message that House Republicans displayed considerable ambivalence—and at times hostility—toward these initiatives while rank-and-file northern Democrats provided strong support.

Throughout much of the 1940s and 1950s, top GOP leaders were sufficiently interested in appealing to African American and pro–civil rights white voters that they avoided outright opposition, even as rank-and-file party members refused to back strong actions. For example, after an FEPC bill was reported from the liberal-dominated House Labor Committee in 1945, it languished for months in the Rules Committee. The GOP's 1944 platform had endorsed FEPC legislation, making party members reluctant to oppose it publicly (see chapter 10). Yet within the Rules Committee, Republicans helped southern Democrats block the bill, at times leaving meetings when a southern member's absence would have otherwise provided a window of opportunity for bill supporters. Louis Ruchames notes that the Republicans were "theoretically in favor but actually opposed to the legislation."[70]

A House GOP Conference meeting in September 1945—called to plan a program for the upcoming election—supports the idea that rank-and-file House Republicans increasingly came to see civil rights as a losing bid for African American votes that contradicted their party's opposition to "big government." The meeting, which was intended to be confidential, included a discussion of the place of civil rights on the party's agenda.[71] Charles La Follette, a liberal Republican from Indiana, challenged party members to sign the discharge petition for the fair employment practices bill that was stuck in the Rules Committee. La Follette claimed that his civil rights support had helped him win a substantial share of the African American vote in his district and noted that "I definitely do feel that there is a great mass of voters who will go to the Republican Party because they know that they cannot get any help out of the Democratic Party, if we make a positive step in that direction."[72]

La Follette, whose NOMINATE score made him the third most liberal House Republican, was greeted with disdain by his colleagues. James Mott (R-OR) countered that "We don't want any FEPC in the state of Oregon. We don't want any communistic legislation that will require a private employer who employs a certain number of men to make any choice whatever." Mott added that the issue "will do us political damage." Republican Ross Rizley (R-OK) added that the national party platform's endorsement of FEPC had been put there "wholly and solely for political expediency, and that alone. How in the world are you going to take the position that the Republican Party has taken and the position that I have taken in order to get elected down in Oklahoma, that we are against bureaucracy, and then set up one of the greatest bureaucracies that would ever be known, this FEPC?"[73] Rizley's speech was greeted with applause, in contrast to the silence that greeted La Follette. Following the conference meeting, Republican Howard Knutson (R-MN) estimated that 90 percent of the attendees were opposed to a permanent FEPC.[74]

The mood of the conference is also indicated by the reaction when John Jennings Jr. (R-TN) lambasted the FEPC: "To say that anybody can come along and say to a man that you can't take people you know and that are efficient and that are trustworthy to run your business, is un-American, and we cannot afford to stultify ourselves by undertaking to do that sort of thing. The decent colored people in my country don't want it. A few agitators want it. And certainly the Jews don't need it. My God, they are taking care of themselves." The conference minutes note that laughter greeted Jennings's comment.[75]

Undeterred, La Follette soon launched a Senate campaign highlighting his support for civil rights and labor unions, even winning the endorsement of the CIO-PAC. His opponent, William Jenner (R-IN), made no secret of his hostility to FEPC, flatly telling Indiana African Americans that "there would be no state FEPC and he didn't want them to talk about it."[76] Republican state convention delegates nominated Jenner by a 1,994 to 105 vote.[77] After his defeat, La Follette abandoned the GOP, claiming that "I am convinced it is not the party in which the goal of racial equality and the elimination of discrimination based on false prejudice can be advanced."[78] In the staunchly Republican state of Indiana, there is little doubt that the brand of Republicanism espoused by Jenner—against unions and big government, and skeptical of civil rights initiatives such as FEPC—resonated with the party's activists and electoral base, while La Follette's positions put him far outside the party mainstream. After leaving the GOP, La Follette would go on to become a national director of the ADA.[79]

The observation that the percentage African American in GOP districts predicted civil rights discharge petition signatures prior to 1948, but not afterward, is also consistent with the idea that the La Follette strategy of appealing to African American voters through civil rights support gradually faded from the scene amid electoral setbacks. A private letter from GOP leader Joseph Martin (R-MA)—himself a supporter of at least mild civil rights legislation—assessed the problem as follows: "Our greatest difficulty is that in districts where the colored vote predominates, only Democrats have been elected, and that has made it difficult to arouse the enthusiasm you would normally expect among the Republicans."[80] Nationally oriented party leaders—such as presidential aspirants and Senate candidates in heavily urban northern states—continued to see an incentive to back at least modest civil rights measures in order to maintain some appeal to African American voters who could hold the balance of power in a close election (see chapter 10).[81] But most House Republicans came from more rural, conservative areas of the North and had little electoral or personal interest in pursuing civil rights.

Where rank-and-file Republicans showed little interest in civil rights in this period, the issue continued to be a significant concern for northern liberal Democrats. As discussed in chapter 9, civil rights was a prime motivation for liberal organizing in Congress in the mid-1950s, which culminated in formation of the Democratic Study Group (DSG). The DSG played a key role in overcoming Republicans' reluctance to sign the discharge petition for the legislation that became the Civil Rights Act of 1960. With the legislation buried in the Rules Committee, a coalition including the NAACP, UAW, AFL-CIO, and American Jewish Congress launched a major lobbying campaign seeking discharge signatures, complemented by a full day of floor speeches from DSG members.[82] Several of the DSG speeches accused GOP leader Charlie Halleck (R-IN) of urging Republicans not to sign the discharge petition, charging that his motivation was to maintain his party's alliance with southern conservatives.[83] In one speech, Judiciary chair Emanuel Celler (D-NY) claimed that while Republicans have "pronounced time and again that they are for civil rights, [they] do nothing to bring a civil rights bill forward. They help stymie the bill in committee; they help stymie the bill by refusing to sign the petition. I call that sheer rank hypocrisy."[84]

When the press did not cover the floor speeches, the DSG tried a new tactic: the group had members approach the clerk's desk where the discharge petition was held, ostensibly to study the petition's contents but really to compile a list of the members who had signed. The DSG assembled a full list, which showed that 145 of the 175 signatures were from Democrats. The group then leaked the list of signatories to the *New York Times*, while helpfully sending ballpoint pens to each of the Republicans who had yet to sign the petition.[85] The absence of GOP support proved embarrassing for party members, leading to several new signatures. With the petition approaching the threshold number of 218, Halleck "allowed the Republicans on the [Rules] committee to join the four northern Democrats in sending the bill to the floor."[86]

The qualitative evidence from the Republican Conference minutes and the DSG's maneuvering complements the clear patterns revealed in the quantitative data on civil rights support: by the mid-1940s support for pushing civil rights initiatives to the House floor had become tied to Democratic partisanship and economic liberalism among northern members of Congress. Indeed, civil rights now constituted one of the key identifying issues for northern liberal Democrats, just as rank-and-file Republicans demonstrated a far more ambivalent stance toward these initiatives. As a result, northern Democrats were poised to be far more responsive as the civil rights movement mobilized with increasing success in the 1960s, forcing the issue to the top of the national agenda.

IMPLICATIONS: SHAPING THE POLITICAL AGENDA

One potential objection to reliance on evidence from discharge petition signatures, bill sponsorships, and floor speeches is that northern Democrats' activity generated minimal legislative results prior to the 1960s. Congress did not enact a major civil rights bill until 1957, and even that legislation was notable for its weakness. One might wonder about the actual stakes of the legislative battles of the 1930s–1950s, given the scant legislative output. Perhaps the skirmishes surrounding civil rights were merely an opportunity for members on all sides to position-take for their constituents while the real business of governing continued on track for the Democrats.

Against this view, I argue that the civil rights drives in the House reflected an ongoing battle for the future of the Democratic Party that had important political consequences. By working with civil rights activists to mount aggressive discharge petition campaigns, members repeatedly forced civil rights onto the legislative agenda. In doing so, liberal Democrats heightened the political visibility of an issue that southern Democrats (and many top

Democratic leaders) hoped to suppress. As shown below, the press gave considerable coverage to the legislative battles of the late 1930s and 1940s, and many southern conservatives believed that there was a realistic possibility that Congress would enact some of this legislation. Civil rights advocates in Congress worked in collaboration with the NAACP, CIO, and other groups to push legislation that helped give concrete, programmatic meaning to the new version of labor-oriented liberalism that first developed in the late 1930s. In doing so, they sharpened the cleavage between the two wings of the Democratic Party and amplified the association between "true" New Deal liberalism and civil rights support.[87]

Press Coverage of Civil Rights Legislative Initiatives

A crucial challenge for the NAACP and other civil rights groups was to focus political attention on the rampant discrimination confronting African Americans. Nationally oriented Democratic leaders, such as Franklin Roosevelt, had little interest in a widely publicized debate on civil rights that would only highlight Democratic divisions. Civil rights advocates, however, sought to force their bills onto the House floor during these same years. Did these legislative drives garner national attention? Were they simply a minor sideshow, receiving scant notice given everyone expected the final act would be a successful southern filibuster? Or were they instead major political events, focusing attention on an issue that southern Democrats and many national leaders desperately hoped to avoid?

To begin to answer this question, I searched for front-page stories on civil rights legislation in the *Washington Post* and *New York Times* from 1931 to 1950. The search required that the headline or subtitle of the front-page story mention either FEPC, lynching, or the poll tax and that the text of the story refer to the House or Senate, along with mention of a bill, measure, or legislation.[88] This is a stringent test: numerous other front-page stories discussed civil rights legislation but did not include FEPC, lynching, or the poll tax in their headline.[89]

As figure 8.9 demonstrates, prior to 1935 civil rights legislation received only modest coverage on the front page of the *Times* and *Post*. However, starting with the 1935–36 legislative drive for the antilynching bill—which featured a Senate filibuster and a discharge petition that reached 218 signatures in the House—considerably more attention was paid to civil rights issues.[90] There were eleven front-page stories in 1935–36 that include one of the key terms in the headline. The successful discharge petition drive for antilynching legislation in 1937 led to an even bigger jump in coverage in the Seventy-Fifth Congress, with a total of forty-two front-page stories on civil rights legislation. Passage of the House version of the bill in April 1937

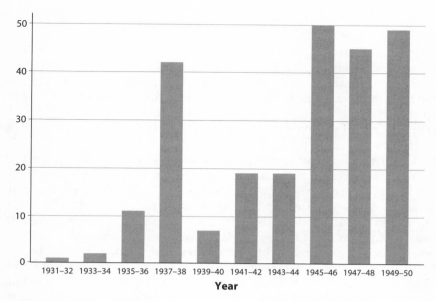

FIGURE 8.9. Front-page stories mentioning civil rights issues in headline, *New York Times* and *Washington Post*. Story must also mention Congress. Search terms used: ((fepc OR "f.e.p.c." OR "fair employment" OR "lynch*" OR "anti-lynch" OR "poll tax" OR "anti-poll tax") AND (congress OR house OR senate OR senator OR representative)) AND (bill OR measure OR legislation). The search also required that the headline or title of the story include the terms (fepc OR "f.e.p.c." OR "fair employment" OR "lynch*" OR "anti-lynch" OR "poll tax" OR "anti-poll tax").

sparked several front-page stories in the *Post* and the *Times*, putting Democratic divisions on prominent display.[91] The ensuing Senate filibuster generated far more front-page coverage, including numerous stories highlighting southern Democrats' anger with their fellow partisans for pushing the bill.[92]

The numbers fall off a bit in 1939–42 amid the run-up to war, but even in 1941–42 there were nineteen front-page stories with a headline mentioning civil rights. Coverage again increased in 1943–44 and 1945–46, with fifty front-page stories in the latter Congress, many focused on the FEPC fight. News coverage continued to be extensive in the late 1940s, amid Truman's reelection campaign and the ensuing FEPC push in the Eighty-First Congress (1949–50). This level of coverage cuts against the notion that civil rights was simply kept off the political agenda in the 1930s and 1940s.

Southern Democrats' Response

One might still wonder whether southern Democrats viewed all this publicity accorded to civil rights as a true threat, or instead as an opportunity for members on all sides of the debate to posture for their constituents, safe in the knowledge that the measures pushed onto the agenda would never be enacted. A major flaw in this reasoning is that elected officials did not at all take for granted that civil rights legislation would fail in the late 1930s or the 1940s.

An early example of growing southern concern about the prospect of civil rights legislation being enacted occurred in 1937, when House Judiciary Committee chairman Hatton Sumners (D-TX) backed an effort to substitute a weaker antilynching bill sponsored by the sole African American Democrat, Arthur Mitchell (D-IL), for the Gavagan measure. The NAACP's fierce opposition was sufficient to defeat Sumners's effort on the floor, but Sumners was among ten southerners who voted to consider the Mitchell bill.[93] The willingness of a southern leader like Sumners to vote to consider Mitchell's antilynching bill suggests the depths of their apprehension that Congress might pass meaningful civil rights legislation.

When the Gavagan bill reached the Senate, many observers—including southerners—expressed the view that it would pass despite the looming filibuster. Press coverage widely reported that the bill was expected to be enacted.[94] Following report of the bill from the Senate Judiciary Committee on a 13–3 vote, the *New York Times* noted that southern leader Tom Connally (D-TX) predicted that "it looked as though the bill would be passed."[95] During the initial floor debate, Josiah Bailey (D-NC), who had filibustered the 1935 bill, declared, "I feel that the bill is sure to pass. If it should not pass now, I am sure it will pass in January or February." Bailey continued that though he fiercely opposed the bill, he was confident it was unconstitutional and would have no effect in practice.[96] Connally also suggested during the initial floor debate that the bill was likely to pass, but he claimed to take comfort in the knowledge that "when Representatives and Senators, under the whip and spur of expediency to get votes, are willing to pass any kind of legislation, then I thank God that we have a Supreme Court to keep us back within our jurisdiction."[97]

Although Wagner's initial effort to force a vote in November 1937 was derailed by pressure to take up a housing bill, the New York senator successfully insisted that the measure be made the unfinished business for the session convening in January 1938. Wagner confided to the NAACP's White that "I am absolutely convinced that this victory [the Senate commitment to make the measure an item of unfinished business] means the passage of the bill early next winter."[98] Amid widespread reports that White and the NAACP had evidently lined up a sufficient number of votes for cloture, the *Atlanta*

Constitution noted that "under the present circumstances, [southern sena-
tors] have said they saw no prospect of talking the bill to death."[99] Southerners' private letters also expressed considerable pessimism, with Theodore
Bilbo (D-MS) writing a constituent that "I am afraid it is going to pass regardless of what we say or do."[100] In the end, however, most Senate Republicans refused to back cloture, providing southerners with a triumph that
many had not expected when the battle started.[101]

Despite their 1938 victory, southern senators' private papers reveal that
they continued to harbor serious doubts that they would prevail in subsequent filibuster battles. When a handful of moderate southerners indicated
they might support the poll tax bill when it came onto the agenda, Connally
warned that with a fractured southern bloc, "being in a decided minority, we
don't get very far."[102] A few years later, amid the 1948 civil rights push, John
Stennis (D-MS) warned in a private letter that "we are in the midst of a real
battle where the outcome is uncertain. These battles have been won for the
past fifteen years by a filibuster, but at that time the Southern Senators held
many key positions and controlled the machinery of the Senate. This is not
true today."[103]

Southern conservatives' correspondence reveals that they believed that
the passage of a poll tax ban in the 1940s was quite likely, notwithstanding
their filibuster efforts. Harry Byrd, leader of the Virginia Democratic machine, was particularly attuned to the need to adapt in case the poll tax was
banned. In a 1945 letter marked confidential, Byrd asked local politician
E. W. Senter for advice on what actions the state legislature could take "in
the event the poll tax is repealed."[104] During the 1948 renewed push for
voting rights legislation, Senator A. Willis Robertson (D-VA)'s letter to Byrd
regarding the conservatives' chances in upcoming elections by no means
took the success of southern obstruction for granted: "If by any chance the
poll tax should be repealed before next November the vote of the left wing
group against the State ticket added to the Republican vote could be serious.
The situation, of course, could be measurably helped if the Senate does not
invoke cloture and we succeed in the defeat of the so-called Civil Rights
bill."[105] A year later, Howard Smith wrote Byrd to consult further about
what actions to urge in the Virginia legislature if "Congress repealed the
poll tax in the next session."[106] In a letter sent to Byrd in August 1949, Virginia's Pulaski County treasurer J. F. Wyson also noted the need to be ready
for a state response, writing that "we are agreed that on the poll tax Congressional action is almost certain to come in the winter or early spring of
1950."[107]

More generally, the southerners' papers from the 1940s and early 1950s
show that they viewed it as quite plausible that civil rights supporters would
succeed either in obtaining cloture or in changing the Senate's rules to limit
obstruction.[108] Finley writes that leading southern senators in the 1940s

"depicted the civil rights fight in national political terms as a battle in which the South, even in the Democratic Party, was steadily losing ground." Amid Truman's 1949 civil rights push, Richard Russell (D-GA) wrote to one constituent that "we are in a desperate situation here" and told another that "we must bravely face discouragement and probable defeat in our fight to stave off this vicious legislation."[109] Russell Long (D-LA) wrote in 1949 that "I fear that we are going to lose a couple of rounds in the Civil Rights fight" before the end of the current session. Long also noted the NAACP would not be satisfied with limited successes, and "the northern wing of our party cannot resist the pressure that will be brought for the total abolition of segregation."[110] Even after southerners triumphed in their obstruction of the FEPC, Russell noted that "we have held the bridge up until now ... [but] it is disheartening to see how the advocates of this monstrosity [FEPC] increase in strength each year." He continued that "the odds against us are very heavy."[111]

These southerners clearly did not regard northern liberals' efforts to push civil rights legislation as part of a mere sham battle that allowed them to showcase their commitment to their constituents. Instead, the liberal initiatives were part of an all-out struggle for the future of the Democratic Party and of the country.

CONCLUSION: CIVIL RIGHTS AND THE DEMOCRATIC COALITION

As it turned out, such southern leaders as Russell were overly pessimistic about their prospects for success in the short term. With southern senators working as a well-organized team, the filibuster proved to be a powerful weapon.[112] Equally important, top Democratic leaders generally provided only tepid support, at best, for rank-and-file liberals' efforts to force action.[113] Meanwhile, southern Democrats found important allies among the Republicans, both in their defensive efforts to block civil rights and in their moves to go on offense against their northern liberal copartisans. As Republican support for civil rights initiatives continued to recede in the mid- to late 1940s (see fig. 8.2), discharge petition drives generally came up short, minimizing the place of civil rights on the congressional agenda in the late 1940s and early 1950s. At the same time, southerners provided vigorous support for Republicans' successful efforts to weaken the labor unions that northern liberals relied on so heavily for their electoral support.[114]

Yet southern Democrats' longer-term fears were justified. The new politics of civil rights that took shape in Congress in the late 1930s and early 1940s signaled the development of a novel political coalition, in which labor unions, African American groups, and northern urban liberals were aligned on one side, with southerners on the other. Southerners fought back against this coalition by sponsoring antilabor legislation and by putting the brakes on many other New Deal initiatives. Yet this southern resistance only reinforced the message that southern conservatives constituted a critical enemy to liberal aspirations. Ultimately, the southerners were correct in their intuition that they could not coexist permanently in the Democratic Party alongside the emerging liberal wing. There could be no bargain that was mutually acceptable to these two fundamentally incompatible groups. Once the liberals became a force to be reckoned with, all that remained for the Democratic Party was a long, slow collapse from within.

By pushing civil rights initiatives to the House floor, rank-and-file Democrats clarified the meaning of mainstream liberalism as an ideological formation that encompassed civil rights. Democratic state parties and legislators complemented these efforts as they too pursued civil rights initiatives. The coalition of CIO unions, African Americans, and urban liberals that was forged in the late 1930s thus was able to work with midlevel party actors to define the policy aspirations of the liberal wing of the Democratic Party. The federated nature of American parties and the local roots of rank-and-file members of Congress constituted important resources for civil rights activists as they battled to overcome a national political alignment that had been premised on avoidance of racial issues.

In this way, much of the important political work of the racial realignment had largely been completed by the end of the 1940s. The same story holds both for the mass public and for midlevel actors such as state parties and northern rank-and-file members of Congress: Democratic partisanship and economic liberalism were each linked to greater civil rights support, while economically conservative Republicans were especially skeptical.

However, both Democratic and Republican national party elites had strong reasons to continue to straddle civil rights issues, thus abetting southern filibusters. Preferences had largely been realigned, but it required the direct action of grassroots activists to force civil rights to the very top of the national agenda, pressuring national leaders to finally choose sides. Evasion was no longer an option with disorder in the streets. In that context, the linkages forged in the late 1930s and the 1940s meant that northern liberal Democrats would be primed to be the most responsive, while many Republicans would see the political and ideological logic of allying with southern whites. Part 3 tells the story of the battle for control of each national party, with a focus on the interplay among civil rights activists, midlevel party actors, and top party leaders.

PART 3

The National Parties Respond

CHAPTER 9

Facing a Changing Party

DEMOCRATIC ELITES AND CIVIL RIGHTS

WHETHER ONE EXAMINES mass attitudes, the platforms of northern state parties, or the behavior of rank-and-file northern House Democrats, it is clear that, contrary to the conventional wisdom, the realignment on civil rights did not occur suddenly in 1964. The shift was, in fact, far along by the mid-1940s. However, we must remember that the conventional wisdom on this point is conventional for a reason: it is not without an apparent basis in the empirical record. In fact, as Carmines and Stimson correctly emphasize, national Democratic platforms generally took a vague stand on civil rights in the decades prior to the peak of the civil rights movement, typically devoting less space to the issue than the Republicans and often taking a less forthright stand in favor of action.[1] Clearly, there is a puzzle here. Why did a party that had, in effect, become liberal on matters of race continue to place such weak civil rights planks in its national platforms for twenty years?

The first part of this chapter seeks to reconcile the long-noted tepidness of the national Democratic Party platform on civil rights in the 1940s and 1950s with the evidence presented in this book that the civil rights realignment had been underway from the late 1930s. The central argument is that the halfhearted platform statements on civil rights were anything but uncontroversial within the Democratic Party and, indeed, did not truly represent the wishes of the conventions that approved them. Rather, the weak stance of the national party was the result of a desperate effort on the part of national elites to keep the party—and their power—intact. These leaders were struggling to contain the war between contending regional factions, each of which enjoyed its own electoral power base and each of which was willing, at times, to force confrontations that threatened to unravel the party as a whole. A survey of convention delegates from 1956 reinforces the evidence from the qualitative accounts, suggesting substantially greater support for civil rights among rank-and-file Democratic delegates than among Republican convention delegates, despite the GOP's similar platform outcome.

The second part of this chapter asks why national Democratic elites eventually surrendered in this struggle, completing the realignment at the national level. The key claim is that national leaders had very limited room to maneuver given civil rights supporters' takeover of much of the party apparatus below them. Contrary to standard portrayals of Democratic leaders—particularly President Lyndon Johnson—exercising tremendous agency on matters of race, the argument here is that these men, important figures though they surely were, acceded to forces that had long been at work within their party, and that were brought to the point of unbearable pressure by the civil rights movement. Johnson's skillful maneuvering on behalf of the Civil Rights Act of 1964 helped assure its passage while mitigating the need for damaging compromises. But Johnson's actions reflected his beliefs about what it would take to lead a Democratic Party that had been remade below him over the course of his career, rather than a personal choice to transform his party.

This account suggests that we can best understand the relationship between protest activity and elite agency in the civil rights case in terms of multiple intersecting trajectories. The constituency changes and shifts in ideological alignments highlighted in earlier chapters made the Democratic Party a more receptive home for racial liberals starting in the late 1930s. But it was the protest, litigation, and legislative strategies adopted by movement activists that turned this baseline receptivity into a clear program that took center stage in political battles.

The looming threat of mass protest during the mobilization for World War II forced employment discrimination onto the legislative agenda, and the ensuing conflicts over the FEPC helped turn civil rights into a defining commitment for many urban liberals. The blow-up at the Democratic convention in 1948 reflected the early civil rights movement's success in raising the political salience of the issue and in gradually gaining influence in northern state Democratic parties and among rank-and-file Democratic representatives. The more intense mobilization campaign that began with the Montgomery bus boycott of 1955–56 and accelerated in the early 1960s ratcheted up the pressure to take a stand, ultimately leading to Kennedy and Johnson's legislative drive.

In each case, from A. Philip Randolph's March on Washington Movement through Martin Luther King's nonviolent direct-action campaign, movement activists pursued their own agenda of making racial oppression a top political issue. Although many activists had ties to the Democratic Party stemming from the coalitional reshuffling of the New Deal, their actions were not governed by concern for the party. Indeed, they pursued disruptive protests even when party leaders asked them to stand down. Activists took advantage of opportunities—such as the U.S. government's growing concern with its international reputation in the Cold War context—that Democratic leaders surely would have liked them to pass up.[2] Crucially, as Democratic leaders grappled with how to respond to this activist pressure, they did so on a political ground constructed by the coalition of labor unions, African Americans, Jews, and other urban liberals that had incorporated civil rights into the liberal program. In this way, it is the intersection of early coalitional changes and recurrent, escalating rounds of movement activism that explains the timing and substance of national Democrats' shift on racial policy.

NATIONAL DEMOCRATS AND THE PLATFORM-WRITING PROCESS, 1940–56

While northern state Democratic platforms provided much stronger support for civil rights measures than did their Republican counterparts from the mid-1940s onward, the national Democratic platform fell far short of civil rights advocates' hopes, with the notable exception of 1948. Republican national platforms were hardly clarion calls for aggressive action, but they were typically roughly as strong as the national Democratic platforms prior to the 1960s.[3]

Nonetheless, an examination of the platform-approval process in the 1940s and 1950s reveals an important difference between the two parties. The tepid GOP civil rights platforms reflected the broadly shared party position in favor of mild civil rights measures but opposed to vigorous national, enforceable protections. Although a handful of prominent Republicans from urban, liberal states with substantial African American populations did advocate for a stronger civil rights stand, they were easily outnumbered by mainstream party leaders who favored minimal action. Furthermore, there was almost no groundswell from rank-and-file GOP delegates in support of stronger action. Chapter 10 narrates these platform discussions as part of a broader account of Republicans' move toward racial conservatism.

By contrast, the straddle that Democrats adopted was intended to mask the war that was underway between northern and southern factions for control of the party, a war in which northerners were progressively gaining the upper hand. Repeatedly, top national leaders struggled to force northern liberals to stand down and accept a weak civil rights plank. Given the leverage enjoyed by presidential nominees over national conventions—rooted in the imperative of holding the party together for the purpose of winning an electoral vote majority—party leaders often were able to win approval of the resulting compromise platform. However, unlike with the Republicans, a large proportion of Democratic delegates—likely a majority of the convention—favored stronger civil rights action. Repeatedly, the same coalition of African

Americans, unions, and urban liberals that pushed for pro–civil rights state party platforms also strenuously advocated for a strong national platform. While they often faced disappointment at the national level, their increasing victories at the state level and in winning over rank-and-file Democrats in the House of Representatives indicated that they were gradually succeeding in their bid to take over the party.

A broad-based liberal push for a strong civil rights plank in the national Democratic platform first became evident in 1944, amid the wartime movement activism that helped put the FEPC on the political agenda. In earlier years African Americans had pushed Democratic platform writers to endorse civil rights legislation, but they received little backing from other major players within the party.[4] But the 1944 Democratic convention in Chicago featured a pitched battle over the future of the party, in which civil rights figured prominently.

As in 1936 and 1940, African American groups urged the platform committee to include a robust civil rights plank. But this time they were joined by the very public backing of the CIO. Indeed, news coverage referred to the "CIO plank" on civil rights, which CIO president Philip Murray formally presented to the platform committee. This proposal included an FEPC with enforcement power, an end to the poll tax, and broad protections for voting rights. In a speech to the platform committee, Murray declared that "God help America if, after this war is won overseas, we should find ourselves plunged here at home into a terrifying war of hatred because of intolerance, race, religion or color." Speaking to "cheers from the crowded gallery," Murray added that "I plead on behalf of my organization for the inclusion of a plank on this vital issue, a plank that people will understand. They want to know that the Democratic party has taken a courageous stand on this all-important issue."[5]

Southern Democrats' outraged reaction to the CIO plank made civil rights the central issue in platform deliberations. The *Chicago Defender* observed that "the bristling, hot Negro issue had the Democratic convention proceedings completely tied in knots this week," resulting in a two-day delay in reporting the platform.[6] *New York Times* reporter Turner Catledge highlighted the platform committee's struggles, noting "the chief problem it was wrestling with tonight was a racial plank which would cut a center course between the Southern Democrats ... and Northern and Western delegates demanding a statement of policy against discrimination."[7] Catledge correctly predicted that the deadlock would be resolved only when Roosevelt sent over a compromise platform. The *Defender* criticized the compromise ultimately dictated by Roosevelt as a "weasel-worded" dodge.[8] Still, in a departure from earlier years, national party leaders now had to struggle against bottom-up pressure from the liberal wing of the party to take a clear stand on civil rights.

Alongside the civil rights plank, Vice President Henry Wallace served as a lightning rod for the broader conflict over the direction of the Democratic Party that played out in Chicago. Although Roosevelt's civil rights advocacy had been far from aggressive, southerners identified Wallace as a symbol of the administration's move toward an alliance with African Americans. A 1943 survey of southern county chairmen revealed that many believed the New Deal administration now constituted a grave threat to Jim Crow. A South Carolina chairman wrote that "the National Democratic Party will have to choose between the South and the negroes of the North," while others warned of a southern bolt if the administration did not pay more attention to the "rights of the Southern white Democrats."[9] Following the *Smith v. Allwright* (1944) Supreme Court decision outlawing the white primary, former Mississippi governor Mike Conner declared that the national Democratic Party had become a "New Deal Party" that embraced "un-American and undemocratic philosophies of government." Louisiana governor Sam Jones added that the "New Deal high command hopes to use the war as an instrument for forcing the social 'equality' of the Negro upon the South."[10] With Roosevelt too popular to take on directly, disaffected southerners turned their fire on Wallace, who had made himself unacceptable through his unabashed embrace of both the CIO and civil rights.

Previewing the convention, Arthur Krock of the *New York Times* depicted Wallace as "the overwhelming choice of the 'old' New Dealers, of the CIO and its Political Action Committee, of The Daily Worker and its following, of many Negro leaders, of numerous left-wing publicists, of Democratic organizations where union labor is in control (such as Pennsylvania)."[11] The *New Republic* warned that if the convention "appeases the Southern Republocrats" by dismissing Wallace and adopting a weak civil rights platform, it runs the risk of seeing liberals, labor, and African Americans stay home.[12] These southern reactionaries, however, found an ally in many big-city machine mayors who distrusted Wallace for his extreme liberalism and unwillingness to work through the traditional party apparatus.

Wallace's ties to the CIO, African Americans, and the 100% New Dealer wing of the party were on clear display at the convention itself. His nomination was seconded in a fiery speech by UAW vice president Richard Frankensteen, who brought "into the open a battle that has been raging behind the scenes" by declaring that "the people are through with smoke-filled rooms and political bosses."[13] Frankensteen claimed that party bosses from Chicago, Jersey City, and Tammany Hall were setting Democrats up for defeat by blocking the choice of the American people. In his own speech on Roosevelt's behalf, Wallace declared that "the future belongs to those who go down the line unswervingly for the liberal principles of both political democracy and economic democracy regardless of race, color, or religion. In a political, educational, and economic sense there must be no inferior races.

The poll tax must go. Equal educational opportunities must come. The future must bring equal wages for equal work regardless of sex or race. Roosevelt stands for all this."[14]

Although the party establishment was, in the end, able to keep Wallace off the ticket, press coverage of the convention suggests that the rank-and-file delegates likely favored his candidacy.[15] Indeed, the *New York Times* reported that the anti-Wallace leaders were taken aback at the convention when they found that "Wallace showed greater strength among the delegates than some of them had expected and his backers were becoming almost evangelical as they sought to make the contest an out-and-out showdown between the 'right-center' and 'left' elements of the party." These leaders grew even more disturbed when "the Vice President received a prolonged ovation from the delegates and the galleries as he came into the stadium."[16] By contrast, when Chicago mayor Edward Kelly nominated the moderate Scott Lucas of Illinois as an alternative to Wallace, he was "bombarded with hisses and boos" in his home city.[17] On the initial ballot for vice president, Wallace won a plurality of the votes, though he fell short of the needed majority amid the numerous favorite-son candidates. In the end, however, the trump card held by Wallace's opponents was that the convention as a whole was unwilling to take any major actions that Roosevelt disapproved.[18]

Liberal observers complained bitterly after the convention, but some also saw encouraging signs. The *New Republic* editorialized that the defeat of Wallace at the hands of the "worst elements" of the party—the machines and southern Tories—had resulted in "the serious disaffection of Northern liberals, trade unionists and Negroes, in the states which Mr. Roosevelt most badly needs to win."[19] The *Nation*'s Freda Kirchwey attributed Wallace's defeat to the lack of organization and preparation among his supporters but claimed that most delegates on the floor favored his renomination.[20] Kirchwey concluded that the "lines have been drawn more sharply; an open division has been made between reactionaries and progressives.... The Battle of Chicago has opened a new phase of an old war."[21] Liberal journalist Bruce Bliven shared the view that "liberals, trade unionists, and Negroes ... were contemptuously dismissed" in Chicago but argued that liberals "are stronger at this moment than they have ever been before. They are closely allied with millions of trade unionists who are for the first time politically conscious and politically organized. They are working with all minorities who suffer discrimination. While the New Deal was historically an accident, it has resulted in great gains."[22] Bliven predicted that liberals would eventually capture the Democratic Party, now that the battle lines were clear.

Four years later national party leaders once again sought to keep a lid on civil rights at the convention but this time faced a better-organized liberal opposition. Although observers today often credit Harry Truman for his forthright civil rights advocacy in 1948, his team tried to step back from the forceful program he had outlined early in the year as the signs of a full-fledged southern revolt grew during the spring.[23] Truman talked less about civil rights in his speeches in the weeks leading up to the convention, and the administration worked for adoption of a vague platform that might keep most southerners onboard. DNC chairman James Howard McGrath and platform committee chairman Representative Francis Myers of Pennsylvania were charged with implementing this strategy.[24]

But civil rights advocates in the NAACP, CIO, and ADA had other plans. In the view of the liberals, civil rights "had become the most pressing question of domestic policy," making a straddle intolerable.[25] The threat from the left posed by Henry Wallace's Progressive Party—which sought to leverage its civil rights support to take votes from Truman—added to the urgency for liberal Democrats to take a clear stand.

Well before the convention met, the ADA had identified civil rights as a wedge that could be used to separate liberals from conservatives in the party.[26] Meanwhile, the CIO-PAC's director, Jack Kroll, met with Senate candidate Hubert Humphrey before the platform committee sessions, promising full CIO support for a strong civil rights plank.[27] When the platform committee convened, Walter White of the NAACP testified that a weak plank would cause Democrats' reputation as a party of reform to perish. The CIO's secretary treasurer, James A. Carey, also called for a forceful civil rights stand, noting that "we must not seek to evade responsibility for this minimum program of civil rights by placing blame on a small minority of willful men."[28]

Even so, party leaders had control of the platform committee and were able to defeat the NAACP-ADA-CIO alternative. In the words of *Time*, "the party's worried leaders had done their best to produce something which, if it failed to please everyone, at least would not rile anyone very much. They had kept in touch with Harry Truman, whose cautious advice had been to keep the specific points of his so-called 'civil rights' program out of the platform."[29]

Following this setback, Humphrey came under intense pressure from national leaders—including Truman, McGrath, and Senate leader Alben Barkley—to give up. But the ADA held an all-night caucus that came out strongly in favor of forcing a floor vote on a strong civil rights plank. Humphrey decided to push ahead, working with other ADA and CIO leaders to line up big-city bosses such as Chicago's Jacob Arvey and New York City's Ed Flynn and Pennsylvania governor David Lawrence to back the revolt. The shift on the part of the urban bosses proved crucial; combined with the many delegates with ADA or CIO ties, it provided the liberals with a majority over the southerners and administration forces. They triumphed on a dramatic 53–47 percent vote.

While Humphrey's speech at the convention is appropriately remembered as a key turning point, its success depended not just on the delegates' sentiment in favor of civil rights but also on the shifting calculus among the city bosses. With the growing African American population in northern cities, a public vote against a firm stand on civil rights had become politically risky. The liberal journalist Robert Bendiner writes that "to delegates with large labor and Negro constituencies the dilemma was sharp: go along with the party leadership and risk reprisals at home, or break ranks and hope for the best in November."[30] One city boss put his considerations a bit more colorfully: "This is the only way we can win the election, by stirring up the minorities and capturing the cities.... And besides, I'd also like to kick those southern bastards in the teeth for what they did to Al Smith in 1928."[31]

The roll call on the so-called ADA plank underscored the changes that had occurred earlier in the 1940s at the state level. Delegates from the eight northern states that had adopted a firm pro–civil rights platform in 1941–47 voted 326–10 for the ADA plank; by contrast, delegates from the ten northern states with platforms that took a weaker civil rights stance in 1941–47 favored the liberal plank by a mere 109.5–100.5 margin.[32] More generally, within the North, urban states with a liberal electorate, relatively high unionization, and a substantial African American and Jewish population were more likely to vote in favor of the strong plank.[33]

Truman dismissed Humphrey and his allies as "crackpots" immediately after the civil rights plank was approved, but as the historian Timothy Thurber observes, the convention had taken an important step forward in redefining liberalism to include civil rights.[34] Indeed, the South's open revolt only increased the pressure on Truman to prevent Wallace's Progressive Party from siphoning off votes from the left in northern cities. In the months following the convention, Truman took on a more aggressive pro–civil rights tone, issuing an executive order desegregating the military and closing the campaign with a series of speeches in northern cities that emphasized his commitment to civil rights. These efforts helped solidify African American support for the Democrats, while undercutting Wallace's appeal.[35] Truman may have wished to avoid a direct confrontation with the South at the Democratic convention, but once liberal troops forced the party to go on record, he ended up defending the Democratic Party's civil rights liberalism from attacks both on the right and on the left.

Although racially liberal Democrats had won the platform battle, on the eve of the 1948 general election it seemed probable that their triumph would be a pyrrhic victory, costing their party the election. In response to the Democrats' strong civil rights position, many southern Democrats supported the States' Rights Democratic Party. With New York governor Thomas Dewey seen as the frontrunner throughout the fall campaign, the Dixiecrat revolt could have been the final nail in Truman's coffin. Of course, in the end Strom Thurmond did not serve as a spoiler, carrying only four southern states, and Truman defeated Dewey. However, the close call led party leaders to redouble their efforts to straddle civil rights at future conventions. As a result, Democratic civil rights statements in the national platforms throughout the 1950s were careful attempts at compromise, not angering either side enough to cause a walkout, but not at all reflective of party activist sentiment on civil rights either.[36]

The platform deliberations in 1952 once again featured dramatic testimony by the liberal, pro–civil rights contingent. The Leadership Conference on Civil Rights, a coalition of dozens of groups formed in 1950, led the charge, as "northern demands for a strong civil rights plank roared through the Democratic National Convention platform hearings."[37] Walter White testified on the LCCR's behalf and was joined by CIO leader Carey, as well as leaders of the ADA, American Jewish Committee, and Anti-Defamation League.[38] Carey told the committee that the CIO considered civil rights to be one of the "most important issues" and claimed that "millions of members" of the CIO demanded fair employment legislation.[39] The *New York Times* reported that the platform committee "appeared to be much impressed by the towering strength of the pressure that had been put upon it" in "one of the best organized hammer bodies seen in action at a party convention in many years."[40] The main goal of civil rights forces was to gain an explicit endorsement of enforceable fair employment legislation.

Notwithstanding the strength of the pro–civil rights sentiment, Democratic National Committee chairman Frank McKinney had been careful to stack the platform committee with advocates of compromise. It was chaired by House majority leader John McCormack and included a majority that favored placating the South.[41] Amid rumors that the plank would represent a step back from the 1948 platform, the ADA's chair Francis Biddle threatened a floor fight, claiming that he could muster 654 votes—a majority of the convention—on behalf of a "thoroughly effective civil rights plank."[42] When told that a strong civil rights plank might lead to a southern walkout from the convention, UAW president Walter Reuther responded that he did not expect the South to act on this threat, "but if it so chooses, let this happen; let the realignment of the parties proceed."[43]

In the end, however, the national leadership got the better of the liberal advocates. John Sparkman, a moderate Democratic senator from Alabama (and the party's vice presidential nominee) and Representative William Dawson (D-IL), an African American associated with Richard Daley's Chicago machine, worked together to write a compromise plank. While the language of the platform was similar to 1948, liberals lost on their central goal of winning an FEPC endorsement. The presiding officer of the convention, House Speaker Sam Rayburn, gaveled the draft language through on a voice vote, thereby eliminating the need for delegates to take a recorded, public position. Although the compromise language passed, few seemed satisfied with it. The Mississippi and Georgia delegations formally opposed the plank as going too far, while many liberals, including the sixty black delegates whom Representative Adam Clayton Powell (D-NY) led off the convention floor in protest, did not think it went far enough.[44]

For all the party leaders' efforts to submerge the issue, however, it is worth noting that civil rights had dominated much of the coverage of the 1952 convention. The *Times* noted that "from the start, the civil rights issue ... had been in the minds of all Democrats assembled in Chicago. The fight had become so hot and concentrated that such matters as foreign policy, national defense, governmental expenditures, taxes and the scandals developed by Capitol Hill investigations took lower place." In that context, the Democrats' nominee, Adlai Stevenson, could only avoid a clear stance for so long. In August 1952 the reluctant Stevenson finally came out in favor of the Humphrey-Ives FEPC bill pending in Congress, thus staking out a more forceful pro–civil rights stand than that of the GOP nominee, Eisenhower. [45]

The story of the 1956 Democratic platform's civil rights plank followed a similar narrative arc. Civil rights had played a significant role in the 1956 nomination race, with both Averill Harriman and Estes Kefauver challenging Stevenson from the left on civil rights by strongly endorsing the *Brown* decision.[46] In response, the still-reluctant Stevenson sounded a stronger pro–civil rights message before the California primary, which he won decisively, racking up big majorities in African American precincts.[47] Before the platform hearings began, labor unions issued a series of resolutions calling for a strong civil rights platform stand, as did state party conventions in Michigan, New York, and Wisconsin. The LCCR once again coordinated efforts, and the NAACP was joined by the ADA and labor leaders in testifying for a strong plank before the platform committee.[48] The ADA's chair, Joseph Rauh, insisted that "a forthright liberal platform on all issues including civil rights is necessary even if it arouses opposition of the Eastlands, the Byrds, and the Thurmonds."[49]

But McCormack was back as chair of the platform committee, which party leaders once again stacked with supporters of compromise. Interestingly, even Humphrey—with his eye firmly on the vice presidential nomination—was cautious in his advocacy for a strong plank, setting himself apart from the ADA's "nonpolitical" leaders.[50] The platform committee reported a vague plank, which avoided endorsement of the recent *Brown* decision or a call for an FEPC. The platform even included a statement recognizing "the existence of honest differences of opinion as to the true location of the Constitutional line of demarcation between the Federal Government and the States" and acknowledging "the vital importance of the respective States in our Federal Union."[51] In response to the weak platform proposal, NAACP executive secretary Roy Wilkins, Reuther, and Senator Herbert Lehman (D-NY) led nearly three hundred delegates in planning a floor challenge.[52] This sent a scare into party leaders, who recognized that "the North and West have the preponderance of the votes at this convention."[53]

Given the underlying views of the delegates, the key was to avoid a roll-call vote on the minority report advocating a strong plank. Several top Democratic leaders—including former president Truman and Eleanor Roosevelt—urged civil rights supporters to stand down and not force a vote.[54] In the end, presiding officer Sam Rayburn ruled that the "ayes have it" on the voice vote to adopt the platform plank and refused to recognize the New York delegation when it sought a roll call.[55] In a postmortem on the convention, the *Washington Post* credited three "old party pros" with staving off a damaging roll call showdown: McCormack, Rayburn, and Truman. Once again, national leaders' interest in holding together the precarious North-South coalition triumphed at the convention, even as more and more state Democratic parties, activists, and rank-and-file members of Congress were embracing civil rights and seeking an open confrontation.

A Window into Convention Delegate Views

The qualitative discussion above suggests that the national platform adopted by Democrats was out of step with the views of most delegates in 1956 (and implicitly in earlier years). There is also quantitative evidence supporting the claim that the mild Democratic civil rights platform masked greater delegate support for civil rights than was present among GOP convention delegates. As it happens, political scientist Herbert McClosky conducted a pathbreaking survey of national convention delegates in 1956.[56] Of 6,848 delegates and alternates, McClosky received responses from 1,788 Democrats and 1,232 Republicans.[57] The survey included several items tapping into civil rights views. Figure 9.1 summarizes the party gap on these items, both for all delegates and among northern delegates.

The question with the clearest policy content asked whether "enforcement of Supreme Court decisions on segregation" should be "increased," "decreased," or "kept as is." In the full sample, Democrats favored increased enforcement by a 47–26 percent margin. By contrast, just 24 percent of Republicans favored increased enforcement, while 34 percent wanted the government to decrease its efforts.[58]

The gap between the parties is even more substantial if one focuses attention on northern delegates: northern Democrats favored increased enforcement by a 57–13 percent margin, compared to the 27–25 percent margin favoring increased enforcement for Republicans. Among southern delegates, Democrats and Republicans were equally anti–civil rights: 59 percent of southern Democrats favored less enforcement, compared to 58 percent of southern Republicans. Roughly equal shares of southern Democrats (20%)

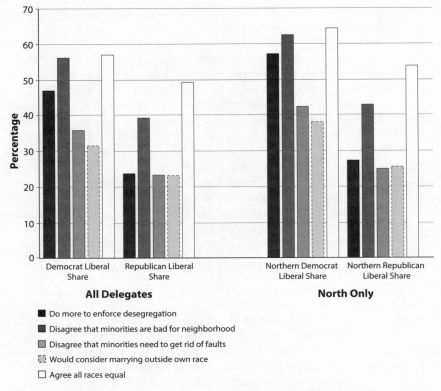

FIGURE 9.1. Comparison of share of Democratic and Republican convention delegates with liberal racial views, 1956, all delegates and northern delegates only

and southern Republicans (15%) favored increased enforcement.[59] On the whole, the evidence is clear: even as the Republican national platform was about as pro–civil rights as the Democratic platform, the actual Democratic delegates were far more pro–civil rights than their GOP counterparts.

One might worry that the presence of a Republican president may have made Republican delegates reluctant to call for greater enforcement than the administration was currently undertaking, but other items that tap into more general racial attitudes suggest a similar interparty gap. For example, the survey asks whether respondents agree or disagree that "the trouble with letting certain minority groups into a neighborhood is that they gradually give it their own atmosphere." While 61 percent of the Republicans agreed with this statement, just 44 percent of Democrats agreed. Once again, the gap was even bigger when one focuses on the North: 58 percent of northern

Republicans agreed that minorities are bad for a neighborhood, while 38 percent of Democrats shared this view.

Republicans were also significantly more likely than Democrats to agree that minority groups would be better liked if they simply got "rid of their harmful and irritating faults" and were less likely to be able to imagine marrying outside their race.[60] Finally, Republicans were somewhat more likely than Democrats to agree that "when it comes to the things that count most, all races are certainly not equal": where 55 percent of Republicans agreed with the statement, just 40 percent of Democrats agreed. Outside the South, 51 percent of Republicans agreed that all races are not equal, while 33 percent of Democrats shared the view. These responses underscore that racial prejudice was a persistent feature in both parties in the 1950s, but the consistent story is nonetheless that Democratic delegates had more racially liberal attitudes than did Republicans.

One might also ask which Democrats were especially likely to favor civil rights. The McClosky survey provides some hints that are consistent with the mass-level evidence in chapter 5 and with the constituency correlates of civil rights support in state platforms and among rank-and-file members of Congress. Union members were more pro–civil rights than were nonmembers, both overall and within the North. Thus among northern Democrats, 67 percent of union affiliates favored increased desegregation efforts, compared to 55 percent of non–union members.[61] Jewish Northern Democrats favored increased enforcement by an overwhelming 81–2 percent margin, as did 94 percent of African American Democrats.[62] Northern Democrats who lived in a large city favored increased enforcement by a 61–12 percent margin, compared to the smaller 48–18 percent margin among northern delegates from small towns or farm areas.

Finally, self-identified liberal northern Democrats were especially pro–civil rights, favoring stronger enforcement by a 70–7 percent margin, compared to the 36–20 percent margin among moderates, and the 47–23 percent plurality actually favoring *weaker* enforcement among the small number of northern conservative Democrats.[63] One sees a parallel relationship among northern Republicans: while the small number of liberals favored stronger action on desegregation (50%–9%, N = 54), the far more numerous conservative Republicans favored decreased enforcement by a substantial margin (38%–20%, N = 172). In other words, delegates who were in line with the national party in terms of general ideology—liberal Democrats and conservative Republicans—were especially far apart in their civil rights views even in 1956.

The convention delegate survey helps to understand the political meaning of the national platforms adopted by the two parties in the 1940s and 1950s. Although the Democratic and Republican platforms in 1956 ended up in a similar place—with halfhearted statements that left civil rights leaders deeply dissatisfied—this similarity owed mainly to top Democratic leaders' efforts to suppress the substantial support for civil rights within the party rather than the sincere views of the delegates themselves. Indeed, the Democratic national convention delegates came from the same middle level of state and local party officials and activists that had been transforming the Democratic Party's stance on civil rights at the state level since the early 1940s. As civil rights became a part of the standard liberal program, party leaders had to struggle mightily to adopt a platform that was less supportive of civil rights than most of the delegates favored. By contrast, for Republicans, the mild calls for action on civil rights roughly corresponded to the views of rank-and-file party officials and activists.

THE CIVIL RIGHTS MOVEMENT AND NATIONAL PARTY ELITES

The election of 1956 would prove to be the last national campaign in which advocates of avoiding a clear stand on civil rights would maintain control of the Democrats' national platform or of the national party more generally. Although party leaders' strategy had been out of sync with the rank-and-file partisans below them for more than a decade, they were able to keep a lid on the pressure to take a decisive stand so long as civil rights was not at or near the top of the nation's political agenda. The civil rights movement played a decisive role in upsetting that calculus.

It is important to emphasize that the developments in the late 1950s were not the first time that civil rights activism forced the hand of reluctant national leaders. As discussed in chapter 4, Roosevelt agreed to issue the executive order creating the FEPC only when A. Philip Randolph threatened to bring a massive protest march to Washington at a time when Roosevelt desperately hoped to avoid disruption of his war mobilization. A few years later civil rights activists played a critical role in generating Truman's 1948 civil rights program. An ambitious effort to register southern African American voters in the lead-up to the 1946 election had given rise to sickening violence. In response, civil rights activists created the National Emergency Committee Against Mob Violence in August 1946. The committee, which included the NAACP, Urban League, CIO, and AFL, met with Truman, insisting that he take action. Truman's creation of the President's Committee on Civil Rights in December 1946 was a direct response to this activism, ultimately leading to the unveiling of the president's ambitious civil rights program in February 1948.[64] Meanwhile, a long campaign to integrate the military—which included Randolph's threats of a draft boycott unless Jim Crow was ended in the armed forces—finally came to fruition with Truman's July 1948 executive order barring discrimination.[65]

Even so, these earlier civil rights mobilizations were not sustained long enough to force a permanent shift in Democratic leaders' approach. Civil rights movement activity was fairly low in the late 1940s and early 1950s, making life somewhat easier for national Democratic leaders.[66] But the *Brown* decision in 1954 was soon followed by intense battles over school integration in Little Rock and other southern cities. The Montgomery bus boycott, which began in December 1955, was an especially important moment because it signaled the launch of a more aggressive, concerted direct-action campaign that would spread across the South.

Taeku Lee shows that it was in 1956, amid the bus boycott, that several indicators of public attention to civil rights began to take off. For example, after receiving only limited attention in the *New York Times* from 1949 to 1955, civil rights coverage increased dramatically in 1956 and stayed above its earlier levels for the remainder of the civil rights era.[67] Similarly, the volume of constituent mail to the president on civil rights increased substantially in 1956 and 1957. Perhaps most significantly, the percentage of the public rating civil rights as the most important problem facing the country rose above 10 percent for the first time in 1956. A substantial portion of the public continued to rate civil rights as the top problem for several more years, with the share peaking at about one-third of citizens in 1963 and 1964 amid southern authorities' violent response to civil rights protests.[68]

Longtime liberal backers stepped up their attention to civil rights in the context of this increased activist mobilization. Indeed, as the bus boycott unfolded, the AFL-CIO announced a $2 million drive to promote civil rights legislation. The union's head, George Meany, spoke out against a "foot-dragging approach" and instead said labor had to "go all the way" in fighting for civil rights legislation.[69] At the same time, the UAW's Reuther made clear that his patience with Democratic leaders' moderate approach had waned. Nelson Lichtenstein writes that "after the 1954 *Brown* decision and the Montgomery bus boycott pushed civil rights issues to the top of the liberal agenda, Reuther told an ADA audience 'If the Democratic Party tries to straddle the civil rights issue, I for one will not support it.' "[70] Not long after this 1956 speech, Reuther commented that "We are sick and tired of the civil rights runaround practiced by the present leadership of both political parties."[71]

Leading Democratic politicians recognized that the intensified push by the civil rights movement—and the public attention generated by the violent response of white southerners—had made it much harder to avoid taking a stand. Eisenhower's improved performance among African American voters in the 1956 election, alongside the loud complaints of such African American leaders as Adam Clayton Powell that Democratic leaders had failed to stand up to the South, added to the sense of urgency.[72] Richard Bolling (D-MO), the longtime liberal House Democrat with close ties to Democratic leaders, recalled that the recent *Brown* decision and increased mobilization by the NAACP had increased the pressure on the leadership to act. According to Bolling, "liberal organizations and segments of the trade-union movement were becoming increasingly vocal in support of effective civil rights measures: No more posturing—pass a bill."[73] In this new political context marked by increased civil rights movement mobilization, the long-standing strategy adopted by most national Democratic leaders—straddle civil rights in an effort to prevent an intraparty explosion—finally began to give way.

National Democratic Leaders Finally Respond

For some two decades, most of the Democratic Party's top congressional and national committee leaders had attempted to sidestep the pressure to act on civil rights, without explicitly backing southern racists. Senate Democratic leaders Alben Barkley (D-KY) and Scott Lucas (D-IL) repeatedly discouraged efforts to force long floor debates on civil rights bills and sought to give priority to other measures rather than confront southern filibuster threats.[74] When Lyndon Johnson became Democratic leader in 1953, southern civil rights foes gained even greater sway with the upper chamber's leadership. As leader, Johnson pursued a delicate dance of maintaining close ties to the southern conservatives who were his strongest backers while seeking to appear sufficiently moderate on civil rights to maintain his viability as a presidential contender.[75]

On the House side, Speaker Sam Rayburn had offered no support to the repeated civil rights discharge petition drives, and his leadership team desperately sought to maintain cordial relations with both southern conservatives and northern liberals.[76] Rayburn prevented the Democratic Caucus from even meeting to discuss legislation, fearing that such sessions would only exacerbate the party's divisions. Although Majority Leader McCormack hailed from liberal Massachusetts, he collaborated with Speaker Rayburn in seeking to keep a lid on pro–civil rights activists, both in the House and in his role as platform committee chairman.

But the growing mobilization by the civil rights movement made these leaders' disconnect from the rank-and-file partisans below them unsustainable. One sign of change atop the Democratic hierarchy occurred soon after the 1956 election, as DNC chair Paul Butler moved to associate the party with civil rights. Interestingly, Butler had been the southerners' choice for DNC leader in 1954. Early in his tenure he sought to conciliate the South, noting he does not consider segregation a party issue.[77] But Butler moved to the left on civil rights after the 1956 election.[78]

A key initial move was the creation of a new Democratic Advisory Council (DAC). The council was "regarded as an attempt to give a more authoritative voice to elements that would be largely submerged by the conservative reign in Congress" and was viewed as a "challenge" to Lyndon Johnson's leadership. Pushed by the "Northern and urban elements who blamed the conservative Southern leadership in Congress" for the disappointing 1956 election results, the council was expected to urge a program for "liberal and enlightened social progress." The *New York Times* argued that the initiative represented a "phase in the developing struggle between the liberal and conservative wings over the party's future."[79]

The DAC's five-person steering committee had a "liberal, pro–civil rights complexion," with just a single southern member.[80] Rayburn and Johnson pointedly refused to participate in the council's deliberations, but the new body offered an institutional voice for liberals pushing for a more forthright party stance on civil rights.[81] Soon after its formation, the council's first policy declaration included an explicit call for Congress to pass civil rights legislation in the current session.[82] Later in September 1957 the DAC called on Eisenhower to take more decisive action in Little Rock and declared that Arkansas governor Orval Faubus's stand against integration "does not represent the position or the policy of the Democratic party."[83] A few weeks later the DAC issued another strong statement on civil rights, "reflecting the predominant Northern Democratic sentiment that the time for appeasement is over."[84] In keeping with this view, Butler declared that the national Democratic Party "will not pull back, surrender or in any way withdraw from" its advocacy for civil rights and school integration.[85]

Press accounts make clear that it was the turmoil at Little Rock—and the more general growing sense of crisis in the South—that heightened northern leaders' willingness to take on the South. The *Washington Post* reported that "more so since Little Rock than before," a substantial segment of the northern wing of the party now agree with the idea that "the Democratic Party would be better off without the South than to continue to be embarrassed by the Southern segregationists in the party."[86] Likewise, *CQ Weekly* observed that "the Little Rock controversy in the Fall of 1957 brought" DNC chair Butler "directly into conflict with the South."[87]

In case anyone doubted whether the DAC's pro–civil rights stance reflected a broader shift by Butler, he predicted in an October 1958 television appearance that Democrats would "adopt a 'no compromise' civil rights plank" and declared that those in the party who "don't want to go along on the racial problem and the whole area of human rights ... are going to have to take political asylum wherever they can find it, either in the Republican Party or a third party.... I certainly would hope they would take leave of the Democratic Party."[88] A year later Butler argued that the mounting attention to the civil rights issue made it unlikely that the party would nominate a southerner or southwesterner as president.[89] Southerners sought to replace Butler as DNC chair with a moderate, but even one of his critics conceded that the chairman's "strong civil rights stand" would make a challenge untenable: "Butler's managed to make it a fight between himself and Faubus; on that basis, he can't possibly lose."[90]

Butler was by no means alone among party leaders in seeking to pressure congressional leaders to take a clearer stand in favor of civil rights. Averill Harriman—a presidential contender in 1956 and governor of New York (1955–58)—joined Michigan governor Mennen Williams as powerful voices for civil rights on the Democratic Advisory Council's Steering Committee. Soon after joining the committee, Harriman and Williams scheduled a governors' conference on civil rights to be attended by governors whose states had adopted a fair employment practices law.[91] Twelve states were invited to the conference, which was held in December 1957; all but one had a Democratic governor. Williams and Harriman hoped to use the conference as a way to commit Democrats to civil rights and to counter the Southern Governors' Conference. Follow-up conferences were held in January 1959 and March 1960, with fifteen states represented at the latter event. In each case the conference urged forceful action on civil rights. Williams also enlisted the Democratic Midwest Governors' Conference in March 1960 to push strong civil rights views on national Democrats.[92]

The efforts of such nationally prominent Democrats as Butler, Harriman, and Williams were reinforced by moves within Congress to organize liberal forces. Inspired by the Southern Manifesto—the 1956 attack on the *Brown* decision signed by 101 southern members of Congress—Eugene McCarthy (D-MN) put together a network of liberal House Democrats hoping to wrest control of the party's direction from the more conservative leadership.[93] The group issued a statement, signed by eighty House Democrats, that called for a range of liberal initiatives, including a section on civil rights that proposed the "enactment of legislation designed to eliminate illegal and unconstitutional discrimination affecting the right to vote and the right to engage in gainful occupation, and designed also to insure full protection of the law, of the enjoyment of the security of person and of the rights of citizenship."[94] The group, nicknamed "McCarthy's Mavericks," formed a rudimentary whip system in 1957 and offered assistance to liberal House candidates in the 1958 election.[95]

Seeking to capitalize on the Democratic wave in that election, the liberals decided to become more formally organized. The liberal leaders sent out an invitation for a meeting that led to the creation of the Democratic Study Group. Interestingly, the only specific issue mentioned in the invitation text was civil rights, which it labeled "one pressing matter still unresolved."[96]

Following the first meeting, one of the group's leaders, Lee Metcalf (D-MT), sent a letter again highlighting concern for civil rights and noting that Judiciary chairman Emanuel Celler (D-NY) would attend the next meeting to discuss strategy on the pending civil rights discharge petition. A few months later the DSG issued a formal program, which put "effective civil rights legislation" first on its list of priority legislation.[97] The group also set up several task forces, including one on civil rights. Where Speaker Rayburn had taken a hands-off approach when civil rights supporters sought to overcome committee gatekeeping, the DSG aggressively fought to force the legislation to the floor.[98] By 1960 Rayburn responded to the rank-and-file pressure within his party by signaling that he privately supported the discharge petition drive to bring the 1960 Civil Rights Act to the House floor.[99]

In short, civil rights was the focal point as liberals organized in the House of Representatives to challenge the party's more conservative leadership and move the party in a more clearly progressive direction. These rank-and-file House Democrats were linked both to a network of civil rights organizations with strong ties to the liberal wing of the Democratic Party and to a growing set of prominent party leaders outside Congress who saw a liberal stance on civil rights as crucial to their party's future. Again, this emphasis on civil rights as a policy priority occurred in the context of the renewed civil rights movement activism of the mid- to late 1950s. It had been much easier for Democratic leaders to sidestep pleas to act on civil rights before Little Rock, the Montgomery bus boycott, and the more general nonviolent direct action campaign taking hold in the South.

The Democratic convention in 1960 underscored the gains that liberals had made at the top levels of the party. Butler passed over senior congressional leaders in selecting the platform committee. Instead, he chose outspoken civil rights advocate and ADA cofounder Chester Bowles to chair the committee. Philip Perlman, vice chair of the platform committee, also had strong ADA ties and was a member of the Democratic Advisory Council.[100]

Walter Reuther and the UAW reinforced Butler's efforts to move the national party. During the nomination battle, Reuther pressed the major Democratic candidates to take a clear stand in favor of civil rights. As part of his effort to win over the UAW, Senator John F. Kennedy endorsed the union's old-age health insurance bill and "became far more visible in his commitment to civil rights legislation." In a private meeting, Reuther and Jack Conway pressed Kennedy on civil rights, with Kennedy finally standing up and asserting, "All right. There's no question. The Negroes are right."[101] As the nomination contest unfolded, the UAW organized informal sessions with representatives from the Kennedy, Humphrey, and Stevenson camps to ensure all would cooperate in providing civil rights liberals with control of the critical convention posts and committees.[102]

Once again, liberal organizations testified in favor of a strong civil rights plank, but this time they were on the inside rather than the outside looking in. Joseph Rauh appeared before the committee to "present ADA's position on the 'single most important issue,' the question of civil rights."[103] Bowles worked with Harris Wofford of Pennsylvania to write a plank that clearly

committed the national party to an aggressive civil rights program. The platform pledged full support for African American voting rights, elimination of
literacy tests and poll taxes, full implementation of the *Brown* decision, creation of the FEPC, an end to discrimination in federal housing programs,
and to provide the Justice Department with the power to initiate civil suits
to prevent the denial of civil rights. Senator Sam Ervin of North Carolina
sought amendments in the committee to water down the plank, but his effort was "howled down ... by voice vote."[104] When southerners challenged
the plank on the convention floor, they were met with boos, and the outcome
showed that "the South again stood alone."[105] Just 27 percent of the delegates at the convention represented the South, and delegates from outside
the region showed little interest in coming to their assistance; the region had
become an isolated minority in the national party's deliberations.[106] For the
first time, civil rights leaders were pleased with a national Democratic platform drafted with the support of top Democratic leaders, rather than having
to work with insurgents to try to force the party's hand.[107] With the sit-in
movement spreading across the South and civil rights in the national headlines, the pressure to take a clear stand was much stronger than in the past,
and liberals were now well positioned within the national party to shape the
content of that stand.

The liberals' triumph was not yet complete, however. The party's nominee,
Kennedy, had been forced to voice support for a strong civil rights program
in order to secure the party's nomination.[108] As part of these efforts, Kennedy's team had "unequivocally assured" the liberal and labor forces that
"Johnson would never be Jack Kennedy's choice" for vice president.[109] But
Kennedy's personal commitment to civil rights was limited at best, and his
search for an Electoral College majority led to the selection of Lyndon Johnson as vice president. When the news broke, Rauh was in tears and Reuther
"was livid with rage, profane in anger."[110] Bitter cries that they had been
"double-crossed" spread throughout the liberal forces, with the Michigan
delegation, along with California, New York, and Wisconsin, threatening a
floor fight.[111] Governor Williams of Michigan—who had backed Kennedy
after receiving assurances of his civil rights support—voted against Johnson
in the voice vote on the convention floor.[112] Indeed, although the presiding
officer declared Johnson the victor on the vote, observers noted that it was
actually "about evenly divided" between yeas and nays.[113]

Even as the Johnson nomination rankled liberals, Kennedy had been nominated to lead a party in which civil rights advocates now enjoyed a clear
majority—and a far stronger institutional place than just a few years earlier.
Before Johnson's nomination was accepted on the floor, the son of the South
offered a "foursquare endorsement of the party's civil rights plank."[114] During
the campaign, Kennedy was careful to position himself just to Nixon's left on
civil rights. His call to Martin Luther King, Jr., when the civil rights leader

was imprisoned in Georgia was a key moment, signaling his support and drawing a contrast to Nixon's indecision.[115] The Kennedy campaign printed a million pamphlets highlighting the episode, distributing them at African American churches right before the election. In the end, Kennedy won the African American vote by a 68–32 percent margin, allowing him to capture the presidency while narrowly losing the white vote.[116]

Once in office, Kennedy continued to face the conflicting imperatives of responding to intraparty pressure to act on civil rights and of avoiding a full breach with southern Democrats that would jeopardize their support for other aspects of his program. At first Kennedy attempted to sidestep his party's pledge to act on civil rights, delaying the introduction of legislation and refusing to back the initiatives introduced by rank-and-file members of Congress.[117] The president did not send a civil rights message to Congress until late February 1963, and even that message focused on reporting on executive actions while recommending only mild legislative measures.[118]

But the dramatic violence in Birmingham, Alabama, that unfolded in early May 1963—in which Bull Connor turned fire hoses and attack dogs on peaceful protesters—forced Kennedy to change his approach.[119] As Rowland Evans and Robert Novak observe, the violence and public attention meant that "any further delay of civil rights legislation was out of the question."[120] The administration finally signaled that it would introduce a major bill. Civil rights activists—including representatives from the AFL-CIO, Democratic Study Group, and Leadership Council on Civil Rights—pressed the administration to include strong fair employment, public accommodations, and desegregation language. The bill itself, however, was more limited: it did not include fair employment practices, restricted the public accommodations provisions to enterprises with a substantial impact on interstate commerce, and left the executive branch with discretion on whether to cut off funds to schools that failed to integrate.[121] Even with these limitations, Kennedy's program was hailed as a bold civil rights push. But there should be no mistaking that the pressure to act came from civil rights protests and the ensuing southern violence: a few months after the administration bill was introduced, the *Washington Post*'s Chalmers Roberts concluded that "Kennedy had no intention of pushing civil rights legislation this year until the eruption in Birmingham convinced him it was imperative."[122]

When the bill went to the House of Representatives, Judiciary Committee chairman Celler referred the bill to a subcommittee with a clear civil rights majority. The subcommittee pushed the bill well to the left, expanding the public accommodations provision, adding a fair employment practices section, making the cutoff of federal funds to recalcitrant school districts mandatory, and extending voting rights protections. The administration argued that this bill could not gain sufficient Republican support to pass the Senate and persuaded Celler and other liberals to back a bipartisan compromise in the full committee that was stronger than the initial Kennedy bill but not quite as bold as the subcommittee's alternative.[123] The revised bill included a fair employment practices title and a broad provision for the attorney general to intervene in civil rights cases, though the voting rights section was watered down.

The employment provisions of the act constituted a crucial addition; Lichtenstein argues that "the trade union movement was primarily responsible for the addition of FEPC, now rechristened the Equal Employment Opportunities Commission (EEOC) to the original Kennedy bill."[124] To win Republican votes, it was necessary that the antidiscrimination provisions apply to unions as well, a provision that Meany backed.[125] Reuther occupied a high place in the civil rights councils advocating for a strong bill, and the UAW worked with the LCCR to keep up grassroots pressure on Congress and the White House to act.[126]

Following Kennedy's assassination, the big question was whether the southerner Johnson would pursue Kennedy's civil rights program.[127] Johnson's embrace of the civil rights bill—and his success in pushing it through Congress—is generally seen as the crucial moment in the civil rights realignment.[128] Indeed, Johnson's famous quote about having "delivered the South to the Republican Party" encapsulates the view that the Texan was the key player in the civil rights drama.

But Johnson's civil rights stand emerged from a clear political calculus: the main threat to holding on to the Democrats' presidential nomination in 1964 was a challenge from the left—most ominously from Robert Kennedy. To forestall such a challenge, Johnson had to establish himself as a liberal. Given the redefinition of liberalism that had taken place over the preceding two decades—and amid the intense civil rights protest movement of the early 1960s—taking a strong civil rights stand was essential to proving Johnson's liberal bona fides.

As soon as he took office, Johnson met individually with key civil rights leaders—including Martin Luther King, Jr., the NAACP's Roy Wilkins, and Joseph Rauh—and made clear he would push hard for enactment of strong legislation.[129] Johnson later told Doris Kearns that "I knew that if I didn't get out in front of this issue, they [the liberals] would get me. They'd throw up my background against me.... I couldn't let that happen. I had to produce a civil rights bill that was even stronger than the one they'd have gotten if Kennedy had lived. Without this, I'd be dead before I could even begin."[130] As Evans and Novak note, Johnson had less flexibility to compromise on the specifics than Kennedy: "if he trimmed away as Kennedy probably would have done to wedge the bill through the Senate, Johnson would be excoriated by the civil rights movement, by organized labor, and by liberals. On this issue, Johnson's political imperatives as a *Southern* President foreclosed compromise."[131]

With the intense civil rights mobilization on the ground—and the vicious, violent response to that mobilization—the nation's attention was focused squarely on civil rights, meaning that Johnson's advocacy could not be merely rhetorical. The new president not only provided a clear endorsement of Kennedy's civil rights program in his first address to Congress days after the assassination but also threw himself and his administration into the challenge of rounding up the necessary votes. In doing so, Johnson turned a constraint—his need to win over northern liberals—into an opportunity to push forward a broad-ranging liberal program, with civil rights as a centerpiece but also including the Great Society's educational and antipoverty initiatives.

The story of the passage of the Civil Rights Act of 1964 has been told from a wide range of perspectives. All credible accounts must reckon with the critical role of the civil rights movement's nonviolent activism, which generated the public attention and pressure that created the sense of urgency for political elites to act. Where some accounts also emphasize Johnson's personal importance, others rightly draw attention to a range of other legislative actors, including Hubert Humphrey, Judiciary Committee Republican William McCulloch, and Senate Republican leader Everett Dirksen.[132]

Nonetheless, two key facets of the complex battle warrant emphasis in evaluating Johnson's role in the civil rights realignment. First, the all-important negotiations with Dirksen and the Republicans to gain the necessary votes for cloture primarily involved concessions that weakened the bill to meet GOP objections. In other words, while Republicans provided crucial votes for the bill's passage, they sought more moderate legislation than the president, Democratic leaders, and northern liberal Democrats. In particular, Dirksen had serious doubts about the increased federal power inherent in the legislation.[133] Liberal Democrats worked with civil rights groups to stir up as much grassroots pressure as possible to persuade Dirksen to swallow these objections.[134] The concessions Dirksen gained were far less than he asked for initially but did impose limitations on the EEOC's enforcement powers, barred racial preferences, protected employer ability tests, and made clear that the integration provisions did not affect de facto segregation.[135]

Second, in pursuing the strongest possible bill, Johnson was keenly aware that excessive compromises risked a revolt on his left flank. The efforts of core constituents within the party he hoped to lead had moved the proposed legislation to the left before he took office. He understood that the liberal, labor, and civil rights groups essential for a smooth nomination campaign were scrutinizing his every action on civil rights and were treating his stance on the issue as the single most important indicator of his commitment to the liberal cause. In that context, any compromises had to have the support of key civil rights and labor leaders. The president's message to Senate Democratic leaders that they must gain Robert Kennedy's approval for any decisions on the civil rights bill was a clear indicator of Johnson's goal of inoculating himself against a challenge from the left.[136] Johnson's uncanny legislative skills warrant appreciation, but his deployment of those skills to pass the strongest possible civil rights bill was rooted in a sharp political imperative.

The 1964 election appeared to vindicate Johnson's strategy in the short term. After coasting to his party's nomination, the president trounced Barry Goldwater in November. As chapter 10 discusses, Goldwater's rise reflected a deep-seated shift in the GOP that was every bit as important as liberals' capture of the Democratic Party, and one with implications for the national balance of power that were a far cry from the 1964 election outcome.

The drive for civil rights legislation continued after the election. Although Johnson advised King in December 1964 that a pause was necessary before moving on to securing full voting rights for African Americans, direct action by movement activists forced the issue again to the top of the agenda.[137] King led a series of demonstrations in Selma, Alabama, starting in mid-January 1965. Thousands of protestors, including King, were soon jailed.[138] The violent repression by state authorities when King attempted to lead a march from Selma to Montgomery proved to be the final straw: television coverage of state troopers attacking peaceful protestors with tear gas, whips, and clubs galvanized public attention. Johnson quickly responded with a speech before a joint session of Congress where he backed the bill making its way through Congress and famously echoed King's formulation that "we shall overcome."[139]

The unity—outside of the South—that greeted Johnson's call would soon give way to a far more divisive racial politics. These divisions and strains—both within the Democratic coalition and in the country as a whole—were never far below the surface and set crucial limits on what civil rights liberals would accomplish (see chapter 11). But for the moment, advocates could celebrate twin legislative accomplishments—the Civil Rights Act of 1964 and the Voting Rights Act of 1965—that reflected the culmination of a decades-long campaign.

CONCLUSION

National party leaders occupy a seemingly ambiguous position in the story of the civil rights realignment. As African American activists and voters entered the Democratic coalition starting in the 1930s, Democratic leaders were generally slow to respond. Franklin Roosevelt was the first of several top Democrats to temporize when it came to civil rights, in the hope of holding together his party's increasingly uneasy North-South coalition. With the exception of the 1948 convention floor fight, national leaders typically proved successful in adopting a platform that avoided the kind of strong language that would lead to a southern bolt. Meanwhile, the party nominated presidential candidates who were broadly acceptable to both northern liberals and southern conservatives.

This rough balancing act fell apart amid the intensified civil rights mobilization of the late 1950s and the 1960s. By pushing the issue to the top of the nation's political agenda, the civil rights movement made it much harder for political leaders to avoid taking a clear stand. The position that Democratic leaders ultimately adopted—supporting strong civil rights legislation— was rooted in the remaking of the Democratic Party that had begun in the late 1930s. By the mid-1940s "liberalism," as it was conventionally understood, included support for civil rights as a key marker. A coalition of African Americans, unions, Jews, and urban liberals had worked successfully to move northern state Democratic parties into the pro–civil rights camp. They had also won over a solid majority of northern Democrats in the House of Representatives, who cooperated with civil rights activists to force initiatives onto the floor for a vote. The same individuals and groups who were the main foot soldiers and allies of the civil rights movement were also key members of the urban liberal coalition that was at the core of the northern Democratic Party.

With northern state parties firmly in the hands of civil rights liberals who had come to view decisive action as imperative, the South found itself isolated and with far fewer votes in national councils—such as nominating conventions—than their northern counterparts. Prior to the direct action campaign and violence of the late 1950s and early 1960s, southerners could withstand their minority status through alliances with top national leaders, such as Stevenson, Johnson, and Rayburn, who were not keen to see a liberal takeover of the entire party. These leaders were centrally concerned with the damage to the national party of losing the South and also may well have wondered whether a majority of voters nationwide favored forceful action on civil rights.[140] But even nationally minded leaders—such as DNC chair Butler, and eventually Presidents Kennedy and Johnson—altered their calculus amid the intense focus on civil rights brought about by the protests and violence broadcast nightly on the national news.

This account of political change challenges the idea that there was a single pivotal moment at which the Democratic Party became a pro–civil rights party. As a federal party in which both northern liberals and southern conservatives enjoyed independent electoral power bases, no single set of interests and no single logic dominated the party from the late 1930s through the 1960s. Instead, the contending sides fought a long-term war for control, in which liberals gradually gained the upper hand. Within the North—which controlled a solid majority of votes at the Democratic national convention— the constituency changes of the mid- to late 1930s allowed civil rights supporters to capture state parties and to win over rank-and-file House members over the next decade. In this initial period, civil rights advocates succeeded in making civil rights a key element of the liberal program, but they still had to contend with national leaders who struggled to keep the South inside the party tent.

These national leaders finally gave ground in the late 1950s and early 1960s in response to the intense mobilization campaign undertaken by the civil rights movement. The creation of the Democratic Advisory Council, the 1960 platform fight in which liberals were, for the first time, in control of the party machinery, Kennedy's 1963 legislative initiative, and Johnson's relentless 1964–65 drive each qualify as important moments in solidifying the association between the national Democratic Party and civil rights liberalism.

But stepping back, we ought to see these maneuvers by national leaders as a product of the confluence of two distinct but related political trajectories. The coalitional and ideological transformation of the Democratic Party that began with the entry of the CIO and African American voters in the mid- to late 1930s meant that the pressure to take a pro–civil rights position would be stronger for Democratic leaders than for Republican elites. However, overcoming national leaders' interest in avoiding a clear stand would require a campaign of direct action by civil rights advocates that would bring their concerns to the top of the nation's political agenda. By thinking of parties as complex historical composites and of political change in terms of multiple, intersecting trajectories, we gain a richer understanding of the contributions of both movement activists and party elites in national Democrats' ultimate embrace of racial liberalism.

CHAPTER 10

Lincoln's Party No More

THE TRANSFORMATION OF THE GOP

IN ACCOUNTS OF the racial realignment, Barry Goldwater often occupies a position that is the mirror image of Lyndon Johnson's. Where the southerner Johnson overcame his ties to arch-segregationists and decisively moved his party to the left on civil rights, Goldwater—despite his past NAACP membership—forged the GOP's alliance with southern racial conservatives. Goldwater voted against the Civil Rights Act of 1964 and campaigned for president on a platform that found common cause with southerners furious at Johnson's civil rights advocacy. After the Goldwater campaign of 1964, Republicans would no longer be identified as occupying a similar position to Democrats' on civil rights.[1]

But just as Johnson's racial liberalism had deep roots in the Democratic Party, Goldwater's rise reflected long-standing currents within the GOP. The Arizona Republican played an important role in bringing those currents together and articulating them in a politically powerful way, but the GOP's alliance with southern racial conservatives found a strong foundation in the opinions of ordinary Republican partisans, activists, and officeholders, and in institutional changes that provided a vehicle for southern racial conservatives to become an important constituency in nominating conventions.

Indeed, much of the basis for Republicans to adopt a more racially conservative position on civil rights was in place by the 1940s. As shown in chapter 5, white Republican voters in the North tended to be more racially conservative than their Democratic counterparts from the late 1930s onward, and economically conservative Republicans were especially likely to be racially conservative. The survey evidence suggests that the same voters who expressed skepticism of expanding the New Deal welfare state and promoting labor rights were, in general, also skeptical of calls for vigorous governmental action to secure African Americans' civil rights.

At the same time, Republicans' support among African Americans had begun a precipitous decline with the 1936 election. Many Republican officials came to believe that it was unlikely that African American voters would return to the party, particularly given that African Americans tended to be closer to northern Democrats not just on civil rights policy but on a range of other issues as well (see chapter 6). As such, the pull of African American voters on most GOP politicians was quite limited. There continued to be Republicans who advocated that the party pursue African American votes, but the persistent shift of African American partisanship to the Democrats tilted this debate in favor of those promoting an alternative strategy.

Faced with no important constituency within the GOP pushing for a strong pro–civil rights stand, midlevel party actors provided less civil rights support than their Democratic counterparts did by the mid-1940s (see chapters 7 and 8). As northern Democratic state parties increasingly included civil rights in their platforms and pursued action in state legislatures, Republicans took a more guarded stance in state platforms and often blocked bills from coming to a vote in state legislatures. Meanwhile, rank-and-file House Republicans gave less support to initiatives such as antilynching legislation than they had in the past and opposed the passage of fair employment legislation. The typical House Republican—an economic conservative representing a relatively rural district—had little interest in promoting civil rights.

This chapter first asks why the national Republican Party—as represented by its platform and presidential nominees—continued to express at least a mildly progressive stance on civil rights for so many years after the base of the party had moved to the right of northern Democrats on the issue. Starting in 1937, as southern Democratic elites first became identified with opposition to the New Deal, political entrepreneurs and journalists began to discuss the viability of a conservative North-South alliance. The rise of the "conservative coalition" in Congress showed that northern Republicans and southern Democrats could make common cause on a range of issues. Yet for the next two decades, the GOP repeatedly chose presidential candidates who spurned the kind of all-out appeal to states' rights that might cement an alliance with southern racial conservatives.

This disconnect reflected the internal power dynamics in the national GOP. During these years the moderate northeastern wing of the party had decisive influence over presidential nominations, repeatedly defeating the more conservative wing associated with Ohio senator Robert Taft. Where many Taft Republicans viewed an alliance with the South as the path both to conservative control of the national party and to a potential governing majority, members of the northeastern faction feared alienating African American voters who were increasingly concentrated in the big northern swing states. With the southern GOP largely a shell party in the hands of patronage-minded politicians, the Taft wing lacked the votes to dominate the GOP national convention. Instead, conservative candidates for the presidential nomination lost out to moderates who relied heavily on overwhelming support in states such as New York and New Jersey.

Yet even the moderates at the top of the ticket increasingly turned to southern whites as a potential source of votes in the late 1940s and the 1950s, while paying less attention to African Americans. This meant adopting a straddle on civil rights designed to appeal in the South without entirely writing off northern African Americans.[2] In contrast to the situation in the Democratic Party, this straddle was the site of little contestation for Republicans. Where the Democratic conventions repeatedly featured pitched battles on matters of race, civil rights was generally not a major issue at the GOP conventions. The small number of African American delegates continued to advocate for a strong stand, but they were far more isolated than their Democratic counterparts given that no other group within the party viewed civil rights as a priority. For this straddle to move to an all-out alliance with the South, however, would require a change in the internal party balance in favor of the conservative wing.

The chapter proceeds to ask why the national GOP eventually did embrace southern racial conservatives. A crucial part of the answer is that southern Republican Party organizations entered the national GOP as full players. When conservative politicians first began to talk about a realignment in the late 1930s, and again in the early 1950s, there was no GOP organization on the ground in most southern states. But President Eisenhower invested heavily in building genuine Republican Party organizations in the South. Eisenhower hoped that this new GOP would be rooted in middle-class, urban southerners motivated by issues other than segregation.[3] However, the intense civil rights mobilization of the late 1950s and northern Democrats' increased control of the national Democratic Party spurred a growing number of angry southern whites to enter the new Republican organizations. By 1959–62 the conservative movement had captured these organizations, tipping the balance in the national GOP away from the Northeast.

With the South a real player in nomination politics, the conservative wing of the party was finally in a position to nominate a candidate of its choice, one who would cement the long-sought alliance between the Taft wing of the GOP and the Dixiecrat wing of the Democratic Party. The conservative activists found such a candidate in Goldwater, who emerged in the late 1950s as a spokesperson for an aggressive rendition of conservatism that embraced the "states' rights" position on race relations. Goldwater's stance echoed that of earlier advocates of realignment, but the rise of southern Republican parties, along with the hostility of many northern rank-and-file Republican voters and officials toward civil rights advances, put him in a position to succeed.

In several ways, the shift in the national GOP's stance parallels that of the Democrats. As with the Democrats, the Republican transformation was rooted in the views of mass- and midlevel party actors. Ordinary Republican voters' skepticism of civil rights legislation, alongside the movement of

African Americans out of the GOP camp, provided a permissive backdrop for efforts to forge a coalition with white southerners. Conservative Republicans—including a handful of top leaders—pushed for such a coalition as soon as signs of southern alienation from the New Deal appeared in the late 1930s, but most party leaders preferred to avoid the kind of explicit alliance with southern segregationists that they believed would undermine the party's standing in the Northeast. Just as state parties provided a power base for northern Democrats to pursue their battle to move their party to the left on civil rights, conservatives drew on the new southern Republican Party organizations as a key resource in their struggle to defeat the northeastern moderates atop the GOP. In both cases, the "party" was not a coherent entity governed by a single logic or set of interests; instead, it was a battlefield, in which the contending sides prosecuted their battle for control while drawing on their own independent electoral bases.

There also was a distinct ideological element to the drive to bring together the conservative Republicans of the Midwest and southern segregationists, paralleling the ideological shift occurring among the Democrats. Starting in the late 1930s, Republican advocates of a coalition with the South emphasized the fit between their antistatist, limited government attacks on the New Deal and southerners' interest in defending Jim Crow. "States' rights" became a language that united criticism of the New Deal's economic policies with resistance to government policies to prevent racial discrimination. These conservative Republicans embraced and sought to reinforce the ideological cleavage that the rise of the CIO, the entry of African Americans into the New Deal coalition, and southern reactionaries' turn against labor-oriented liberalism had opened up. Ardent New Dealers and their conservative Republican opponents could agree that the central issue in politics was whether the national government would have the power to reorder economic and social relations against the will of the states. The alignment between racial and economic conservatism evident at the mass level by the late 1930s shows that this cleavage was not confined to elites.

Indeed, although some accounts have noted the role of intellectual elites in bringing racial conservatism together with economic conservatism, the process began long before William F. Buckley's *National Review* crashed onto the political scene in 1955.[4] Political entrepreneurs, acting on the ground, saw the coalitional opportunity created by southern opposition to the labor-infused direction of the New Deal and articulated a conservative vision emphasizing states' rights and limited government that was well suited to appeal in the South. These efforts failed to capture the national GOP when they were first launched in 1937 and revived in 1950–52, but they finally succeeded once southerners recognized that the national Democratic Party was in the firm control of their enemies.

One important difference between the Democratic and Republican stories, however, has to do with the relationship between the civil rights movement and the actions of top party leaders. Among Democrats, it was the intensification of the civil rights movement that forced the hand of top party leaders. The civil rights movement played a more indirect, permissive role for Republicans. By compelling national Democrats to take a clear stand, the civil rights movement exacerbated the disaffection of southern conservatives, widening the opening for the Goldwater movement to win over converts in the region.[5] In the North, economically conservative Republican voters had long shown skepticism toward civil rights initiatives; the turmoil of the 1960s helped turn this skepticism into outright anger, which again became a key resource for the Goldwater movement. From this perspective, the Goldwater movement capitalized on the intersection of two initially distinct political trajectories: the coalitional changes at lower levels of the party system dating back to the New Deal years and the disruption sparked by the civil rights movement.

The next section traces the relationship between the national GOP's moderate-conservative cleavage and the party's treatment of civil rights in the presidential campaigns of the 1940s and 1950s. The chapter then turns to the early conservative efforts to forge an alliance with disillusioned southern Democrats, and the party-building efforts in the South that ultimately paved the way for the success of those efforts. The final section reassesses Goldwater's rise, arguing that it found a strong basis at the mass and mid-levels of the party, and in conservatives' widespread reaction against the disruption associated with the civil rights movement.

THE NATIONAL GOP AND CIVIL RIGHTS, 1940–56

Political observers of the 1940s and 1950s often distinguished between the GOP's conservative congressional wing and its moderate presidential candidates.[6] The congressional wing found its base in the Midwest and Plains states and was epitomized by "Mr. Republican," Robert Taft.[7] The heart of the conservative coalition in Congress, these Republicans not only eagerly worked with southern Democrats to attack New Deal labor policies but also fought against enactment of an FEPC with enforcement powers and often cooperated with southerners to stymie other civil rights initiatives (see chapter 8). The sentimental choice of party conservatives in the 1948 and 1952 presidential races, Taft was a leading opponent of a strong FEPC, observing in 1946 that "it is just about as difficult to prevent discrimination against negroes as it is to prevent discrimination against Republicans. We know the latter is impossible."[8]

However, the more moderate, northeastern wing of the party had predominant control over presidential nominations in the 1940s and 1950s. The two biggest delegate blocs at the convention belonged to New York and Pennsylvania.[9] When combined with New Jersey and New England, these nine states controlled a majority of the delegates required to win the nomination.[10] Party leaders from these states generally believed that Republicans' path back to power ran through the big urban states of the Northeast and upper Midwest, where a moderate party image was an asset. Robert Novak observes that starting in 1940, realistic top GOP leaders saw the need to nominate presidential candidates "to the left of the party consensus" in order to compete with the Democrats.[11] These leaders wrote particularly strong civil rights planks in 1940 and 1944, when they still held out hope of winning back a substantial share of African American votes.

In many ways, the 1940 campaign represents the modern high point of forthright civil rights advocacy by the national GOP. The party's nominee, Wendell Willkie, was clearly identified with the most liberal party faction, pledging to maintain most of Roosevelt's New Deal policies.[12] The three leading candidates initially had been the isolationist conservatives Taft and Arthur Vandenberg (R-MI), and New York attorney general Thomas Dewey, who had avoided a clear position on the war. Amid news of the German blitzkrieg and France's surrender, the internationalist Willkie emerged the victor, riding a last-minute popular wave of support. On the critical vote in the 1940 contest, Willkie trounced Taft by a 223 to 33 margin in the Northeast and Mid-Atlantic states, while losing the rest of the delegates by a 344 to 208 margin.[13]

Willkie worked hard to win over African American voters. The 1940 platform declared that "discrimination in the civil service, the army, navy, and all other branches of the Government must cease." It also called for ensuring universal suffrage for African Americans and for antilynching legislation. Willkie appealed for African American support in his acceptance speech and in several campaign speeches, in which he contrasted his program with the administration's lack of action on behalf of African Americans.[14] In a mid-September Chicago speech, Willkie declared that "there are some things we must do before this democracy can claim to be reaching anything near perfection. And one of these is to completely eliminate in this country any discrimination between people because of race or religion."[15] Sugrue observes that Willkie took a "pro–civil rights position more forceful than any that had come from the party of Lincoln since the last days of Reconstruction."[16] Despite Willkie's vigorous civil rights advocacy, however, the GOP won just 32 percent of the African American vote.[17]

Although Willkie's liberalism across a range of issues placed him outside of the mainstream of even the northeastern GOP, his successor, Thomas Dewey, also came from the party's moderate wing. Dewey had spoken out

forcefully against racial discrimination during his 1942 gubernatorial campaign in New York, although he also received much criticism in the African
American press prior to the 1944 election for initially failing to vigorously
support proposed fair employment legislation in New York.[18]

As part of the national GOP's continuing efforts to appeal to African
American voters, the 1944 platform supported an investigation of discrimination in the armed forces, antilynching legislation, a constitutional amendment to end the poll tax, and "the establishment by Federal legislation of
a permanent Fair Employment Practice Commission." The FEPC plank was
especially important, earning praise from the NAACP's Walter White as "unequivocal and excellent" and providing a sharp contrast with the Democrats' silence on the subject.[19] Despite these strong promises, Dewey spoke
less about civil rights during the campaign than had Willkie and did not
come out in favor of the FEPC legislation pending in Congress until just two
weeks before the election.[20]

Dewey's limited civil rights advocacy during the campaign was reflective
of the national GOP's ambivalence. The moderate, northeastern wing of the
party continued to hold out hope of winning African American votes in
swing states. Yet the base of the party—both its ordinary voters and its core
supporters in the business community—opposed fair employment legislation. The result was a platform endorsement of the FEPC but little effort to
back that promise up.

Indeed, some senior Republicans acknowledged the strategic calculus they
faced following Dewey's poor showing among African Americans, whom he
lost by a 68–32 percent margin.[21] In an especially frank statement, the incoming Republican Speaker of the House of Representatives—and former
Republican National Committee chair—Joe Martin (R-MA) told a prominent African American Republican leader in December 1946 that the "FEPC
plank (in the 1944 Republican platform) was a bid for the Negro vote, and
they didn't accept the bid .... I'll be frank with you. We are not going to pass
the FEPC bill, but it has nothing to do with the Negro vote. We are supported mainly by New England and Middle Western industrialists who would
stop their contributions if we passed a law that would compel them to stop
religious as well as racial discrimination in employment."[22]

The GOP nominated the moderate Dewey over Taft once again in 1948
but this time dropped its platform endorsement of an FEPC, instead offering vague support for "such legislation as may be necessary" to maintain
"equal opportunity to work," along with a call for an end to the poll tax and
segregation in the armed forces.[23] African American leaders judged the platform to be a step back, with A. Philip Randolph leading a group of protesters after the platform committee refused to hear complaints from African
American delegates.[24] But the plank reflected national leaders' effort to straddle the issue. With southern Democrats in open revolt against the Truman

administration, Dewey's campaign hoped that a vague position on civil rights would allow the Republican to compete in both the urban North and the South. Dewey barely discussed civil rights in his campaign, offering just a few isolated mentions and generally ignoring African American voters.[25]

Dewey's team even sent his conservative rival, Taft, into the South to campaign, where he told a South Carolina audience that the Republican Party's policies "are far more in accord with the views of the South than the policies of the Truman administration." Southern white newspapers interpreted Taft's statement "to mean that a Dewey administration will 'go easy' on civil rights."[26] Taft also told a Florida audience that Republicans wanted to promote material gains while "maintaining the liberty of the local community," which again was interpreted as a nod to the states' rights position on race.[27] Dewey himself did not travel to the South, but his campaign hoped that the mixed signals—a platform vaguely supportive of civil rights coupled with the use of conservative surrogates in the South—would win southern votes without costing support in the North. But in the end Dewey polled just 23 percent of the African American vote and did not win a single southern state.[28]

The moderate northeastern wing maintained control of the national party in the 1952 campaign. Eisenhower defeated Taft for the nomination by winning the vast majority of delegates from the Northeast. On the key convention ballot, Eisenhower won the Northeast and Mid-Atlantic states by a 300–68 margin over Taft. He actually lost the rest of the country, by a 432–295 margin. New York loomed especially large, giving Eisenhower a 92–4 landslide.[29]

Although Eisenhower, like Dewey, was the candidate of the party's moderate northeastern wing, his team sought a milder civil rights plank than the party had adopted in 1944 and 1948. The platform endorsed "federal action toward the elimination" of lynching and poll taxes, along with "enacting federal legislation to further just and equitable treatment in the area of discriminatory employment practices." But it specified that action on job discrimination "should not duplicate state efforts to end such practices; [and] should not set up another huge bureaucracy." In a clear appeal to states' rights, the platform asserted that "it is the primary responsibility of each State to order and control its own domestic institutions, and this power, reserved to the states, is essential to the maintenance of our Federal Republic." The federal government's role is to take "supplemental action within its constitutional jurisdiction" to oppose discrimination.

The forty African American delegates met to discuss the proposed platform and agreed that it represented a substantial retreat. But they found themselves isolated within the party and were persuaded not to introduce futile and divisive amendments on the floor. The plank was ultimately adopted with little struggle.[30] The *Washington Post* observed that the "Democrats' preoccupation with the civil rights issue contrasted with the relatively little time consumed by the Republicans on the problem during the past two weeks."[31] With no consequential constituency within the party pushing for a strong civil rights stand, Eisenhower's team had the flexibility to pursue a tepid plank with little surrounding controversy.

The vague platform gave Eisenhower the opportunity to compete effectively in much of the South. The Democratic governors of Louisiana and South Carolina, Robert Kennon and Jimmy Byrnes, publicly supported Eisenhower over Adlai Stevenson, as did Harry Byrd of Virginia.[32] Eisenhower was the first Republican in years to campaign actively in the South, appearing with leading Democratic politicians such as Byrnes.[33] While making it clear that he believed in equal opportunity, Eisenhower avoided emphasizing civil rights in his speeches. Eisenhower's refusal to back the FEPC gave him a critical edge over Stevenson in the battle for southern white voters.[34] A cartoon printed in the *Defender*—"Ike at the Dike" (fig. 10.1)—was one indication of African Americans' concerns about Eisenhower's appeals to southern segregationists.

By October, fifty-six southern newspapers had endorsed Eisenhower, compared to twenty-nine for Stevenson.[35] Meanwhile, press coverage pointed to the Republican's southern potential amid dissatisfaction with Democrats on civil rights.[36] On Election Day Eisenhower won approximately 50 percent of the white vote in the supposedly solid South.[37] While most of his gains came in the peripheral South, Eisenhower received 49 percent of the vote in South Carolina.

A similar dynamic played out four years later in 1956. A handful of Republicans seeking election in states with large African American populations—such as Everett Dirksen in Illinois—pushed for a strong platform stance. But observers pointed to the small audiences at the GOP platform hearings on civil rights, which contrasted with the heavy attendance among Democrats. In the end, Eisenhower dictated the plank's contents—a vague straddle—and faced criticism mainly from the small number of African American Republicans.[38] Eisenhower once again ran as a moderate on civil rights, avoiding a clear stand on the *Brown* decision. As in 1952, Republicans did well in the Rim South; Eisenhower won Florida, Texas, Louisiana, Virginia, Kentucky, and Tennessee and came close in North Carolina (49%) and Arkansas (46%).

Still, the Eisenhower administration proved willing to send troops into Little Rock to enforce the *Brown* decision in 1957, while also promoting and signing the (admittedly weak) Civil Rights Act of 1957 (see below). These decisions underscore the continuing reluctance of national Republican leaders to cement an alliance with states' rights southerners. Other voices within the party—particularly from its conservative wing—were more eager to foster such a realignment, which they believed would shift political power away from the "me-too" Republicans of the Northeast and offer a genuine conservative alternative to New Deal liberalism. For these efforts to succeed,

Ike At The Dike... *by commodore*

FIGURE 10.1. "Ike at the Dike," cartoon from 1956 campaign. Reproduced with permission from the *Chicago Defender*.

however, southern whites had to first abandon hope of winning back control of the Democratic Party, and genuine GOP organizations were needed to incorporate these alienated southern segregationists.

REPUBLICANS TURN TO THE SOUTH

The push for an explicit alliance between conservative Republicans and southern segregationists began in 1937 as southern Democratic elites first became disenchanted with the incorporation of African Americans and industrial labor into the New Deal coalition. In a November 1937 letter to Carter Glass (D-VA), former senator (and arch-conservative) George Moses (R-NH) wrote, "You and I have often discussed realignment but you have always raised the color question. This condition no longer exists. Jim Farley and the Roosevelt largess have made the colored vote in the North impregnably Democratic. Therefore, with the color line obliterated, why cannot those of us who are free, white, and twenty-one get together and do a job as effective as Mussolini did when he made his march upon Rome?"[39]

Meanwhile, Alf Landon—still smarting from his landslide defeat in 1936—talked of creating a "coalition ticket" for 1940 that would unite southern conservatives with Republicans. Landon asked Arthur Vandenberg to "explore with some of your Southern Democrat friends just what we would be up against in those states in the way of getting a new name on the ticket." Vandenberg replied that "my 'hunch' runs in [the] direction" of a 1940 realignment, and he explored ideas for a coalition ticket over the next year.[40]

In seeking such an alliance, prominent Republicans emphasized that their party was the true heir to the Jeffersonian tradition of limited government and states' rights. Highlighting this ideological commonality, Republican National Committee chairman John Hamilton told the Alabama state GOP convention in 1938 that the Republicans are the "only organized champion of the Jeffersonian philosophy" and asserted that "there is today no insurmountable barrier between the real Democrats of the South and the Republican party."[41] Hamilton argued that only "deep-seated loyalty that comes from years of loving and serving their party keeps many southern Democrats today from formally and openly repudiating it under its present leadership" and claimed—with no irony intended—that the South must join with Republicans "if America is to be preserved as a land of opportunity without classes, if free enterprise—for which the south has always fought—is to be reestablished."[42] Hamilton followed the Alabama speech with a visit to Monticello on July 4, 1938, where he laid a wreath at Jefferson's grave, and with an address at the University of Virginia on the "Aims of the Republican Party."[43] Hamilton's overtures attracted the notice of the NAACP's Walter White, who wrote to the RNC chair to express concern that individuals "high in the councils" of the GOP had told him that "the Republican Party's former attitude towards the Negro had been the chief, if not the sole, barrier to breaking up the solid South and that since the Republican Party had lost the Negro vote it was now determined to go after the South."[44]

In Congress, Vandenberg worked actively with Josiah Bailey (D-NC) in an effort to unite conservative Democrats and Republicans behind a formal statement of principles. Bailey drafted the so-called Conservative Manifesto in December 1937 following a series of meetings attended by anti–New Deal Democrats and Republicans. The manifesto included "maintaining states' rights" as one of its core points. Though not aiming to create a new party,

Bailey and Vandenberg hoped to forge a broad foundation for conservatives to stand on, consolidating opposition to the New Deal and crystallizing opinion among dissident groups.[45] But Senate Republican leader Charles McNary of Oregon—a member of the party's moderate wing—sabotaged the effort by disclosing the plot to the press. Vandenberg was furious at McNary, writing that "premature publicity—thanks to treachery—ended the episode. The next time we want to plan a patriotically dramatic contribution to the welfare of the country, we shall let no one in who is not tried and true."[46]

Still, it is an oversimplification to attribute the failure of the realignment push to McNary. Instead, it spoke to the significant challenges facing the idea of uniting Republicans and conservative Democrats in a formal coalition. Given Roosevelt's extraordinary popularity among southern voters, few southern Democrats in Congress were eager for a formal break with the administration. Moreover, with the national Democratic Party's continued willingness to straddle on civil rights, most southern Democrats believed their best strategy was to fight within the party apparatus. The failure of Roosevelt's own 1938 purge effort—which also aimed to create an ideological realignment—meant that southern conservatives could continue to win and hold office as Democrats for years to come.

From the GOP side, party leaders came to believe that Roosevelt's second-term struggles made it possible to compete for majority status without the need for an alliance with southern conservatives. The Republicans' huge gains in the 1938 midterms—eighty-one House seats, six Senate seats, and a dozen governorships—sparked hope that the GOP could soon win back the White House. Diluting the party's brand by allying with southern Democrats seemed unnecessary—and potentially counterproductive—given that more optimistic outlook.[47] Furthermore, as noted above, the northeastern wing of the party that controlled presidential nominations favored moderate candidates who could compete in swing states such as New York, New Jersey, and Pennsylvania, rather than the sort of arch-conservatives who might bring together the rural Midwest and the South.

By 1950, in the aftermath of the Dixiecrat 1948 bolt and amid deep southern anger over Truman's civil rights advocacy, a group of conservative Republicans, frustrated with their party's continued failures in presidential elections, revived the idea of a regional realignment rooted in appeals to "states' rights." The two leading supporters of this movement were strong backers of the conservative, Taft wing of the party: incoming Republican National Committee chairman Guy Gabrielson and Senator Karl Mundt of South Dakota.

In 1950 Gabrielson embarked on a speaking tour of the South in an effort to drum up support for a proposed "unity ticket" of Republicans and southern Democrats in the next presidential election. Gabrielson proposed that the Dixiecrats and Republicans nominate the same men for president and vice president. This would allow the two groups to coalesce behind a common slate, without requiring southerners to mark a ballot for a candidate labeled as "Republican." One of the Dixiecrat participants in the discussions referred to the idea as a "trial marriage at the top."[48]

Gabrielson again toured the South in 1951, noting in a Little Rock speech that southern anger at Truman had made it the GOP's "great hunting ground."[49] In a speech in Atlanta, Gabrielson claimed the GOP would pitch its southern campaign around the idea of "states running their own affairs and the cutting down of Federal bureaucracy in Washington."[50] Gabrielson made an even more explicit appeal for Dixiecrat support during a February 1952 speech to Alabama Republicans, in which he argued that only semantics separated Dixiecrats from the GOP: "The Dixiecrat party believes in states' rights. That's what the Republican Party believes in."[51] Once again, conservative Republicans were drawing on the same ideological appeal that would later form the basis of Goldwater's southern drive.

Gabrielson's efforts were reinforced by Mundt, who traveled the South in 1950–52, giving a series of speeches touting the idea of a realignment. Mundt's Senate colleagues appointed him as vice chair of the Senate Republican Campaign Committee in 1951, as "part of a long-range program to build up Republican strength in the South."[52] Mundt maintained that Republicans and southern Democrats have similar philosophies and should unite on a common ticket for the 1952 election in order to defeat the "socialistic" New Deal Democrats.[53] To foster this coalition, the Republican Party would select a nominee who was acceptable to the South and would drop from its platform planks that were "repugnant to the South and an insult to your traditions."[54] Mundt was even willing to go so far as to push for a states' rights southerner—such as Harry Byrd or Richard Russell—as the Republican vice presidential nominee.[55]

A handful of other conservative Republican senators, such as Joe McCarthy of Wisconsin and Owen Brewster of Maine, endorsed Mundt's effort.[56] By the fall of 1951 Mundt and his plan had received enormous publicity, including a cover story in *U.S. News and World Report*, interviews on every important syndicated talk show, and a debate segment on CBS radio's *Peoples' Platform*, a popular roundtable-style debate program. During the CBS debate, Mundt advocated for a platform plank "in the field of discrimination" that returns to "the great and noble American concepts of states' rights which the New Deal today has entirely scuttled."[57] In another radio appearance, Mundt debated Hubert Humphrey, who agreed with the South Dakota conservative that having southern Democrats and Republicans in the same party would get the parties "cleared up on the basis of issues," quipping that a southern Democrat is just a "conservative Republican with a southern accent."[58]

A *Collier's* magazine exchange between Mundt and his chief liberal Republican critic, Representative Clifford Case of New Jersey, in July 1951 nicely summarized both the logic of Mundt's proposal and its risks. In his article, "Should the G.O.P. Merge with the Dixiecrats?," Mundt argued that the "South is the natural and logical source of new strength for the Republican party." Mundt cited the "strong political kinship" between southern Democrats and Republicans: "their viewpoint is similar, their fears are similar. They both stand against an overpowerful central government, and for maintenance of local and state responsibilities." The South Dakota senator sought to convince southern Democrats that their only hope was to ally with Republicans, since "there is not a chance for Southern Democrats to recapture their former party. It is irrevocably committed to a viewpoint that is not Southern, and to non-Southern special interest groups." Meanwhile, he claimed Republicans would be happy with a Harry Byrd (D-VA), Walter George (D-GA), or Richard Russell (D-GA) on their ticket. Mundt concluded that saving America from socialism "can't be done without Dixie. The key to America's political future is in the South."[59]

Case responded that America instead needed a forward-looking Republican Party that would ally itself with the "progressive forces in Southern labor, industry, and agriculture—not with the Dixiecrats." While Case admitted that Mundt's proposed realignment might win southern states for the GOP, he believed that these gains would be outweighed by the loss of electoral votes from the North. Case maintained that a Dixiecrat-Republican coalition could not win in New York, New Jersey, Pennsylvania, Michigan, or Connecticut—all of which Dewey had won in 1948. Instead, to build a national majority, the GOP needed to argue for progress on civil rights, housing, social security, and health care, while promising greater economy and efficiency than the Democrats.[60]

In thinking about the long-term viability of Case's and Mundt's alternative strategies, it is important to emphasize that Case's general liberal outlook placed him outside of the party's mainstream in Congress. Hailing from a liberal district in the Northeast, Case had ADA scores between 1950 and 1963 that ranged from a low of 61 (in 1951) to a high of 100 (in 1952). Similarly, his DW-NOMINATE score placed him well to the left of all but a handful of Republicans. By contrast, Mundt's first-dimension NOMINATE score was right at the Senate GOP median (0.26), and his ADA scores ranged from 0 to 25 during these years.

Nonetheless, Gabrielson's and Mundt's efforts did not come to fruition in the 1952 campaign. Case may have been far from the mainstream of the congressional GOP, but his reticence to forge an all-out alliance with the South was shared by other northeastern Republicans, who worried about creating an extreme party image in the closely contested northern states.[61] These northeastern and mid-Atlantic Republicans continued to dominate the

GOP nominating convention. At the same time, Truman's decision not to run for reelection, coupled with the ability of national Democratic elites to force a moderate civil rights platform through their convention, made it less likely that southern Democrats would break entirely from their party. Perhaps most important, however, Dwight Eisenhower's campaign seemed to demonstrate that a moderate candidate who straddled the civil rights divide could compete in both the big northern swing states and in much of the South. Yet Eisenhower would ultimately contribute to changes in the southern GOP that would redound to the benefit of his conservative party rivals.

Eisenhower and Party Building in the South

Eisenhower's electoral success had complicated implications for the GOP's long-term stance on civil rights. In keeping with his moderate political brand, Eisenhower sought to avoid taking a decisive stand that would alienate either southern whites or northern African Americans. Eisenhower's approach to the *Brown v. Board of Education* case is illustrative. The Truman administration had filed a brief challenging "separate but equal" in December 1952 as part of the pending *Brown* case, and the Supreme Court invited the new administration to take a position as well. In preparing the brief, Eisenhower instructed Attorney General Herbert Brownell not to take a direct position on the case and sought "to separate himself from personal accountability for the Justice Department's stance." Once the *Brown* decision was issued, Eisenhower pointedly refused to endorse it. A few years later he did send troops into Little Rock to enforce the Court's decision, but he also made it clear that this action was taken with considerable reluctance.[62]

Similarly, Eisenhower's strategy leading up to the adoption of the Civil Rights Act of 1957 reflected considerable ambivalence. Brownell—a New Yorker and one of the remaining strong civil rights liberals in the GOP—pushed for an aggressive bill, but Eisenhower and other senior administration officials collaborated with such Senate conservatives as Minority Leader William Knowland (R-CA) to water down the bill before it was introduced.[63] During the legislation's long journey through Congress, there were many occasions when it was not entirely clear whether the president supported all the elements of his own bill.[64] When Richard Russell attacked part 3 of the proposed legislation—which would have given the Justice Department broad power to seek injunctions to protect individuals from denials of civil rights—Eisenhower refused to endorse this crucial provision.[65] Indeed, in the days before part 3 was dropped, Eisenhower told a press conference that he could not take a position on the controversy because he had reread the section and "there were certain phrases I didn't completely understand."[66]

Eisenhower's moderation on civil rights went hand-in-hand with his effort to revive the Republican Party in the South. Eisenhower believed that his success in 1952 showed that the GOP could compete successfully in the region.[67] But where Mundt and Gabrielson had sought an alliance with the South rooted in an explicit appeal to states' rights conservatism, Eisenhower understood that allying with the Dixiecrats would boost the conservative wing of his party, threatening his effort to identify the GOP with "Modern Republicanism." Instead, Eisenhower sought to develop southern party organizations that could provide a vehicle for the growing urban middle class in the region to join the GOP. A straddle on civil rights would allow these economically conservative southerners to join the Republican Party, without creating an extreme image that would threaten the party's viability in northern swing states. Ironically, however, as southern disaffection with national Democrats grew and as civil rights rose to the top of the national agenda, these revived southern state party organizations became an instrument for Eisenhower's more conservative rivals to take over the GOP.

In the years before Eisenhower took office, national Republican leaders—most notably Herbert Hoover—had aided "lily-white" factions in taking control of southern state parties from the so-called black-and-tan organizations that had dominated much of the southern GOP.[68] But these southern party organizations did not amount to much on the ground in most states, constituting little more than hollow institutional shells for delivering patronage.

In that context, southern delegations were fought over in party conventions, but the fights were as much about patronage and control of local party machinery as they were about ideology. Despite Taft's status as the more conservative candidate in the 1948 and 1952 nomination fights, southern delegations split nearly evenly on the critical votes in the nominating contests.[69] In 1948 Dewey actually edged Taft in the South, 107–104. Four years later Taft did win the South, but only by a bare 119–103 margin, which failed to compensate for Eisenhower's huge lead in the Northeast and Mid-Atlantic states.

Eisenhower came into office determined to create a more substantial southern GOP. Soon after the election, he formed the Committee on the South to develop a "long range program for expanding the Republican Party" in the region.[70] Eisenhower and his team hoped to replace the so-called post office Republicans—officials focused on securing patronage appointments rather than winning elections—with a new generation of Republicans committed to building a viable party apparatus.[71] The initial efforts led to the recruitment of new party chairs in several states, but progress was slow. When Meade Alcorn became RNC chair in 1957, he reported that in most southern states there was still "no Republican organization.... No office, no staff, no telephone, no program of party action, no effort to develop candidates, no effort to do anything" other than send delegates to the national party convention.[72]

Rather than give up, Eisenhower launched Operation Dixie, pouring more funding into the effort and creating a new Southern Division at the RNC. Former Virginia Republican state chair I. Lee Potter led the new division and traveled across the South in 1957–58 to attend party conventions, help select local leaders, and set up party headquarters.[73] The backlash against Eisenhower's decision to send troops into Little Rock briefly stalled these efforts, but the president continued to pour funds and talent into the region. By 1960 "every southern state party finally had a headquarters, a long-term strategic plan, and candidate recruitment programs in the works."[74] Indeed, Operation Dixie "brought forth a bumper crop of GOP candidates" to run for Congress in 1960.[75]

Eisenhower's vision for Operation Dixie was that it would create a Republican Party based primarily in the growing urban areas of the South, appealing to upper middle-class professionals rather than traditional segregationists. A solid majority of upper-income urban southern whites had voted for Eisenhower, and the president believed that he could win over more moderate southern Democratic supporters. In most cases, the candidates recruited by the Southern Division during the Eisenhower years did not emphasize segregation as an issue and instead highlighted their economic conservatism.[76]

Even so, Eisenhower's team was not above siding with lily-white racists when it suited their goal of building viable state parties. For example, the Eisenhower administration favored hard-core segregationists in their battle for control of the Mississippi Republican Party with longtime African American leader Perry Howard. After Little Rock, the head of the lily-white organization renounced his party affiliation in protest, seemingly giving Howard an opening to make a comeback. But Eisenhower instead gave control over patronage to white conservative Wirt Yeager, who was a critic of Eisenhower's own civil rights record. The lily-whites remained dominant in the state GOP. Yeager proved to be a much more active leader than Howard, beginning a drive to "build the Mississippi GOP into a vehicle for conservatives who felt estranged from the national Democratic Party."[77]

Still, for the most part, Eisenhower's party-building efforts were premised on fostering a moderately conservative party with a base in the "new South." This would change when William Miller, a brash conservative Representative from upstate New York, took over the RNC in 1961. Miller expanded Operation Dixie's funding but was far more open to recruiting segregationists than Eisenhower had been.[78] Doubting that young urban professionals were a sufficient party base for the GOP to win the South, Miller and his allies saw the rural Deep South as increasingly receptive to the party's entreaties.

With Miller's support, the Southern Division of the RNC was "fully funded and more active than any other [party] division" in the early 1960s.[79]

Indeed, by 1964 the RNC was spending nearly one-third of its expenditures on Operation Dixie, and more than 87 percent of counties in the South had a Republican chair and vice chair.[80] Young Republican operatives took control of state parties across the South, selling an aggressive brand of conservatism that explicitly linked racial and economic issues.

Under Miller, the RNC backed well-known segregationists as candidates for office. In South Carolina, columnist William Workman challenged incumbent Democratic senator Olin Johnston in a 1962 campaign based largely on the claim that southern Democrats' ties to the national Democratic Party made them unreliable on the race issue. The segregationist Workman's campaign "perfectly crystallized what the Republican party was up to in the South—and the incredible progress it would make."[81] He spoke in front of Confederate flags, likened Kennedy to Hitler, and argued that Johnston was too close to the Democratic Party to defend "the southern way of life."[82] Workman won an impressive 43 percent of the vote against the longtime incumbent, a "historic achievement for the South Carolina GOP."[83]

Meanwhile, Alabama Democrat Lister Hill barely survived a challenge from Republican James Martin, who had "passed word" that Hill was "soft on integration."[84] In accepting the state GOP Senate nomination, Martin called for "a return to the Spirit of '61—1861, when our fathers formed a new nation."[85] Taking advantage of "increased hostility and tension produced by white perceptions of the Kennedy Administration's racial policies," Martin captured 49 percent of the vote in November, nearly unseating Hill.[86] The Workman and Martin campaigns signaled that southern conservatives could run as Republican segregationists and threaten once-safe Democratic incumbents.

It was not long before Eisenhower's allies recognized that their efforts had ended up strengthening their ideological rivals within the GOP. In an oral history, former RNC chairman Alcorn charged that their program's "whole purpose was perverted" as the new leaders "took over the Operation Dixie machinery and attempted to convert it into a lily-white Republican organization. They did succeed in some states, I'm sorry to say."[87] Daniel Galvin concludes that Operation Dixie had "unwittingly laid the groundwork for Eisenhower's more conservative successors to move the party in a direction he had not intended for it to go. By helping to create 'empty vessels' that could easily be captured and politically converted, Eisenhower's sub-rosa partisanship had contributed to the rightward drift of the GOP."[88]

Even before Eisenhower had left the scene, there were signs that the new state party chairmen in the South had their own ideas about how they might fit into the party's future. In April 1959 the GOP state chairmen in twelve southern states "agreed among themselves that their representatives on the platform writing Resolutions Committee will operate as a unit to champion the conservative viewpoint, especially on civil rights and the general area of states' rights." The *Washington Post* observed that "a unified bloc" of southern votes "could be decisive in close fights on civil rights and other platform issues."[89] Although frustrated at the 1960 convention (see below), the southern delegates would prove critical once conservatives found a candidate whom they could rally around.

THE GOLDWATER MOVEMENT

While Eisenhower's victory had temporarily quieted the talk of a conservative takeover of the GOP, conservative political entrepreneurs grew increasingly frustrated with the president's moderation during his second term. With southerners ever more estranged from the national Democratic Party and with civil rights rising on the nation's political agenda, talk of a realignment once again became common on the right. This section traces the rise of the Goldwater movement, emphasizing that it drew on a deep base of support at the mass and midlevels of the GOP, and that its ultimate success depended both on the new role played by southern state party organizations and on a widespread reaction against the civil rights movement among conservative voters in both the South and the North. The script had largely been set in motion decades earlier by conservative advocates of a realignment, but these developments put Goldwater in a position to deliver on its promise to transform the GOP.

A key figure in forging the alliance between Taft conservatives and southern whites was activist and radio host Clarence Manion. Working closely with South Carolina Democratic representative William Jennings Bryan Dorn, Manion initially proposed that conservatives get behind Arkansas governor Orval Faubus as a candidate in the 1960 southern Democratic primaries, while backing a conservative Republican in the GOP's northern primaries. When both inevitably lost their nomination contests, the two would join forces to form a third party that brought together Dixiecrats and Taftites.[90]

In laying out this scenario, Manion viewed Barry Goldwater as the obvious choice to take up the conservative banner in the GOP contest. Goldwater had already established himself as a conservative star when he broke from the Eisenhower administration in April 1957, condemning its excessive spending. A year later Goldwater declared that the way for the GOP to achieve majority status was to "let the party stop copying the New Deal." Goldwater quickly became identified as the "most articulate spokesman" for grassroots conservative discontent with Eisenhower's Modern Republicanism.[91] At this stage, Goldwater had not been associated with racial conservatism—indeed, he had voted for the Civil Rights Act of 1957.

This would change, however, when Goldwater visited the South in 1959. The Arizona senator used a speech to Mississippi Republicans to openly criticize Eisenhower's decision to send troops to Little Rock, claiming that "most Republicans across the country" also disagreed with the president.[92] Goldwater suggested that "the general feeling among Republicans is to let the states handle [school] segregation" and for the national government to stay out of the dispute. In an attack line sure to appeal in the South, Goldwater accused Chief Justice Earl Warren of being a "socialist" unfit for his position.[93]

Goldwater made an even bigger splash a few weeks later when he was invited to headline a Republican state convention in Greenville, South Carolina. Local segregationist, antiunion industrialists Gregory Shorey and Roger Milliken had sponsored the event as part of their efforts to build on the nascent Republican organization in the state. In his speech, which was televised live throughout South Carolina, Goldwater declared that the *Brown* decision should "not be enforced by arms" because it was "not based on law."[94]

Goldwater's speech received a hero's welcome and sparked a sensation across the state. The raucous reception for Goldwater in the heart of the South persuaded Manion that he did not need to rely on Faubus to win over southern whites. Instead, Goldwater could appeal to both northern and southern conservatives. Manion launched a Draft Goldwater organization in June 1959.[95]

This early interest in Goldwater was not confined to the South. A November 1959 Goldwater speech at the Western States' GOP Meeting in Pasadena was again greeted with a boisterous reception—one that contrasted sharply with the activists' tepid response to the moderate New York governor, Nelson Rockefeller.[96] Following the speech, the *Los Angeles Times* recruited Goldwater to write a column for its editorial page that would appear three times a week.

To spread the word about Goldwater's ideas to a still wider audience, Manion hired young activist Brent Bozell to ghostwrite *Conscience of a Conservative*. The 123-page book became a manifesto for conservatives dissatisfied with me-too Republicanism. The book declared that segregation was abhorrent but argued that it was up to the states, not Congress or the courts, to stop it. Again, this appeal to states' rights as a basis to oppose action on civil rights could draw on and extend decades of conservative criticism of the New Deal on similar grounds. A total of 500,000 copies were in print by November 1960.[97]

As a sitting vice president with ties to both moderates and conservatives, there was little doubt that Nixon would emerge as the GOP nominee in 1960. Yet conservatives across much of the United States viewed Goldwater as a hero and pushed for inclusion of the Arizona senator on the ticket, perhaps even in the top spot. Following a Goldwater speech criticizing Nixon's complacent attitude toward the South, the South Carolina GOP convention pledged its presidential delegates to the Arizona senator.[98] Goldwater insisted that he did not want the nomination, but state party chair Gregory Shorey refused to back down. Louisiana and Arizona also pledged their delegates to Goldwater for the first ballot. Numerous College Republican and Young Republican groups endorsed Goldwater for vice president. Youth for Goldwater soon had about sixty chapters on college campuses.[99]

As the GOP convention began, Nixon was receiving warnings that party activists were moving toward Goldwater. Indeed, delegates "were besieged with postcards and telegrams plumping Goldwater" for the ticket.[100] Both *Newsweek* and the *New York Times* observed that top GOP leaders conceded that in a truly open convention, Goldwater would be the vice presidential nominee.[101] The *Times* referred to Goldwater as the "chief spokesman for his party's conservative wing" and as the "new glamour boy and white hope" of Republican conservatives.[102]

Despite the grassroots activist support for Goldwater, Nixon had the delegates to control the convention, and he viewed Nelson Rockefeller as the more immediate threat to party unity. The acknowledged leader of eastern liberal Republicans, Rockefeller had gone public with a threat to "take a walk" from the campaign due to his concern that the emerging party platform was too conservative.[103] Nixon met with Rockefeller at his home and agreed to a series of concessions that became known as the "Compact of Fifth Avenue." Among other changes, Nixon agreed to a strong civil rights plank to assure "aggressive action to remove the remaining vestiges of segregation or discrimination in all areas of national life—voting and housing, schools, and jobs."

Conservatives were outraged by what they called the "Sellout of Fifth Avenue." Goldwater referred to it as the "Munich of the Republican Party" and claimed that the "handful of liberal militants that are seeking to take control over the Republican Party will inherit a mess of pottage."[104] He was particularly dismayed that Nixon had broken his promise to him that the platform would not include federal action against private job discrimination.[105] The *Times* noted that Goldwater had entered the convention with open support mostly "centered in Southern delegations and far-right fringe groups" but added that "many influential Republican conservatives" from the Taft wing of the party shared his platform protest.[106]

The ensuing fight in the platform committee underscored the growing disconnect between the top national party leadership—such as Nixon—and rank-and-file party activists and officials on civil rights. The platform subcommittee on civil rights, although chaired by a Rockefeller ally, had a clear majority for the anti–civil rights forces led by Texan John Tower. The subcommittee "refused to accept the militant stand of Nixon and Rockefeller" and instead reported out the southern-backed weak plank.[107] As the convention prepared to open, Tower evidently enjoyed the support of a majority of the full platform committee as well, which initially rejected Nixon's call that it revise the subcommittee-approved plank.[108] Robert Novak observes that Rockefeller, who represented the old eastern forces who had "engineered the Willkie-Dewey-Eisenhower nominations," was demanding a platform "more liberal than the convention was apt to accept in a free vote."[109]

But Nixon insisted that the plank be changed, summoning committee members who disagreed with his position and calling in personal favors to persuade them to switch. The strong precedent that the party nominee dictate the platform enabled Nixon to strengthen the civil rights plank by a 56–28 vote, though his team allowed abstentions from those "reluctant to allow chits to be cashed against their conservatism."[110] Still, the intensity of opposition to the liberal platform indicated that the "party was increasingly becoming a redoubt for those who either wished blacks ill or viewed them with indifference."[111]

The platform fight boosted Goldwater's profile within the party. Although he continued to back Nixon publicly, Goldwater now reluctantly agreed to have his name placed in nomination as a favorite son by Arizona. This would allow him to deliver a high-profile speech withdrawing his name. The boisterous floor demonstration for Goldwater, accompanied musically by "the strains of Dixie," signaled his rising status—along with its southern foundation.[112] The *Washington Post* commented that Goldwater had entered the convention with few votes in sight, but that there had been "an astonishing clamor for him in Chicago" with his buttons and hats "in evidence all over the place."[113] Rick Perlstein writes that the "Goldwater ranks had swelled far beyond" the troops that had come to Chicago. His supporters now included "disgruntled platform drafters, most of the Southern delegations, [and] old Taftites who thought they had come to Chicago to rubber-stamp decisions made from on high."[114] Novak concurs that the convention featured "a spontaneous mass movement" for Goldwater and showed Nixon and his supporters that "they had a phenomenon on their hands."[115]

Despite his anger about Nixon's compromise with Rockefeller, Goldwater kept up a high profile during the 1960 campaign. He delivered 177 speeches across twenty-six states for the ticket. During one swing through South, Goldwater declared that "there's hardly enough difference between Republican conservatives and the Southern Democrats to put a piece of paper between."[116]

Meanwhile, both Goldwater and Rockefeller grew frustrated by Nixon's refusal to choose sides in the battle between the liberal and conservative wings. Rockefeller believed Nixon had "completely neglected the massive Negro vote in Harlem and Brooklyn" during the campaign and complained that he had tried but failed "to talk Nixon into canceling some of his Southern expeditions and concentrating on the big Northern urban vote and particularly the Negro vote." Goldwater, for his part, believed Nixon was faltering because he had gone too far to the left to try to win "a Negro vote that was irrevocably Democratic." When vice presidential nominee Henry Cabot

Lodge promised an African American in Nixon's Cabinet—a promise Nixon backed away from—Goldwater was aghast, fearing "that Lodge was alienating Southern voters, with no real prospect of gains among Negroes."[117]

Following Nixon's defeat, Goldwater continued to gain recognition as the leader of resurgent conservatives. His opinion column became the fastest growing feature in the Times Mirror Syndicate's history, reaching more than one hundred newspapers by summer 1961.[118] Writing in the *Wall Street Journal*, Novak claimed that the GOP was marching to the right in the wake of Nixon's defeat, "in a procession toward conservatism led by grass-roots party workers with members of Congress following along." As evidence, Novak observed that local Republican groups were showing "overwhelming demand for speaking appearances by conservative leader Sen. Barry Goldwater" and few demands for Rockefeller, who lacked appeal "among party workers outside the Eastern seaboard."[119] By 1961 it "was sinking home to party leaders that Goldwater was by far the most sought-after speaker at party functions across the country."[120]

Goldwater eagerly responded to the demand for his appearances. He gave 225 speeches across the country in 1961, including many in the South, where his popularity continued to grow.[121] In a speech in Atlanta in November 1961, Goldwater reiterated his opposition to the federal government imposing integration and pledged to "bend every muscle I have to see that the South has a voice [at the next GOP convention] on everything that affects the life of the South." When asked after the speech whether the GOP should give up on the African American vote, Goldwater responded that Republicans "could not 'outpromise the Democrats' in seeking the support of members of that race."[122] In private settings, Goldwater assured his southern backers not to worry about his earlier ties to the NAACP. Goldwater told South Carolina's Workman that his membership in the group had ended over a decade ago and was irrelevant because "in the interim my most bitter enemies have been the NAACP." Goldwater made clear that he saw little virtue in the group, observing that it was "beholden to every socialistic cause in America."[123]

Consistent with the line taken in these Goldwater appearances, his friends and backers developed a plan by January 1962 for conservatives to win the White House for the first time since the 1920s. The road map explicitly divided voters into ethnic and racial groupings, arguing that the African American is now a "steadfast Democrat," such that "no amount of Republican crusading for Negro rights could outweigh the magnetic attraction of the Democratic Party's social welfare programs. Anyway, the Northern Negro had come to think of the Democratic Party in terms of the Northern integrationist, not the Southern segregationist. Thus, it would be extremely difficult for the Republicans to outdo the Democrats in championing civil rights, even if they tried." As a result, the first priority for conservatives is to "soft-pedal civil rights ... forget all the sentimental tradition of the party of Lincoln. Because the Negro and Jewish votes are irrevocably tied to the Democrats anyway.... But it might work wonders in attracting white Southerners into the Republican Party." Interestingly, Goldwater himself did not yet entirely buy into the argument that he could be elected president, believing that no candidate could win the GOP nomination without support in the big northeastern states, where he recognized his brand of conservatism remained an unlikely sell.[124]

The Draft Goldwater Movement

In the face of Goldwater's reluctance, conservative activists began a concerted effort to draft him for 1964. This movement drew on important forces transforming the GOP: most important, the rise of genuine southern party organizations and the alienation of southern white Democratic voters from their party provided a solid base for a conservative candidate.[125] At the same time, northern white conservatives were also deeply skeptical of civil rights advances and eager to embrace a candidate who could unite conservatives of the North and South.

Starting in summer 1961, Clif White, a conservative with roots in the Young Republican National Federation, worked with the publisher of *National Review*, William Rusher, and Ohio freshman representative John Ashbrook to plot the takeover of the party. At a December 1961 meeting, White "unfurled a map of the United States and explained the grand strategy." Crucially, "White explained that a convention could be won *without* the Northeast," which his counterparts understood "was a revolution." The key to victory would be the Midwest, Southwest, and South. White noted that the South's "delegates wouldn't be available to the highest bidder as in the old 'post office' days. Now there were real Republican organizations in Dixie. And their members worshiped Goldwater." Furthermore, 43.4 percent of the convention's delegates would come from the South and West, compared to just 35 percent in 1940.[126]

White believed the South would also prove the key in November. An early Draft Goldwater document argued that the Arizona senator could win by running up a 128–0 Electoral College margin in the South even as he lost the Northeast by 118–11. The text declared that "Goldwater will give 'the solid South' dramatic new meaning! *This is the key to Republican success!*"[127]

As White and his colleagues launched the "Suite 3505" group to nominate Goldwater, they understood that strength among grassroots activists would be crucial. They would start with the precinct meetings that selected county conventions, which in turn chose national delegates. If conservative activists showed up at each stage of the contest, they could capture a majority without the need for support from northeastern liberals and moderates.[128]

The ensuing Draft Goldwater movement had the feeling of a crusade, with the crusaders especially strong in the South. White had little trouble in ensuring that there were strong Goldwater organizations in place in Texas, Mississippi, and Louisiana. Indeed, an early Texas straw poll gave Goldwater 1,115 votes to 90 for Rockefeller, and the Texas GOP's 1962 state convention adopted a resolution urging Goldwater to seek the presidency.[129] But Goldwater's support was not confined to the South. In August 1962 Republicans in the state of Washington approved a resolution declaring Goldwater the party's only genuine spokesman.[130]

Even as Goldwater denied interest in running for the White House, the draft movement continued to show strength in state conventions. Oklahoma Republicans resolved at their 1963 convention that Goldwater "champions the political beliefs of the Oklahoma Republican party," which was "the closest thing to a delegate pledge state law would allow." In May 1963 South Carolina's Republican county chairmen unanimously voted to constitute themselves as the state's Draft Goldwater Committee.[131] Writing in 1963, Evans and Novak declared that "the South is a Goldwater citadel" and noted that the Goldwater "boom is the closest thing to a spontaneous mass movement in modern American politics."[132]

Goldwater's rise inspired heated debate at the June 1963 RNC annual meeting, in Denver. "Goldwater kitsch was everywhere," in sharp contrast to Rockefeller's "empty hospitality suite."[133] Evans and Novak declared that the meeting was evidence of the "transformation" underway in the GOP, as "the aggressive postwar club of conservative young Republicans from the small states of the West and South are seizing power, displacing the eastern Party chiefs who have dictated Republican policy and candidates for a generation."[134] The easterners maintained that Goldwater was unacceptable and expressed dismay at the "unmistakable signs that party leaders from outside the industrialized states of the eastern seaboard were seriously contemplating transforming the Republican Party into the White Man's Party."[135]

Those southern and western party officials were in no mood to make concessions to their eastern counterparts. They were willing to write off New York, Pennsylvania, New Jersey, and Michigan to the Democrats, in the hope that Goldwater would sweep the South. One border state chairman warned that "the eastern boys are just going to have to get it through their heads that they're not top dogs any more."[136] Amid the increased racial tensions unleashed by the civil rights movement, "a good many, perhaps a majority of the party's leaders, envisioned substantial political gold to be mined in the racial crisis by becoming in fact, though not in name, the White Man's Party." Novak quotes an "astute party worker's" ominous comment over the breakfast table: "Remember," the worker noted, "this isn't South Africa. The white man outnumbers the Negro 9 to 1 in this country."[137]

Despite the intense grassroots conservative energy, Goldwater's drive to the nomination was by no means smooth. After Goldwater amassed a big lead in the early polls, the Kennedy assassination fed a backlash against extremism that threatened the conservative's support. Soon after, Goldwater stumbled during several television performances and press conferences, making numerous impolitic statements. Furthermore, the Suite 3505 group clashed with Goldwater's Arizona advisers on strategy, creating organizational disarray.[138]

Still, White's team proved skillful at amassing delegates. After Goldwater lost New Hampshire's primary (and its fourteen delegates), White noted that he had already won four times as many delegates from Georgia, North Carolina, and South Carolina. Following Goldwater's win in the Indiana primary on May 5, White's "secret ledger" showed that he had amassed 400 delegates, which constituted four-fifths of the delegates selected to date and over 60 percent of the 655 needed to win.[139] The public side of the nomination contest climaxed with Goldwater's narrow victory in the California primary in June. The Arizonan likely did not need California to secure the nomination, though it was an important indication that he could mount a credible campaign in November.[140]

The northeastern and mid-Atlantic delegates continued to stand for a more moderate party image at the 1964 convention, but now they were easily outvoted. The Goldwater-dominated platform committee drafted a weak civil rights plank: eliminating discrimination, it claimed, is "a matter of heart, conscience and education, as well as of equal rights under law." Goldwater's opponents challenged the plank on the floor with a liberal alternative affirming the constitutionality of the recently passed Civil Rights Act of 1964 and calling for legislation to implement school desegregation and to enforce voting rights. On the key convention roll call, delegates from the Northeast and Mid-Atlantic voted overwhelmingly for the more liberal plank, 309–46. But the region's delegates were now isolated against the more conservative Midwest, West, and South. Southern delegates voted 324–1 for the conservative plank, and the remainder of the delegates (i.e., those from states outside the South, Northeast, and Mid-Atlantic) voted 527–99 for the conservative plank.[141] Goldwater's nomination and the hard-right platform signaled the ascension of a new leadership group in the Republican Party, one in which southern whites and Taft-wing conservatives had displaced the old eastern moderates as the driving force.

Midlevel Party Actors and the Goldwater Movement

The organizational work of Clarence Manion, Clif White, and other conservative political entrepreneurs constitutes a crucial part of the Goldwater story. But it is important to emphasize that this work could not have succeeded had there not been a receptive audience in both the mass and midlevels of the GOP. Most pointedly, the ability to capture precinct and county conventions—in both the South and much of the rest of the country outside the Northeast—depended on a message that resonated with party officials and activists. These were not outsiders launching a hostile takeover of the Republican Party. In much of the United States, this *was* the Republican Party.

Comprehensive evidence on the preferences of midlevel party actors is not easily available, but useful indicators can be pulled together from a variety of sources. Recall that McClosky's survey in 1956 showed that Republican convention delegates were significantly more conservative on racial issues than were Democratic delegates, even as the two parties approved platforms with similarly vague positions (see chapter 9). Accounts of the 1960 GOP convention (discussed above) also suggest that rank-and-file delegates favored a more conservative civil rights position than Nixon and Rockefeller dictated. In April 1963 *Congressional Quarterly* polled the 1960 delegates and found that 46 percent favored Goldwater, compared to the 34.5 percent who preferred Rockefeller. In the poll, Goldwater dominated the South— with its revitalized party organizations—by a 182–66 margin, while also posting leads in the Midwest and West, trailing Rockefeller only in the East.[142] Novak finds Goldwater's lead "deeply significant" because it showed that the "perennial party workers" who had attended the Nixon-dominated convention actually favored Goldwater's conservative approach.[143]

A survey of California delegates to the 1960 and 1964 national conventions underscores both the general racial conservatism of the 1960 delegates and the particularly high degree of racial conservatism among Goldwater supporters.[144] Among other issues, the delegates were asked their position on a state referendum to repeal the Rumford Fair Housing Act, a controversial antidiscrimination law passed by the legislature. The 1960 Nixon delegates from California backed repeal of the Rumford Act by a 63.5–36.5 percent margin.[145] This again reinforces the view that even as the GOP adopted a liberal platform in 1960, rank-and-file delegates were hardly strong civil rights supporters. Goldwater's 1964 California delegates outpaced even this high degree of civil rights opposition: 83 percent of Goldwater delegates backed repeal of the Rumford law, with just 17 percent in favor of keeping the act. By contrast, a whopping 93 percent of Democratic delegates to the 1964 convention opposed repeal of the Rumford Act.[146] Of the fourteen issues examined in the California delegate survey, only right-to-work laws, national health insurance, and the war on poverty registered partisan polarization levels similar to that observed for fair housing policy.

The California survey also makes clear that the Goldwater delegates were not newcomers who had infiltrated party affairs. Goldwater delegates were actually more deeply entrenched in the GOP organization than were members of Rockefeller's proposed delegate slate. A higher proportion of Goldwater delegates were members of their county committee and of the state central committee. Furthermore, nearly twice as many Goldwater delegates had attended a past GOP national convention in an official capacity, suggesting a longer period of party service. The Goldwater delegates also had contributed more money to the GOP in the 1962 election campaign than had the Rockefeller delegates.[147]

A survey of party officials in Ohio tells a similar story about polarization on civil rights at the midlevel of the parties in the early 1960s. Thomas Flinn and Frederick Wirt surveyed county Democratic and Republican leaders early in 1962 and included many of the same items McClosky had asked about in 1956, such as his question on whether the government should increase or decrease its effort to enforce integration.[148] Flinn and Wirt report an 18-point gap (on a 100-point scale) between Democratic and Republican officials in their support for government enforcement of integration. This degree of polarization was similar to the party gap on such proposals as increasing taxes on high incomes (20 points) and increasing corporate taxation (also 20 points). In short, Republican Party officials and activists in core northern states—such as California and Ohio—were well to the right of their Democratic counterparts on civil rights *before* Goldwater's nomination and, indeed, provided a supportive context for the Arizona senator's push for a conservative GOP stance on civil rights (see also chapter 7 on state party platforms and chapter 8 on rank-and-file House members).

Mass Opinion and the Goldwater Movement

One might ask whether the Goldwater phenomenon was limited to this midlevel of the GOP—to state and local party officials and activists—or instead had a genuine mass base. As shown in chapter 5, economically conservative Republican voters in the North were less supportive of key civil rights initiatives than were economically liberal Democratic voters as far back as the late 1930s. While racial policy was far from a salient concern for conservative Republican voters in this earlier era, the intense civil rights movement activism of the late 1950s and early 1960s changed this dynamic. The turmoil in the streets—and eventual governmental response—turned this baseline skepticism among conservative northern Republicans into a potent political phenomenon, particularly when combined with southern conservatives ready to bolt from the Democratic Party.[149]

Survey evidence provides an important window into the partisan and ideological correlates of civil rights views during this period. Starting in May 1962, Gallup asked respondents whether the current administration was pushing "too fast," "too slow," or "about right" on racial integration. The results reinforce the message that Goldwater's racial conservatism found

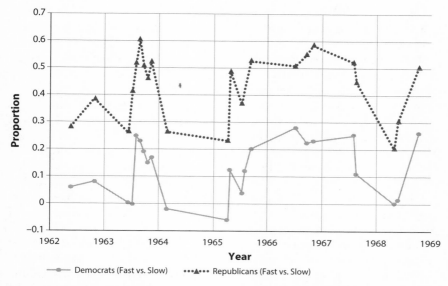

FIGURE 10.2. Comparison of views on integration, northern Republicans and northern Democrats. Proportion responding that the administration is pushing "too fast" minus proportion responding "too slow."

a receptive audience among many Republican partisans and economic conservatives in the early 1960s.

Figure 10.2 compares the responses of northern Republicans and northern Democrats to the integration question from 1962 to 1968, with higher values indicating a greater share of "too fast" responses relative to "too slow" responses. From the start—even before the Kennedy administration finally took a forthright stand in favor of strong civil rights legislation in June 1963—Republicans were much more likely than Democrats to believe that the administration was moving too fast on integration. Thus 48 percent of northern Republicans with an opinion believed the administration was pushing too fast in surveys conducted from May 1962 through May 1963, while just 27 percent of northern Democrats held this view. Fewer Republicans than Democrats, by contrast, believed the administration was moving too slowly.[150] Once the administration took a strong stand, the share of Republicans who believed it was moving too fast increased further, to 61 percent in polls from June 1963 through May 1964; the share of Democrats holding that view also increased, but to a much more modest 33 percent. Following the Goldwater debacle, northern Republicans continued to believe the administration was moving too fast on civil rights, consistently outpacing their Democratic counterparts. The two series move in parallel from 1962 through 1968, with the size of the partisan gap remaining essentially unchanged.

Throughout the period, economically conservative Republicans were especially likely to express the view that the administration was pushing too fast on civil rights. In the initial period before Kennedy put forward a civil rights bill, 57 percent of economically conservative northern Republicans accused the administration of pushing too fast (by contrast, just 14 percent viewed the administration as moving too slowly). From June 1963 through May 1964 fully 69 percent of economically conservative Republicans believed the administration was pushing too fast, with just 11 percent saying it was moving too slowly.[151] If one thinks of economically conservative Republicans as the core of the Goldwater movement in the North, these voters were primed to support a candidate expressing doubt about the pace of change on civil rights.

Indeed, when one examines Goldwater supporters directly, the importance of racial issues comes to the fore. From the start, Goldwater found his greatest support among southern whites. For example, in the early Gallup polls on the GOP nomination contest conducted in 1963, Goldwater was the first choice of 45 percent of southern whites, compared to just 30 percent of northern whites.[152] An astounding 90 percent of those southern Goldwater supporters interviewed in 1963 claimed that the administration was pushing too fast on integration, compared to 74 percent of southern whites who did not back Goldwater at the time. Among northern white Republicans, 69 percent of early Goldwater backers believed the administration was pushing too fast on civil rights, compared to 60 percent of Republicans who backed other candidates for the nomination. These relationships held up over the course of the campaign: southern whites provided the greatest support for Goldwater's nomination, and, in both the South and North, Goldwater backers were more likely to see the administration as pushing too fast on integration than were supporters of other candidates.

The widespread view among economically conservative Republicans and Goldwater supporters that the administration was pushing too hard on civil rights can be viewed as the flip side of the progress brought about by the civil rights movement. The protests had created an urgent situation in which most national political elites—including many Republicans—recognized that something must be done. At the same time, the tense conditions sparked a conservative reaction that would reverberate throughout the political system. Goldwater's pollster reported that racial backlash had become a potent appeal in much of the North, while the press speculated about how racial strife could cost the Democrats among white northerners.[153]

An early warning sign came in April 1963, when Berkeley, California, voters repealed a fair housing ordinance that the city council had passed in January; a postelection survey revealed that white Republicans had voted for repeal by an 87–9 percent margin, while white Democrats had backed keeping the ordinance by 60–37 percent.[154] Conservatives' success in Berkeley gave momentum to the successful statewide initiative to repeal the Rumford Fair Housing Act the following year.[155]

For the first time since the Civil War, the race question "had become a truly national issue of immediate concern to tens of millions of [white] voters." Northern members of Congress found, "to their amazement," that "a good bit of" the outpouring of constituent mail was "hostile and antagonistic" to the civil rights movement.[156] One representative from a suburban district in the North reported receiving "a bundle of letters … each betrayed deep-seating anxieties" over racial integration.[157] Another northern Democratic senator—a backer of Kennedy's civil rights program—commented that "for the first time I'm getting mail from white people saying 'wait a minute, we've got some rights too.'"[158] Even as the white South was a key foundation for the Goldwater movement, Novak concludes that "what really breathed new vigor into the Goldwater-for-President drive was the Negro revolution's impact in the North."[159]

While mass-based skepticism of civil rights advances had been related to economic conservatism back in the late 1930s and the 1940s (see chapter 5), much had changed in the interim. Southern whites were now far more prepared to vote for a Republican presidential candidate than they had been twenty years earlier; these southern whites could now participate effectively in GOP nomination politics through revitalized state party organizations; and, for the first time in generations, civil rights had become a voting issue among many white northerners—both for liberal supporters of change and for conservative opponents.

CONCLUSIONS

Throughout the 1940s and 1950s, even as ordinary Republican voters, members of Congress, and state parties provided less support for civil rights than did northern Democrats, the national GOP's presidential candidates and platforms positioned the party close to and sometimes even to the left of the lukewarm moderation of the national Democratic Party. This disconnect reflected the strength of the moderate, northeastern wing of the party in presidential nominating conventions, which generated a set of candidates who were, on balance, more pro–civil rights than were rank-and-file Republican partisans. Indeed, given that the GOP's presidential candidates represented the more pro–civil rights wing of the party through 1960, it is striking that even these candidates increasingly opted to woo southern white conservatives while campaigning less actively for African American votes.

The idea of creating a truly conservative party through an alliance of northern Republicans and southern Democrats had been a recurrent theme of political discussion dating back to the early efforts of George Moses, Arthur Vandenberg, and others in 1937–38. The southern reaction against the CIO and labor-oriented liberalism made it clear to conservative Republican politicians that the rhetoric of "states' rights" and limited government offered an ideological template for joining attacks against the "excesses" of the New Deal with a defense of southern whites' core interests. Indeed, the alignment among economic conservatism, GOP partisanship, and a conservative stance on civil rights at the mass and midlevels of the parties provided a permissive context for national party leaders to embrace an explicit alliance with southern whites. But bringing this alliance to fruition required displacing the control of the northeastern wing over presidential nominations. Ironically, Eisenhower's party-building efforts in the South provided a vehicle for conservative activists to transform the balance of power in the GOP's nomination contests.

The decision to woo the South was less a personal judgment by Goldwater than a concerted strategy adopted by a likeminded group of die-hard conservatives working over the course of several decades to take over the GOP. As Joseph Crespino writes, the choice to "embrace Strom Thurmond, or to recruit segregationist apologists like Bill Workman, or to go hunt any of the other ducks who could help them take back the Republican Party from the Rockefellers, Javits, and other liberal Republicans was not a difficult one." Put simply, the "Goldwaterites needed white southerners badly if they were to take over the party from liberal Republicans."[160] With viable southern Republican state parties in place to send conservative delegations to the national convention, and with many economically conservative northern white Republicans deeply hostile to the burgeoning civil rights movement, the Draft Goldwater movement was well situated to implement the alliance envisioned by Moses and Vandenberg, and elaborated on by Mundt and Gabrielson.

The Goldwater movement had deep political roots, but it is also important to emphasize that the Arizona senator's nomination in 1964 was not inevitable and did not itself signal the complete triumph of the GOP's conservative wing. Had the GOP's moderate wing coordinated on a single candidate earlier in 1964—such as William Scranton of Pennsylvania, who emerged late in the campaign as a Goldwater rival—it is plausible that it would have been able to capitalize on Goldwater's many stumbles to mount a more effective "Stop Goldwater" campaign.

It is equally important to note, however, that even if a more moderate candidate had won the nomination in 1964, that candidate would still have had a strong incentive—as did Nixon in 1960—to woo southern white conservatives alienated by national Democrats' progressive stance on civil rights.[161] Furthermore, just as the conservative movement continued to grow after Nixon's 1960 loss, it seems quite likely that a moderate Republican's defeat in November 1964 would have set the stage for the rise of another conservative star four years later. Indeed, Ronald Reagan, who was catapulted into the California governor's mansion in 1966 partly as a result of his attacks on the state's fair housing law, had become a conservative hero by 1968 while pushing a policy vision broadly similar to Goldwater's program.[162]

Even with Goldwater's 1964 nomination, internal debates about civil rights within the GOP were by no means over. Indeed, Goldwater's landslide defeat provided a resource for moderates eager to move the party back to the political center.[163] Such prominent Republicans as Rockefeller, George Romney, and Gerald Ford (R-MI) continued to push for a moderate stance across a range of issues, including civil rights, that they argued would help the party compete in the Northeast and parts of the Midwest. Yet a brief examination of the 1968 nomination contest reveals the important shift in the balance of power within the party toward racial conservatism.

Romney led the party's liberal wing in 1968, while conservatives rallied to Reagan, and Nixon occupied the middle ground. Romney's progressive record on civil rights was a sharp departure from Goldwater, whom he had refused to endorse in 1964. Reagan, though not an official candidate until the convention opened, was widely viewed as the heir to Goldwater and was especially strong in the South. Nixon carefully positioned himself to the right of the Democrats but avoided Goldwater's identification with segregationists: he expressed support for the *Brown* decision, the Civil Rights Act of 1964, and the Voting Rights Act, while also denouncing busing and advocating for "freedom of choice" plans that would allow parents to select which school their children would attend. Nixon also opposed withholding federal education funds from school districts that were slow to integrate and promised to appoint conservatives to the Supreme Court.[164]

Timothy Thurber suggests that, had Romney won in 1968, he would not have pursued Nixon's racially divisive policies in office. Thus the Michigan governor's failure "represented a lost opportunity to remake the Republican Party along racially more progressive lines." However, Thurber also acknowledges that Romney "faced an uphill battle" to win the nomination.[165] Rank-and-file Republican voters were hardly in a mood to push for civil rights initiatives: in the last Gallup poll before the convention, fully 56 percent of Republicans with an opinion believed the federal government was pushing too fast on integration, compared to 24 percent who believed it was not pushing fast enough.[166] Even had a progressive Republican such as Romney somehow emerged as the nominee, he would have faced a rank-and-file Republican electorate, conservative congressional wing, and GOP activist class that was deeply skeptical of civil rights initiatives.

The obstacles to a Romney nomination also included the South's considerable strength at the GOP convention, which forced Nixon to move further to the right on civil rights to secure southern delegates' votes. Indeed, Nixon beat back the rising Reagan threat at the convention by reassuring southern delegates that he would slow down school integration, fight busing, push the courts to show restraint on social issues, and select a vice presidential candidate acceptable to conservatives.[167] Where Nixon in 1960 had made a deal with Rockefeller to secure his path to the White House, eight years later he had to accommodate southern racial conservatives such as Thurmond and Tower to assure his nomination.[168]

The balance of power within the party had shifted, so that satisfying southern conservatives now loomed as more important than reassuring the so-called Rockefeller wing of the party. The Goldwater debacle in 1964 had not reversed this crucial change, which represented the culmination of a long process that dated back to the first signs of an alignment among racial conservatism, economic conservatism, and Republican partisanship evident in the Roosevelt era.

Much like the shift among national Democrats traced in the previous chapter, the GOP transformation began decades before Goldwater entered the political scene and was rooted in developments at the mass- and mid-levels of the party. From the late 1930s onward, conservative political entrepreneurs saw the opportunity afforded by southern disaffection with the direction of the New Deal and believed that an ideological appeal framed around states' rights had the potential to create a coalition of midwestern economic conservatives and southern racial conservatives. Top party leaders representing the moderate wing of the GOP were able to resist an all-out alliance with southern segregationists in the 1940s and 1950s, but the revitalization of southern party organizations under Eisenhower combined with white backlash against civil rights advances to pave the way for the Goldwater movement's triumph. The flip side of civil rights activists' success in forcing Democratic national elites to take a clear stand was that southern segregationists were now fully available for a new generation of Republican leaders and activists to mobilize, while economically conservative northern Republican voters' skepticism toward civil rights left them ready to embrace a racially conservative candidate.

CHAPTER 11

Conclusions

THE STORY OF the civil rights realignment is often told as one in which national party elites—Lyndon Johnson and Barry Goldwater—triggered a dramatic reshuffling of party positioning on racial issues. This book instead argues that top Democratic and Republican leaders were actually among the last to move. Johnson's civil rights embrace ratified changes that had remade his party over the preceding thirty years, while Goldwater's alliance with southern racial conservatives was made possible by earlier developments at the mass and midlevels of his party.

After briefly recapping the main argument and findings, this concluding chapter considers the implications of the civil rights realignment for the study of political change more generally. I then discuss lessons that this case offers for theories of political parties and conclude with reflections on what the historical developments of the 1930s–1960s tell us about the contemporary politics of race in America.

THE CIVIL RIGHTS REALIGNMENT: A RECAP

In contrast to accounts that treat the civil rights realignment as driven by the decisions of top Democratic and Republican leaders in the 1960s, which then reverberated throughout the party system, this book has argued that the civil rights realignment was rooted in changes in the constituency base of the Democratic Party that took place starting in the mid-1930s. These changes—and the reaction they sparked—reshaped the meaning of "liberalism" to incorporate civil rights. Even as national party elites had strong incentives to resist this reformulation of liberalism, the federal nature of American parties and the election of members of Congress through separate geographic constituencies provided a channel for civil rights advocates to capture the national Democratic Party from below. These same institutions also ultimately allowed the Goldwater movement to overtake the moderate national GOP leaders who had also sought to straddle civil rights issues. The civil rights movement forced national elites to choose sides in the 1960s, but the ground on which these leaders made their choices had been set in place by earlier developments at the mass and midlevels of the party system.

Part 1 traced the process through which civil rights was incorporated into the mainstream liberal project in the late 1930s and early 1940s. When the New Deal was launched in 1933, most Democratic politicians, policy advocates, and political observers did not view civil rights as part of the liberal program. Although there were individual liberals who advocated for civil rights, few white liberals viewed the race "problem" as bound up with the success of liberalism. Indeed, when white liberals attacked Roosevelt for his timidity, they highlighted his failures to back organized labor, to rein in business power, and to fully fund recovery efforts, not his steadfast avoidance of civil rights. The most radical New Dealers envisioned a major transformation in America's political economy, but this meant taking on corporate power, not Jim Crow. Indeed, for early New Dealers, the main obstacle to turning Democrats into a truly liberal party was not southern conservatism but rather the continued influence of economically conservative, probusiness northeastern Democrats.

Even as Roosevelt avoided a clear stand on civil rights, three developments in the mid- to late 1930s established important linkages between civil rights and New Deal liberalism. First, the emergence of northern African Americans as a potentially important source of votes for northern Democrats in 1934–36 gave more rank-and-file Democratic politicians an incentive to show concern for civil rights. Second, the rise of the CIO as the leading edge of New Deal liberalism sharpened the political battle lines. The CIO's outspoken civil rights advocacy—which stemmed both from its internal organizing imperatives and from its broader programmatic vision—meant that the group now most associated with an ambitious reading of the New Deal's goals was also associated with the civil rights cause. Southern Democrats' furious response to these two developments in the late 1930s constituted the third key shift. Where southern Democrats had provided crucial backing for the New Deal during Roosevelt's first term, many southern politicians viewed the CIO's rise and African Americans' incorporation into the Democratic Party and the labor movement as an existential threat to the racially oppressive "southern way of life." Conservative southern Democrats were soon the most consequential opponents of labor-sponsored expansions of the New Deal, cooperating with Republicans to push investigations and legislation that sought to undermine organized labor, and along with it, the liberal agenda more generally.

African Americans activists, working in cooperation with the CIO and other urban liberals, capitalized on World War II to tighten these connections. The early civil rights movement forced such issues as fair employment practices and military integration onto the political agenda in the early 1940s. Although the CIO and other urban liberals had expressed support for civil rights before the war, the battles over the FEPC in the early to mid-1940s raised the political visibility of civil rights issues and thus encouraged liberal leaders and groups to give civil rights a more prominent place in their program. By the end of the war, support for civil rights had become a key marker of one's identity as a liberal.

In sum, the rise of the CIO, alongside the entry of African Americans, Jews, and urban liberals into the New Deal coalition, meant that the core supporters of the New Deal in the North were also among the groups most closely associated with support for civil rights. At the same time, southern Democrats' hostility toward the CIO as well as civil rights meant that African Americans were no longer alone. Rather, they stood united with the rest of the northern New Deal coalition against southern Democrats, who were increasingly viewed as enemies not only of civil rights but also of liberalism as a whole.

Part 2 demonstrated that this new liberal coalition—and its broader interpretation of liberalism—took firm hold at the mass- and midlevels of the Democratic Party long before the 1960s. Notably, even ordinary voters evidently participated in the realignment early on, as economically liberal white northern Democrats were substantially more likely to back key civil rights initiatives by the early 1940s than were economically conservative Republicans.

This mass-based support among white liberals provided a permissive context for northern Democratic politicians to back civil rights, but the entry of millions of African American voters into the party coalition acted as a force multiplier. The economic liberalism (and material interests) of African Americans predisposed them to support the New Deal, notwithstanding its many accommodations with the Jim Crow South. Keenly understanding that the GOP alternative of turning relief and employment policy over to the states would pave the way for even more discrimination, African Americans responded to the racism inherent in many New Deal initiatives not by condemning the programs but by working to expand their scope. While older African Americans' long-standing ties to the GOP kept many from identifying with the Democratic Party during the Roosevelt years, younger cohorts affiliated with the Democrats throughout the New Deal era. Soon after the 1948 election, even older African Americans moved decisively to the Democrats. The combination of growing Democratic partisanship and the migration of African Americans to the North in the 1940s meant that African Americans had become an important constituency for many northern Democratic politicians, providing a direct incentive to be identified as pro–civil rights.

At the midlevel of the party system, both northern state parties and rank-and-file members of Congress vigorously responded to the new liberal coalition's civil rights push. A content analysis of several hundred state party platforms from the 1920s–1960s shows that northern state Democratic parties surpassed their Republican counterparts in their civil rights support by the mid-1940s. Pro–civil rights platforms were more likely in states with a high African American population. States with a large Jewish population and with high rates of unionization and urbanization also had more liberal civil rights platforms. Qualitative evidence supports the argument that African American activists, along with Jews, unions, and urban liberals, played a key role in pushing state Democrats to back civil rights.

Rank-and-file members of the House of Representatives displayed broadly similar dynamics. Analysis of recently discovered discharge petition data shows that northern Republicans had provided greater support for civil rights in the early to mid-1930s, but that northern Democrats caught up by about 1940 and easily surpassed northern Republicans by 1945. Democrats from urban and unionized areas were especially likely to back civil rights initiatives. Although district African American population does not predict Democrats' discharge petition support, other indicators—such as bill sponsorships—suggest that representatives were more likely to take an active pro–civil rights role when they had a large African American constituency. At the same time, rank-and-file Republicans gradually moved away from their earlier civil rights advocacy, not only opposing the FEPC but providing less support than in the past for antilynching and poll tax legislation. Again, among northern state parties and rank-and-file members of Congress, the racial realignment was largely completed in the 1940s.

Still, part 3 makes clear that transforming the mass and midlevels of both parties was not itself sufficient to complete the national partisan realignment. Liberals still had to overcome the resistance of national party leaders, who had long fought to contain the pressure to take a clear stand on civil rights. From 1944 to 1956 rank-and-file Democratic activists and convention delegates favored a more liberal stance on civil rights than did national leaders, but—with the exception of 1948—national elites succeeded in preventing the approval of either platform language or a presidential nominee unacceptable to white southerners. However, civil rights movement activists—again acting alongside other members of the liberal coalition—worked to force the issue to the fore, eventually leaving leaders with no choice but to take sides. Critically, by the time the issue rose to the top of the national agenda, the liberals enjoyed a clear majority within the Democratic Party; southern conservatives, by contrast, had been reduced to an isolated minority. Amid the intensified civil rights movement mobilization of the mid- to late 1950s, Democratic National Committee Chair Paul Butler and other top Democratic leaders finally embraced the pro–civil rights forces. For the first time, the platform committee was firmly in the hands of civil rights liberals in 1960 and framed a platform that won wide support from all but the much-weakened southerners.

Among Republicans, ambitious politicians on the right understood by the late 1930s that southern disillusionment with the New Deal's direction created an opening to unite economic and racial conservatives through appeals to "states' rights." But the party's more moderate national leaders—who drew their greatest support from the Northeast—had reservations about explicit cooperation with southern conservatives. Thus while the weaker support for civil rights among ordinary GOP partisans, elected officials, and state parties generated the potential for a new coalition to form, the national party nominated presidential candidates and framed platforms that largely straddled the civil rights issue in the 1940s and 1950s. Ironically, the moderate Eisenhower's party-building efforts in the South—which generally did not draw on racial appeals—provided a crucial boost to advocates seeking to turn the GOP in a more conservative direction. The Goldwater movement drew its greatest support from these new southern party organizations, bringing together disaffected southern Democrats and more traditional conservative northern Republicans.

THE CIVIL RIGHTS CASE AND THE STUDY OF POLITICAL DEVELOPMENT

This study argues that the roots of the civil rights realignment rest in changes in the Democratic coalition that took hold in the late 1930s and early 1940s. The rise of the CIO, coupled with the incorporation of African American voters into the Democratic coalition and the southern backlash against CIO-sponsored extensions of the New Deal, forged a new understanding of liberalism that finally incorporated civil rights as a significant element. The association between New Deal liberalism and civil rights support at the constituency level established a crucial basis for the party realignment on race.

Translating this early shift into an actual change in *national* party alignments required the confluence of two forces. First, the relatively independent electoral bases of state parties and rank-and-file members of Congress provided an institutional foothold for those seeking to redefine the parties' stance toward civil rights. Political fragmentation allowed pressure for change and adaptation to trickle up gradually without requiring an immediate confrontation with national leaders. Second, the African American–led civil rights movement pushed the issue to the top of the national agenda, forcing politicians to choose sides. These two factors reinforced each other: civil rights activists encouraged Democratic politicians to put legislation onto the agenda at the state and national levels; these legislative efforts then further raised the salience of the issue and sharpened the divisions between pro– and anti–civil rights forces.

More broadly, the civil rights case suggests that one cannot understand large-scale political transformations by focusing on only a single institution or a narrow time window. Instead, the intersection of long-term political trajectories proved critical.[1] The reshaping of the party system in the 1930s constitutes the first trajectory. The initial rise of the New Deal coalition in the North—and Republicans' turn to antistatism—had little direct connection to civil rights concerns. The new groups that backed the New Deal—CIO unionists, African Americans, Jews, and other urban liberals—were not attracted to the Democrats by the party's (weak) civil rights stand. But their presence in the party coalition had a crucial impact on how the party positioned itself on racial issues over the ensuing decades.

Along the second political trajectory, civil rights movement activists worked to push the issue higher on the national agenda through direct action. Although these activists often had ties to the Democratic Party dating from the New Deal era, the civil rights movement's strategy was not dictated by the Democrats' partisan concerns. From A. Philip Randolph's March on Washington Movement through the voter registration campaigns in the South in the early 1960s, movement activists capitalized on available opportunities, regardless of how those maneuvers fit in with the goals of Democratic politicians. In sum, the civil rights movement played a decisive role in making civil rights salient, while the earlier reshuffling of coalitions in the 1930s and 1940s shaped the impact of that issue's salience for the party system as a whole.

Similarly, Goldwater's capture of the GOP was set off most immediately by the reaction against the civil rights movement, yet its roots can be found in the coalitional and ideological changes at lower levels of the party that date back to the New Deal, along with the southern party-building efforts of the 1950s. Understanding the connections between the changes in the New Deal era and the ultimate reshuffling of national party positions on civil rights therefore requires tracing the interplay of voters, activists, state parties, members of Congress, and national party leaders over several decades.

While I have not aimed to put forward a theory that explains all party realignments, the interaction between geographic decentralization and movement activism that proved important in this case may have implications for understanding other transformations in party alignments, particularly when the top leaders of both parties have a stake in keeping an issue off of the agenda. Two potential cases to examine through this lens are the rise of abolitionism in the 1830s–1850s and the currency issue in the 1870s–1890s. In both cases, the existing party lines were premised on suppression of an issue that cross-cut each party's coalition.

In the 1830s–1850s third parties played a much greater role in generating the partisan transformation than in the modern period. Nonetheless, even in this earlier period, antislavery activists' strategy bears important parallels to the modern civil rights movement. As Corey Brooks argues in his impressive new book, political abolitionists worked through third parties to raise the visibility of slavery on the political agenda.[2] Abolitionists focused much of their attention on Congress, where they used petitions, legislative initiatives, and protracted battles to elect the House Speaker as opportunities to force a public debate regarding slavery, which in turn allowed them to transmit their arguments to a much wider audience. Just as civil rights discharge petitions overcame the gatekeeping of southern committee barons in the late 1930s and the 1940s, political abolitionists found openings to force a debate that both parties' leaders sought to avoid. This debate then pressured reluctant northern politicians to take a stand, notwithstanding their leaders' wishes. One conjecture that arises from the civil rights case is that federalism and the locally rooted constituencies of individual members of Congress provided key institutional footholds for political abolitionists as they built momentum for their cause.

Where the slavery issue eventually gave rise to a new party—and the destruction of the once-competitive Whig Party—the currency issue resembles the civil rights case more closely in that one party shifted ground to incorporate a new issue commitment. National Democratic leaders—such as Samuel Tilden and Grover Cleveland of New York—had resisted the calls for inflation that arose from agrarian interests within the party starting in the 1870s. These leaders believed that winning the White House required New York's electoral votes, and they were keenly aware that the financial interests in that state fervently opposed currency expansion. But the political ground gradually shifted below top Democratic leaders, allowing William Jennings Bryan and his populist allies to gain control at the national convention in 1896. The civil rights case suggests the hypothesis that state parties and locally based politicians may have provided an institutional mechanism for pro-inflation activists to gradually gain the upper hand within the national Democratic Party, notwithstanding the opposition of many top leaders. The populist movement's efforts to heighten the salience of the currency issue also may have played a role that is broadly analogous to that of the civil rights movement, forcing national elites to take a clear stand on an issue that they had sought to straddle for nearly two decades. In both the antislavery and currency cases, attention to the intersection of long-term political trajectories—involving both movement activists and midlevel party actors—may illuminate how party lines were transformed despite the resistance of top party leaders.

The idea that political development is driven by the intersection of multiple long-term trajectories also has broader methodological implications for the study of politics. Experimental approaches and other strong research designs that allow one to identify the causal effect of a single independent variable on an outcome of interest have put empirical political science research on a much sounder footing over the past decade. By leveraging random assignment—or exogenous shocks and interventions that approximate random assignment—these designs allow one to assess the impact of a causal (treatment) variable by comparing the observed value of the dependent variable for different values of the "treatment." The great benefit of this approach is that it holds constant the many confounding variables that stand in the way of sound causal inference. The control group provides a valid "counterfactual"—telling us what we would expect to observe in the absence of the key causal variable.

Yet many complex political phenomena, particularly large-scale historical changes, are not amenable to such designs. This is not just due to the data limitations that often plague historical work. Isolating the impact of a single variable is less useful when a transformation is the product of interactions across multiple layers of the political system. In that context, there is no single, adequate counterfactual that can be used as the basis for comparison to the observed outcome.

Rather than sidestepping efforts to explain such substantively important developments, one can draw on a wide range of data sources at several levels of the political system—including opinion surveys, state party platforms, new measures of congressional behavior, and content analysis of news coverage—to gain substantial explanatory leverage. Systematically tracing the interplay of multiple historical processes over time can yield insight into the sources of political development even when clean causal identification is simply not possible.

The Civil Rights Case and Political Parties

Multimethod historical analysis can also provide us with a level of nuanced theoretical insight that is difficult to generate when research questions are framed more narrowly. In this case, the civil rights realignment has important implications for our understanding of political parties. Two key claims stand out: First, the civil rights case puts in sharp relief the limitations of thinking of parties as coherent entities governed by a single overriding logic. Second, it highlights both the contributions and limitations of thinking of parties as coalitions of group demanders.

Scholars have often treated the coalition forged by Roosevelt as a stable equilibrium rooted in a North-South bargain to ignore the race question in order to build the welfare state and win elections.[3] There is much truth to this assessment: in particular, Roosevelt and other top New Deal leaders were keenly aware of the need to keep southern racial conservatives onboard and thus sought to avoid taking a stand on racial issues. The New Deal was compromised from the start by the perceived need to accommodate the

South. This perspective is consistent with a range of theories of parties: it fits comfortably both with Anthony Downs's idea that parties are teams of politicians that cooperate to win power and with the increasingly influential view that coalitions of intense policy-demanding groups use parties to secure the policies they care about most (see discussion of the latter below).[4]

But a closer examination reveals that the Democratic Party was being torn apart from within from the late 1930s onward. While national leaders wanted to avoid issues that divided the party, the rank-and-file members of the party's contending southern and northern wings had their own agendas. Southern Democrats worked closely with Republicans to launch investigations targeting labor unions and to promote legislation reducing union power.[5] In this way, one party faction sought to undercut the group that was the most important mobilization instrument for electing members from the opposing faction. For their part, rank-and-file northern Democrats signed discharge petitions to force civil rights bills to the House floor, directly challenging southerners' central policy commitment. For all of national party leaders' efforts to suppress Democrats' deep divisions, the political actors on the ground understood that the rendition of New Deal liberalism put forward by the CIO and other urban liberals starting in the late 1930s was incompatible with conservative southern Democrats' understanding of their interests. This realization gave each side a strong incentive to undercut the core interests of the other in struggling for control of the party.

Given the sharp political battles lines drawn in the late 1930s between urban racial liberals and southern conservatives, the most striking feature of the realignment is not Johnson's and Goldwater's 1964 choices but rather that it took so long for civil rights advocates to complete their capture of the national Democratic Party and for racial conservatives to emerge atop the GOP. Indeed, it may seem puzzling at first that the national leaders of *both* parties generally sought to avoid taking a clear stand on civil rights in the 1930s–1950s. In a two-party system, one would normally expect that if an issue is too dangerous and divisive for one party to handle, the other party would have an incentive to seize on that issue.[6]

One potential answer to this apparent puzzle is uncertainty: it was not entirely clear to political observers at the time whether the winning strategy was to forge a liberal coalition on pro–civil rights lines (as the Democrats eventually did) or to unite the economic and racial conservatives of the Midwest, Sunbelt, and South (as Republicans eventually chose). Johnson's landslide victory seemed to signal that the former strategy was the winning one, but it was not long before political analysts were touting the success of Nixon's "Southern Strategy."[7] One could argue that in a context of severe uncertainty, risk-averse parties might prefer the status quo to a sharp departure.

But uncertainty is only part of the answer. Crucially, neither party was a unified actor deciding on the best course for its electoral future. Instead, the competing party factions put forward very different visions of what was in their party's electoral interests, and there was no neutral arbiter in a position to order these conflicting claims.[8]

Among Republicans, an alliance with white southern racial conservatives promised to empower the more conservative, midwestern Taft wing of the party while undermining the place of the moderate, northeastern wing. As shown in chapter 10, northeastern and mid-Atlantic moderates had the decisive say in GOP national conventions in the 1940s and 1950s. These politicians believed that a moderate party image on both economics and race was the best way to win governor's races and Senate seats in big urban states such as New York, Pennsylvania, New Jersey, Illinois, Michigan, and California, and to secure an Electoral College majority. Presidential nominees Thomas Dewey and Dwight Eisenhower were keen to win additional votes from disaffected southern whites, but they did not want to remake the GOP as a conservative party. When the Goldwater movement gained the upper hand, the Eisenhower moderates were aghast at the implications for their vision of the GOP. Even if an embrace of racial conservatism was in the long-term electoral interests of the national Republican Party, it threatened the political future of the Rockefellers, Scrantons, and Romneys of the party. These politicians believed that a party brand that sells in Mississippi and South Carolina would not work in New York, Pennsylvania, and Michigan.[9]

For Democrats, the two warring camps disagreed bitterly about which path forward would allow the party to thrive. A third group—nationally oriented top party leaders—had a stake in preventing either faction from emerging victorious. Most top party leaders saw the prospect of a decisive break with the South as posing an unacceptable risk to the party's electoral vote and congressional majorities, yet these same leaders also understood that the northern wing was too large and important to flout. Under these conditions, most national leaders positioned themselves as moderates with ties to both factions. Speaker Sam Rayburn, Majority Leader John McCormack, Senate leaders Alben Barkley, Scott Lucas, Ernest McFarland, and Lyndon Johnson, and presidential contenders such as Adlai Stevenson sought to avoid a clear identification with either northern liberals or southern conservatives. Having staked their power on construction of a moderate party brand, these leaders saw the rise of northern liberals—as reflected by the formation of the pro–civil rights Democratic Advisory Council and the Democratic Study Group a few years later—as a threat to their own influence over the party's direction, regardless of whether the liberals' strategy was in the long-term electoral interests of the national party. In sum, as both parties grappled with civil rights, no one was in a position to impose a unified, coherent strategy; instead, party transformation arose from an often-bitter factional struggle in which changes at the mass and midlevels eventually tilted the balance of power.[10]

As discussed throughout this book, the civil rights case also has important implications for the theory of political parties put forward by John Zaller, Kathleen Bawn, and their collaborators.[11] By placing groups at the center of party theory, this so-called UCLA School illuminates a core logic of party positioning. There is no question that groups and group interests loom large in the civil rights case: Democrats' support depended critically on the party's African American, Jewish, and labor union constituents, while Republican opposition to the FEPC, in particular, owed much to the party's ties to business.[12] Parties are, in an important sense, coalitions of intense policy demanders. If one seeks to understand how each party positions itself on issues of the day or which candidates are likely to have a realistic chance of winning a party's presidential nomination, assessing the views of the party's major constituency groups is the right place to start.

At the same time, the civil rights case underscores important features of party politics that are in tension with the assumption that parties are coherent entities reflecting stable coalitional bargains. Most important, American parties are federal in structure, with the result that politicians in different states and congressional districts answer to different core constituent groups. There is no guarantee that these constituencies will view one another as allies when it comes to the major policy challenges facing the country. Indeed, at times, politicians with one kind of electoral base (e.g., northern liberal Democrats) and those with a very different base (e.g., southern Democrats) may view weakening the other party faction as essential to their own political future.

If each faction that was entrenched in a party had a veto over the acceptance of new coalition entrants, such conflicts might not occur. But southern Democrats of the 1930s—arguably the most deeply rooted party faction imaginable—had no such veto power when African American voters and CIO unions entered Roosevelt's coalition in the 1930s. Many southerners inveighed against the incorporation of these new constituency groups into the party and sought to undermine their influence. But they failed in this endeavor because northern Democrats quickly learned that these new entrants would help them win elections in their own states and districts.[13]

Rather than coherent entities with a single defining logic, parties are historical composites that incorporate multiple competing interests and logics. In that type of setting, the actors competing to shape the party's direction will have strong incentives to draw on a wide range of power bases. In the civil rights case, the contending sides sought to enlist ordinary voters, movement activists, organized groups, state parties, rank-and-file members of Congress, and national party elites as they prosecuted their battle for control of the party. Analyses of the civil rights realignment miss much of the important action if they focus on just one set of actors or one political trajectory since it was the interactions across these layers that drove the transformation.

These interactions also had an ideological dynamic that tends to be obscured if one thinks primarily in terms of specific policy demands. The entry of the CIO and African Americans into the Democratic coalition and the burgeoning alienation of southern conservative Democrats together created a new ideological cleavage that was then reinforced by the efforts of movement activists to raise the salience of civil rights issues. This new cleavage constrained the ability of groups and top party leaders to manage coalitional stresses. The CIO and its allies put forward a broad vision fusing concerns about "class" and "race" in a drive that threatened the central pillars of the South's political economy. Most top Democratic leaders were wary of this fusion, yet by the end of World War II, support for civil rights had become a critical indicator of a politician's liberal bona fides.

The new ideological cleavage also created opportunities for conservative Republicans seeking to seize control from the party's moderate leaders. Appeals to states' rights could be deployed to link white southerners' resistance to racial progress and labor organizing with one of conservative Republicans' favored lines of attack against the New Deal. Although these appeals did not immediately lead southerners to bolt outright from their longtime home in the Democratic Party, the two groups cooperated on a range of issues in Congress. The "conservative coalition" that dominated much of congressional politics from the late 1930s through the early 1960s imposed sharp limits on the New Deal's economic initiatives and was especially successful in limiting labor unions' progress.[14] In the longer term, as southerners steadily lost influence in the Democratic Party, Republicans' invocation of states' rights would serve as the basis for their formal incorporation into the GOP fold.

The behavior of southern whites over a long span of political history is especially useful for thinking about the nature of American parties. One might view southern whites as simply another intense policy demander. From this perspective, the race issue and memories of Reconstruction kept southern whites as stalwart Democrats for nearly a century following the Civil War; these voters moved to the Republicans once the parties' positions on their paramount issue—race—finally switched decisively.

Yet the striking unity of southern white voters—first in voting for Democrats for decades after the Civil War and, more recently, in voting for Republican candidates by overwhelming margins—suggests that more might be going on. Notwithstanding accounts suggesting that the South's "exceptionalism" has become a thing of the past, southern white voters are arguably nearly as distinctive today as they were in the 1940s.[15] In the 2012 election Barack Obama won just 34 percent of the white vote in the South and polled a paltry 26 percent among whites in the five Deep South states of Alabama, Mississippi, South Carolina, Georgia, and Louisiana. By contrast, Obama won about 49 percent of the white vote outside the South.[16] For comparison, the South's presidential vote was about 18–20 percent more Democratic than the rest of the country during the Roosevelt years. More generally, Republicans have achieved a degree of dominance among southern whites—particularly native southern whites—that has re-created something close to a "New" Solid South. Indeed, as of 2015, not a single Democrat represents a majority white district in the Deep South; the few House Democrats from Mississippi, Alabama, Georgia, South Carolina, and Louisiana are African Americans representing majority minority districts.

This southern white distinctiveness is perhaps more deeply rooted than any specific policy demand. Instead, it arguably reflects an interlocking set of racial, sectional, and religious identities and animosities. Many southern whites view the groups associated with the contemporary Democratic Party—racial and ethnic minorities, feminists, gays and lesbians, secular voters, and "liberals" more generally—as opposed to their own core values. Enduring sectional and cultural identities and animosities are not necessarily contrary to a theory of parties focused on "intense policy demanders," but they at least suggest that the kinds of coalitions that are formed are far from arbitrary.[17]

Indeed, one can see many of the partisan changes that have taken place since the 1960s and 1970s as closely intertwined with southerners' realignment to the Republican Party. It is well-known that a wide range of issues that cross-cut party lines prior to the 1970s—gun control, environmentalism, gay rights, abortion rights, and feminism—now divide the parties, with Democrats siding with liberals and Republicans with conservatives. It is wrong to see the shifts on each of these issues as separate cases of new policy demanders being incorporated into one party or the other. Instead, the shifts across issues were mutually reinforcing: as southern whites moved into the Republican Party, the Democratic coalition gradually lost its rural, socially traditionalist constituency. To take but one example, southern evangelicals were among the leading forces within the GOP pushing the party to embrace the socially conservative position on abortion and gay rights. Dislodging southern white voters from the national Democratic Party can be viewed as the first, crucial step in the sweeping changes in party politics over the past four decades.[18]

Just as southern white voters had anchored the Democratic Party for a full century following Andrew Jackson's rise, they now anchor the Republican Party, with their racial, cultural, and sectional identities helping shape the structure of the entire party system.[19] American parties are coalitions of intense policy demanders, but they are also (often) deeply rooted, sectionally based organizations. While an earlier generation of scholarship grappled with the relationship among political ideologies, sectional cleavages, and

narrower interests, newly available data on public opinion and state platforms may allow for an even richer understanding of the roots and logics of
American party coalitions.[20]

The Civil Rights Realignment, Backlash, and the Politics of Race Today

Beyond its implications for understanding the New Deal and for theories of
political parties, the dynamics of the racial realignment from the 1930s–
1960s has much to tell us about the politics of race since the mid-1960s. The
legislative achievements of 1964–65 represented a moment of triumph and
hope, but even then the signs of trouble were not far from the surface.

There is a rich literature on the politics of racial backlash from the 1960s
onward.[21] Civil rights opponents did not disappear from the scene in the
wake of the 1964 election. Even as explicit racial appeals lost their political
viability, politicians found numerous other ways to tap into racial animus
to promote their electoral and policy goals.[22] The rise of the carceral state—
and the imprisonment of a vast share of the African American population—is
only the most glaring reminder of the continued centrality of racial injustice
in American politics.[23]

Several studies have drawn connections between the cleavages present before 1964 and subsequent developments. For example, Anthony Chen shows
that critics of affirmative action in the 1970s and 1980s echoed the attacks
made by conservative opponents of fair employment practices legislation
decades earlier.[24] The evidence in this book complements Chen's account:
conservative "backlash" was not an artifact of new demands raised by civil
rights activists after 1964 but instead had deep roots in long-standing conservative skepticism of civil rights initiatives.

At the same time, the evidence concerning white public opinion presented
in chapter 5 shows that conservative Republicans would not be the only
obstacles facing civil rights advocates going forward. Northern white Democratic voters were more supportive than Republicans when it came to many
civil rights initiatives, but they differed little from their GOP counterparts
when it came to racial prejudice and policies that encourage close social
mixing. As fair housing and school busing rose onto the agenda, it should
not be surprising that many of these white Democrats provided bitter opposition to the civil rights agenda. The limited progress after 1964 reflected
not just conservative Republican opposition but also the enduring tensions
among northern Democrats on racial issues.[25]

One should not, however, conclude from this rank-and-file racism that
white working-class Democrats have always stood in the way of civil rights
progress. Instead, on many issues, including fair employment practices, such

Democrats gave substantially more support to civil rights than did their GOP counterparts. The active support for civil rights that came from many labor leaders—particularly in the CIO but also in key AFL-CIO unions after the 1955 merger—was at least in part mirrored at the rank-and-file level, even if with less consistency than among CIO leaders (see chapter 5).[26] The politics of racial resentment since the 1960s has clear linkages to the patterns evident in the mass public before the civil rights era yet does not negate the role played by labor unions in forging the liberal civil rights coalition.

The widespread racism that was evident in the 1960s continues to shape racial politics to this day. In that context, Barack Obama's presidency inspired both claims that we had finally reached a new era in race relations and considerable frustration that not much actually changed on the ground, notwithstanding the hopeful rhetoric of 2008.[27]

The civil rights case of the 1930s–1960s may illuminate why the pace of change under Obama proved so disappointing to liberal critics. In contrast to the view that Lyndon Johnson moved his party to embrace racial liberalism, this book has argued that the change in party alignments depended on an earlier transformation at the mass and midlevels of the parties, which intersected with the activism of the civil rights movement to transform the ground on which Johnson stood.

Obama, by contrast, found himself leading a Democratic Party in which the voices pushing for dramatic action on race constituted but one of several factions, none of which commanded a clear majority. The contemporary Democratic Party consists of a wide range of groups—each with its own priorities—but there is no overarching sense of a "liberal agenda" that links together these priorities into a unified program in which the individual parts are seen as intimately connected. In the 1940s–1950s, liberals understood that progress on civil rights was essential to the broad project of defeating the conservative coalition, and thereby paving the way for fulfilling the New Deal's potential across a range of policies. Today's Democratic Party looks more like a coalition of narrow, intense policy demanders than did the liberal coalition led by the CIO and its allies. This is arguably part of the *problem* confronting the Democrats, rather than a constant feature of American party politics.

Some have argued that a focus on racial issues has stood in the way of creating the kind of wide-ranging coalition that is needed for liberalism to regain its momentum and confront the urgent challenge posed by escalating income inequality.[28] From this perspective, it was only in the 1960s that the cause of social democracy became linked to racial justice in the United States—and this linkage is what ultimately brought down the liberal project. But this gets the history wrong. By the time of World War II, the liberal coalition identified civil rights as a critical front in the battle for economic and social progress, and its members understood that defeating southern defenders of Jim Crow was essential for liberalism's future. Indeed, much of the moral fervor that fed the liberal project in the 1940s came precisely from its linkage to the cause of racial justice.

Still, even if racial justice were a priority within the Democratic Party, the evidence presented here suggests that an external force would be necessary to precipitate elite action on the issue. For policy to change, it was not enough for individual Democratic politicians to adopt pro–civil rights positions in the 1940s and 1950s. Overcoming the entrenched opposition to progress demanded that politicians make civil rights a top legislative priority. This, in turn, required a cascade of protest that made it clear the status quo could not be sustained. Johnson's willingness to take the political risks inherent in his civil rights push depended on a social movement forcing the issue to the top of the national agenda, something he alone would not and could not have accomplished.[29]

Nonetheless, even in the absence of a major mass movement for racial justice, changes in the demographic composition of the parties and the country at large may once again gradually transform the Democratic Party from below. The rise of Latinos as a key element in the Democratic coalition has already generated significant pressure on national Democrats to take action on deportation and citizenship policies. It may be that as the base of the Democratic Party increasingly comes to rest on a population that is "majority minority," the balance of pressures on party elites will shift.

Shifting the group composition of the parties is likely a necessary but not sufficient condition for major policy change. The CIO and its urban liberal allies in the 1930s and 1940s were important not just as stand-alone groups within the Democratic Party. Their significance rested as well in developing, articulating, and aggressively pursuing a broader programmatic vision that linked together the aspirations of a range of distinct groups. The bitter response to this program forged a clear division in which southern conservatives were identified on one side and African Americans, unions, Jews, and other urban liberals on the other. A challenge facing contemporary liberals is once again forging a politics in which reformers seeking progress for particular groups do not see themselves as isolated claimants on the party system but instead as part of a much broader ideological coalition with common aims and shared enemies.

Notes

Chapter 1: Introduction

1. Edward G. Carmines and James A. Stimson, *Issue Evolution: Race and the Transformation of American Politics* (Princeton, NJ: Princeton University Press, 1989).

2. Thomas Edsall and Mary Edsall, *Chain Reaction: The Impact of Race, Rights, and Taxes on American Politics* (New York: Norton, 1992), 7.

3. Ibid., 7, 35–36; John R. Zaller, *The Nature and Origins of Mass Opinion* (Cambridge: Cambridge University Press, 1992), 12–13.

4. Carmines and Stimson, *Issue Evolution*; Zaller, *Nature and Origins of Mass Opinion*, 11–13.

5. The content of "racial liberalism" changed over time; several policies under consideration in the 1960s–1970s—e.g., busing and affirmative action—were not part of the political conversation in the 1930s. Racial liberalism is defined here in relative terms, reflecting where actors stand on the policies pursued by civil rights advocates at the particular moment in time. This allows one to assess the relative positions of the parties and the degree of alignment between civil rights and economic policy views but not the absolute level of racial liberalism. Racial conservatism is understood here as occupying the opposite end of this underlying spectrum, identified by opposition to the policies pursued by civil rights advocates.

6. Joseph Califano, *The Triumph and Tragedy of Lyndon Johnson* (New York: Simon and Schuster, 1992), 55.

7. Margaret Weir, "States, Race, and the Decline of New Deal Liberalism," *Studies in American Political Development* 19 (October 2005): 157–72.

8. Doug McAdam and Karina Kloos, *Deeply Divided: Racial Politics and Social Movements in Post-War America* (New York: Oxford University Press, 2014), 79, 68.

9. David Karol, *Party Position Change in American Politics: Coalition Management* (New York: Cambridge University Press, 2009), 109–22.

10. William H. Riker, "The CIO in Politics, 1936–1946" (PhD diss., Harvard University, 1948).

11. The first New Deal featured the emergency recovery and relief legislation of 1933–34, while the second New Deal was highlighted by several landmark laws adopted in 1935: the Social Security Act, the National Labor Relations Act, the Wealth Tax Act, and the Emergency Relief Appropriation Act (which led to the Works Progress Administration). The labor, tax, and relief laws of the second New Deal became touchstones of partisan and ideological conflict and were seen as reflecting a turn away from Roosevelt's initial effort to forge an all-class alliance. See William E. Leuchtenburg, *Franklin D. Roosevelt and the New Deal, 1932–1940* (New York: Harper & Row, 1963), chaps. 4 and 7.

12. Sean Farhang and Ira Katznelson, "The Southern Imposition: Congress and Labor in the New Deal and Fair Deal," *Studies in American Political Development* 19 (2005): 1–30.

13. In this book I define the "South" to include the eleven states of the Confederacy, along with Kentucky and Oklahoma. The remaining states are referred to as the "North."

14. See Richard P. Young and Jerome S. Burnstein, "Federalism and the Demise of Prescriptive Representation in the United States," *Studies in American Political Development* 9 (Spring 1995): 1–54, for the argument that federalism enhanced the influence of African Americans once the Great Migration created a critical mass in key northern states. See Theda Skocpol, *Protecting Soldiers and Mothers* (Cambridge, MA: Harvard University Press, 1992), for analysis of how federalism afforded groups the opportunity to mobilize at the grassroots level and through federated organizations to promote policy development in the realm of social welfare policy.

15. Urban politics often provided an entryway for African American politicians and voters into Democratic politics. See, e.g., James Q. Wilson, "Two Negro Politicians," *Midwestern Journal of Political Science* 4, 4 (1960): 346–69; Harold Gosnell, *Negro Politicians: The Rise of Negro Politics in Chicago* (Chicago: University of Chicago Press, 1967). As discussed in chapter 9, machine Democrats—newly sensitive to the increased number of African American voters in the wake of wartime migration—played a key role in the liberal triumph at the 1948 Democratic convention, when they sided with the pro–civil rights forces over the objections of national party leaders. See also Thomas Sugrue, *Sweet Land of Liberty: The Forgotten Struggle for Civil Rights in the North* (New York: Random House, 2008), 111–15.

16. The presidential ambitions characteristic of many senators give them a national orientation that cuts against the local roots emphasized here. As a result, senators constitute a mixed case: some northern Democrats downplayed civil rights in service of their national strategy (e.g., John Kennedy), while others, such as Hubert Humphrey, used civil rights advocacy as a launching pad to national prominence. Although the quantitative analysis focuses on the House, chapters 8–10 incorporate the maneuvering in both chambers.

17. The antislavery and currency cases are briefly discussed in chapter 11.

18. In countries with multiparty systems, third parties likely play a key role in bringing demands for new policies to the forefront when those policies threaten the leading parties' existing strategies. Given the institutional obstacles to third parties in the United States, it may be that federalism allows state parties to play a somewhat analogous role in providing a vehicle for new issue demands. In Canada, which had what has been called a two-and-a-half-party system for many years, the New Democratic Party (NDP) used its control of provincial governments as a showcase for health insurance reform, which contributed to eventual national-level policy innovation. (It is worth noting that Canada combines third parties *and* federalism; this combination may be especially potent as third parties are able to engage in provincial policy experimentation.) I thank Paul Pierson and Richard Valelly for suggesting this line of thinking.

19. See Richard F. Bensel, *Sectionalism and American Political Development, 1880–1980* (Madison: University of Wisconsin Press, 1984), 150–52; Bensel, "Sectionalism and Congressional Development," in *The Oxford Handbook of the American Congress*, ed. Eric Schickler and Frances E. Lee (New York: Oxford University Press, 2011), 771–73; Ira Katznelson, Kim Geiger, and Daniel Kryder, "Limiting Liberalism: The Southern Veto in Congress, 1933–1950," *Political Science Quarterly*, 108, 2 (1995): 283–306; and Robert C. Lieberman, *Shifting the Color Line: Race and the American Welfare State* (Cambridge, MA: Harvard University Press, 1998), 23–25.

20. See Lieberman, *Shifting the Color Line*, for an important treatment of the Social Security case.

21. Walter White, *A Man Called White: The Autobiography of Walter White* (New York: Viking, 1948), 169–70.

22. For the revisionist view, see Kevin J. McMahon, *Reconsidering Roosevelt on Race* (Chicago: University of Chicago Press, 2004). For a critical account of the New Deal's approach to the race issue, see Ira Katznelson, *When Affirmative Action Was White* (New York: Norton, 2005); Katznelson, *Fear Itself: The New Deal and the Origins of Our Time* (New York: Liveright, 2013). Desmond S. King and Rogers M. Smith offer the helpful formulation that Roosevelt operated within both what they refer to as the "white supremacist" and the "egalitarian transformative" institutional orders in American politics, perpetuating racial discrimination in some ways while also undermining its hold in other ways. King and Smith, "Racial Orders in American Political Development," *American Political Science Review* 99 (February 2005): 75–92.

23. See, e.g., Farhang and Katznelson, "Southern Imposition"; Katznelson, Geiger, and Kryder, "Limiting Liberalism."

24. Edsall and Edsall, *Chain Reaction*, 6–13; Michael Omi and Howard Winant, *Racial Formation in the United States,* 2nd ed. (New York: Routledge, 1994), chap. 7; Donald R. Kinder and Lynn M. Sanders, *Divided by Color: Racial Politics and Democratic Ideals* (Chicago: University of Chicago Press, 1996), chaps. 8 and 9.

25. Eric Schickler and Kathryn Pearson, "Agenda Control, Majority Party Power, and the House Committee on Rules, 1939–1952," *Legislative Studies Quarterly* 34, 4 (2009): 455–91.

26. As Farhang and Katznelson, "Southern Imposition," show, the New Deal changed in other ways as well in the late 1930s and the 1940s. The emphasis on government planning that many early New Deal advocates pushed gave way to a focus on fiscal policy in the 1940s. This turn away from planning was partly rooted in shifts in the South, though it also had roots in broader shifts in public opinion. See Eric Schickler and Devin Caughey, "Public Opinion, Organized Labor, and the Limits of New Deal Liberalism, 1936–1945," *Studies in American Political Development* 25, 2 (2011): 162–89. The move to fiscal policy did not, however, eliminate the threat posed by the CIO and African Americans' broad agenda to southern Democrats or temper southerners' eagerness to rein in the industrial labor movement.

27. Kathleen Bawn, Martin Cohen, David Karol, Seth Masket, Hans Noel, and John Zaller, "A Theory of Political Parties: Groups, Policy Demanders, and Nominations in American Politics," *Perspectives on Politics* 10, 3 (2012): 571–97; Karol, *Party Position Change*; Marty Cohen, David Karol, Hans Noel, and John Zaller, *The Party Decides: Presidential Nominations Before and After Reform* (Chicago: University of Chicago Press, 2008).

28. Bawn et al., "Theory of Parties," 585. Bawn et al. cite as evidence a study of candidate positioning, which finds that candidate positions "nearly all reflect the positions of their national party agendas, with only modest trimming in response to local conditions" (593). Though based in part on a 1996 candidate survey, the earlier study uses a dimensional scaling of roll-call voting from 1874 to 1996 to show that "throughout this period congressional candidates have primarily espoused the ideology associated with the national party." See Stephen Ansolabehere, James M. Snyder Jr., and Charles Stewart III, "Candidate Positioning in U.S. House Elections," *American Journal of Political Science* 45, 1 (2001): 136.

29. Bawn et al., "Theory of Parties," 574.

30. See Karol, *Party Position Change*, chap. 4; Anthony Chen, *The Fifth Freedom: Jobs, Politics, and Civil Rights in the United States, 1941–1972* (Princeton, NJ: Princeton University Press, 2009).

31. Celler was first elected in 1922 and served fifty years in the House.

32. For the view of national elites as party coalition managers, see Karol, *Party Position Change*; Bawn et al., "Theory of Parties," 581.

33. These cases are also not isolated instances in American history. For example, the feud between progressive and old guard Republicans in the first decades of the twentieth century is another case in which two geographically based factions, each with an independent electoral base, put forward opposing programs that reflected a deep division over commitments of ideology and interest.

34. See Adam Bonica, "Mapping the Ideological Marketplace," *American Journal of Political* Science 58, 2 (2014): 367–87, on campaign contribution networks.

35. Karen Orren and Stephen Skowronek, *The Search for American Political Development* (Cambridge: Cambridge University Press, 2004); Eric Schickler, *Disjointed Pluralism: Institutional Innovation and the Development of the U.S. House* (Princeton, NJ: Princeton University Press, 2001).

36. The Wagner Act is a good example of the idea that policy can "make" politics. In this case, a legislative change contributed to the growth of a new interest—industrial labor unions—that then transformed the balance of power within the Democratic Party and in American politics more generally. At the same time, the CIO's triumphs provoked a backlash in which the opponents of union power—southern Democrats and northern Republicans—coalesced to rein in organized labor. This opposition distinguishes the Wagner Act from some other landmark cases (such as Social Security) in which a policy created a self-sustaining politics. On policy feedback, see Andrea Campbell, "Policy Makes Mass Politics," *Annual Review of Political Science* 15 (2002): 333–51; see also David Plotke, "The Wagner Act, Again: Politics and Labor, 1935–1937," *Studies in American Political Development* 3 (1989): 104–56.

37. Devin Caughey, "Congress, Public Opinion, and Representation in the One-Party South, 1930s–1960s" (PhD diss., University of California, Berkeley, 2013).

38. Bawn et al. ("Theory of Parties") do not argue that all policy demanders are narrow. But their account emphasizes *particular* demands rather than overarching ideological crusades.

39. John Gerring shows that Republican antistatism began to take hold in 1928. This initial shift became more pronounced as Republicans sought grounds to critique the New Deal in the 1930s. See Gerring, *Party Ideologies in America, 1828–1996* (New York: Cambridge University Press, 2001).

40. One might ask if this is Whig history, in which one can find the early roots of the realignment that succeeded, but there were a range of other, equally plausible alternatives that did not occur (even though they too had roots in the 1930s). However, when one examines political debates in the late 1930s and the 1940s, discussions of realignment invariably focused on the potential for Republicans (or a new party) to bring southern racial conservatives together with northern economic conservatives, and for Democrats (or a new party) to unite union labor, African Americans, and other liberal forces under a common banner. In other words, from 1937–38 onward, discussions of realignment focused on the anomalous position of southern conservatives in the party system and on the race-labor nexus.

41. In a recent study, Hans Noel highlights the importance of public intellectuals in constructing ideology, including modern liberalism. While this is an insightful contribution, I contend that elite discourse is not sufficient to generate a meaningful ideological cleavage. Midlevel party actors and voters can also play a crucial role and certainly did so in the case of the civil rights realignment. See Noel, *Political Ideologies and Political Parties in America* (Cambridge: Cambridge University Press, 2014).

42. Orren and Skowronek, *Search for American Political Development*.

43. As chapter 3 discusses, a handful of Democratic politicians—such as Joseph Guffey of Pennsylvania—experimented with using civil rights appeals as part of their efforts to attract African American votes. The gestures of politicians such as Guffey likely influenced some African American voters but were not sufficiently visible or salient to account for the alignment between New Deal liberalism and racial liberalism among white voters.

44. See Jacquelyn Dodd Hall, "The Long Civil Rights Movement and the Political Uses of the Past," *Journal of American History* 91, 4 (2005): 1233–63.

45. See Mary L. Dudziak, *Cold War Civil Rights: Race and the Image of American Democracy* (Princeton, NJ: Princeton University Press, 2001). The Cold War also constrained the civil rights movement's opportunities. As Carol Anderson argues, rising anti-communism undermined the movement's efforts to draw on appeals to human rights—and to enlist the United Nations—as part of its strategy. See Anderson, *Eyes off the Prize: The United Nations and the African American Struggle for Human Rights, 1944–1955* (New York: Cambridge University Press, 2003).

46. Paul W. Holland, "Statistics and Causal Inference," *Journal of the American Statistical Association* 81 (1986): 945–60.

47. Chen, *Fifth Freedom*. See also Chen, "'The Hitlerian Rule of Quotas': Racial Conservatism and the Politics of Fair Employment Legislation in New York State, 1941–1945," *Journal of American History* 92 (2006): 1238–64.

48. Karol, *Party Position Change*, chap. 4. See also Karol, "Realignment without Replacement: Issue Evolution and Ideological Change among Members of Congress," paper presented at the Annual Meeting of the Midwest Political Science Association, Chicago, April 15–18, 1999; Jeffery Jenkins, Justin Peck, and Vesla Weaver, "Between Reconstructions: Congressional Action on Civil Rights, 1890–1940," *Studies in American Political Development* 24 (2010): 57–89; and Jeffery Jenkins and Justin Peck, "Building toward Major Policy Change: Congressional Action on Civil Rights, 1941–1950," *Law and History Review* 31, 1 (2013): 139–98.

49. Taeku Lee, *Mobilizing Public Opinion* (Chicago: University of Chicago Press, 2002). See also Anthony Chen, Robert Mickey, and Robert Van Houweling, "Explaining the Contemporary Alignment of Race and Party: Evidence from California's 1946 Ballot Initiative on Fair Employment," *Studies in American Political Development* 22 (2008): 204–28.

50. Noel, *Political Ideologies and Political Parties*. Two recent, important contributions focus on southern partisan change. Joseph Lowndes's book on the rise of the southern GOP, *From the New Deal to the New Right: Race and the Social Origins of Modern Conservatism* (New Haven, CT: Yale University Press, 2009), argues that the Republican takeover of the South can be traced to developments in the late 1940s and 1950s, when strategists and leaders fused racial and economic conservatism, thus creating a unique form of American conservatism that had distinctive appeal in the region. Robert Mickey's landmark *Paths out of Dixie: The Democratization of Authoritarian Enclaves in America's Deep South* (Princeton, NJ: Princeton University Press, 2015), focuses on variation in how elites in the Deep South responded to the challenges posed by the movement to democratize their political and social institutions.

51. This book also builds on the burgeoning historiographic literature on civil rights in the North. For example, Sugrue's magisterial *Sweet Land of Liberty*, 111–21, offers a brief but important account of how civil rights activists turned to state and local politics when their opportunities at the national level were limited by the conservative coalition's influence in Congress. More generally, Sugrue provides the most comprehensive account of how activists generated the bottom-up pressure to force civil rights onto the agenda in

the North (and nationally), even as they confronted pervasive racial prejudice in the region. See also Robert O. Self, *American Babylon: Race and the Struggle for Postwar Oakland* (Princeton, NJ: Princeton University Press, 2003).

52. Carmines and Stimson, *Issue Evolution*, date the connection to the 1960s; Lee, *Mobilizing Public Opinion*, dates it to the late 1950s.

53. Interestingly, economic liberalism is more consistently related to support for desegregation than is partisanship.

54. Brian D. Feinstein and Eric Schickler, "Platforms and Partners: The Civil Rights Realignment Reconsidered," *Studies in American Political Development* 22, 1 (2008): 1–31.

55. See chapter 10 for survey evidence on GOP voters' views of Kennedy's civil rights policies.

Chapter 2: Race: The Early New Deal's Blind Spot

1. The CIO had a substantial communist contingent, and communists were among the strongest civil rights backers. Nonetheless, the CIO as a political organization—notwithstanding frequent charges of communism—was able to establish itself as a key member of the Democratic coalition.

2. White, *Man Called White*, 169–70.

3. See, e.g., Edward S. Robinson, "Trends of the Voter's Mind," *Journal of Social Psychology* 4 (1933): 265–84; William E. Leuchtenburg, *Franklin D. Roosevelt and the New Deal, 1932–1940* (New York: Harper & Row, 1963), 9–13. The Republican platform hedged on prohibition, arguing that it is not a "partisan political question" and emphasizing the range of views Republicans held on the policy. Even so, the Democrats' avowed wet stance made it clear that the GOP was the best hope for prohibition's defenders.

4. As quoted in Leuchtenburg, *Roosevelt and the New Deal*, 9.

5. Editorial, "How Shall We Vote?" *The New Republic* (hereafter *TNR*), August 17, 1932, 4–6.

6. See, e.g., Oscar Villard, "The Bipartisan Hypocrisy of Politicians," *Nation*, September 21, 1932, 247.

7. See Samuel Lubell, *The Future of American Politics* (New York: Harper and Brothers, 1952), 35–43; Walter Dean Burnham, *The American Party Systems: Stages of Political Development* (New York: Oxford University Press, 1967), 301.

8. "Smith Defies Roosevelt at 'Harmony' Banquet," *Los Angeles Times* (hereafter *LAT*), April 14, 1932, 1.

9. See, e.g., Arthur Krock, "Republicans Hail Signs of Smith Rift," *New York Times* (hereafter *NYT*), April 15, 1932, 1; "Bunk Cannot Win: Al Smith Assails Those Who Put Class against Class," *Chicago Tribune*, April 14, 1932, 1.

10. Raskob was a longtime executive at Du Pont and General Motors.

11. Ernest Jerome Hopkins, "Goodbye to Mr. Raskob," *TNR*, March 2, 1932, 63–65.

12. TRB, "Washington Notes," *TNR*, August 17, 1932, 16–17.

13. Ibid., 17. In another story the *New Republic* noted that Roosevelt's efforts had been focused on "placating the industrial and conservative East" (TRB, "Washington Notes," August 10, 1932, 342–43).

14. TRB, "Washington Notes," *TNR*, October 5, 1932, 206.

15. Oscar Villard, "Bipartisan Hypocrisy," *Nation*, September 21, 1932, 247.

16. Hopkins, "Goodbye to Mr. Raskob," 63–65.

17. Paul Y. Anderson, "The Moronic Conventions," *Nation*, June 22, 1932, 697–99.

18. For an excellent analysis of the Southern Caucus, see Ruth Bloch Rubin, "Intraparty Organization in the U.S. Congress" (PhD diss., University of California, Berkeley, 2014).

19. Frank Walsh was a prominent labor lawyer in the 1920s and 1930s. Originally from Missouri, he moved to New York, where he became a progressive leader and chair of the New York Power Authority.

20. Ralph Coghlan, "Missouri—a Threat and a Promise," *Nation*, November 2, 1932, 422–24.

21. Johnson is a more complicated case than Douglas or Woodin, but his policies at the NRA clearly favored business interests over labor and, over time, he became identified with probusiness conservatives. See Ellis Hawley, *The New Deal and the Problem of Monopoly* (Princeton, NJ: Princeton University Press, 1966).

22. Ira Katznelson, *Fear Itself: The New Deal and the Origins of Our Time* (New York: Liveright, 2013).

23. Jonathan Mitchell, "Mr. Roosevelt on Stilts," *TNR*, November 29, 1933, 69–71.

24. Stephen Skowronek, *The Politics Presidents Make*, rev. ed. (Cambridge, MA: Belknap Press, 1997), chap. 7, pt. 1.

25. *Congressional Intelligence* compiled the list for *Collier's*. A handful of additional roll calls were unrelated to economic liberalism and so are excluded (e.g., a naval expansion bill). None of the votes related to racial policy. The cases where the administration was identified on the conservative side were roll calls relating to spending (the Economy Act and related legislation), the Veterans Bonus, and currency expansion (silver).

26. Boas would also play an important role in debunking so-called scientific racism through his anthropological studies. See Lee D. Baker, "Columbia University's Franz Boas: He Led to the Undoing of Scientific Racism," *Journal of Blacks in Higher Education* 22 (Winter 1998–99): 89–96.

27. The full text of the plan was obtained from the Paul U. Kellogg Papers, University of Minnesota Library, Social Welfare History Archives, Box 36, Folder 341.

28. See Katznelson, *Fear Itself*, on the radical potential of the early New Deal.

29. Kellogg Papers, Box 36, Folders 341 and 342.

30. Raymond Gram Swing, "Issues before the New Congress," *Nation*, November 21, 1934, 582–83.

31. Editorial, "A New Party—the Program," *TNR*, May 29, 1935, 60–61.

32. Haakon M. Chevalier, "Farmer-Labor Conference," *TNR*, June 17, 1936, 172–73.

33. "Third Party Move Balked at Parley," *NYT*, June 1, 1936, 2.

34. Both La Follette's 1924 platform and the platform adopted by the pro–La Follette Conference for Progressive Political Action omitted mention of civil rights. See Donald Bruce Johnson and Kirk Harold Porter, *National Party Platforms, 1840–1972* (Urbana: University of Illinois Press, 1973), 252–56. There were a handful of exceptions to the tendency to keep civil rights out of liberal programmatic statements. Most notably, the League for Independent Action did include a discussion of lynching and civil rights in its lengthy 1932 platform. See Nathan Fine, "A Four Year Presidential Plan 1932–1936," *The American Labor Year Book, 1932*, vol. 13 (New York: Labor Research Department of the Rand School of Social Science), 102–16. However, coverage of the league generally did not mention civil rights concerns (see, e.g., Editorial, *Nation*, July 20, 1932, 46; Devere Allen, "A Program for Revolt," *Nation*, July 27, 1932, 80–82; John Dewey, "Prospects for a Third Party," *TNR*, July 27, 1932, 278–80).

35. "How They Are Voting," *TNR*, September 30, 1936, 223–24.

36. "How They Are Voting: IV," *TNR*, October 21, 1936, 304.

37. Ibid., 305. Wise referred explicitly to state legislators in New York who were worried about the value of securities.

38. Ibid. Since southerners were not backing the GOP, it is clear this was a reference to Al Smith and his northeastern allies. Kellogg adds that neither the *New Republic* nor the *Nation* commented on the lack of a civil rights plank in the Democrats' national platform.

See Peter John Kellogg, "Northern Liberals and Black America: A History of White Attitudes, 1936–1952" (PhD diss., Northwestern University, 1971). In June 1936 the *New Republic* presented a sixteen-page special supplement, "Balance Sheet of the New Deal," that reviewed the New Deal's accomplishments and limitations. The extensive discussion of New Deal social welfare programs never mentioned African Americans' exclusion from benefits. African Americans were specifically included only in the final section, "Minorities and Civil Liberties," which praised the Roosevelts' opposition to social discrimination, noted that the AAA had hurt both African American and white sharecroppers, and claimed the NRA had given some help to African American workers.

39. "What I Expect of Roosevelt," *Nation*, November 14, 1936, 571–74, and November 28, 1936, 627–29. The statement by Socialist Norman Thomas did criticize Roosevelt for giving reactionaries a "free hand in the South in return for their political support" but does not explicitly discuss civil rights (ibid., 571). None of the other eleven statements even alludes to African Americans.

40. "The Next Four Years: The Constitution," *TNR*, January 13, 1937, 317–21.

41. Noel, *Political Ideologies and Political Parties*, 149–50.

42. I used the search terms (Scottsboro or lynch*) and "Roosevelt" to identify stories.

43. See, e.g., "Robinson Explains Our Peace Stand," *NYT*, May 26, 1933, 5; "Exchange Bill May Be Held Up," *LAT*, March 6, 1934, 3; Arthur Krock, "Subtlety Marks Maneuvering on Tax Proposals," *NYT*, June 25, 1935, 18.

44. The Southern Tenant Farmers' Union, which organized on a biracial basis, began to bring racial issues to the fore in fighting against the oppressive conditions facing both white and African American tenant farmers. Some left-wing administrators in the AAA sided with the nascent union, but they were purged in 1935 by Secretary of Agriculture Henry Wallace, who feared that the movement would damage relations with southern leaders such as Robinson. See David Eugene Conrad, *The Forgotten Farmers: The Story of Sharecroppers in the New Deal* (Urbana: University of Illinois Press, 1965).

45. "The Good Soldier," *Time*, July 15, 1935, 19–21.

46. "Taxmaster," *Time*, June 1, 1936, 10–12. *Time* published a similar story on House Ways and Means Committee chairman Robert Doughton of North Carolina, noting that Doughton had "reported out the new liquor tax law, the bill for renewing the life of RFC, the reciprocal tariff bill, the tax bill and got them all passed by the House in the form in which the Administration wanted them." "Ten Men at a Table," *Time*, April 30, 1934, 13.

47. "Mr. Commonsense," *Time*, June 3, 1935, 11–12. *Time* also referred to Garner as "a real political power in a politically powerless office." This depiction was common in press coverage of the vice president during Roosevelt's first term.

48. See Caughey, *Congress, Public Opinion, and Representation*. See also Sean Farhang and Ira Katznelson, "The Southern Imposition: Congress and Labor in the New Deal and Fair Deal," *Studies in American Political Development* 19 (2005): 1–30; and Ira Katznelson and Quinn Mulroy, "Was the South Pivotal? Situated Partisanship and Policy Coalitions during the New Deal and Fair Deal," *Journal of Politics* 74 (2012): 604–20.

49. Caughey, *Congress, Public Opinion, and Representation*.

50. Krock, "Tide Sweeps Nation," *NYT*, November 7, 1934, 1, 3.

51. See, e.g., Editorial, "How Shall We Vote?" *TNR*, August 17, 1932, 4–6; Chevalier, "Farmer-Labor Conference," 172–73.

52. See Nancy J. Weiss, *Farewell to the Party of Lincoln: Black Politics in the Age of FDR* (Princeton, NJ: Princeton University Press, 1983), chap. 7.

53. See Raymond Wolters, "The New Deal and the Negro," in *The New Deal: The National Level*, ed. John Braeman, Robert H. Bremmer, and David Brody (Columbus: Ohio State University Press, 1975), 188–93; and Harvard Sitkoff, *A New Deal for Blacks* (New York: Oxford University Press, 1983), 70–73.

54. Wolters, "The New Deal and the Negro," 191–93, 197–99.

55. Sitkoff, *New Deal for Blacks*, 48, 52–55.

56. Ibid., 56; Eleanor Ryan, "Toward a National Negro Congress," *New Masses* 4 (June 1935): 14–15.

57. "New Deal Love Has Its Limits," *Chicago Defender*, July 11, 1936, 16. As chapter 3 shows, the *Defender*'s coverage of the New Deal became more positive after 1936.

58. See Sitkoff, *New Deal for Blacks*, 345, on the negative coverage. Interestingly, very few news stories used the term "Black Cabinet" in the 1930s. A ProQuest search for the term found no stories in the *New York Times*, *Washington Post*, or *Chicago Tribune* and just a small handful of stories in the *Chicago Defender*.

59. A copy of the signed petition was obtained from the Edward P. Costigan Papers, Archives, University of Colorado at Boulder Libraries, Box 42, Folder 16.

60. "Delaware Likely to Go Republican," *NYT*, October 27, 1934, 6. Buck later served in the Senate, where his voting record placed him among the most conservative Republicans (e.g., his first-dimension DW-NOMINATE score in 1943–44, his first Congress as a senator, was the tenth most conservative in the entire chamber). At his first National Governor's Conference, Fitzgerald of Michigan sponsored a resolution opposing federal control of relief expenditures; it was rejected by the more liberal governors ("Governors Back Principles of NRA," *NYT*, June 15, 1935, 3). Fitzgerald was defeated in 1936 but came back two years later, besting liberal Frank Murphy in a race marked by attacks on the pro-CIO Murphy for his alleged radicalism. Landon was identified with the moderate wing of his party at the time but was by no means a New Dealer.

61. This was in an era when university presidents (and academics more generally) were not necessarily liberal. For example, Yale president James Angell, who signed the NAACP petition, publicly criticized the New Deal's excessive taxation and overly generous relief policies ("Angell Bids Nation Yield Some Rights to Keep Democracy," *NYT*, November 20, 1936, 1, 17).

62. A handful of individuals who signed Kellogg's plea to expand the New Deal also signed the NAACP petition, including Ernst, Kirchwey, and Mason. As noted above, this suggests that there was overlap between individual civil rights supporters and New Deal backers, but the NAACP list is also noteworthy for its inclusion of such New Deal critics as the Republicans Fitzgerald, Buck, and Landon.

63. Johnson and Porter, *National Party Platforms*, 318.

64. Sugrue, *Sweet Land of Liberty*, 23–24.

65. Hugh T. Murray, Jr. "The NAACP versus the Communist Party: The Scottsboro Rape Cases, 1931–1932," *Phylon* 28, 3 (1967): 276–87.

66. "Negro Editors on Communism," *Crisis* (April 1932): 117.

67. Ibid., 117–19; and "Negro Editors on Communism," *Crisis* (May 1932): 154–56.

68. "Negro Editors on Communism" (May 1932): 154.

69. On Vann's anticommunism, see Andrew Buni, *Robert L. Vann of the Pittsburgh Courier: Politics and Black Journalism* (Pittsburgh: University of Pittsburgh Press, 1974), chap. 10.

70. Ronald D. Rotunda, *The Politics of Language: Liberalism as Word and Symbol* (Iowa City: University of Iowa Press, 1986), 14.

71. See, e.g., Donald Young, "Some Effects of a Course in American Race Problems on the Race Prejudice of 450 Undergraduates at the University of Pennsylvania," *Journal of Abnormal and Social Psychology* 22 (October–December 1927): 235–42.

72. M. H. Harper, "The Social Beliefs and Attitudes of American Educators," *Teachers College Contributions to Education* 294 (1927).

73. See, e.g., Claude Arnett, *The Social Beliefs and Attitudes of American School Board Members* (Emporia, KS: Emporia Gazette Press, 1932); E. Salner and H. H. Remmers,

"Affective Selectivity and Liberalizing Influence of College Courses," *Journal of Applied Psychology* 17 (August 1933): 349–54; and A. J. Harris, H. H. Remmers, and C. E. Ellison, "The Relation between Liberal and Conservative Attitudes in College Students, and Other Factors" *Journal of Social Psychology* 3 (1932): 320–36.

74. Raymond R. Willoughby, "A Sampling of Student Opinion," *Journal of Social Psychology* 1 (1930): 164–69.

75. Percival Symonds, "A Social Attitudes Questionnaire," *Journal of Educational Psychology* 16 (May 1925): 316–22. A partial exception is Floyd Allport and D. A. Hartman, "The Measurement and Motivation of Atypical Opinion in a Certain Group," *American Political Science Review* 19 (November 1925): 735–60. Allport and Hartman use seven issues in assessing radical, conservative, and reactionary opinions; one of the seven is attitudes toward the Ku Klux Klan (KKK). Other issues include views of the League of Nations, President Coolidge, legislative control of the Supreme Court, prohibition, the distribution of wealth, and graft in politics. Needless to say, a few of these issues bear some relationship to New Deal era cleavages, but several others do not fit at all. Allport and Hartman code those who want the KKK suppressed as radical and those who approve of it as reactionary; the focus of the study is on the common personality features of those with such "atypical" opinions. The authors label those in the "middle" on the KKK issue as "conservative," as compared to the "extremists" (743).

76. See Duane F. Alwin, Ronald L. Cohen, and Theodore M. Newcomb, *Political Attitudes over the Life Span* (Madison: University of Wisconsin Press, 1991). The scale did include one item asking whether democracy works well if the unintelligent and uneducated have the vote, which might be taken as a very indirect indicator of views toward southern voting restrictions. The question did not mention race or the South.

77. George B. Vetter, "The Measurement of Social and Political Attitudes and the Related Personality Factors," *Journal of Abnormal and Social Psychology* 25 (1930): 149–89.

78. Respondents opposed to laws discriminating against such unions are coded as liberals, and those who wish to encourage "the biological intermixture of the races" are coded as radicals.

79. Reactionaries were those who said that whites should continue subjugating "the darker or inferior races." There was no "conservative" response option; radicals were those suggesting that other races are justified in combining to displace the white race from its unjust domination.

80. Vetter classifies the sample—drawn from several colleges—into such categories as conservative, reactionary, liberal, and radical. Interestingly, while conservatives are predominantly Republican, reactionaries are nearly evenly divided between Democrats and Republicans. Liberals are more likely to be Democrats than Republicans, but nearly two-thirds of the liberals were either Socialists or nonpartisan (by contrast, only about 22% of reactionaries and 8% of conservatives were nonpartisan, with no conservative Socialists and 2% of the reactionaries). The vast majority of radicals were Socialists or nonpartisan (85%), with just 10% Democrats and 2% Republican. Vetter finds that regular church attenders were more likely to be reactionary or conservative, while those rarely attending church were likely to be liberal or radical, though this may in part be rooted in the many items that tapped directly into religious teachings (e.g., birth control, abortion). It is also worth noting that Vetter's racial attitude measures were sociological in content (interracial marriage; social subjugation) and were far removed from the issues that were soon to dominate debates over civil rights, such as voting rights, public accommodations, and job discrimination.

81. See, e.g., Ira Katznelson, Kim Geiger, and Daniel Kryder, "Limiting Liberalism: The Southern Veto in Congress, 1933–1950," *Political Science Quarterly* 108 (1993):

283–306; David M. Kennedy, *Freedom from Fear: The American People in Depression and War* (New York: Oxford University Press, 1999), 764; Richard M. Dalfiume, "The 'Forgotten Years' of the Negro Revolution," *Journal of American History* 55 (June 1968): 90–106; and Richard M. Valelly, *The Two Reconstructions: The Struggle for Black Enfranchisement* (Chicago: University of Chicago Press, 2004), 153–54.

Chapter 3: Transforming Liberalism, 1933–1940

1. See Frank Kent, "The Revolt in the South," *Wall Street Journal* (hereafter *WSJ*), August 3, 1937, 4; James T. Patterson, *Congressional Conservatism and the New Deal* (New York: Oxford University Press, 1967), chaps. 3 and 8.

2. Cf. Bawn et al., "Theory of Political Parties."

3. See Eric Foner, *Reconstruction: America's Unfinished Revolution, 1863–1877* (New York: Harper Collins, 2011); Richard M. Valelly, *The Two Reconstructions: The Struggle for Black Enfranchisement* (Chicago: University of Chicago Press, 2004).

4. Robert L. Zangrando, *The NAACP Crusade against Lynching, 1909–1950* (Philadelphia: Temple University Press, 1980), 68–69.

5. Henry Lee Moon, *Balance of Power: The Negro Vote* (Garden City, NY: Country Life Press, 1948), 106.

6. Ibid., 106. See also Allan Lichtman, *Prejudice and the Old Politics: The Presidential Election of 1928* (Lanham, MD: Lexington Books, 1979), chap. 7.

7. See discussion in chapter 2.

8. Charles Halt, "Joseph F. Guffey, New Deal Politician from Pennsylvania" (PhD diss., Syracuse University, 1975), 31–33.

9. "Smith-for-President Campaign Launched," *Pittsburgh Courier*, August 25, 1928, 1.

10. Buni, *Robert L. Vann*, 178–79.

11. Ibid., 191.

12. Joseph Alsop and Robert Kintner, "The Guffey: Biography of a Boss, New Style," *Saturday Evening Post*, March 26, 1938, 5–6.

13. Samuel John Astorino, "The Decline of the Republican Dynasty in Pennsylvania, 1929–1934" (PhD diss., University of Pittsburgh, 1962), 176–77.

14. Ibid., 178. See also Editorial, "Millions Will Turn Lincoln's Picture to the Wall," *Pittsburgh Courier*, September 17, 1932, 13.

15. Editorial, "The Parting of the Ways," *Pittsburgh Courier*, August 27, 1932, 10.

16. Astorino, "Decline of the Republican Dynasty," 189.

17. Buni, *Robert L. Vann*, 196–201.

18. Halt, "Joseph F. Guffey," 122.

19. Buni, *Robert L. Vann*, 218.

20. *Literary Digest*, September 7, 1935, 18.

21. On the partisan change in Philadelphia, see Matthew J. Countryman, *Up South: Civil Rights and Black Power in Philadelphia* (Philadelphia: University of Pennsylvania Press, 2006), chap. 1.

22. Frank Kent, "The Great Game of Politics," *LAT*, March 11, 1938, 5.

23. Alsop and Kintner, "The Guffey," 5–7, 98–102.

24. Ibid., 7.

25. Thomas T. Spencer, "The Good Neighbor League Colored Committee and the 1936 Democratic Presidential Campaign," *Journal of Negro History* 63, 4 (1978): 307–16.

26. The rallies were conducted as far south as Kentucky and Maryland. "Roosevelt Gets Colored Units Support at Rally," *Washington Post*, September 22, 1936, 2.

27. Spencer, "Good Neighbor League," 311; Donald R. McCoy, "The Good Neighbor League and the Presidential Campaign of 1936," *Western Political Quarterly* 13 (December 1960): 1011–21.

28. "26 Negro Rallies Back Roosevelt," *NYT*, September 22, 1936, 4.

29. Frank Kent, "Great Game of Politics," *Wall Street Journal*, September 8, 1936, 6.

30. Harold L. Ickes, *The Secret Diary of Harold L. Ickes* (New York: Simon and Schuster, 1953), entry for October 4, 1936, 689.

31. Nahum Brascher, "Conventions of 2 Parties Contrasted," *Chicago Defender*, July 4, 1936, 1, 18.

32. William Allen White, *What It's All About: Being a Reporter's Story of the Early Campaign of 1936* (New York: Macmillan, 1936), 67, 73, 75.

33. Bunche, "The Negro in Political Life," 580. Bunche does credit the New Deal with some direct benefits for African Americans. He emphasizes the role of AAA cotton referendums in the South in beginning to challenge prevailing racial hierarchies in the region: "the participation of Negroes in those elections, and on an equal basis with whites, is of the utmost significance in the South" (577).

34. David Karol, *Party Position Change in American Politics: Coalition Management* (New York: Cambridge University Press, 2009), chap. 4.

35. Robert H. Zieger, *The CIO: 1935–1955* (Chapel Hill: University of North Carolina Press, 1995), 83. Thomas Sugrue agrees that "there were enough black workers in key northern industries that it would be difficult to organize plantwide or industrywide without their support." See Sugrue, *Sweet Land of Liberty*, 35.

36. Zieger, *The CIO*, 84.

37. Robert H. Zieger, *John L. Lewis: Labor Leader* (Boston: Twayne, 1988), 99–100.

38. Michael Goldfield, "Race and the CIO: The Possibilities for Racial Egalitarianism during the 1930s and 1940s," *International Labor and Working-Class History* 44 (Fall 1993): 1–32.

39. Sugrue, *Sweet Land of Liberty*, 35.

40. Sitkoff, *New Deal for Blacks*, 180–81; Nelson Lichtenstein, *The Most Dangerous Man in Detroit: Walter Reuther and the Fate of American Labor* (New York: Basic Books, 1995), 30–31.

41. Zieger, *John L. Lewis*, 100.

42. Sitkoff, *New Deal for Blacks*, 182–90.

43. Anthony David Di Biase, "Labor's Non-Partisan League, 1936–1941" (MS thesis, University of Wisconsin, 1962), 3–7.

44. Steve Fraser, *Labor Will Rule: Sidney Hillman and the Rise of American Labor* (New York: Free Press, 1991), 368.

45. Labor's Non-Partisan League, *Labor's Non-Partisan League: Its Origin and Growth* (Washington, DC, 1939), 7.

46. Paul W. Ward, "Wooing the Negro Vote," *Nation*, August 1, 1936, 20; Frank Kent, "A Solid Black Belt?," *WSJ*, June 30, 1938, 4.

47. Riker, "The CIO in Politics," 127–38.

48. Sean Savage, *Roosevelt: The Party Leader, 1933–1945* (Lexington: University Press of Kentucky, 2014), 89.

49. TRB, "Washington Notes," *TNR*, September 9, 1936, 129.

50. TRB, "Washington Notes," *TNR*, September 16, 1936, 155.

51. Editorial, *Nation*, November 7, 1936, 535, 536.

52. "Plan for Labor Party Advanced by Election," *NYT*, November 8, 1936, E5.

53. Sidney Olson, "Vote Is Called Labor Pledge by Roosevelt," *Washington Post*, November 10, 1936, X1.

54. LNPL, *Labor's Non-Partisan League*, 4; Di Biase, "Labor's Non-Partisan League," 10.

55. LNPL, *Labor's Non-Partisan League*, 5.

56. "Partisan League," *Time*, August 24, 1936, 19.

57. As quoted in Zieger, *John L. Lewis*, 90.

58. See, e.g., "C.I.O. Fights for Liberals," *LAT*, June 30, 1938, 8.

59. LNPL, *Labor's Non-Partisan League*, 10.

60. I used the ProQuest Historical Newspapers database, searching for front-page stories mentioning all of the following keywords: "sit-down," "strike or strikers," and "General Motors" or "Chrysler."

61. Melvyn Dubofsky and Warren Van Tine, *John L. Lewis: A Biography* (New York: Quadrangle, 1977), 271.

62. Schickler and Caughey, "Public Opinion, Organized Labor, and New Deal Liberalism," 170–72.

63. See Riker, "The CIO in Politics," 97; Di Biase, "Labor's Non-Partisan League," 25–26.

64. "Berry Labor Group Backs Court Plan," *NYT*, February 17, 1937, 2.

65. "Labor Group Votes a Court Bill Drive," *NYT*, March 9, 1937, 15.

66. Fraser, *Labor Will Rule*, 376.

67. Ibid. On the Court fight more generally, see Joseph Alsop and Turner Catledge, *The 168 Days* (New York: Doubleday, 1938).

68. J. David Greenstone, *Labor in American politics* (New York: Knopf, 1969), 9–18, 39–52. On the expansive agenda and activities of CIO unions, see also Riker, "The CIO in Politics," chaps. 1 and 3; and Kevin Boyle, "'There Are No Union Sorrows That the Union Can't Heal': The Struggle for Racial Equality in the United Automobile Workers, 1940–1960," *Labor History* 36, 1 (1995): 5–23.

69. Charles Michelson, *The Ghost Talks* (New York: G. P. Putnam's Sons, 1944), 170–80.

70. Stanley High, *Roosevelt—and Then?* (New York: Harper and Brothers, 1937), 196.

71. The CIO succeeded in defeating Davey in the Democratic primary. The victory was a pyrrhic one, however, as Republicans captured the governorship in November.

72. The early New Deal had its own radical potential, with comprehensive planning and government control of industry advocated by prominent administration figures (see Katznelson et al., "Limiting Liberalism," 283–306). But Roosevelt himself refused to identify his project with any particular faction's vision, frustrating those who sought to identify the New Deal with a radical vision for remaking America's political economy (see Skowronek, *Politics Presidents Make*, chap. 7, part 1).

73. The search terms used were ("Anti-New Deal*" OR "Anti-administration*" OR "New Dealer*" OR "New Deal Democrat*" OR "100 per cent New Deal*" OR "100 percent New Deal*" OR "100% New Deal*") AND (Congress OR House OR Senate OR representative OR senator), with a limitation to front-page stories.

74. While the number of front-page stories mentioning organized labor in relation to the New Deal fell in 1939 compared to 1938, this partly reflected the smaller total number of stories with the "New Dealer"/anti-administration search terms in that year compared to 1938. The percentage of front-page stories treating organized labor as a New Deal supporter was 25% in 1938 and 21% in 1939.

75. "LNPL Watches Votes Cast by Congressmen," *CIO News*, February 26, 1938, 3; see also "CIO Attacks Filibuster on Lynching Bill," *CIO News*, January 29, 1938, 4

76. "Brophy Raps Lynching at Negro Parley," *CIO News*, March 26, 1938, 6.

77. "1940 Legislative Summary," *Labor Non-Partisan League National Bulletin*, December 20, 1940, 3.

78. "What the Senate Did," *CIO News*, Special Supplement, August 19, 1946, 2–3.

79. Riker, "The CIO in Politics," 102–4.

80. "CIO Attacks Filibuster on Lynching Bill," *CIO News*, January 29, 1938, 4.

81. See, e.g., "Lewis Urges Unions to Push Legislation," *CIO News*, April 29, 1940, 3.

82. See, e.g., "Brophy Raps Lynching at Negro Parley," *CIO News*, March 26, 1938, 6; "Lewis Addresses Negro Congress," *CIO News*, April 29, 1940, 1.

83. Sitkoff, *New Deal for Blacks*, 187.

84. "Brophy Raps Lynching at Negro Parley," *CIO News*, March 26, 1938, 6.

85. "Issue New Pamphlet: CIO and the Negro Worker," *CIO News*, April 29, 1940, 6; "Equal Opportunity," *CIO News*, May 6, 1940, 2–4, 6.

86. Lewis also promised that "labor will not rest until the right to vote becomes the right of every citizen, unhampered by such devices as the poll tax."

87. "Lewis Invites National Negro Congress to Join Labor League," *CIO News*, April 29, 1940, 5.

88. "Lewis Sets C.I.O. against Any 'Deals' for Bridges Group," *NYT*, November 17, 1938, 1, 21. For other examples, see "Filibuster Holds in Night Session," *NYT*, January 25, 1938, 6; "Mine Union Votes Bigger C.I.O. Fund," *NYT*, February 1, 1938, 8; "Lewis Miners Cut Last Tie with A.F.L.," *NYT*, February 2, 1938, 1; "Asks NLRA Rules on Federal Work," *NYT*, December 22, 1938, 10.

89. Sitkoff, *New Deal for Blacks*, 187.

90. I searched the *New York Times* online archive for stories mentioning the CIO and either African Americans or civil rights issues (search terms: "lynch" and variants thereof, "negro" or variants thereof, or "colored"). The resulting stories were counted only if they link the union movement or union leaders to civil rights support or support for African American interests more generally, or if the story links the opponents of civil rights to the opponents of unions. Stories that discuss African American support for the labor movement were also counted.

91. Kent, "Solid Black Belt," 4. As Roosevelt's national support faded amid his setbacks of 1937–38, Kent observed that the one contrary trend is that "the President today is stronger than ever with the CIO and the colored people" (Frank Kent, "Effect Unknown," *WSJ*, January 13, 1938, 6).

92. Christopher Baylor, "First to the Party: The Group Origins of the Partisan Transformation on Civil Rights," *Studies in American Political Development* 27 (October 2013): 1–31.

93. Lester B. Granger, "Industrial Unionism and the Negro," *Opportunity* 14 (January, 1936): 29, 30. A September 1936 editorial in the *Crisis* adopted a more optimistic tone, concluding that African Americans would likely find the CIO to be a hospitable home given the UMW's record of providing equality for African American workers in the mining industry. The editorial thus recommended that black workers join the new labor organization ("Editorial," *Crisis*, September 1936, 273).

94. James S. Olson, "Race, Class, and Progress: Black Leadership and Industrial Unionism, 1936–1945," in *Black Labor in America*, ed. Milton Cantor (Westport, CT: Negro Universities Press, 1969).

95. "CIO Drives to Organize Race Steel Workers," *Defender*, August 8, 1936, 4.

96. "NNC to Give Cooperation to CIO Drive," *Defender*, August 29, 1936, 4.

97. Sitkoff, *New Deal for Blacks*, 184; High, *Roosevelt*, 207; "Negroes Honor Lewis," *CIO News*, May 6, 1940, 2.

98. Sugrue, *Sweet Land of Liberty*, 35–36; Olson, "Race, Class, and Progress," 155; August Meier and Elliott Rudwick, *Black Detroit and the Rise of the UAW* (Oxford: Oxford University Press, 1979), 22.

99. Granger, "Views and Reviews: New Inter-Racialism," *Defender*, November 6, 1937, 16.

100. "Interracial Meet Draws Big Throng," *Defender*, September 25, 1937, 7.

101. "A. L. Foster Urges Employers to Give Race an Even Break," *Defender*, April 10, 1937, 4; Meier and Rudwick, *Black Detroit*, 22.

102. As quoted in Sitkoff, *New Deal for Blacks*, 180.

103. See Raymond Wolters, *Negroes and the Great Depression: The Problem of Economic Recovery* (Westport, CT: Greenwood, 1970), chap. 11.

104. Sugrue, *Sweet Land of Liberty*, 40. See also Meier and Rudwick, *Black Detroit*, 22–23.

105. Wolters, *Negroes and the Great Depression*, 305.

106. Ibid., 329.

107. Report of Resolutions Committee, July 3, 1936, 4, Papers of the NAACP, Microfilm Vol. 1, Reel 9.

108. Editorial, "Industrial Unions and the Negro Worker," *Crisis*, September 1936, 273.

109. "Blood for the Cause," *Crisis*, July 1937, 209.

110. George Schuyler, "Reflections on Negro Leadership," *Crisis*, November 1937, 327–28.

111. "From the Press of the Nation," *Crisis*, January 1939, 19.

112. Meier and Rudwick, *Black Detroit*, 20–22.

113. Roy Wilkins, "'Mind Your Own Business,'" *Crisis*, August 1937, 241. See also George S. Schuyler, "Reflections on Negro Leadership," *Crisis* 44 (November 1937): 328. Younger militants in the city did not share the Detroit NAACP leadership's support for Ford. Sugrue points out that the NAACP's youth councils provided early backing to the UAW's efforts (*Sweet Land of Liberty*, 40).

114. For an excellent discussion of developments across several northern cities, see Beth Tompkins Bates, "A New Crowd Challenges the Agenda of the Old Guard in the NAACP, 1933–1941," *American Historical Review* 102, 2 (1997): 340–77. See Meier and Rudwick, *Black Detroit*, chaps. 2 and 3, on this gradual process in Detroit.

115. See, e.g., "C.I.O. Advocates Labor Equalities throughout South," *Defender*, June 12, 1937, 3.

116. "N.Y. Subway Porters Get Promotions," *Defender*, August 13, 1938, 7; "First Witnesses Heard in Probe of TVA," *Defender*, September 17, 1938, 10; "Sharecropper Arrest Seen as Blow at CIO," *Defender*, October 8, 1938, 6.

117. "Midwest Hits WPA Retrenchment Program," *Defender*, January 28, 1939, 10; "Begin Fight to Get Anti-Lynch Bill Vote," *Defender*, April 8, 1939, 1.

118. "St. Louis Lawyer Seeks School Board Post," *Defender*, March 18, 1939, 4; "Police Terror Arouses Race," *Defender*, July 1, 1939, 3; "Map Laws to End Jim Crow in New Jersey," *Defender*, June 17, 1939, 6.

119. "40 Deported from Coast by Police," *Defender*, September 2, 1939, 1.

120. Sugrue, *Sweet Land of Liberty*, 39. Similarly, Bates credits young militants with pushing NAACP leaders to shift their priorities toward working-class interests: "the legacy of new-crowd networks, such as those formed by the NNC at the local level, may lie as much in the influence they had reordering priorities of the old guard within the NAACP as in contributing to a realignment of power relations in black communities" (Bates, "A New Crowd Challenges the Old Guard," 375). Bates argues that White and Wilkins had been persuaded to alter the NAACP's "agenda and tactics" by 1939 (370). See also Zangrando, *NAACP Crusade*, 137.

121. See Olson, "Race, Class and Progress," for examples.

122. Editorial, "Loose Talk about Labor," *Pittsburgh Courier*, August 28, 1937, 10.

123. "A Year of the CIO," *Pittsburgh Courier*, September 18, 1937, 10; see also Buni, *Robert L. Vann*, 282; Schuyler, "Reflections on Negro Leadership," 328.

124. See, e.g., "Labor, a United Front," *Defender*, June 5, 1937, 16.

125. "C.I.O. Groups Elect 3 Race Men at Meet," *Defender*, November 27, 1937, 3.

126. See "Lewis Backs CIO Support of Anti-Lynching Bill," *Defender*, December 17, 1938, 1; "Firing of 18 Race Workers Stirs Harlem," *Defender*, April 9, 1938, 6; "Whites Aid Race in Harlem in Campaign for Employment," *Defender*, June 11, 1938, 10; "C.I.O. Advocates Labor Equalities throughout South," *Defender*, June 12, 1937, 3; "Sharecropper Arrest Seen as Blow at CIO," *Defender*, October 8, 1938, 6.

127. To identify stories, the following search terms were used in ProQuest's Chicago Defender archive: ((lynchi* OR negro* OR colored*) AND (CIO OR C.I.O. OR U.A.W. OR UAW OR "Congress of Industrial" OR "industrial union" OR "John L. Lewis" OR "industrial organization")) AND at.exact("Article" OR "Correspondence" OR "Military/War News" OR "Feature" OR "General Information" OR "Review" OR "Front Matter" OR "Editorial Cartoon/Comic" OR "Commentary" OR "Front Page/Cover Story" OR "Editorial" OR "Undefined" OR "News" OR "Letter To The Editor").

128. Editorial, "Opportunity Justice," *Defender*, August 20, 1938, 16.

129. In 1936 six *Defender* stories noted the NNC's connection to the CIO as compared to two mentioning the NAACP in connection to the CIO. In 1939 eight stories highlighted the NAACP/CIO tie, compared to six for the NNC. The following year eighteen stories in the *Defender* tied the NAACP to the CIO, compared to thirteen stories noting the NNC/CIO connection.

130. See, e.g., "No Color Ban in Auto Union, Leader Claims," *Los Angeles Sentinel* (hereafter *Sentinel*), April 29, 1937, 1; Editorial, "Helps Us All," *Sentinel*, March 18, 1937, 1; "Workers Support CIO Plan," *Afro-American*, February 13, 1937, A16; "Scabs Attack CIO Organizer," *Afro-American*, June 19, 1937, 1. For details on the *Afro-American*'s coverage of the CIO, see Andor Skotnes, *A New Deal for All? Race and Class Struggles in Depression-Era Baltimore* (Durham, NC: Duke University Press, 2013), chap. 10.

131. "Labor Leadership," *Afro-American*, July 17, 1937, 4.

132. Horace R. Cayton and George S. Mitchell, *Black Workers and the New Unions* (Chapel Hill: University of North Carolina Press, 1939), 202.

133. Sitkoff, *New Deal for Blacks*, 184.

134. Riker, "The CIO in Politics," 82.

135. See, e.g., Cayton and Mitchell, *Black Workers*; Paul Frymer, *Black and Blue*, 2007; Gary Gerstle, "Working Class Racism: Broaden the Focus," *International Labor and Working-Class History* 44 (Fall 1993): 33–40.

136. Zieger, *The CIO*, chaps. 4 and 7. There is no doubt that the CIO's leaders and organizers were generally more pro–civil rights than were rank-and-file members, though even ordinary union members provided greater civil rights support than did other whites (see chapter 5 for evidence). Some critics have also argued that the CIO often accommodated racial segregation in the South, particularly when mainstream leaders displaced communists or other left-wing radicals. See Goldfield, "Race and the CIO," 1–32; Marshall Stevenson, "Beyond Theoretical Models: The Limited Possibilities of Racial Egalitarianism," *International Labor and Working Class History* 44 (Fall 1993): 45–52.

137. See, e.g., Frank Winn, "Labor Tackles the Race Question," *Antioch Review* 3, 3 (1943): 341–60; Louis Kesselman, *The Social Politics of FEPC: A Study in Reform Pressure Movements* (Chapel Hill: University of North Carolina Press, 1948); Robert Korstad, "The Possibilities for Racial Egalitarianism: Context Matters," *International Labor and Working Class History* 44 (Fall 1993): 41–44.

138. Robert Korstad and Nelson Lichtenstein, "Opportunities Found and Lost: Labor, Radicals, and the Early Civil Rights Movement," *Journal of American History* 75, 3 (December 1988): 786–811; Boyle, "There Are No Union Sorrows," 5–23.

139. Sugrue, *Sweet Land of Liberty*, 89.

140. On the SCHW, see Patricia Sullivan, *Days of Hope: Race and Democracy in the New Deal Era* (Chapel Hill: University of North Carolina Press, 1996).

141. Sullivan, *Days of Hope*, 115; William Brewer, "The Poll Tax and the Poll Taxers," *Journal of Negro History* 29, 3 (1944): 260–99. The CIO actively worked with poll tax ban advocates even before this group formed. For example, the *Defender* reported on a strategy meeting in poll tax bill sponsor Lee Geyer's (D-CA) office at which the CIO, NAACP, NNC, and even some AFL officials strategized on how to pass the bill despite the opposition of the "southern Tory bloc" ("C.I.O. and A.F. of L. Join to Wipe Out Poll Tax," *Defender*, March 2, 1940, 2).

142. Thomas Krueger, *And Promises to Keep: The Southern Conference for Human Welfare, 1938–1948* (Nashville, TN: Vanderbilt University Press, 1967), 44–47.

143. "March on Washington Set for Spring to Push FEPC," *Defender*, March 2, 1946, 1, 8.

144. Kesselman, *Social Politics of FEPC*, 146–51.

145. "Anti-Lynchers Move into Action," *Defender*, August 31, 1946, 4.

146. Alvin Johnson, "What I Expect of Roosevelt," *Nation*, November 14, 1936, 573.

147. Caughey, *Congress, Public Opinion, and Representation*.

148. Irving Bernstein, *The New Deal Collective Bargaining Policy* (Berkeley: University of California Press, 1950), 114.

149. *Congressional Record* (hereafter *CR*), June 19, 1935, 9679. Similarly, Smith declared that "I am opposed to this bill because it is obviously unconstitutional.... We have no earthly power under the Constitution to legislate with respect to labor disputes except those labor disputes which directly affect interstate commerce." He predicted that the law would be overturned by the Supreme Court and argued that "too many of the reserve powers of the States have been taken away by judicial interpretation and other means" (ibid., June 19, 1935, 9692–93).

150. Ibid., 9707.

151. Bernstein, *New Deal Collective Bargaining*, 116.

152. "Wrangle 5 Hours on Sit-Down Ban," *NYT*, April 3, 1937, 3.

153. "Byrnes Defeated: But Compels Colleagues to Take Recorded Vote on Labor Policy," *NYT*, April 6, 1937, 1. These members were each explicitly included in the list of New Dealers opposed to the Byrnes amendment.

154. Republicans voted 12–3 in favor of the amendment.

155. "Party Lines Drawn," *NYT*, April 9, 1937, 1, 3.

156. Ibid.

157. Northern Democrats voted 167–30 against the investigation. Southern party members narrowly backed the investigation, 52–49. Republicans supported the investigation by a 75–9 vote. A year later Dies capitalized on another chance to go after the CIO. When the House approved Dies's proposal to create a committee to investigate un-American activities, the Texan quickly turned the committee's sights on the sit-down strikes. The committee charged that Michigan's governor, the liberal New Dealer Frank Murphy, had aided the strikes, which the committee sought to attribute to communists.

158. See Zieger, *The CIO*, chap. 4, on the union's southern drive.

159. *CR*, June 30, 1937, 6637; "South Will Repeal C.I.O., Cox Asserts," *NYT*, July 1, 1937, 2. Later in 1937 newspapers noted evidence that the KKK had revived as part of southern efforts to ward off the CIO's racial and alleged communist agenda ("Klan, Shorn of Power, Seeking to Regain It," *NYT*, September 19, 1937, 68; "Says Klan in South Will War on C.I.O.," *NYT*, October 17, 1937, 24; "Klan Drive Is Seen as Fight on C.I.O.," *NYT*, October 31, 1937, 6).

160. Kent, "Revolt in the South," 4.

161. "Connally Chides Wagner on Labor," *NYT*, November 18, 1937, 1, 14.

162. *CR*, November 17, 1937, 67.

163. Ibid., 80.

164. Ibid., 71.

165. *CR*, January 12, 1938, 381.

166. *CR*, November 17, 1937, 76. Southern opponents of the lynching bill also tried to divide northern Democratic supporters of the bill by charging that it might be used to prosecute unions (see, e.g., *CR*, July 26, 1937, 7593–94). But the CIO did not waver in its support for the bill.

167. "Smith's Racial Issue," *NYT*, September 4, 1938, 37; see also "Smith Is Victor in Carolina Vote," *NYT*, August 31, 1938, 1, 5.

168. "Negro Issue Raised in South At 'Purge': Old-Line Southerners Tell Voters New Deal Threatens White Supremacy," *NYT*, August 23, 1938, 5; see also Walter Brown, "Sense and Nonsense along the Potomac," *Charleston News and Courier*, August 7, 1938, 4.

169. "George Asks Fight on 'One-Man Rule,'" *NYT*, August 16, 1938, 1, 2.

170. "Senators Look into Ambitions of John L. Lewis," *Chicago Tribune*, March 29, 1937, 1, 6.

171. "Smash A.F. of L.! Stalin's Order, Inquiry Hears," *Tribune*, October 19, 1938, 2.

172. Russ Stone, "Blitzkreig against the Labor Board," *TNR*, January 22, 1940, 106–7.

173. See Schickler and Pearson, "Agenda Control and the Committee on Rules,"; Caughey, *Congress, Public Opinion, and Representation*.

174. These estimates derive from pooling the dozens of polls from 1937 that asked about vote choice in 1936. By comparison, Roosevelt only barely won in small towns and farm areas in 1940 (53%–47% in both cases, based on vote recall in Gallup polls conducted in 1941), while continuing to win in cities by approximately 20 points. Outside the South, Roosevelt actually lost narrowly in both farm areas and small towns in 1940, while continuing to win by a big margin in cities.

175. Gallup used a five-category class measure in this poll. "Average +" was the top class category, consisting of about 14% of public; there is a class cleavage in voting but it is impressive how well Roosevelt ran across the boards.

176. See Gallup poll 76, Roper Archive, April 1937.

177. "Undeclared War," *Time*, March 20, 1939, 11–13.

178. Ibid., 12. For the earlier assessment of Harrison, see "Taxmaster," *Time*, June 1, 1936, 12. Amid the growing ideological divisions in 1937, Roosevelt had offered crucial backing to Alben Barkley in his one-vote victory over Harrison to succeed Joseph Robinson as Senate Democratic leader after Robinson's death. Roosevelt's move was widely understood as an indicator that he viewed Harrison's loyalty to the New Deal as suspect (see Patterson, *Congressional Conservatism*, chap. 4).

179. The search term in Proquest Historical database was (Garner w/15 ("conservativ*")). An examination of the individual stories indicates that they are a valid indicator of views of Garner (i.e. in the vast majority of cases, Garner is being referred to as a conservative).

180. Stanley High, "Party Purge," *Saturday Evening Post*, August 21, 1937, 17.

181. "Young Democrats Cheer Demands for a Third Term," *NYT*, August 12, 1939, 1, 5.

182. Gallup Poll 145, January 1939. Hopkins and Wallace were both northern liberals; Barkley represented Kentucky but was a key administration supporter as Senate leader. This was the same Champ Clark who had been praised by the *Nation* in 1932 as a paragon of liberal hopes (Coghlan, "Missouri—a Threat and a Promise," 422–24).

183. Gallup Poll 160, June 1939.

184. Ibid. An August 1938 Roper poll also asked respondents whether various political figures were radical, liberal, conservative, or reactionary (Roper/Fortune Survey 2). Roosevelt was viewed as a liberal by 51%, radical by 18%, conservative by 9%, and reactionary by 3%. Garner was viewed as conservative by 39% and as reactionary by 3%; just 21% viewed him as liberal, and 2% as radical. The conservative-liberal ratio for Garner was similar to Republican stalwart Arthur Vandenberg (19% conservative, 8% liberal, but many more nonresponses).

185. When the *New Republic* considered Garner's presidential prospects in August 1938, it labeled him "a New Deal threat," noting that after having been "one of the most enthusiastic helpers that the 'Boss' had in Congress" before 1937, Garner was now commenting on New Deal legislation with "increasing acerbity" (Jonathan Mitchell, "Garner, Texas Bogey Man," *TNR*, August 31, 1938, 91–93).

186. The search terms used were ("Anti-New Deal*" OR "Anti-administration*" OR "New Dealer*" OR "New Deal Democrat*" OR "100 per cent New Deal*" OR "100 percent New Deal*" OR "100% New Deal*") AND (Congress OR House OR Senate OR representative OR senator), with a limitation to front-page stories.

187. The number of stories meeting the search requirement increases from 8 to 76 in 1933 but is still well below the levels observed in later years (e.g., 335 in 1938).

188. The criticism from the left was mainly in articles on the third-party movement by William Lemke, which offered a mix of agrarian radicalism and Coughlinite proto-fascism. Lemke won less than 2% of the vote.

189. A single member of Congress can be counted more than once if he is mentioned in multiple front-page stories. The results are substantively unchanged if one counts each member only once per year.

190. Twelve front-page stories from December 1935 through December 1936 mention the Liberty League as a critic of the New Deal and Roosevelt.

191. In 1936 eleven front-page stories in the *New York Times* identify Ely as a New Deal critic; ten stories characterize Reed in this manner; and seven note John Davis's role.

192. "'Grass Roots' Open War on New Deal; Boom Talmadge," *NYT*, January 30, 1936, 1.

193. "Talmadge Ready to be a Candidate," *NYT*, December 16, 1935, 1.

194. Where twenty-one *New York Times* front-page stories pointed to Smith's opposition to Roosevelt in 1936, five discussed Talmadge.

195. Indeed, it was not long before Harrison was referred to as a key leader of a bloc of "moderates" opposed to the 100% New Dealers (see "New Dealers Turn to Garner as Key to Congress Plans," *NYT*, December 31, 1938, 1).

196. Prior to 1938 the number of front-page stories that fit this description (including a mention of at least one member of Congress depicted as either pro– or anti–New Deal) was never higher than twenty-seven. In 1938 there were eighty-nine such stories, with fifty-eight the following year.

197. Caughey, *Congress, Public Opinion, and Representation.*

198. Schickler and Pearson, "Agenda Control and the Committee on Rules."

199. "Ninth Inning Rally," *TNR*, October 5, 1938, 238.

200. See, e.g., "Washington Notes: Planters' Punch," *TNR*, March 16, 1938, 162; "Congress Adjourns," *TNR*, June 29, 1938, 200; "Mr. Roosevelt, Ringmaster," *Nation*, January 15, 1938, 63–64; Editorial, *Nation*, March 5, 1938, 257–58.

201. See, e.g., "Anti-Labor Congressman," *CIO News*, May 19, 1941, 4.

202. "Many Gains Won by Labor, Election Results Indicate," *CIO News*, November 11, 1940, 1; "No Upsets in South; Poll Tax Helps Reactionaries Win," *CIO News*, November 11, 1940, 6. This was by no means an isolated use of this imagery. For example,

an article titled "The Best Argument for Poll Tax" featured pictures of "reactionaries" Howard Smith, Gene Cox, and Martin Dies, all of whom the *CIO News* argued could survive only because of the restricted electorate of the poll tax (April 22, 1940, 8).

203. "Opportunity Justice," *Defender*, August 20, 1938, 16.

204. "Le Berethon Thinks U.S. Should Correct Stand on Treatment of Negroes," *Defender*, January 7, 1939, 6.

205. "Mr. Lewis Speaks His Mind," *Defender*, April 13, 1940, 14.

206. Similarly, only 31% of the *Defender* stories from 1933 to 1936 took note of ways in which African Americans benefited from the New Deal; 57% of the stories did so in 1938–40. In addition, 29% of the early stories (1933–36) highlighted limits in how the New Deal benefited African Americans, while just 9% of the stories in 1938–40 did so. The search terms were: "new deal*" and (Roosevelt or Congress* or House or Senate or representative* or senator*); the search was limited to front-page stories and editorials. A total of 116 stories were initially coded, but a small number were dropped when it turned out the mention of the "new deal" was only incidental.

207. Noel, *Political Ideologies and Political Parties*, 149–50.

208. Kellogg, *Northern Liberals and Black America*, 3.

209. Among northern Democrats in Congress, the most prominent anti–New Deal members included John O'Connor and Royal Copeland of New York, William King of Utah, Edward Burke of Nebraska, Guy Gillette of Iowa, Alva Adams of Colorado, and Peter Gerry of Rhode Island. O'Connor was the lone target of Roosevelt's purge to lose in 1938, with Copeland dying the same year; King and Burke left Congress in 1940, with Adams departing two years later, and Gerry in 1946. On the northern conservatives, see James T. Patterson, "A Conservative Coalition Forms in Congress," *Journal of American History* 52, 4 (March 1966): 757–72.

Chapter 4: Liberalism Transformed:
The Early Civil Rights Movement and the "Liberal Lobby"

1. See Richard M. Dalfiume, "The 'Forgotten Years' of the Negro Revolution," *Journal of American History* 55 (June 1968): 90–106; and Dalfiume, *Desegregation of the U.S. Armed Forces* (Columbia: University of Missouri Press, 1969). The war's impact on the civil rights movement was not entirely positive. On this theme, see Kevin Kruse and Stephen Tuck, "Introduction," in *Fog of War: The Second World War and the Civil Rights Movement*, ed. Kruse and Tuck (New York: Oxford University Press, 2012). Along these lines, Julian Zelizer shows that conservatives actually gained ground in Congress during the war, solidifying the dominance of the GOP–Southern Democratic coalition (Zelizer, "Confronting the Roadblock: Congress, Civil Rights, and World War II," in Kruse and Tuck, *Fog of War*). Even so, however, the wartime mobilization contributed to the development of a liberal coalition in support of civil rights that increasingly gained influence within the northern Democratic Party (see discussion below). See also Philip Klinkner and Rogers Smith, *The Unsteady March: The Rise and Decline of Racial Inequality in America* (Chicago: University of Chicago Press, 1999), on the relationship between war and civil rights progress.

2. Ira De A. Reid, "Special Problems of Negro Migration during War," *Milbank Memorial Fund Quarterly* 25, 3 (July 1947): 284–92.

3. Reid estimates that 89% of northern African Americans lived in urban areas, while 63.5% of the southern African American population was rural. Ibid.

4. Wilson, "Two Negro Politicians"; Gosnell, *Negro Politicians*.

5. Dalfiume, "Forgotten Years," 99–100.

6. Sugrue, *Sweet Land of Liberty*, 40. See also Korstad and Lichtenstein, "Opportunities Found and Lost."

7. Moon, *Balance of Power: The Negro Vote* (Garden City, NY: Country Life Press, 1948).

8. Recall that Hoover pursued southern white votes by promoting lily-white organizations in the region, jettisoning the older, black-and-tan factions. Smith's team turned down *Pittsburgh Courier* editor Robert Vann's offer for help with African American voters.

9. Dalfiume, "Forgotten Years," 98.

10. Sugrue, *Sweet Land of Liberty*, 46–47.

11. Ibid., 57. The order was drafted by White House assistant Joseph Rauh, who would become a key civil rights leader active in the ADA and other liberal groups. See Andrew Edmund Kersten, *Race, Jobs, and the War: The FEPC in the Midwest, 1941–1946* (Urbana: University of Illinois Press, 2000).

12. *CR*, September 11, 1941, 7395–96.

13. On the FEPC's performance, see Kersten, *Race, Jobs, and War*; Louis Ruchames, *Race, Jobs, and Politics: The Story of FEPC* (New York: Columbia University Press, 1953); and Merl E. Reed, *Seedtime for the Modern Civil Rights Movement: The President's Committee on Fair Employment Practice, 1941–1946* (Baton Rouge: Louisiana State University Press, 1991).

14. Kersten, *Race, Jobs, and War*, 102.

15. Sugrue, *Sweet Land of Liberty*, 71–72.

16. "A Double Victory Campaign Gains Country-Wide Support," *Pittsburgh Courier*, February 14, 1942, 1. On the Double-V campaign more generally, see Harvard Sitkoff, "Racial Militancy and Interracial Violence in the Second World War," *Journal of American History* 58 (1971): 668–81. The wartime publication of Gunnar Myrdal's *American Dilemma* (New York: Harper & Row, 1944) provided an additional resource for civil rights activists seeking to highlight the deep conflict between the so-called American Creed and the reality of American racial practices.

17. Dalfiume, *Desegregation of the Armed Forces*, chaps. 2–6.

18. Katznelson, *Fear Itself*, chap. 6.

19. Lichtenstein, *Most Dangerous Man*, 208.

20. Thomas Sancton, "The Race Riots," *TNR*, July 5, 1943, 9. Following the initial rioting over housing in Detroit in 1942, the *New Republic* editorialized that those seeking to block African Americans from housing "were assuredly doing Hitler's work" ("Race Riot," March 9, 1942, 317).

21. "Defeat at Detroit," *Nation*, July 3, 1943, 4.

22. Sancton, "Something's Happened to the Negro," *TNR*, February 8, 1943, 177.

23. I. F. Stone, "Capital Notes," *Nation*, January 23, 1943, 115–16.

24. Sancton, "Race Riots," 11–12.

25. Ibid., 12. A year earlier Sancton had criticized Roosevelt for putting too many conservatives in charge of the war effort. He quoted an African American newspaperman who wondered whether "the President worried at all at the way people like Talmadge and Dixon are whipping up race-hate in a cold-blooded attack on the New Deal." Sancton argued that Roosevelt needed to take such opponents on directly ("Poor Morale in Washington," *TNR*, September 14, 1942, 305–7).

26. African American liberals, of course, challenged Roosevelt throughout (see chapter 2).

27. Nelson Lichtenstein, "Politicized Unions and the New Deal Model," in *The New Deal and the Triumph of Liberalism*, ed. Sidney M. Milkis and Jerome M. Mileur (Amherst: University of Massachusetts Press, 2002), 135–65.

28. *This Is Your America*, reprinted in Joseph Gaer, *The First Round: The Story of the CIO Political Action Committee* (New York: Duell, Sloan and Pearce, 1944), 17–48.

29. *The People's Program for 1944*, reprinted in Gaer, *The First Round*, 185–212.

30. James C. Foster, *The Union Politic: The CIO Political Action Committee* (Columbia: University of Missouri Press, 1975), chap. 2.

31. Italics in original. *The Negroe in 1944*, reprinted in Gaer, *The First Round*, 468.

32. "P.A.C. to Poll Congressmen on Their Stands," *LAT*, December 28, 1945, 7. The CIO-PAC kept up this drumbeat in future elections. For example, in the voter guide included in the *CIO News*, the PAC highlighted the failure of the GOP-controlled Eightieth Congress to act on civil rights legislation: "The GOP majority, showing little enthusiasm, alibied that southern poll-taxers would filibuster against the proposals" (July 19, 1948). In tallying the Eightieth Congress's failures, CIO president Philip Murray underscored that it had "ignored our country's need for strengthened civil rights." The scorecard itself included the House vote on the poll tax bill and a House vote to allow southern states to evade court decisions on desegregating schools (which the *CIO News* noted was "opposed by CIO and liberal groups as forcing U.S. to approve racial discrimination policies").

33. Louise Overacker, "Presidential Campaign Funds, 1944," *American Political Science Review* 39 (October 1945): 899.

34. Ibid., 920–21. NCPAC was created in July 1944 as way for progressives supportive of organized labor, but outside unions, to participate in the CIO-led drive.

35. Riker, "The CIO in Politics," 125–39. As a point of comparison, the top industry for pro-Democratic spending was Hollywood; the CIO-PAC and NCPAC spent roughly five times as much as Hollywood on behalf of Democrats (Overacker, "Presidential Campaign Funds," 916–18).

36. Sullivan, *Days of Hope*, 131.

37. "Mr. Hannegan's Troubles in Fight for Party Control," *US News*, April 26, 1946, 65; see also Editorial, "Political Patterns," *Nation*, April 13, 1946, 417.

38. "Mr. Hannegan's Troubles," 65–66.

39. "Rebel Yell," *Newsweek*, April 8, 1946, 21.

40. "Political Roundup: War among the Democrats," *TNR*, June 3, 1946, 793. Conservative southern Democrats had grown increasingly vitriolic in their attacks on the New Deal during the war. In the aftermath of the Court's white primary decision, Mississippi governor Mike Connor charged that African Americans now dominated the "New Deal party." Louisiana governor Sam Jones made similar claims; see Jason Morgan Ward, "'A War for States' Rights': The White Supremacist Vision of Double Victory," in Kruse and Tuck, *Fog of War*, 139–40.

41. "Ex-Pacifists Favor War If Necessary: Liberals Headed by Niebuhr Form Committee Giving Up Stand of Two Decades," *NYT*, April 29, 1941, 9.

42. "Navy Stands by Its Jim Crow Policy," *Defender*, July 26, 1941, 6.

43. "La Guardia Raps Armed Services Jim Crow," *Defender*, June 6, 1942, 7.

44. As quoted in Peter John Kellogg, "The Americans for Democratic Action and Civil Rights in 1948: Conscience in Politics or Politics in Conscience," *Midwest Quarterly* 20 (1978): 51.

45. "Leaders Urge President to Throttle Riot Danger," *Defender*, July 10, 1943, 20.

46. "Platform for Progressives," *TNR*, May 8, 1944, 646.

47. "The Unholy Alliance," *TNR*, May 8, 1944, 658.

48. Ibid., 643. The role of the "unholy alliance" in blocking both racial and economic initiatives featured prominently in several *New Republic* stories (see, e.g., James Loeb Jr, "The Next Congress: I. The Chances for a Progressive Senate," *TNR*, October 9, 1944, 449–52; and Loeb, "The Next Congress: II. Prospects in the House of Representatives," *TNR*, October 16, 1944, 487–90). The alliance had set back liberalism by killing the National Resources Planning Board, undermining price controls, passing antilabor legislation, defeating the poll tax ban, and blocking a federal ballot for soldiers. The prominence that the UDA and *New Republic* gave to racial discrimination in their programmatic

statements during the war was increasingly typical of liberal advocates. For example, in a major speech celebrating her twenty-fifth anniversary with the *Nation*, Freda Kirchwey outlined a "Program of Action" that emphasized both the need to "break the hold in each party of its Dieses, its Hoffmans, its Cotton Ed Smiths, its Ham Fishes" and "the wiping out of every form of legal discrimination, political or economic, against any racial or religious group" (Freda Kirchwey, "Program of Action," *Nation*, March 11, 1944, 300–305).

49. Sullivan, *Days of Hope*, 236–37; see also Clifton Brock, *Americans for Democratic Action: Its Role in National Politics* (Washington, DC: Public Affairs Press, 1962), 51.

50. Brock, *Americans for Democratic Action*, 52.

51. Jennifer Delton, *Making Minnesota Liberal: Civil Rights and the Transformation of the Democratic Party* (Minneapolis: University of Minnesota Press, 2002), xxiv–xxvi.

52. "Douglas: His Policy," *TNR*, June 28, 1948, 20–21.

53. Kellogg, "Americans for Democratic Action," 54–57.

54. Delton, *Making Minnesota Liberal*, 119–20.

55. As quoted in Kellogg, "Americans for Democratic Action," 57.

56. Ibid.

57. Robert Bendiner, "Rout of the Bourbons," *Nation*, July 24, 1948, 91–92.

58. As quoted in Kellogg, "Americans for Democratic Action," 60; see also Timothy N. Thurber, *The Politics of Equality: Hubert H. Humphrey and the African American Freedom Struggle.* (New York: Columbia University Press, 1999), chap. 2. See chapter 9 below for a more detailed discussion of the 1948 convention fight.

59. See, e.g., "Nation's Top Liberals Meet to Push 'Fair Deal' Program," *Defender*, April 9, 1949, 2.

60. Roger Biles, *Crusading Liberal: Paul H. Douglas of Illinois* (Dekalb: Northern Illinois University Press, 2002), 44.

61. As quoted in Brock, *Americans for Democratic Action*, 112.

62. See, e.g., "Reprisals on Foes of Truman Sought," *NYT*, December 12, 1948, 77.

63. "Action Memorandum," December 7, 1949, reprinted in Hearings before the House Select Committee on Lobbying Activities, "Americans for Democratic Action," July 11 and 12, 1950, 116.

64. ADA press release, reprinted in Hearings, "Americans for Democratic Action," 118–19.

65. Ibid., 118; see also "Asks Priority for F.E.P.C.: A.D.A. Board Bids Congress Push Civil Rights," *NYT*, December 18, 1949, 4.

66. As quoted in Brock, *Americans for Democratic Action*, 104.

67. Arthur Krock, "The Superior Articulation of the Left: II," *NYT*, July 19 and 19, 1949; Holmes Alexander, "The '50 Campaign Will Show What We Can Expect of ADA," *LAT*, September 14, 1949, A5.

68. Louis Martin, "Nation's Top Liberals Meet to Push 'Fair Deal' Program," *Defender*, April 9, 1949, 2; Louis Martin, "Liberals Pledge Crusade for Enactment of Civil Rights," *Defender*, April 16, 1949, 1.

69. As quoted in Brock, *Americans for Democratic Action*, 138.

70. See, e.g., "ADA 'Scores' Congressmen on Records," *Washington Post*, August 20, 1952, 2; John M. Couric, "Democrats Lead in Voting Liberal, ADA Finds," *Washington Post*, September 24, 1953, 9; Robert C. Albright, "'Liberal' Votes on Hill Tallied," *Post*, September 12, 1955, 9; "ADA Says Poll Shows Democratic Liberalism," *Washington Post*, August 10, 1956, 22; and Warren B. Francis, "Political Group Hits California Delegation," *LAT*, November 15, 1951, 9.

71. Even in some years where there were no relevant roll-call votes, the ADA published a scorecard evaluating Congress as a whole that attacked the failure to act on civil rights. For example, while there were no civil rights votes in 1948, the ADA's "Congressional

Audit" listed Congress's inaction on the FEPC, the poll tax, and antilynching legislation as important failures ("Congressional Audit: Balance Sheet for the 80th Congress," *ADA World*, July 1948, 4–5). The ADA was equally harsh in criticizing the Democratic Eighty-First Congress; its review of the 1949 session highlighted the "spectacular failures on Taft-Hartley repeal, civil rights and aid to education," and the following year it called the lack of civil rights legislation "the most conspicuous failure of the 81st Congress," while listing the FEPC roll call and a roll call on segregation in the military as key votes (see "Congressional Supplement," *ADA World*, October 28, 1949, 1A; "Congressional Supplement," *ADA World*, September 1950, 1A–4A).

72. Brewer, "Poll Tax," 277.

73. Kesselman, *Social Politics of FEPC*, 31. See also "March on Washington Set for Spring to Push FEPC," *Defender*, March 2, 1946, 1.

74. "Fifty Fail to 'Crash' Anti-Red Civil Rights Conference Here," *Washington Post*, January 16, 1950, 1, 7.

75. Donald R. McCoy and Richard T. Ruetten, *Quest and Response: Minority Rights and the Truman Administration* (Lawrence: University Press of Kansas, 1973), 191.

76. "Fifty Fail to 'Crash'," 1, 7.

77. Ibid, 7.

78. See, e.g., "900 from 35 States at Rights Meet," *Defender*, March 1, 1952, 1; "Reuther Demands Ban on Filibuster," *NYT*, February 19, 1952, 22.

79. There were several other cases in which the NAACP spoke about a single element of pending legislation but did not express a view of the overall bill. The tallies presented here, however, include only cases where the NAACP expressed an overall view of legislation (support for or opposition to).

80. Sitkoff observes that the NAACP leaders worked with the CIO in lobbying for housing, better wages, and Social Security expansion (*New Deal for Blacks*, 257). Such CIO leaders as Philip Murray and Walter Reuther also served on the NAACP board. Reuther was on the board from 1949 until his death in 1970 (Lichtenstein, *Most Dangerous Man*, 315–16). Murray served from 1947 until his death in 1952 (NAACP, "Four New Members to NAACP Board," January 10, 1947, in Papers of the NAACP, Part 1, Reel 14). See also annual reports of the NAACP, 1947–52. (Murray is listed as a member of Board of Directors every year.)

81. This data spans 1948–1955.

82. This occurred when the Jewish League Against Communism—a small group associated with fervent anticommunism that set it apart from mainstream Jewish organizations—testified in favor of the Internal Security Act of 1950.

83. This is based on the *Congressional Quarterly Almanac* coding.

84. Moon, *Balance of Power*, 143, notes that an NAACP-sponsored declaration—signed by the leaders of numerous African American organizations—"closely paralleled the program supported by the CIO-PAC," including civil rights, social security expansion, full employment legislation, price controls, and prounion policies.

85. Hearings before the House Select Committee on Lobbying Activities, "Americans for Democratic Action," July 11 and 12, 1950, 2.

86. Ibid., 68.

87. Korstad and Lichtenstein, "Opportunities Found and Lost," 799–800.

88. Kellogg, *Northern Liberals and Black America*, 309.

89. Lichtenstein, *Most Dangerous Man*, 315–16.

90. "Truman Blasts GOP Smear, Says He Is a Liberal," *Kansas City Plaindealer*, October 27, 1944, 2. See also Kesselman, *Social Politics of FEPC*, 209.

91. Garson, *Democratic Party and Sectionalism*, 136–38. Garson's source is an unsigned memo to Truman, Official Files 40, Truman Papers.

92. Bendiner, "Rout of the Bourbons," 92.

93. McAdam and Kloos, *Deeply Divided*, chap. 2. McAdam and Kloos attribute the dearth of grassroots movement activism in these years in large part to the pervasive influence of the second "Red Scare," which made dissent suspect.

Chapter 5: Civil Rights and New Deal Liberalism in the Mass Public

1. See Adam J. Berinsky and Eric Schickler, "The American Mass Public in the 1930s and 1940s," National Science Foundation, Collaborative Research Grant, 2006–09; Berinsky, Schickler, and Jasjeet Sekhon, National Science Foundation, Political Science Program Grant, "The American Mass Public in the Early Cold War Years," 2012–15; Berinsky and Schickler, "The American Mass Public in the 1930s and 1940s" [computer file]. Individual surveys conducted by the Gallup Organization, Roper Organization, NORC, and the Office of Public Opinion Research [producers], 1936–1945. For more detailed information on the samples and weights, see Adam J. Berinsky, Eleanor Powell, Eric Schickler, and Ian Yohai, "Revisiting Public Opinion in the 1930s and 1940s," *PS: Political Science and Politics* 44, 3 (2011): 515–20. As it turns out, the survey weights do not affect any of the substantive results presented. The weights are used for all the surveys where they are available (i.e., all polls conducted through 1945).

2. See Carmines and Stimson, *Issue Evolution*.

3. Interestingly, as discussed below, economic liberalism is more consistently related to support for desegregation than is partisanship.

4. Thomas J. Sugrue, "Crabgrass-Roots Politics: Race, Rights, and the Reaction against Liberalism in the Urban North, 1940–1964," *Journal of American History* 82, 2 (September 1995): 551–78.

5. Cf. Carmines and Stimson, *Issue Evolution*; Zaller, *Nature and Origins of Mass Opinion*, chap. 1.

6. Bawn et al., "Theory of Parties," 575.

7. When both party identification and presidential vote are included in the same survey, the relationship with racial liberalism is similar across both indicators.

8. The appendix tables and appendix figures are available via http://press.princeton .edu/titles/10750.html.

9. Questions about farm and defense policy were not included because it was not clear what the economically "liberal" position was on these items in the context of the 1930s–1950s.

10. On this approach, which Andrew Gelman has labeled the "secret weapon," see Gelman and Jennifer Hill, *Data Analysis Using Regression and Multilevel/Hierarchical Models* (New York: Cambridge University Press, 2007).

11. The results look substantively the same if one instead estimates the models using logit. Since the level of support for the various items generally ranges from about 30% to 70% (rather than being near the extremes), I focus the presentation on the easier-to-interpret OLS coefficients.

12. As in the rest of the book, the South is defined as the eleven Confederate states plus Kentucky and Oklahoma.

13. As discussed in chapter 9, Truman was inconsistent in his emphasis on civil rights in 1948. However, the announcement of his program early that year, combined with the Democratic platform's endorsement of aggressive action during the summer, sent the clearest signal of civil rights support by national Democrats prior to the 1960s.

14. Zangrando, *NAACP Crusade against Lynching*, 18–19. The spread of the idea of national policing—with the rise of prohibition—also helped make antilynching legislation a more politically feasible strategy (see Christopher Waldrep, "National Policing, Lynching, and Constitutional Change," *Journal of Southern History*, 74 (August 2008): 589–626.

15. See appendix (available at http://press.princeton.edu/titles/10750.html) for details. The one exception, which showed a wider margin in support of action against lynching, is the June 1947 Gallup poll. In that poll, 70% supported federal action, with 21% opposed. The June 1947 question asks whether the federal government should be able to intervene in lynching cases "if it thinks the State Government does not deal with it justly." The other 1947–50 items do not specify that the state government may have acted unjustly. In addition, the June 1947 question immediately followed an item about a notorious Greenville, South Carolina, lynching case. The question wording and context likely explain the much higher support registered in the poll.

16. Landon voters supported the measure by 63%–22%, while Roosevelt voters favored it 60%–25%.

17. The percentage of respondents classified as "liberal" varies across surveys, depending on the particular questions. In general, the share of economic liberals in the South is slightly lower than in the North. The absence of a relationship in the South in the last poll (see fig. 5.1C) could be due to problems with the economic liberalism item in that survey. The only economic liberalism measure concerned what to do about the budget deficit. Respondents were coded as liberal if they opposed domestic spending cuts and as conservative if they favored spending cuts and no tax hikes. Some 72% of southerners were coded as conservative, with just 13% moderate and 15% liberal. Most surveys had questions that more clearly tapped into economic liberalism and that had less skewed response distributions.

18. Adding demographic controls to the models using partisanship to predict views on antilynching legislation also does not affect the results. Controls for demographics (which are used in a consistent manner across the surveys) include age, gender, occupation/class (professional, labor, poor), region (Northeast, Midwest, West), urban and farm residence, phone ownership, and, when available, union membership and education. For southern respondents, a control is also included for the Rim South as opposed to the Deep South.

19. Paul M. Sniderman and Edward H. Stiglitz, *The Reputational Premium: A Theory of Party Identification and Policy Reasoning* (Princeton, NJ: Princeton University Press, 2012). See also Matthew Levendusky, *The Partisan Sort: How Liberals Became Democrats and Conservatives Became Republicans* (Chicago: University of Chicago Press, 2009).

20. In this survey, 42% of Democrats qualified as "sorted" (i.e., economically liberal), compared to 39% of Republicans (i.e., economically conservative). Across all the surveys with civil rights items, about half of the partisans were sorted, with the share of sorted Republicans a bit higher than that for Democrats. While sorted Republicans tend to be better educated than unsorted Republicans, the reverse holds for Democrats: economic liberalism was more concentrated among less educated Democrats in the 1930s–1940s.

21. When I estimate a model pooling the data across surveys with a separate dummy variable for each partisan-ideological group (i.e., economically liberal Democrats, moderate Democrats, and so on), economically liberal Democrats are 22 points more likely to support action against lynching than are economically conservative Republicans. Within each partisan group, one observes a clear tie between economic views and support for federal action. For each ideology level, Democrats are more likely to support federal action than are Republicans. The model includes a separate intercept for each survey. See appendix figure 5.1 for the estimates.

22. See "House Prepares for Passage of Anti-Lynching Bill," *Washington Post*, April 8, 1937, 28; and "House Sidetracks Anti-Lynching Bill," *NYT*, April 8, 1937, 24. In the Senate, however, Republicans proved less willing than northern Democrats to back cloture—though in other cases in this period, Senate Republicans provided greater support than their Democratic counterparts (see Jenkins, Peck, and Weaver, "Between Reconstructions").

23. Brewer, "Poll Tax"; Krueger, *Promises to Keep*, chap. 3.

24. The point estimate for Democratic presidential vote choice is 0.06 (SE = 0.01)—corresponding to a 6-point party difference—when it is the sole independent variable (other than the intercept for each survey) and falls slightly to 0.05 (SE = 0.01) when economic liberalism is added to the model. The point estimate for economic liberalism is 0.06 (SE = 0.01) in the latter model.

25. Dalfiume, *Desegregation of Armed Forces*.

26. The text read: "Should negro and white soldiers serve together in all branches of the armed forces?" See appendix table 5.2 for the overall marginal distribution.

27. If one compares consistent Democratic voters—i.e., those voting for FDR in 1940 and intending to vote Democratic for Congress in 1942 and for FDR in 1944—to consistent GOP voters (defined analogously), the gap is a bit more substantial: core Democratic voters split evenly on integrating the military (46%–46%), while Republicans opposed integration by a substantial 57%–37% margin.

28. Chen, *Fifth Freedom*.

29. Civil rights opponents often defended their opposition to proposed legislation by claiming that the states, not the federal government, ought to act against discrimination. By asking about state laws, the Gallup item avoids this consideration about the appropriate level for governmental action.

30. Neither question mentions religion or ethnicity. This makes it less likely that responses were driven by attitudes toward Catholics, Jews, Italians, etc.

31. The form that asked about working alongside people of other races included a question about government ownership of the electric companies instead of the railroads. Opponents of government ownership of electric companies also oppose requiring integrated workplaces by an overwhelming 60%–33% margin; supporters of government ownership are more closely divided, opposing integrated workplaces by just a 9-point margin.

32. Economic views are coded based on views on government ownership of industry and government help for the unemployed.

33. See Chen, Mickey, and Van Houweling, "Explaining Contemporary Alignment of Race and Party," for an aggregate level analysis of a California fair employment referendum that shows similar patterns.

34. Similarly, 19% of southern liberals backed requiring employees to work in integrated workplaces, compared to 11% of moderates, and 6% of conservatives. In this survey, a little over one-quarter of southern whites were classified as economic liberals (compared to about 33% in the North).

35. Republican and Democratic voters are identified based on their choice in the preceding election (so the 1944 presidential election is used for the March 1948 item).

36. A dummy variable provides a separate intercept for each survey.

37. Devin Caughey, Michael Dougal, and Eric Schickler, "The Policy Bases of the New Deal Realignment: Evidence from Public Opinion Polls, 1936–1952," paper presented at the American Political Science Annual Meeting, Chicago, September 2013. The paper employs a dynamic group-level item-response model. Similar to factor analysis, item-response models treat observed survey responses as indicators of a respondent-level latent trait. There are too few questions per respondent to apply a conventional individual-level item-response model, so Caughey et al. instead use a group-level model, which generates estimates of average liberalism in different subpopulations (e.g., states). The subpopulation estimates are smoothed with a hierarchical model that includes a national intercept and all the geographic and/or demographic predictors that define the groups. To allow for change over time, the group means and parameters of the hierarchical model are allowed to evolve in each year. On this estimation approach, see Devin Caughey and Christopher

Warshaw, "Dynamic Estimation of Latent Opinion Using a Hierarchical Group-Level IRT Model," *Political Analysis* 23 (Spring 2015): 197–211.

38. The graph includes only estimated correlations for years in which there were racial liberalism survey items. Labor questions were asked in all years. See appendix figure 5.4 for scatterplots between state-level racial and labor liberalism for 1937, 1942, 1947, and 1950.

39. If one examines a comprehensive state economic liberalism measure, including both labor and nonlabor issues, the results are much the same: as of 1937, there is almost no relationship between this comprehensive measure and racial liberalism (r = 0.19); the relationship is much larger by 1942 (r = 0.63) and remains of similar magnitude through the rest of the 1940s.

40. When one examines aggregate opinion in the South, there is also a clear relationship between racial liberalism and labor liberalism. This relationship is considerably stronger in the 1940s than at the start of the period and is also stronger for labor liberalism than for nonlabor economic issues.

41. See Sugrue, *Sweet Land of Liberty*, on the persistence of prejudice and discrimination in the urban North in the 1940s–1960s.

42. For example, the same NORC survey showed FDR voters were 8 points more likely than Republicans to say that African Americans are as intelligent as whites.

43. See Paul M. Sniderman and Edward G. Carmines, *Reaching Beyond Race* (Cambridge, MA: Harvard University Press, 1997).

44. A 1944 NORC survey included several items that tap into this dimension. Northern white Roosevelt voters look very similar to their GOP counterparts when it comes to eating in integrated restaurants, having an African American nurse, or having an African American move in next door. The party gap for each item is less than 3 points.

45. The same surveys show a much bigger gap in views when it comes to lynching, fair employment, the poll tax, and Truman's civil rights program as a whole. The wording of the travel desegregation item is confusing, suggesting that some caution ought to be used in interpreting its results.

46. In the Roper survey, 40% of Democrats favor a national law against job discrimination, compared to 27% of Republicans.

47. The question asked, "What about you? Are you in favor of desegregation, strict segregation, or something in between?" The same 1972 survey shows that northern Democrats are somewhat more supportive of school integration than are Republicans but are no more supportive of fully integrated housing than are Republicans.

48. Northern white Democrats, by contrast, were less likely to criticize Kennedy from the right than were Republicans.

49. This gap holds up if one restricts the sample to respondents old enough to vote in 1936.

50. A full 74% of new FDR voters in 1940 (after having either not voted or voted for another candidate in 1936) backed the poll tax ban, while just 60% of new Willkie voters backed the ban. By contrast, just 4 or 5 points separate 1936 FDR and Landon voters on this item.

51. A further piece of suggestive evidence is that northern Democratic House members were less likely to sign discharge petitions for civil rights initiatives in the 1930s than were Republicans. Democrats began to catch up with Republicans after 1937 and surpassed them in the early 1940s. If northern Democratic partisans had been more pro–civil rights than Republicans well before 1937, their representatives in Congress had been out of step with them for a prolonged period. It is more plausible that Democrats in Congress moved soon after their constituents rather than having been out of touch with them for years (see chapter 8 on the discharge petitions).

52. See, e.g., Sniderman and Carmines, *Reaching beyond Race*; Kinder and Sanders, *Divided by Color*; Nicholas A. Valentino and David O. Sears, "Old Times There Are Not Forgotten: Race and Partisan Realignment in the Contemporary South," *American Journal of Political Science* 49, 3 (2005): 672–88.

53. The earliest surveys do not include both civil rights policy and prejudice items in the same poll, but the surveys that include prejudice items show only a weak, inconsistent tie between prejudice and partisanship. In later surveys with both prejudice and policy items, the relationship between New Deal liberalism and civil rights support is robust to controlling for prejudice measures.

54. Carmines and Stimson, *Issue Evolution*; Zaller, *Nature and Origins of Mass Opinion*. See also Elisabeth R. Gerber and John E. Jackson, "Endogenous Preferences and the Study of Institutions," *American Political Science Review* 87, 3 (1990): 639–56.

55. Carmines and Stimson, *Issue Evolution*, 55–57.

56. Changes in question wording require some caution in interpreting the relative size of the estimates. But close inspection of the wording and response distributions over time provides no basis for thinking that the later questions artificially reduced the party gap (e.g. by having a more lopsided response distribution).

57. The question wording was: "Opinions differ as to how certain racial and religious groups are treated in this country. Which of these three ideas comes closest to expressing your opinion of what the real situation is? (A) Racial and religious groups are, on the whole, as well treated as they should be; (B) While certain racial and religious groups in this country are sometimes not treated as well as they should be, we are now improving the situation as fast as is practical; (C) Certain racial and religious groups in this country are treated very badly, and some strong measures should be taken to improve the situation." Republicans were also more likely to say that these groups are treated as fairly as they should be treated (response option A).

58. Zaller, *Nature and Origins of Mass Opinion*; Adam J. Berinsky, *In Time of War: Understanding American Public Opinion from World War II to Iraq* (Chicago: University of Chicago Press, 2009).

59. One can also reject the idea that the partisan divide emerged only when civil rights issues affected the North. Some of the issues discussed above directly affected only the South (e.g., lynching, the poll tax), while others challenged northern race relations (e.g., fair employment practices). The consistency of the partisan and ideological gap across both sets of issues suggests that a narrow explanation—i.e., that Republican voters were willing to target discrimination in the South but not the North—does not hold up.

60. A separate intercept is included for each survey. For the age categories, the model includes dummy variables for 21–34 year olds and 35–50 year olds; respondents over 50 are the excluded category. For region, the model includes indicators for the Midwest and West, with the East excluded. For education, there are dummy variables for "some high school," high school graduates, and "some college"; "no high school" is the excluded category. Protestants are the excluded category for the analysis of religious groups.

61. Since religion is asked in only a handful of surveys, the estimate for Jews is limited to the FEPC items and is based on just three polls. But later polls, which do include religion, also show Jews to be more racially liberal than non-Jews. Notice that the impact of education is actually negative for the FEPC, though it is, as one might expect, positive in predicting support for antilynching legislation.

62. These estimates again come from a model pooling the surveys with FEPC questions; a separate intercept is included for each survey. Controlling for religion (Jewish, Catholic) reduces the number of surveys from thirteen to three, but the coefficient for Democratic vote choice remains robust when dummy variables for religious groups are included alongside the other demographic controls (0.104, SE = 0.02).

63. For example, in predicting support for the FEPC, the size of the economic liberalism coefficient goes from 0.17 (SE = 0.01) with no demographic controls to 0.13 (SE = 0.01) when a full array of demographics are included.

64. The lynching model is estimated for all polls starting in December 1937. The fair employment questions are drawn from all of the relevant Gallup surveys from 1945–53. The results tell the same story when support for banning the poll tax is the dependent variable (see Online Appendix Figure 5.5).

65. While the tie between civil rights views and partisanship is stronger for those with more education, this may have little to do with the particular features of civil rights as an issue area. When one examines the relationship between party identification and economic issue views, one finds a similar pattern: the most educated respondents typically show tighter constraint than the less educated. On this tendency more generally, see Zaller, *Nature and Origins of Mass Opinion*; and Philip Converse, "The Nature of Belief Systems in Mass Publics," in *Ideology and Discontent*, ed. David E. Apter (New York: Free Press, 1964).

66. Cues from intellectuals—highlighted by Noel, *Political Ideologies and Political Parties*—likely played a role in forging these connections, but the extent to which the connections spanned across different groups (even reaching into the South, when it comes to the economic liberalism–racial liberalism tie), suggests that broader forces were at work as well (see chapters 3–4 for additional discussion of these broader forces).

67. For example, Jewish leaders were strong backers of the FEPC, and this support was mirrored at the mass level as 87% of Jews in the 1945–53 Gallup surveys favored the FEPC.

68. Bawn et al., "Theory of Parties."

Chapter 6: The African American Realignment and New Deal Liberalism

1. Karol, *Party Position Change*, 106.

2. Everett Carll Ladd and Charles D. Hadley, *Transformations of the American Party System* (New York: Norton, 1978), 59–60; Weiss, *Farewell to Party of Lincoln*, chap. 10.

3. High, *Roosevelt—and Then?*, 203–4.

4. Carmines and Stimson, *Issue Evolution*, 46; James T. Kenneally, "Black Republicans during the New Deal: The Role of Joseph W. Martin, Jr.," *Review of Politics* 55 (Winter 1993): 139.

5. McCoy and Ruetten, *Quest and Response*, 97–98.

6. Moon, *Balance of Power*, 213. Walter White sent Truman a copy of the book in May 1948 (McCoy and Ruetten, *Quest and Response*, 98).

7. Alexander Heard, *A Two-Party South?* (Chapel Hill: University of North Carolina Press, 1952), 231–32.

8. See Katznelson, *When Affirmative Action Was White*; Wolters, "New Deal and the Negro."

9. See, e.g., Eleanor Ryan, "Toward a National Negro Congress," *New Masses* 4 (June 1935): 14–15; John G. Van Deusen, "The Negro in Politics," *Journal of Negro History* 21 (July 1936): 273–74; Ralph J. Bunche, "The Negro in the Political Life of the United States," *Journal of Negro Education* 10 (July 1941): 567–84.

10. See, e.g., Katznelson, *When Affirmative Action Was White*, 48; Wolters, "New Deal and the Negro," 194.

11. Ralph J. Bunche, *The Political Status of the Negro in the Age of FDR* (Chicago: University of Chicago Press, 1973). Bunche's report was drafted as a working paper for Gunnar Myrdal's *American Dilemma*.

12. Ibid., 93, 614–18, 624.

13. John B. Kirby, *Black Americans in the Roosevelt Era: Liberalism and Race* (Knoxville: University of Tennessee Press, 1980), chaps. 2 and 6.

14. Sitkoff, *New Deal for Blacks*, 68.

15. Richard Sterner, *The Negro's Share: A Study of Income, Consumption, Housing and Public Assistance* (New York: Harper and Brothers, 1943), 222.

16. Edwin Amenta, *Bold Relief: Institutional Politics and the Origins of Modern American Social Policy* (Princeton, NJ: Princeton University Press, 1998), 158.

17. Sterner, *Negroe's Share*, 247.

18. Moon, *Balance of Power*, 21. See also C. William McKinney, "The Negro in Pennsylvania Politics," *Opportunity* 17 (February 1939): 50–51.

19. James A. Harrell, "Negro Leadership in the Election Year 1936," *Journal of Southern History* 34, 4 (1968): 557, 558.

20. McKinney, "Negro in Pennsylvania Politics," 50. See also Samuel Lubell, *The Future of American Politics* (New York: Harper and Brothers, 1952).

21. Harrell, "Negro Leadership in 1936," 558.

22. Again, while African American leaders backed efforts to ban discrimination by unions, they opposed the efforts of Republicans (and their southern Democratic allies) to overturn the Wagner Act regime or undermine the NLRB.

23. As quoted in Simon Topping, *Lincoln's Lost Legacy: The Republican Party and the African American Vote, 1928–1952* (Gainesville: University of Florida Press, 2008), 62. See also Kenneally, "Black Republicans."

24. Weiss, *Farewell to Party of Lincoln*, 269.

25. Topping, *Lincoln's Lost Legacy*, 62.

26. Thomas H. Reed and Doris D. Reed, "The Republican Opposition," *Survey Graphic* 29, 5 (May 1940): 286.

27. This proposal was put in all capitals. Republican American Committee, "Declaration to the Republican Party," August 24–25, 1945, Papers of the NAACP, vol. 18C, Reel 29.

28. A year earlier, a group of African American Republicans issued a similar statement, which included a condemnation of the "unholy and vicious" alliance of Republicans and southern Democrats in Congress. See Topping, *Lincoln's Lost Legacy*, 86.

29. Ibid., 84–88.

30. Walter White to Joseph Martin, November 9, 1942, Joseph L. Martin Papers, Stonehill College Archives and Historical Collections.

31. See Alonzo L. Hamby, "World War II: Conservatism and Constituency Politics," in *The American Congress: The Building of Democracy*, ed. Julian E. Zelizer (New York: Houghton Mifflin, 2004), 474–92.

32. High, *Roosevelt—and Then?*, 206–12.

33. Lewis's antiwar stand played a big role in motivating his complaints about the Democrats. With its Communist Party support, the NNC also sided with the isolationists during the period of the USSR-German Nonaggression Pact (1939–41).

34. Martha Biondi, *To Stand and Fight: The Struggle for Civil Rights in Postwar New York City* (Cambridge, MA: Harvard University Press, 2003), 41.

35. Delton, *Making Minnesota Liberal*, 143–50; McCoy and Ruetten, *Quest and Response*, 99, 113.

36. Herbert H. Hyman et al., *Interviewing in Social Research* (Chicago: University of Chicago Press, 1954), 159–61, 169–70. Interestingly, the race of the interviewer made little difference when African Americans were interviewed in New York City.

37. The nonresponses by many southern African Americans could reflect intimidation, alienation, or lack of information. Nonetheless, the strong liberalism of those with an

opinion is a clear indicator that southern African Americans were largely on the left when it came to debates about the future of New Deal liberalism.

38. The two exceptions in the North are an evaluative item about labor unions and a question about taxes. It is worth noting that there are six other union-related questions; on all six, northern African Americans are to the left of northern whites. The two exceptions in the South are an item about bankers abusing their power and one about general ideological self-identification.

39. See Caughey, Dougal, and Schickler, "Policy Bases of New Deal Realignment," for a discussion. Note that questions that focus on civil rights are excluded.

40. Since southern African Americans are essentially excluded from most of the polls, the estimates for their liberalism are very noisy. Even so, southern African Americans are consistently well to the left of southern whites.

41. Treating each year as the unit of analysis, northern African American Democratic voters are, on average, 0.25 units more liberal than are northern white Democrats. For comparison, the gap between northern white Democrats and northern white Republicans is 0.72. The focus here is on northern African Americans because of the small number of southern African American voters in this period. However, the limited number of southern African Americans again appear similar to northern African Americans.

42. The two exceptions are 1936 and 1937, when the data on African Americans is quite thin. On average across years, African American nonvoters are 0.11 more liberal than northern white Democratic voters. The gap is even bigger with southern white Democratic voters, who tend to be fairly conservative starting in 1941.

43. From 1941 to 1952 northern African American Republican voters were, on average, 0.42 units more liberal than were northern white Republican voters; northern African American Republicans were just 0.18 less liberal than northern white Democrats.

44. Baylor, "First to the Party."

45. The estimates in figure 6.3 are based on the same group-level, item response model as in figure 6.2 but with the analysis limited to labor policy questions,

46. The results hold up within region: not only were northern African Americans well to left of northern whites, but southern African Americans were also well to the left of southern whites on labor policy.

47. Topping, *Lincoln's Lost Legacy*, 206.

48. Buni, *Robert L. Vann*, 297.

49. Ibid., 297, 298.

50. The 1937 and 1938 results, which show a larger Democratic edge, are based on very small African American samples (N = 157 in 1937 and N = 62 in 1938).

51. The results tell substantively the same story if one restricts the sample to the North to minimize the problem that the Gallup sampling frame changed with respect to inclusion of southern African Americans over time.

52. When one regresses partisanship (coded on a 3-point scale) on age, older voters are significantly more Republican than younger voters in each year prior to about 1952. After 1952 the relationship is generally small and insignificant. On the relationship between cohort and African American partisanship, see Daniel V. Dowd, "Understanding Partisan Change and Stability in the Late Twentieth Century" (PhD diss., Yale University, 1999).

53. Cayton and Mitchell, *Black Workers and New Unions*, 378–80.

54. See Weiss on the apparent class cleavages among African Americans in evaluations of the New Deal (*Farewell to Party of Lincoln*, 283–87).

55. A regression model with fixed effects for year indicates that phone ownership is strongly associated with partisanship prior to 1948 but that the relationship weakens appreciably in 1948–52.

56. This variable is coded based on the interviewer's subjective coding of "class" and the respondent's occupation. Respondents whom the interviewer coded as "average" or above or who had a professional, semiprofessional, or white-collar occupation are coded as "average or above" here.

57. On the importance of linked fate as compared to class in shaping African American partisanship, see Michael C. Dawson, *Behind the Mule: Race and Class in African-American Politics* (Princeton, NJ: Princeton University Press, 1994).

58. College-educated African Americans were more likely to be independents (36%) than those without a high school degree (21%). African Americans with a high school degree were in between the "no degree" and "some college" respondents in their partisanship but closer to the "no high school degree" respondents.

59. African Americans with a high school degree were the most Democratic in this period (56%–19%), though the gap with the "no high school degree" group is not statistically significant. These data pool the surveys from 1953 to 1959.

60. Again, this means that the respondent was rated average or above by the interviewer or was in a professional or white-collar occupation.

61. High school graduates were also more Democratic than nongraduates: 49% identified as Democrats, compared to 22% who were Republicans.

62. Again, those who graduated from high school were in between, giving Democrats a 58%–23% margin.

63. Donald P. Green, Bradley Palmquist, and Eric Schickler, *Partisan Hearts and Minds: Political Parties and the Social Identity of Voters* (New Haven, CT: Yale University Press, 2002).

64. There is little evidence of a partisan shift back to the GOP among African Americans amid the 1956 election, though Stevenson's weak stance on civil rights likely hurt the Democrats among African American voters. It is worth noting that the 20-point vote gap between African Americans and whites in 1956 is only a bit smaller than 1952 (26 points) and actually 1 point higher than in 1960. Chapter 9 argues that the 1956 outcome strengthened the hand of those party leaders arguing that the Democrats needed to take a clearer pro–civil rights stand.

65. Catholics, however, voted for Kennedy by an even larger margin: 78%–22%.

66. But see Mark Brilliant, *The Color of America Has Changed: How Racial Diversity Shaped Civil Rights Reform in California, 1941–1978* (New York: Oxford University Press, 2010), on the growing importance of Latinos and Asian Americans even at this early stage in California.

Chapter 7: State Parties and the Civil Rights Realignment

1. Chen, *Fifth Freedom*, 115–69.

2. Arnold Aronson and Samuel Spiegler, "Does the Republican Party Want the Negro Vote?," *Crisis* (December 1949): 364–68, 411–17.

3. Ibid., 413.

4. Duane Lockard, *Toward Equal Opportunity: A Study of State and Local Anti-Discrimination Laws* (New York: Macmillan, 1968), 47–49. Lockard argues that this was the pattern evident in Connecticut and New York; in other cases, such as Pennsylvania and New Jersey, stricter party control of the agenda allowed the GOP to block legislation altogether.

5. On the importance of state African American population in driving politicians' support for civil rights, see Young and Burnstein, "Federalism and the Demise of Prescriptive Representation in the United States."

6. Several of these variables had similar effects for both Republican and Democratic state parties, but controlling for these factors, Democratic state parties were generally still to the left of their GOP counterparts on civil rights by the mid-1940s.

7. As in Bawn et al., "Theory of Parties."

8. See Feinstein and Schickler, "Platforms and Partners," 6–7.

9. Feinstein and Schickler, "Platforms and Partners." Our source was ProQuest Historical Newspapers; search terms: platform w/30 (democrat# or republic#) and state, May to October 1942/1950. All articles originally appeared in the *Chicago Defender*, *Chicago Tribune*, *Los Angeles Times*, *New York Times*, or *Washington Post*.

10. For example, political scientist Stephen Bailey chaired the Connecticut Democrats' committee in 1950. For platform committee members who were listed without an affiliation, we searched http://politicalgraveyard.com to determine whether they were current or former public officials, or delegates to a national convention.

11. For instance, various coalition groups lobbied New York State Democrats as they framed the party's 1936 platform. These groups include the Association of State Civil Service Employees, which pressed the party to adopt a plank supporting a merit-based system for state employment; a women's organization that urged the party to go on the record in supporting gender-neutral labor laws; and a teachers' group pushing for permanent tenure for schoolteachers. See "Lehman Predicts a Party Victory," *NYT*, September 29, 1936, 21.

12. A more complete description of the positions in the party structure that platform writers and executive committee members tended to occupy is available at http://www.statepartyplatforms.com.

13. Newspaper articles from this period indicate that platform writers took their role as codifiers of party positions seriously. For instance, the *Los Angeles Times* reports in 1956 that the California Republican State Central Committee was deeply divided over whether to include a statement favoring right-to-work laws in that year's state GOP platform, debating the issue for nearly two hours before rejecting the proposed plank. See "Right-to-Work Plank Rejected by GOP Group," *LAT*, April 15, 1956, 2.

14. Feinstein and Schickler, "Platforms and Partners." When platforms proved elusive, on-site researchers were hired to comb through libraries and state archives.

15. This estimate is based on the conservative assumption that all northern state parties approved platforms biennially in all cases in which I lack evidence to the contrary. The twenty-two states are California, Colorado, Connecticut, Hawaii, Illinois, Indiana, Iowa, Kansas, Michigan, Minnesota, Missouri, Montana, Nebraska, New Hampshire, New Jersey, New Mexico, New York, North Dakota, Ohio, South Dakota, Utah, and Wisconsin. Texas and North Carolina were not included in the analysis.

16. The dearth of southern platforms is not a major problem given the purposes of this chapter. Southern Democrats were profoundly racist on virtually every political, economic, and social question. Republican party organizations were mere shell organizations in most southern states prior to the mid-1950s, meaning that one cannot readily compare the two parties there in any case (chapter 10 traces the development of GOP organization in the South from the 1950s onward).

17. Carmines and Stimson, *Issue Evolution*, 56. Carmines and Stimson also construct a "racial priority index," which examines the location in each platform in which a paragraph on civil rights first appears and divides that number by the total number of paragraphs in the platform. Since state party platforms often present issue areas in alphabetical order, a similar analysis would not be useful for the state data.

18. A wide range of civil rights issues, including proposed antilynching legislation and integration of the armed forces, among many other subjects, received national attention during the 1920–68 period. While these and all other civil rights issues are included in the summary score measure, the five issue measures were selected because they were the most commonly referenced civil rights issues in the state platforms. These five issues also were the most politically salient during the late 1950s and 1960s apex of the civil rights move-

ment, each receiving attention in at least one of the major civil rights bills of that period (i.e., the Civil Rights Acts of 1957 and 1964, and the Voting Rights Act of 1965).

19. Feinstein and Schickler conducted all the platform coding after attempting to make the coding criteria as explicit as possible to reduce the likelihood of errors. In an effort to assess intercoder reliability and resolve potential differences in each coder's interpretation of the ratings system, both Schickler and Feinstein coded a subset of sixteen platforms. With one exception (one assigned a summary score of 2 to a particular platform, while the other gave the platform a 1), there was complete agreement between the two coders on every variable for every platform. Although the subjective nature of assigning numerical scores to qualitative accounts makes such work challenging, the fact that the findings were very similar across all three measures gives greater confidence that the results are not driven by idiosyncratic judgments.

20. Carmines and Stimson, *Issue Evolution*, 56.

21. The results are also substantively the same if one focuses on the mean number of paragraphs in a given year rather than the median.

22. A small number of platforms are from odd-numbered years. Two-year election cycles are used in the figure (e.g., 1939 is combined with 1940).

23. The call for specific FEPC legislation led to a score of +4 for the Democratic platform; the vague call for equality scored a +1 for the GOP platform. See "Democrats Rap 'Gravy' in Toll Roads," *Indianapolis Times*, June 22, 1954, 1; "GOP Platform Backs Craig's Toll Road Plan," *Indianapolis Times*, June 25, 1954, 13.

24. This analysis includes odd years since collapsing by period avoids the problem of a small number of cases distorting the results.

25. The raw numbers are sixty-one for the Democrats, three for the Republicans, with the parties equal ten times.

26. If one narrows the region definitions, the results remain robust. For example, state Democratic parties are more pro–civil rights than state Republican parties in the Mid-Atlantic, East Central, West Central, Rocky Mountain, and Pacific states. The only exception is New England, where all but one platform pair in 1945–54 is from New Hampshire, which evidently *is* an outlier in the extent to which the state Democratic Party was slow to embrace civil rights. While civil rights were by no means prominent for either party in the state in the 1940s–1950s—perhaps due to the state's lack of racial diversity and its conservatism—Republicans are a bit more likely to take the liberal position until 1960, when New Hampshire Democrats finally embrace racial liberalism. Data from other New England states both before and after this period suggest that state Democratic parties in the region were to the left of state Republicans. For example, in each cycle from 1938 to 1944, Connecticut Democrats were more pro–civil rights than Republicans, though state Democrats did keep silent on the issue in their 1948 platform (there are no other paired platforms for Connecticut from 1945 to 1962).

27. As before, the 423 paired platforms constitute the sample here.

28. The big increase in Democratic attention to equality in education after *Brown* suggests that the Court's ruling likely had a measurable impact in at least this particular domain. Cf. Gerald Rosenberg, *The Hollow Hope: Can Courts Bring about Social Change?* (Chicago: University of Chicago Press, 1991).

29. The patterns uncovered are robust to alternative specifications of the periods. An extension of the analysis would be to apply the methods for analyzing parameter change over time outlined in Gregory J. Wawro and Ira Katznelson, "Designing Historical Social Scientific Inquiry: How Parameter Heterogeneity Can Bridge the Methodological Divide between Quantitative and Qualitative Approaches," *American Journal of Political Science* 58, 2 (2014): 526–46.

30. The figure displays the change in the expected value (and 95% confidence interval) for platform liberalism when each independent variable is shifted from the 20th to the 80th percentile among northern states.

31. Though the Jewish population is borderline significant in this model, the size of the effect is modest and is not consistent across alternative model specifications. The unionization measure is from 1939 and thus likely has considerable measurement error, which could explain the null result in that case. The Catholic population is also insignificant as a predictor.

32. The point estimate falls short of statistical significance in 1937–50 owing to the large standard error, but it is significant in 1951–62. The substantive magnitude of the point estimate in 1937–50 is still reasonably large: a shift from the 20th to the 80th percentile in African American population is associated with roughly a 0.5 shift in platform liberalism on the 10 point scale.

33. NAACP membership (as a percentage of the state population) is not a significant predictor of Democratic state platform liberalism prior to the 1950s but is positive and significant in 1951–62. Given the high correlation between this measure and the share of the state population that is African American ($r = 0.70$–0.93 depending on the year), it is impossible to tease out whether NAACP organizational strength has an impact net of the share of the population that is African American. Jewish population continues to be a significant predictor if New York State—which is an outlier in terms of its relatively high share of Jewish residents—is dropped from the model.

34. Interestingly, state Democrats' support for civil rights is also related to the degree of liberalism evident in mass opinion, particularly on labor policy. The mass-level liberalism measure is constructed for each year from 1937 to 1952 for three policy domains: racial issues, labor policy, and other (i.e., nonlabor) economic issues (see Caughey, Dougal, and Schickler, "Policy Bases of New Deal Realignment"). None of the state-level attitude measures do much to predict platform liberalism prior to the late 1930s. However, Democratic platforms in states with a liberal mass public are more likely to take a pro–civil rights stand starting in the late 1930s. The relationship is especially strong when views toward labor are used as an independent variable. The mass public's racial liberalism is a less reliable predictor, though this may be because the measure is coarser given the limited number of racial attitudes items. Economic liberalism on nonlabor issues is also related to state parties' civil rights support, though the relationship is less consistent than when labor policy is used as the independent variable. In any case, it does appear that state Democratic parties that face a relatively liberal electorate were more likely to take a pro–civil rights stand starting in the late 1930s.

35. The estimate for the Jewish population is significant in some specifications.

36. I also examined whether civil rights support varied with characteristics of state party organizations. Cohen et al. (*Party Decides*, 112–14) code the openness of Democratic and GOP state organizations based on a careful reading of a detailed American Political Science Association study. See Paul T. David, Malcolm Moos, and Ralph M. Goldman, *Presidential Nominating Politics in 1952*, 5 vols. (Baltimore: Johns Hopkins University Press, 1954). For Democrats, none of the three key variables assessing how convention delegates were selected—openness to ordinary voters; openness to unbossed activists; and the extent to which individual candidates intensively campaign for delegates' support—is a significant predictor of platforms' civil rights support in either 1920–36 or 1937–50. There is, however, a positive association from 1951 to 1962, suggesting that more open state parties were somewhat more responsive. For Republicans, party openness is generally unrelated to civil rights support except that states where individual candidates play a bigger role are more pro–civil rights after 1936. I also considered David Mayhew's measure for party organization *strength*, Traditional Party Organization scores.

See David R. Mayhew, *Placing Parties in American Politics* (Princeton, NJ: Princeton University Press, 1986). At the bivariate level, there does appear to be a relationship: Democratic platforms in states with strong traditional party organizations are more pro–civil rights than those in weak organization states. The same holds true for Republicans. However, the regional concentration of strong organizations in the Northeast and Mid-Atlantic states, in particular—which also tended to be more urban and to have higher African American populations—makes it hard to know how to interpret the relationship. The estimated relationship between traditional party organization scores and platform positioning is much weaker (and generally statistically insignificant) when one controls for urbanization or African American population.

37. The share of the population belonging to the NAACP is also a positive and often statistically significant predictor of GOP platform support for civil rights. The very high correlation with the size of the African American population, however, makes it difficult to isolate the impact of NAACP organizational strength per se.

38. As with the Democrats, the state Catholic population is unrelated to civil rights support prior to the 1950s. Among Republicans, however, it does appear that state Catholic population is positively associated with civil rights support in 1951–62.

39. In states with an African American population above the northern mean, Republicans outpaced Democrats in their civil rights support 20% of the time, while Democrats had the advantage 14% of the time (with the remaining platforms equal). For states with fewer African Americans, Democrats outpaced Republicans in 9% of the cases while Republicans were ahead in no cases.

40. In states with an above-average Jewish population, Democrats outpaced Republicans 52%–10% from 1937 to 1950. Again, the margin was smaller—30% to 11%—in states with a below-average Jewish population. It is worth noting that states that are low in unionization, urbanization, Jewish population, and African American population are more likely to have parties that say nothing about civil rights. However, increases in unionization, urbanization, and Jewish population are associated with a greater response among Democratic state parties than Republican state parties after 1936.

41. Sidney Fine, *Expanding the Frontiers of Civil Rights: Michigan, 1948–1968* (Detroit: Wayne State University Press, 2000), 24. For a similar assessment, see Fay Calkins, *The CIO and the Democratic Party* (Chicago: University of Chicago Press, 1952), 114.

42. Although the platforms for a handful of years were missing, there is no mention of civil rights in the 1932, 1936, 1940, or 1944 platforms.

43. Calkins, *CIO and Democratic Party*, 115.

44. *Michigan CIO News*, March 17, 1948, as quoted in ibid., 115–16.

45. Calkins, *CIO and Democratic Party*, 116–17.

46. Calkins estimates that liberals controlled 750 of the 1,243 delegates at the 1950 state convention. Nearly 500 of the delegates were CIO members. Twenty of 68 state committee members were also CIO members (ibid., 114).

47. On the –4 to +5 scale, the Michigan Democratic platform scored a +4 in 1950, +5 in 1951, and +4 in 1952, 1954, and 1955. The platform score dipped a bit in 1956–57 (+1 and +3) but was a 5 in each remaining year.

48. Fine, *Expanding Frontiers of Civil Rights*, 13.

49. Ibid., 14–15. In much the same way, Pennsylvania Republicans had endorsed FEPC in their platform, yet the GOP governor, James Duff, was unable to persuade the Republican legislature to act. Indeed, all Democrats backed a motion to discharge the bill from committee; all but one Republican opposed it (Aronson and Spiegler, "Does Republican Party Want Negro Vote?" 416).

50. Fine, *Expanding Frontiers of Civil Rights*, 16–17.

51. Ibid., 17–19.

52. Ibid., 21.

53. Biondi, *Stand and Fight*, 18.

54. Chen, "Hitlerian Rule of Quotas," 1249.

55. For example, the 1940 GOP platform argued that the "right to work for compensation should not be abridged or denied by reason of color, race or religion," and its 1942 platform condemned "all laws or governmental practices that discriminate directly or indirectly."

56. Ibid., 1252.

57. Ibid., 1258.

58. As quoted in Biondi, *Stand and Fight*, 19.

59. Chen, "Hitlerian Rule of Quotas," 1260; see also Barry K. Beyer, *Thomas E. Dewey, 1937–1947: A Study in Political Leadership* (New York: Garland, 1979), chap. 7.

60. Biondi, *Stand and Fight*, 42.

61. Ibid., 10, 107–8.

62. Labor's Non-Partisan League of California, *Platform and Program* (San Francisco: The League, 1938), Bancroft Library pamphlet, University of California, Berkeley.

63. "California Assembly Hits Poll Tax," *Labor's Non-Partisan League Bulletin*, June 10, 1941, 7.

64. See "The Watchman," *LAT*, August 15, 1942, 8. The *Los Angeles Times* supported the conservative faction seeking to unseat Olson, but the incumbent survived, with "union leaders dominating the convention" (Editorial, "Democrats on the Defensive," *LAT*, September 20, 1942, A4).

65. Brilliant, *Color of America Has Changed*, chap. 4.

66. Chen, Mickey, and Van Houweling, "Explaining Contemporary Alignment," 215–16.

67. On the labor backing, see "FEPC Front: Labor Groups Endorse FEPC Proposition 11," *Sentinel*, September 26, 1946, 3. On Warren's role and on the partisan voting patterns, see Chen, Mickey, and Van Houweling, "Explaining Contemporary Alignment," 216–17.

68. Aronson and Spiegler, "Does Republican Party Want the Negro Vote?," 412.

69. Brilliant, *Color of America Has Changed*, 130, 160–61.

70. Ibid., 139.

71. Lockard, *Toward Equal Opportunity*, chap. 2.

72. *Boston Daily Globe*, May 15, 1946, 14, as quoted in ibid. The CIO worked closely with the NAACP and American Jewish Committee in pushing for the legislation (J. Mitchell Morse, "Fair Employment in Massachusetts?," *Nation*, March 17, 1945, 293–94).

73. Lockard, *Toward Equal Opportunity*, 37.

Chapter 8: Beyond the Roll Call: The Congressional Realignment

1. Even before Smith took over as chair in 1955, southern Democrats and their conservative Republican allies formed a majority on the committee that repeatedly blocked civil rights initiatives.

2. "Howard Smith Called 'Dictator,'" *Washington Post*, August 19, 1958, B19.

3. See, e.g., McCoy and Ruetten, *Quest and Response*, 196–98, 284–85; Ruchames, *Race, Jobs, and Politics*, 206–12.

4. Topping, *Lincoln's Lost Legacy*, 48; Bensel, *Sectionalism and American Political Development*, 150–51.

5. Gary W. Cox and Mathew D. McCubbins, *Setting the Agenda: Responsible Party Government in the U.S. House of Representatives* (Cambridge: Cambridge University Press, 2005); Cox and McCubbins, *Legislative Leviathan: Party Government in the House* (Berkeley: University of California Press, 1993).

6. As but one example, John Kennedy was careful to frame himself as a moderate acceptable to both regional wings as he sought a spot on a national ticket in the mid-1950s (see Carroll Kilpatrick, "Kennedy, the Moderate," *Washington Post*, October 24, 1957, A13). The quantitative analysis in this chapter focuses on the House, where the data are richer and the complications introduced by senators' multiple potential constituencies are avoided. However, the case discussions in this chapter (and in chapters 9–10) consider Senate politics as well.

7. Recall the finding from the opinion surveys in chapter 5 that economic liberalism is associated with racial liberalism both at the individual level among ordinary voters and at the aggregate level across states.

8. See Sugrue, *Sweet Land of Liberty*, 111–15, and discussion below.

9. Bensel, *Sectionalism and American Political Development*, 150–52; Bensel, "Sectionalism and Congressional Development," 771–73; Katznelson, *When Affirmative Action Was White*, 21, 49–50.

10. Bawn et al., "Theory of Parties."

11. See Farhang and Katznelson, "Southern Imposition," and Katznelson, *Fear Itself*, on the southern onslaught against unions.

12. Cf. Bawn et al., "Theory of Parties."

13. See David R. Mayhew, *America's Congress: Actions in the Public Sphere* (New Haven, CT: Yale University Press, 2002), on the importance of member actions that shape debate in the public sphere.

14. See, e.g., Carmines and Stimson, *Issue Evolution*, chap. 3.

15. For details, see Eric Schickler, Kathryn Pearson, and Brian Feinstein, "Shifting Partisan Coalitions: Support for Civil Rights in Congress from 1933–1972," *Journal of Politics* 72, 3 (2010): 672–89. The results are from a logit model, where the dependent variable is support for civil rights on each roll-call vote. The figure displays the change in probability of a pro–civil rights vote when one compares northern Republicans to Democrats, holding seniority at its mean.

16. See Carmines and Stimson, *Issue Evolution*, chap. 3; Karol, *Party Position Change*, chap. 4.

17. Two votes in which the parties differ substantially are worth noting. In 1937 northern Democrats were far more supportive of an antilynching bill than were Republicans, but the bill was a weak alternative meant to derail a stronger GOP-backed bill (see "House Sidetracks Anti-Lynching Bill," *NYT*, April 8, 1937, 24). When the stronger bill was considered, Republicans were a bit more supportive than northern Democrats. The second vote in which the two parties deviate substantially is on the Powell Amendment of 1956. In that case, more Republicans took the pro–civil rights position than northern Democrats, but because of strategic calculations: northern Democrats were reluctant to vote for the amendment because it threatened to sink aid-to-education legislation.

18. See Joshua D. Clinton and John S. Lapinski, "Laws and Roll Calls in the U.S. Congress, 1889–1994," *Legislative Studies Quarterly* 33, 4 (2008): 511–42.

19. Richard S. Beth, "The Discharge Rule in the House: Recent Use in Historical Context," *Congressional Research Service Report for Congress*, Report 97-856 (Library of Congress, April 2003).

20. On a handful of occasions, the names of signatories were leaked to the press (see discussion below). But this was unusual.

21. Walter Oleszek, *Congressional Procedure and the Policy Process*, 6th ed. (Washington, DC: CQ Press, 2004), 142–43. Members could view the petitions and their signatories.

22. During the time period investigated here, the threshold was 218 signatures in all Congresses except for the Seventy-Second and Seventy-Third, when discharge petitions only needed 145 signatures.

23. Kathryn Pearson and Eric Schickler, "Discharge Petitions, Agenda Control, and the Congressional Committee System, 1929–1976," *Journal of Politics* 71, 4 (2009): 1238–56. Pearson made the original discovery of the discharge petitions at the National Archives while combing through the House Rules Committee's records; prior to this, scholars did not know that the names of the signatories to unsuccessful discharge petitions were available.

24. Richard L. Hall, *Participation in Congress* (New Haven, CT: Yale University Press, 1996); see also David Canon, *Race, Redistricting, and Representation: The Unintended Consequences of Black Majority Districts* (Chicago: University of Chicago Press, 1999).

25. Several of the eleven cases that had fewer signatures were for bills that duplicated similar legislation in the same Congress. For example, in the 77th Congress, discharge petitions were filed against two poll tax bills; one reached the 218 signature threshold, while the other measure gained only 29 signatures. A few other cases were petitions for bills that were seen as more "extreme" at the time (e.g., a fair housing bill in 1949–50 received just twenty-four signatures; nineteen were from northern Democrats, while four were from Republicans and a fifth came from the American Labor Party's Vito Marcantonio of New York).

26. The Republican majority in the Eightieth Congress did bring a poll tax bill to the House floor, which was approved. No discharge petition was necessary as the GOP Rules Committee responded to Republican leaders' request to consider the measure. Southern Democrats claimed that Republicans allowed the bill to the floor as revenge for their vote to uphold President Truman's veto of the GOP tax bill ("Republicans to Push Poll Tax Fight to Avenge South's Vote on Income Levy," *NYT*, June 25, 1947, 9). The bill died in a Senate filibuster, when presiding officer Arthur Vandenberg (R-MI) ruled that cloture cannot be applied to a motion to proceed to consider a bill.

27. The estimates are based on a logit model, estimated separately for each discharge petition.

28. See Schickler, Pearson, and Feinstein, "Shifting Partisan Coalitions," for details.

29. If one estimates a linear regression model controlling for seniority, membership on the committee targeted by the petition, urbanization, African American population, state-level unionization, and district presidential vote, a dummy variable for Democratic partisanship is positive and significant in every Congress from 1947 on; it is positive but falls just short of statistical significance in the Seventy-Ninth Congress (1945–46; $b = 0.113$; $SE = 0.078$; $t = 1.43$). The point estimates from 1947 onward indicate that a shift from a northern Republican to northern Democrat is associated with a 0.2 to 0.5 increase in support on the 0 to 1 scale.

30. Districts that Democrats win by a very narrow margin should be comparable to districts that Republicans win by a very narrow margin. See Schickler, Pearson, and Feinstein, "Shifting Partisan Coalitions," 681–83, for details on this regression discontinuity approach.

31. By contrast, during the Seventy-Third to Seventy-Eighth Congresses, the median Republican signature occurred earlier in the sequence than would be expected from chance in six out of the ten cases (see ibid., 677, for details).

32. See ibid., 678–79. To identify pro–civil rights speeches, the *Congressional Record Index* was searched by hand for the following terms: antilynching, civil rights, colored [citizens, rights, etc.], desegregation, fair employment, fair housing, FEPC, integration, Jim Crow, lynching, Negro [rights, etc.], and segregation. A speech is defined as over four contiguous lines of text delivered by one speaker on any of the above subjects. We exclude all text in the *Congressional Record* that was not delivered orally on the House floor.

33. The difference first becomes statistically significant in the Seventy-Ninth Congress (1945–46). When one adds a control for seniority, the results for the party indicator are

unaffected (junior members during this period were less likely to engage in publicity-seeking activity, including giving floor speeches). See Herbert Asher, "The Learning of Legislative Norms," *American Political Science Review* 67, 2 (1973): 499–513.

34. For 1919–46, bill sponsorships were identified by a systematic search of the *Congressional Record*. The search terms used were civil rights, colored, desegregation, discrimination, fair employment, fair housing, Jim Crow, lynching, negro, pernicious, poll tax, race, segregation, vote, voting, and racial. Bills that were found through the search terms were included only if the bill title and related materials indicated that it was supportive of the African American civil rights struggle. For example, bills that are vague or purely symbolic (e.g., to erect a monument) were excluded. For 1947–72 we obtained data on bill sponsorship from Adler and Wilkerson's Congressional Bills Project website (2012), which starts with the Eightieth Congress. We examined each bill that Adler and Wilkerson classified as pertaining to "general civil rights," "ethnic minority and racial group discrimination," and "voting rights and issues" and determined whether each bill met our criteria for inclusion. Bills with the expressed purpose of limiting civil rights (e.g., H.R. 383 in the Ninety-Second Congress: a bill "[t]o repeal the Civil Rights Act of 1964") were excluded, as were bills that focused on expanding civil rights to groups other than racial minorities (e.g., H.R. 2120 in the Eightieth Congress, a proposed constitutional amendment lowering the voting age to eighteen).

35. See Wendy Schiller, *Partners and Rivals: Representation in the U.S. Senate* (Princeton, NJ: Princeton University Press, 2000).

36. Interestingly, the sole exception to this pattern occurs *after* the 1964 election, when Republicans introduce a large number of identical voting rights bills in the Eighty-Ninth Congress. If one drops duplicate bills from the analysis (i.e., cases in which multiple members of the same party introduce the same bill), the pattern remains the same, but the Eighty-Ninth Congress is no longer an outlier (as there are more unique Democratic bills than Republican bills). If one focuses on the percentage of northern Democrats and Republicans who introduce at least one civil rights bill—again excluding duplicate bills—the results tell the same story as in figure 8.5: northern Democrats surpass northern Republicans as bill sponsors in the Seventy-Sixth Congress, and a higher percentage of Democrats sponsor at least one bill in *every* Congress from 1939 through the end of the 1960s.

37. When there are multiple petitions in a Congress, robust standard errors clustered by member are used.

38. Pearson and Schickler, "Discharge Petitions, Agenda Control, and the Congressional Committee System, 1929–1976." The results are unaffected if these controls are dropped.

39. I use ordinary least squares regression, but the results tell the same story when one uses logit. One difficulty with using logit is that one has to decide which petition to use as the "base" for computing predicting probabilities for those Congresses with multiple discharge petitions.

40. Crucially, the more moderate AFL opposed the version of FLSA that passed the Senate and was before the House when these December 1937 votes were taken. See O. R. Altman, "Second and Third Sessions of the Seventy Fifth Congress, 1937–38," *American Political Science Review* 32 (1938): 1099–1122; and "Green, Lewis Renew Conflict on Wage-and-Hours Proposal," *Washington Post*, December 5, 1937, 2. The CIO-backed Labor's Non-Partisan League pushed hard for the December 1937 bill and even issued a pamphlet, *How Congressmen Voted on Wages and Hour Bill*, targeting members who voted against the measure. Reprinted in Labor's Non-Partisan League, *Pamphlets* (Washington, DC: Labor's Non-Partisan League, 1941).

41. If the two predictors are entered in separate models, the association between the sit-down strike vote and civil rights support is much stronger than the association between first-dimension NOMINATE scores and civil rights support.

42. When one uses the count of prolabor votes (ranging from 0 to 3) instead of the vote on the sit-down strikes, a shift from the minimum to maximum value is associated with a 0.30 shift along the 0 to 1 pro–civil rights scale (95% confidence interval of 0.15 to 0.44). In the same model, a shift from the 20th to 80th percentile of liberalism based on NOMINATE scores is associated with just a 0.02 shift on the civil rights scale (95% confidence interval of –0.05 to 0.08). The same pattern holds if one focuses on predicting "early signers" of the civil rights discharge petition. That is, supporters of the CIO position on the sit-down strikes and Wage and Hour bill were more likely to be among the earliest members to sign the civil rights discharge petitions, indicating that they were among the most intense supporters of the initiatives.

43. The results are much the same if one replaces the DW-NOMINATE indicator with a measure of economic liberalism that makes weaker assumptions about the pattern of change over time in member scores. One such measure, based on all economic roll-call votes in each Congress, uses a dynamic item-response (IRT) model, developed by Caughey (*Congress, Public Opinion, and Representation*). It performs similarly to the original DW-NOMINATE measure in predicting civil rights support among northern Democrats; pro-labor voting outperforms it in predicting northern Democrats' civil rights positions in the Seventy-Fifth to Seventy-Seventh Congresses (1937–42).

44. "LNPL Watches Votes Cast by Congressmen," *CIO News*, February 26, 1938, 3; see also "CIO Attacks Filibuster on Lynching Bill," *CIO News*, January 29, 1938, 4.

45. See Sitkoff, *New Deal for Blacks*, chaps. 5 and 7, on the CIO's early support for the lynching and poll tax bills.

46. Caughey, *Congress, Public Opinion, and Representation*. See also Katznelson et al., "Limiting Liberalism"; Farhang and Katznelson, "Southern Imposition"; and Katznelson and Mulroy, "Was the South Pivotal?," for important works on the relationship between labor voting and general ideological cleavages in Congress during this period.

47. In the Seventy-Sixth Congress, when the count of prolabor votes is entered alongside NOMINATE scores as predictors of civil rights signatures, a shift from minimum to maximum (0 to 5) in prolabor votes is associated with a 0.20 increase in civil rights support along the 0 to 1 scale (95% confidence interval of 0.05 to 0.34), while a shift from the 20th to 80th percentile of liberalism on the NOMINATE scale is associated with a 0.10 shift in civil rights support (95% confidence interval of 0.004 to 0.19). If the two measures are entered in separate models, the marginal impact of labor voting is nearly twice that of a similar magnitude change in NOMINATE scores. In the Seventy-Seventh Congress, NOMINATE is borderline significant when entered alongside prolabor voting (which continues to be strong and significant); however, when the two measures are entered in separate models, the magnitude of the NOMINATE marginal effect is similar to that for prolabor voting: a shift from the 20th to 80th percentile of liberalism using NOMINATE has a marginal effect of 0.16 (95% confidence interval of 0.10 to 0.22), while a shift from the minimum to maximum prolabor voting record is associated with a 0.22 shift in civil rights support (95% confidence interval of 0.09 to 0.35).

48. Among Republicans, labor votes and NOMINATE scores perform similarly to one another in the Seventy-Fifth Congress (both are significant and have similar magnitude marginal effects when entered separately; both fall short of significance when entered in the same model). In the Seventy-Sixth Congress, labor voting is unrelated to Republicans' civil rights support, while NOMINATE scores are a significant predictor. However, in the Seventy-Seventh Congress (1941–42), labor support is a somewhat stronger predictor of civil rights support for Republicans than are NOMINATE scores (i.e., the marginal effects for NOMINATE are smaller than for similar-magnitude shifts in labor voting).

49. A further problem has to do with the unionization data, which is available only at the state, rather than the district, level. For the Seventy-Eighth to Eight-First Congresses,

I also draw on estimates of district-level CIO strength provided by William Riker, "The CIO in Politics."

50. Thomas Ogorzalek, "Cities on the Hill: Urban Institutions in National Politics," ms., Northwestern University.

51. Ogorzalek generously shared the dataset, "House Urban District Demographics, Pre-1962 Congresses."

52. I use robust standard errors clustered by member. As in the earlier analyses, I control for seniority and for membership on the committee targeted by the discharge petition.

53. The standard deviation for each district characteristic used in generating the first differences is based on all northern districts for a given Congress. I use all northern districts, rather than computing the standard deviation separately for each party, so that the magnitude of the change in the independent variable is comparable for both parties. The variation in district characteristics within party is sufficiently large so that a two-standard-deviation shift in the full sample—about 52 percentage points for the urbanization variable—is well within the observed range for each party.

54. The models estimated include all three demographic variables, along with seniority and membership on the committee targeted by the petition. The results are the same if one controls only for urbanization, dropping the other constituency characteristics.

55. For the Seventy-Eight to Eighty-First Congresses, I also substituted estimates of district-level CIO membership provided by Riker ("The CIO in Politics") for the state-level unionization numbers. These estimates likely have considerable error as they rely heavily on CIO convention reports. Furthermore, Riker does not have estimates for districts with very low CIO membership; these districts are coded to have no CIO members in the present analysis, although some surely had a small CIO presence. In any case, the multivariate results for district-level CIO membership are slightly weaker than those for state-level unionization: the CIO share of district population is a strong, significant predictor in the Seventy-Ninth and Eighty-First Congresses but is weak and falls short of statistical significance in the Seventy-Eighth and Eightieth Congresses (1943–44, 1947–48). If one drops the controls for urbanization and African American population, the CIO district membership is significant in each Congress where it is available (1943–50).

56. A two-standard-deviation shift in unionization roughly reflects a 14-point increase. If one drops urbanization and African American population from the model, the results tell the same substantive story. State unionization is generally a strong and significant predictor prior to about 1958 but is insignificant afterward.

57. See Jenkins, Peck, and Weaver, "Between Reconstructions," 67.

58. "The Reminiscences of Joseph A. Gavagan," Oral History, Butler Library, Columbia University, transcription of 1950 interview, 28, 42.

59. These are based on simple logit models, estimated separately for each Congress, where the dependent variable is a dummy variable designating whether the member sponsored at least one civil rights bill. The sole point estimate that falls short of statistical significance misses only narrowly (t = 1.56).

60. Urban population is also a statistically significant predictor of bill sponsorships in most Congresses.

61. Alternatively, the position-taking benefits of bill sponsorship were more attractive to members with a substantial African American population.

62. Papers of the NAACP, Microfilm Part 7, Reel 24. More generally, Whelan highlights the role of grassroots pressure from the NAACP in inducing House Democrats to back the lynching bill discharge petition drives. See Isabelle Whelan, "The Politics of Federal Anti-lynching Legislation in the New Deal Era," MA Area Studies, Institute for the Study of the Americas, 40.

63. The weak results for the African American population variable may also be partly attributable to error that remains even in Ogorzalek's improved measure.

64. If one drops the African American population and union density measures, urbanization does have a significant effect in six of ten cases and is borderline significant in one other Congress. However, the magnitude of the relationship is still smaller than that for Democrats.

65. Again, the figure presents results from the model controlling for all three demographic measures. But the unionization variable is insignificant in each Congress even if one drops the other two demographic measures.

66. A two-standard-deviation shift reflected a 12-point increase in the African American population share. The estimate is statistically significant in the Seventy-Ninth Congress if one drops urbanization and unionization. The tenor of the results is otherwise unaffected by dropping the two other demographic variables.

67. Recall from chapter 6 that African American partisanship shifted decisively to the Democrats in the aftermath of the 1948 election. This, too, may have given GOP politicians less reason to appeal to African American voters.

68. As is evident in figure 8.7, district demographics had only weak effects even without inclusion of NOMINATE scores (which are themselves likely shaped by district characteristics and hence would in part reflect the prior impact of district features to the extent that they are important).

69. The additional district demographic controls are available only starting in 1943. If one controls for both district presidential vote and NOMINATE scores—an admittedly problematic move given that the latter are likely partly rooted in the former—one sees that presidential vote share outpaces NOMINATE as a predictor of civil rights support in the Seventy-Fourth through Seventy-Seventh Congresses (1935–42). By the mid-1940s, however, NOMINATE outperforms the presidential vote share, though this could mean that the influence of district characteristics (e.g., presidential vote) increasingly worked through NOMINATE scores.

70. Ruchames, *Race, Jobs, and Politics*, 201. On GOP strategy on the bill, including the strategic absences, see Will Maslow, "FEPC: A Case History in Parliamentary Maneuver," *University of Chicago Law Review* 13 (June 1946): 407–44.

71. The meeting minutes were obtained from the Joseph L. Martin Papers, Stonehill College Archives and Historical Collections, Conference of Republican Members of the House of Representatives, September 14, 1945, Folder 112.1. Members explicitly noted that the meeting would be confidential, though some news reports did leak out (see Daniel M. Kidney, "Republicans Sit on Their Hands as Colleague Asks FEPC Support," *Washington Daily News*, September 15, 1945, 9). The meeting minutes include numerous comments that would not have been made if members expected the deliberations to become public. For example, much of the discussion focused on how to fight the Truman administration's bid for political credit for some of the benefits of war demobilization. Public relations is often a central concern for parties but is not something members would normally openly strategize about if the press were listening. See Frances Lee, "Making Laws and Making Points: Senate Governance in an Era of Uncertain Majorities," *Forum* 9, 4 (2011), article 3, on party public relations.

72. Conference of Republican Members of the House, 39–40.

73. Ibid., 41, 50–51.

74. Kidney, "Republicans Sit on Their Hands," 9.

75. Conference of Republican Members of the House, 83.

76. "Indiana Republican Heads Hurt FEPC by Deserting LaFollette," *Defender*, July 27, 1946, 4.

77. "Indiana G.O.P. Names Jenner for Senator," *Chicago Tribune*, June 14, 1946, 1.

78. "Indiana Republican Heads Hurt FEPC," 4.

79. "Army's Racial Equality Plan Denounced by Liberal Group," *Washington Post*, October 3, 1949, 7.

80. As quoted in Kesselman, *Social Politics of FEPC*, 202.

81. See also Moon, *Balance of Power*. The two most active Senate GOP backers of civil rights bills in 1949–52 were Irving Ives of New York and Wayne Morse of Oregon. Both had NOMINATE scores that placed them well to the left of the median Republican on the first dimension; by the mid-1950s Morse had defected to the Democrats, charging that the GOP was too conservative on a range of issues.

82. Daniel M. Berman, *A Bill Becomes a Law: Congress Enacts Civil Rights Legislation* (New York: Macmillan, 1962), 74–75.

83. See *CR*, January 27, 1960, 1424–45, 1471–73.

84. Ibid., 1427.

85. See Democratic Study Group Records, Library of Congress Manuscript Division, Part 1, Box 43, Folder 5.

86. Berman, *Bill Becomes a Law*, 78–79.

87. Southerners, for their part, pursued policies that attacked labor unions, thereby undermining core supporters of the Democratic Party in the North (see Farhang and Katznelson, "Southern Imposition"; Schickler and Pearson, "Agenda Control, Majority Party Power, and the Committee on Rules").

88. The search terms used were ((fepc OR "f.e.p.c." OR "fair employment" OR "lynch*" OR "anti-lynch" OR "poll tax" OR "anti-poll tax") AND (congress OR house OR senate OR senator OR representative)) AND (bill OR measure OR legislation OR proposal OR proposes OR ban). The search also required that the header or title of the story include the terms (fepc OR "f.e.p.c." OR "fair employment" OR "lynch*" OR "anti-lynch" OR "poll tax" OR "anti-poll tax"). Cases were dropped if the mention of civil rights was merely as an aside in the story.

89. For example, the measure omits stories that highlight other civil rights issues—such as integrating the military and provision of a federal ballot for overseas soldiers during World War II.

90. The discharge petition, however, came too late in the session to force action in the lower chamber ("Anti-Lynching Petition Puts Solons on the Spot," *Defender*, June 27, 1936, 8). Advocates started much earlier in the next Congress.

91. See, e.g., "House Passes Lynching Bill in Fiery Session," *Washington Post*, April 16, 1937, 1.

92. See, e.g., "Legislation Tied Up: Wagner's Sudden Move to Act on Anti-Lynch Bill Stirs Tempest," *NYT*, August 12, 1937, 1; "Connally Chides Wagner on Labor: In Filibuster on Anti-Lynching Bill, He Calls Senator an 'Outstanding Agitator,'" *NYT*, November 18, 1937, 1; "Help Business First, Bailey Asks Congress; Filibuster Continues," *Washington Post*, November 18, 1937, 1.

93. *CR*, April 7, 1937, 3253.

94. See, e.g., "Anti-Lynching Bill Likely to Pass in Senate," *Chicago Tribune*, August 12, 1937, 7; "Legislation Tied Up," *NYT*, August 12, 1937, 1.

95. "New Child Labor Amendment Put to Senate," *NYT*, June 22, 1937, 1.

96. *CR*, November 17, 1937, 76.

97. Ibid., 64. Southern Democrat Samuel McReynolds (D-TN) also expressed the view that the bill "will be enacted," while hoping that the Court would strike it down ("Expects Black to Sit in Anti-Lynching Case," *NYT*, September 27, 1937, 5).

98. As quoted in Zangrando, *NAACP Crusade against Lynching*, 146.

99. "Roosevelt Opens Congress Today," *Atlanta Constitution*, January 3, 1938, 5. See also Keith Finley, *Delaying the Dream: Southern Senators and the Fight against Civil Rights* (Baton Rouge: Louisiana State University Press, 2008), 34–36.

100. As quoted in Ruth Bloch Rubin, "Intraparty Organization in the U.S. Congress" (PhD diss., University of California, Berkeley, 2014), chap. 4, 18. Bloch Rubin's original source is Theodore Bilbo to J. D. Roberts, January 11, 1938, University of Southern Mississippi McCain Library, Theodore Bilbo Papers, Box 331, Folder "11 January 1938 B." Bloch Rubin offers an important broader analysis of the politics of intraparty organization, arguing that southerners' (realistic) fear that they would lose if they did not improve their organizational capacity led them to forge a strong organization.

101. The Republicans claimed their "no" votes were due to principled opposition to the use of the cloture rule as a tool to shut off debate (see Jenkins, Peck, and Weaver, "Between Reconstructions," 84–86). But many of these same Republicans had voted for cloture for other measures.

102. As quoted in Bloch Rubin, "Intraparty Organization," chap. 4, 21. Bloch Rubin's original source is Connally to David H. Byrd, February 2, 1940, LOC, Connally Papers, Box 126, Folder "Hearings."

103. As quoted in ibid., chap. 4, 22. Bloch Rubin's original source is Stennis to James A. McGraw, February 9, 1948, Mississippi State University Libraries, Stennis Papers, Series 29, Box 1, Folder 2.

104. Harry F. Byrd to E.W. Senter, February 7, 1945, University of Virginia Library Special Collections, Harry F. Byrd Papers, Box 192, Folder "Virginia State Poll Tax." Senter was later selected as a delegate to the 1948 Democratic National Convention and ran for lieutenant governor in 1949.

105. A. Willis Robertson to Harry F. Byrd, August 24, 1948, Byrd Papers, Box 190, Folder "Robertson, A. Willis."

106. Howard W. Smith to Harry F. Byrd, August 15, 1949, Byrd Papers, Box 203, Folder "Correspondence re: Poll Tax and Voting Laws."

107. J. F. Wyson to Harry F. Byrd, August 28, 1949, Byrd Papers, Box 203, Folder "Correspondence re: Poll Tax and Voting Laws."

108. For example, in an August 1948 letter, John Stennis confided to state representative William Winter that "not until the very last moment were we sure that our fight [against the anti–poll tax legislation] would be successful at the special session. It appears certain the fight will be renewed in January and if the proponents are able to change the Senate rules, I'm afraid one or more of the so-called civil rights bills will be adopted" (John C. Stennis to Rep. William Winter, August 17, 1948, Series 29, Box 1, Folder 16, John C. Stennis Papers, Mississippi State University, Starkville). See Finley, *Delaying the Dream*, 112–13, on southerners' deep concern that rules changes to limit obstruction would pass.

109. As quoted in Finley, *Delaying the Dream*, 112. Finley provides several other examples where Russell expresses deep pessimism about the prospects for success in blocking legislation.

110. As quoted in ibid., 123.

111. As quoted in ibid., 134.

112. See Bloch Rubin, "Intraparty Organization."

113. Finley, *Delaying the Dream*, 25, 133.

114. Schickler and Pearson, "Agenda Control, Majority Party Power, and the Committee on Rules"; "Farhang and Katznelson, "Southern Imposition."

Chapter 9: Facing a Changing Party: Democratic Elites and Civil Rights

1. Carmines and Stimson, *Issue Evolution*, chap. 2.

2. See, e.g., Dudziak, *Cold War Civil Rights*.

3. Carmines and Stimson, *Issue Evolution*, 55–57.

4. CIO president John L. Lewis did deliver a series of speeches urging a strong civil rights stand in the party's 1940 platform ("Lewis Hurls Bolt Threat," *LAT*, April 2, 1940,

1; see also "Lewis Threatens Third Party Move to Hit Democrats," *NYT*, April 2, 1940, 1). But Lewis's isolationist crusade divided the union over whether to endorse Franklin Roosevelt at all, greatly limiting the CIO role at the 1940 convention. Lewis's isolationism eventually led him to endorse the Republican Wendell Willkie, though the vast majority of other CIO leaders (and voters) stuck with the Democrats. In contrast to later years, news coverage does not indicate that CIO officials testified before the Democratic platform committee on behalf of civil rights in 1940 (the coverage does discuss testimony from African American groups).

5. "Race Issue Snarls Platform," *NYT*, July 19, 1944, 1, 13.

6. "Negro Issue Ties Up Democrats as Race Plank Takes Spotlight," *Defender*, July 29, 1944, 18.

7. "Democrats Press 'War Chief' Issue; Second Place Open," *NYT*, July 20, 1944, 1, 11.

8. "Negro Issue Ties Up Democrats," 18.

9. As quoted in Garson, *Democratic Party and Sectionalism*, 100. Mickey's *Paths Out of Dixie* also highlights southern conservatives' serious disaffection with Roosevelt in 1943–44, noting Senator Josiah Bailey's threat to form a separate southern Democratic Party to hold the balance of power in the Electoral College (138). Manufacturing, banking, and oil interests in the South even funded an effort by conservatives to deprive Roosevelt of the nomination for a fourth term and to try to force a states' rights national platform (139–40).

10. Ward, "War for 'States' Rights,'" 139–40.

11. Arthur Krock, "Struggle over Wallace to Enliven Convention," *NYT*, July 16, 1944, E3. The African American press treated Wallace as a key ally. In the lead-up to the convention, the *Defender* noted that Wallace had "endeared himself" to the "common man"—"his devotion to the interest of the underdog, whether be he in America or abroad, has registered well with Negroes. His forthright language, following the Detroit riots, his remarks before the Capital Press club, have all struck home" ("Race Question to Plague Democratic Convention in Chicago on Three Fronts," *Defender*, July 15, 1944, 2). The *Defender* concluded that Wallace was a key to keeping African American voters in the Democratic column.

12. Editorial, "Keep Vice President Wallace!" *TNR*, July 17, 1944, 62–63.

13. "Party Drops Wallace in Bitter Floor Fight," *Washington Post*, July 22, 1944, 1.

14. "Addresses by Barkley and Wallace Putting President Roosevelt in Nomination," *NYT*, July 21, 1944, 10.

15. Polling by Gallup also indicated that Democratic voters overwhelmingly favored Wallace for the nomination. When Gallup gave respondents a list of potential candidates for vice president in early July 1944, 57% of Democratic voters chose Wallace, with Barkley second at 20%. Truman was the first choice of just 3% (Poll 322, July 8–13, 1944).

16. "Democrats Press 'War Chief' Issue; Second Place Open," *NYT*, July 20, 1944, 1, 11.

17. "Party Drops Wallace in Bitter Floor Fight," *Washington Post*, July 22, 1944, 1, 2.

18. Before the decision was reached, Catledge had noted that the key factor would be that "no substantial part of the delegates … proposed to do anything not wanted by Mr. Roosevelt" ("Democrats Press War Issue," 1, 11).

19. Editorial, "The Democrats Meet," *TNR*, July 31, 1944, 115–16.

20. See Sullivan, *Days of Hope*, 181–86, for a similar assessment.

21. Freda Kirchwey, "The Battle of Chicago," *Nation*, July 29, 1944, 118–20.

22. Bruce Bliven, "The Liberals after Chicago," *TNR*, August 7, 1944, 152–54.

23. Garson, *Democratic Party and Sectionalism*, chap. 8.

24. Ibid., 272; McCoy and Ruetten, *Quest and Response*, 124.

25. Garson, *Democratic Party and Sectionalism*, 272.

26. Kellogg, "Americans for Democratic Action," 60. See also discussion of ADA strategy in chapter 4.

27. Foster, *Union Politic*, 116.

28. Robert C. Albright, "Platform Writers Are Warned against Giving in to South," *Washington Post*, July 9, 1948, 1.

29. "The Line Squall," *Time*, July 26, 1948, 12.

30. Bendiner, "Rout of the Bourbons," 92.

31. As quoted in Winthrop Griffith, *Humphrey: A Candid Biography* (New York: Morrow, 1965), 155. The source for this quote was Andrew Biemiller, a Wisconsin Democrat and labor leader, who recalled the conversation with an unnamed city boss.

32. The eight states are those adopting at least one platform that scored a 4 or 5 on the civil rights support scale described in chapter 7. These states are California, Connecticut, Illinois, Indiana, Kansas, Minnesota, New Jersey, and New York. The ten states taking a weak position were those that adopted platforms that scored a 0 or 1 from 1941 to 1947; they included Iowa, Michigan, Missouri, Montana, North Dakota, New Hampshire, New Mexico, Ohio, South Dakota, and Utah. Note that two of these ten states were already in the process of being captured by civil rights liberals: Ohio adopted a strong civil rights platform in 1948, and Michigan liberals were just gaining the upper hand within the state party in 1948 (see chapter 7). Both Ohio and Michigan did vote decisively in favor of the strong plank at the national convention, unlike the other eight "late adopters."

33. At the bivariate level, each of these variables was significantly related to support for the liberal civil rights plank. The African American population variable, however, was only significant when an expansive definition of the South—to include the seventeen states that practiced de jure segregation (Katznelson and Mulroy, "Was the South Pivotal?")—was used, as opposed to the usual thirteen-state definition of the South used in this book. In this case, the border states of Missouri, Maryland, West Virginia, and Delaware, each of which had a fairly substantial African American population, voted against the liberal civil rights plank. Interestingly, the four states also voted unanimously against southerners' states' rights plank. These states thus differed markedly both from the Confederate South and from the remaining non-Confederate states.

34. Timothy Thurber, *The Politics of Equality: Hubert H. Humphrey and the African American Freedom Struggle* (New York: Columbia University Press, 1999), 65.

35. William C. Berman, *The Politics of Civil Rights in the Truman Administration* (Columbus: Ohio State University Press, 1970), 122–27.

36. Truman's decision not to run in 1952 underscored the almost impossible task facing Democratic presidents of this era: how to live up to the expectations of the northern liberals who had gained control of much of the party without completely alienating the South. Despite his roots as a border state senator and his effort to gain adoption of a weak civil rights platform in 1948, Truman became identified as an enemy of the South during his time as president. While African American leaders urged Truman to run again, he decided to stand down in part owing to the realization that "his candidacy could have irrevocably split the party. After all, the South in 1952 would simply not tolerate him" (ibid., 196–97). Indeed, Gallup showed Eisenhower leading Truman in the South by a 62%–30% margin in March 1952 (McCoy and Ruetten, *Quest and Response*, 314). As Truman left office, Speaker Rayburn argued that "one of the major causes of the split in Democratic ranks in recent years ... was the championship of civil rights programs by Presidents Truman and Roosevelt" ("Rayburn Predicts New Unity in Party," *NYT*, January 6, 1953, 16). While one might well object to Rayburn's use of the word "championing" for Roosevelt (and perhaps even for Truman), the Speaker was right that the presidency forces decisions that make it harder to paper over party divisions (see Skowronek, *Politics Presidents Make*, 1993). In much the same way, Kennedy—despite his long record

of moderation on civil rights—had alienated much of the South by the time he traveled to Dallas in November 1963 (see Caro, *Passage of Power*, 266).

37. "Democrats Pressed on Civil Rights," *Washington Post*, July 18, 1952, 1.

38. "Democrats Tackle Civil Rights Issue," *NYT*, July 18, 1952, 8.

39. "Democrats Pressed on Civil Rights," 1, 4. Before the hearings, the *Nation* printed a series of statements of platform goals by labor leaders, most of which mentioned civil rights in general or the FEPC specifically (see Kellogg, *Northern Liberals and Black America*, 403).

40. "Democrats Tackle Civil Rights Issue," 8.

41. Berman, *Politics of Civil Rights*, 201.

42. "Democrats Stress Civil Rights Plank," *NYT*, July 19, 1952, 6.

43. As quoted in Allan P. Sindler, "The Unsolid South: A Challenge to the Democratic Party," in *The Uses of Power: Seven Cases in American Politics*, ed. Allan Sindler (New York: Harcourt, Brace, and World, 1962), 233.

44. Berman, *Politics of Civil Rights*, 214, 215.

45. "Party Platform as Adopted Compromises on Civil Rights," *NYT*, July 24, 1952, 1, 16; Berman, *Politics of Civil Rights*, 218–22. Baylor claims that Stevenson "was an improvement over Truman in civil rights" ("First to the Party," 23–24). As noted above, however, Stevenson was only a very reluctant supporter of an FEPC with enforcement powers, unlike Truman. Indeed, Truman's withdrawal from a potential presidential run in 1952 was in part due to his belief that, unlike the more moderate Stevenson, his presence on the ballot would drive the South away from the Democrats permanently (see Berman, *Politics of Civil Rights*, 196–97). Stevenson's initial opposition to an FEPC with enforcement power during the nomination campaign allowed him to win significant support from southerners; as the *Wall Street Journal* wrote soon after his nomination, "on the noisiest state-vs.-Federal issue—a compulsory Federal Employment Practices Commission—Stevenson is more 'liberal' than Ike, but a lot less so than the Fair Dealers" ("Adlai's Ideas: Nominee Stevenson Stands to the Right of Mr. Truman," *WSJ*, July 26, 1952, 1, 2). Stevenson's close adviser, George W. Ball, recalled Truman's aides' frustration in 1952 with Stevenson's moderation on civil rights and other issues (George W. Ball, *The Past Has Another Pattern* [New York: Norton 1982], 117). Four years later, the *Baltimore Afro-American* mournfully contrasted the "disappointing Mr. Stevenson" to Truman's "plain-speaking" advocacy for civil rights ("Democratic Alarm," February 18, 1956, 4), while the *Defender* commented after the election that "Harry Truman took a long-shot gamble … and decided that he could take a stand on civil rights and win without the solid South. Instead Stevenson chose to pit his campaign on moderation and the H-bomb and got completely trounced" (Editorial, "Call for New Leadership: An Editorial," November 17, 1956, 1).

46. John Martin, *Civil Rights and the Crisis of Liberalism: The Democratic Party, 1945–1976* (Boulder, CO: Westview Press, 1979), 106–15; J. W. Anderson, *Eisenhower, Brownell, and the Congress: The Tangled Origins of the Civil Rights Bill of 1956–1957* (University: University of Alabama Press, 1964), 47–50.

47. Anderson, *Eisenhower, Brownell, and Congress*, 63–64. As the national convention started, Stevenson also caused a stir by declaring in an interview that "I have a very strong feeling that the platform should express unequivocal approval of the court's [*Brown*] decision." See Charles A. H. Thomson and Frances M. Shattuck, *The 1956 Presidential Election Campaign* (Washington, DC: Brookings Institution, 1960), 127–28. This was interpreted as a move away from Stevenson's earlier moderate stance.

48. See Anderson, *Eisenhower, Brownell, and Congress*, 106–17; Brock, *Americans for Democratic Action*, 159–61; Martin, *Civil Rights and Crisis of Liberalism*, 108–10.

49. "ADA Urges Dumping of 'Eastlands,'" *Washington Post*, August 5, 1956, A12. Rauh symbolized the close organizational connections among the ADA, labor, and African

American groups. In addition to chairing the ADA, Rauh was the former general counsel for the UAW and a longtime board member of the NAACP.

50. Brock, *Americans for Democratic Action*, 161.

51. Although Baylor claims that "future platforms were at least as liberal on civil rights as the 1948 platform" ("First to the Party," 23), this statement on states' rights and the deliberately vague language of the civil rights plank itself suggests that observers at the time were correct to view the 1956 platform as a step backward. NAACP executive secretary Roy Wilkins and the ADA's Joseph Rauh both argued that the GOP's plank in 1956 was "a shade" stronger than the Democrats, though both were inadequate ("Call GOP Plank 'Shade' Stronger," *Defender*, September 1, 1956, 1). Clarence Mitchell of the NAACP condemned the 1956 Democratic plank as "the biggest pile of fertilizer outside the stockyards" ("'The Biggest Pole of Fertilizer Outside the Stockyards'—Mitchell," *Afro-American*, August 25, 1956, 7). The *Washington Post* concluded that the 1956 Democratic platform "unquestionably ... is a straddle" ("Patches on the Platform," August 16, 1956, 14), while the *Los Angeles Sentinel* depicted the platform as a "shabby sellout to appease a pack of rebels armed with something less than a cause. At best, the plank represents a series of absurd contradictions telescoped into an unholy compromise of the rights of 16,000,000 Americans" ("A Sellout without A Cause," August 23, 1956, A9). Stevenson's acceptance speech in 1956 was also noteworthy for its conciliatory tone on civil rights, renouncing "the extremes of force or nullification" and referring to "the understanding accommodation of conflicting views" ("Stevenson's New America," *Washington Post*, August 19, 1956, E4).

52. Anderson, *Eisenhower, Brownell, and Congress*, 115.

53. "3 'Old Pros' Kept Civil Rights Fight under Control," *Washington Post*, August 17, 1956, 27.

54. Ibid. See also Anderson, *Eisenhower, Brownell, and Congress*, 117–18; Robert Bendiner, "The Compromise on Civil Rights–I," *Reporter*, September 6, 1956, 11–12.

55. Bendiner, "The Compromise on Civil Rights–I," 11–12.

56. See Herbert McClosky, Paul J. Hoffmann, and Rosemary O'Hara, "Issue Conflict and Consensus among Party Leaders and Followers," *American Political Science Review* 54 (June 1960): 406–27.

57. The response rate for the two groups was similar; there were fewer GOP delegates and alternates.

58. This data is restricted to the 1715 actual delegates who responded, but the party gap is very similar if one also includes alternates. I have also explored weighting the data to account for differential response rates across regions; the party gap remained robust when the data were weighted.

59. Consistent with the decline in biracial Republican state parties in the South, a mere 5 of the 173 Republican southern delegates surveyed were African American.

60. On the "harmful faults" item, there was a 12-point gap in party views in the full sample and a 17-point gap in the North. The gap was smaller on interracial marriage: among northerners, 38% of Democrats and 26% of Republicans could see themselves marrying outside their own race. In the full sample, 31% of Democrats and 23% of Republicans could envision marrying a person of another race.

61. Including the South, 63.5% of Democratic union members favored increased enforcement, compared to 43.5% of nonmembers.

62. The number of African American delegates was quite low, however. A total of 27 Democratic respondents were African American, while 91 were Jewish.

63. The sample included 503 liberal northern Democrats, 227 moderates, and just 47 conservatives. Even in the South, the small number of liberal Democrats favored increased

enforcement (43%–28%), while conservatives overwhelmingly favored weaker enforcement (87%–4%). The ideology question wording was: "How would you describe your general political outlook—are you a liberal, a middle-of-the-roader, or a conservative?"

64. See Garson, *Democratic Party and Sectionalism, chap.* 6; Kari Frederickson, *The Dixiecrat Revolt and the End of the Solid South, 1932–1968* (Chapel Hill: University of North Carolina Press, 2001), chap. 2.

65. Dalfiume, *Desegregation of the Armed Forces*, chap. 8.

66. See McAdam and Kloos, *Deeply Divided*, 56–57, for data on movement activity.

67. Lee, *Mobilizing Public Opinion*, 107–9, 145–46.

68. Ibid.; see also Howard Schuman, Charlotte Steeh, and Lawrence Bobo, *Racial Attitudes in America: Trends and Interpretations* (Cambridge, MA: Harvard University Press, 1985). The "most important problem" item is a demanding measure of salience. The percentage rating civil rights as the top problem dipped after its big increase in 1956 and 1957 but remained above the level recorded prior to 1956 and reached a high point in 1963–64 (Lee, *Mobilizing Public Opinion*, 107).

69. "AFL-CIO Will Raise Civil Rights 'War Chest,'" *Washington Post*, May 15, 1956, 11; "Union Commission to Fight Race Bias," *NYT*, May 15, 1956, 1.

70. Lichtenstein, *Most Dangerous Man in Detroit*, 371.

71. As quoted in ibid., 370.

72. See Anderson, *Eisenhower, Brownell, and Congress*, 137–39.

73. Richard Bolling, *House Out of Order* (New York: Dutton, 1965), 175–76. See also James Sundquist, *Politics and Policy: The Eisenhower, Kennedy, and Johnson Years* (Washington, DC: Brookings Institution, 1968), 251.

74. See examples in Zangrando, *NAACP Crusade against Lynching*, 145–46, 162–64; Ruchames, *Race, Jobs, and Politics*, chap. 13; McCoy and Ruetten, *Quest and Response*, chap. 9. This leadership resistance was a recurrent feature of civil rights battles in the Senate. For example, when Robert Wagner sought to force a floor debate on the lynching bill in fall 1937, Barkley tried to prevent Wagner's recognition, but a mix-up allowed Wagner to bring the bill to the floor (see Finley, *Delaying the Dream*, 25; Weiss, *Farewell to Party of Lincoln*, 244–48). Lucas, who served as Democratic Leader in 1949–50, continued Barkley's approach. For example, his decision following Truman's 1948 reelection to emphasize Taft-Hartley repeal and trade legislation—in place of FEPC—outraged liberal leaders such as the ADA's Joseph Rauh and the NAACP (Thurber, *Politics of Equality*, chap. 3). Ruchames characterizes Lucas and other Senate Democratic leaders as "singularly, weak, hesitant, and inactive on the Senate floor" in the face of southern obstruction (*Race, Jobs, and Politics*, 209)

75. Robert Caro, *Master of the Senate: The Years of Lyndon Johnson, Volume 3* (New York: Knopf Doubleday, 2003).

76. Indeed, Democratic leaders pressured rank-and-file members not to sign Joseph Gavagan's 1937 discharge petition for his lynching bill (and pressed those who had signed to withdraw their names). See Zangrando, *NAACP Crusade against Lynching*, 134.

77. Butler also backed efforts to weaken the "loyalty oath" pledge that the party had approved at the 1952 convention. The oath had been adopted in response to the Dixiecrat revolt, which had prevented Truman from appearing as the Democratic candidate on the ballot in four states. The oath required delegates to ensure that the party nominees appear on the state ballot as Democrats with electors pledged to them (Sindler, "Unsolid South," 256–60). With Butler's support, the DNC weakened the pledge in 1956 so that it placed the burden on state parties, rather than the delegates themselves, to "assure that voters in the State will have the opportunity to cast their election ballots" for the party's nominees. The revised pledge placed no obligation on delegates to take any action on behalf of the

national ticket and was seen as a concession to the South (Sindler, "Unsolid South, 269–70; on Butler's position, see "Notable Change Seen in Butler Leadership," *CQ Weekly*, December 5, 1958, 1497).

78. Butler's move may have been attributable to his own presidential aspirations (see Martin, *Civil Rights and Crisis of Liberalism*, 120).

79. "Democrats Push Liberal Program," *NYT*, November 28, 1956, 1, 26. See also Daniel Disalvo, "The Politics of a Party Faction: The Liberal-Labor Alliance in the Democratic Party, 1948–1972," *Journal of Policy History* 22, 3 (2010): 269–99.

80. "Democrats Press Civil Rights Bills," *NYT*, February 18, 1957, 1, 15.

81. On Johnson and Rayburn's refusal, see "Notable Change Seen in Butler Leadership," 1497–99.

82. "Democrats Press Civil Rights Bills."

83. "School Segregation," *CQ Weekly*, September 20, 1957, 1114.

84. Carroll Kilpatrick, "Kennedy, the Moderate," *Washington Post*, October 24, 1957, A13.

85. Earl Mazo, "Butler's Rights Stand Stirs Demand He Quit," *Washington Post*, September 18, 1957, A2.

86. Kilpatrick, "Kennedy, the Moderate," A13.

87. "Notable Changes Seen in Butler Leadership," 1497–98.

88. "Democrats Quarrel," October 24, 1958, 1364; see also DiSalvo, "Politics of a Party Faction," 285.

89. "Butler Discounts Southern Hopes," *NYT*, June 7, 1959, 60; see also Sindler, "Unsolid South," 272.

90. "Notable Changes Seen in Butler Leadership," 1499.

91. Fine, *Expanding Frontiers of Civil Rights*, 184–86.

92. Ibid., 187.

93. Dominic Sandbrook, *Eugene McCarthy: The Rise and Fall of Postwar American Liberalism* (New York: Knopf, 2004), 77.

94. *CR*, January 30, 1957, 1325.

95. See Kenneth Kofmehl, "The Institutionalization of a Voting Bloc," *Western Political Quarterly* 17 (June 1964): 256–72; Disalvo, "Politics of a Party Faction."

96. Kofmehl, "Institutionalization of Voting Bloc," 266.

97. Ibid., 266–67, 270.

98. See discussion in chapter 8 of the DSG public relations campaign to pressure Republicans to sign the discharge petition for the Civil Rights Act of 1960.

99. Berman, *Bill Becomes a Law*, 75.

100. See Brock, *Americans for Democratic Action*, 179; Sundquist, *Politics and Policy*, 251–52.

101. As quoted in Lichtenstein, *Most Dangerous Man*, 355.

102. Ibid.

103. Brock, *Americans for Democratic Action*, 179–80.

104. Ibid.

105. Sundquist, *Politics and Policy*, 252.

106. For the size of delegations by state, see Paul T. David, Ralph M. Goldman, and Richard C. Bain, *The Politics of National Party Conventions* (Washington, DC: Brookings Institution, 1960). In 1956, 28.6% of delegate votes came from the South, but party leaders had stacked the platform committee with moderates willing to placate the region.

107. Anthony Lewis wrote in the *New York Times* that the "astonishing civil rights plank ... signifies a major shift in the controlling forces of the party in the last four years" ("The Civil Rights Plank," *NYT*, July 13, 1960, 20).

108. Fine, *Expanding Frontiers of Civil Rights*, 187–88; Martin, *Civil Rights and Crisis of Liberalism*, chap. 9.

109. Robert Caro, *The Passage of Power: The Years of Lyndon Johnson, Volume 4* (New York: Knopf Doubleday, 2012), 136. Rauh reportedly stated that "he and some of his liberal friends agreed to work for Kennedy in the preconvention campaign upon a specific pledge that Kennedy would not take Johnson as his running mate" (Brock, *Americans for Democratic Action*, 182).

110. Lichtenstein, *Most Dangerous Man*, 355.

111. Brock, *Americans for Democratic Action*, 182–83; Caro, *Passage of Power*, 140.

112. Fine, *Expanding Frontiers of Civil Rights*,189.

113. Caro, *Passage of Power*, 143. Rauh "insists to this day: 'We won the decibel vote' " (Brock, *Americans for Democratic Action*, 183).

114. Lichtenstein, *Most Dangerous Man*, 356. The statement was drafted by the UAW's Jack Conway as part of efforts to forestall a full-blown AFL-CIO revolt. See also "Nominees Appeal for Negro Votes," *NYT*, July 16, 1960, 1.

115. Sundquist, *Politics and Policy*, 254–55; Rick Perlstein, *Before the Storm: Barry Goldwater and the Unmaking of the American Consensus* (New York: Hill and Wang, 2001), 136–37.

116. See http://www.gallup.com/poll/139880/election-polls-presidential-vote-groups .aspx#14.

117. Kennedy did use his executive power on behalf of civil rights, establishing the President's Committee on Equal Employment Opportunity to combat discrimination by government contractors and appointing more than forty African Americans to important government posts in his first two months (see Thurber, *Politics of Equality*, 113).

118. See Sundquist, *Politics and Policy*, 257.

119. In the next six weeks, 127 civil rights bills were introduced in the House of Representatives (ibid., 261).

120. Rowland Evans and Robert Novak, *Lyndon B. Johnson: The Exercise of Power* (New York: New American Library, 1966), 363.

121. Sundquist, *Politics and Policy*, 263.

122. "Politicians Taking a Wary Attitude toward the Civil Rights Question," *Washington Post*, October 20, 1963, A1, A11.

123. Paul D. Moreno, *From Direct Action to Affirmative Action: Fair Employment Law and Policy in America, 1933–1972* (Baton Rouge: Louisiana State University Press, 1997), chap. 8; Sundquist, *Politics and Policy*, 264–65.

124. Lichtenstein, *Most Dangerous Man*, 387–88. Thurber also observes that labor leaders had criticized Kennedy's initial draft from the left and "informed Humphrey that they intended to fight for the inclusion of an FEPC provision" (*Politics of Equality*, 118).

125. Greenstone, *Labor in American Politics*, 342. Moreno notes that the AFL-CIO "vigorously denied that Title VII would hurt organized labor, and regretted Lister Hill's argument to that effect in the Senate.... The AFL-CIO believed that the act helped organized labor by applying the same rule of nondiscrimination that bound unions through the 'fair representation' doctrine to non-union employees" (*From Direct Action to Affirmative Action*, 221).

126. Lichtenstein, *Most Dangerous Man*, 385–88.

127. Evans and Novak, *Lyndon B. Johnson*, 376.

128. See Edsall and Edsall, *Chain Reaction*, 7, 35–36; Carmines and Stimson, *Issue Evolution*.

129. Evans and Novak, *Lyndon B. Johnson*, 378.

130. Doris Kearns, *Lyndon Johnson and the American Dream* (New York: Harper & Row, 1976), 191.

131. Evans and Novak, *Lyndon B. Johnson*, 379.

132. For a balanced account, see David B. Filvaroff, and Raymond E. Wolfinger, "The Origin and Enactment of the Civil Rights Act of 1964," in *Legacies of the 1964 Civil Rights Act*, ed. Bernard Grofman (Charlottesville: University Press of Virginia, 2000).

133. See Timothy Thurber, "The Second Reconstruction," in *The American Congress: The Building of Democracy*, ed. Julian Zelizer (Boston: Houghton Mifflin, 2004), 541.

134. Thurber, *Politics of Equality*, 132–33.

135. Sundquist, *Politics and Policy*, 269; Moreno, *From Direct Action to Affirmative Action*, 214–21.

136. Robert Dallek, *Flawed Giant: Lyndon Johnson and His Times, 1961–1973* (New York: Oxford University Press, 1998), 115.

137. Johnson reportedly told King, "You're right about [voting rights]. I'm going to do it eventually, but I can't get a voting rights bill through in this session of Congress." David Garrow, *Bearing the Cross: Martin Luther King, Jr., and the Southern Christian Leadership Conference* (New York: Quill, 1986), 368. Dallek notes that "Johnson was ambivalent about putting a voting rights bill before Congress early in 1965" but was forced to act by the violence in Alabama (*Flawed Giant*, 212, 213–21).

138. Sundquist, *Politics and Policy*, 271–22.

139. Dalleck, *Flawed Giant*, 218–19.

140. Consistent with much prior work, the analysis of opinion data in chapter 5 reveals considerable ambivalence in the mass public when it comes to vigorous governmental action against discrimination throughout the 1930s–1960s (see Schuman et al., *Racial Attitudes in America*, for a comprehensive analysis of aggregate opinion toward civil rights policy). While economically liberal Democrats were more supportive of most civil rights initiatives than were economically conservative Republicans, the position of the median voter nationally varied across issues and was not always favorable to the liberal side.

Chapter 10: Lincoln's Party No More: The Transformation of the GOP

1. See Carmines and Stimson, *Issue Evolution*; Zaller, *Nature and Origins of Mass Opinion*, 12–13; Edsall and Edsall, *Chain Reaction*, 7, 35–36.

2. While the 1960 platform—discussed in detail below—reflected an exception to this trend, it provoked a conservative backlash that underscored the growing influence of civil rights opponents in the national GOP.

3. In this way, his vision echoed V. O. Key's aspirations for the future of southern politics. See Key, *Southern Politics in State and Nation* (New York: Knopf, 1949), 671–75.

4. Noel sees intellectual elites on the left drawing these connections before the 1950s, but with respect to the right, he argues that the "significant intellectual transformation on race" began in the 1950s with the launch of the *National Review* and related developments (Noel, *Political Ideologies and Political Parties*, 152).

5. See McAdam and Kloos, *Deeply Divided*, 96–104.

6. See, e.g., William S. White, *The Taft Story* (New York: Harper & Brothers, 1954), 106–15; Nelson Polsby, *Congress & The Presidency* (Englewood Cliffs, NJ: Prentice Hall, 1964), 11; James McGregor Burns, *The Deadlock of Democracy: Four-Party Politics in America* (Englewood Cliffs, NJ: Prentice Hall, 1963).

7. See James T. Patterson, *Mr. Republican: A Biography of Robert A. Taft* (Boston: Houghton Mifflin, 1972).

8. As quoted in ibid., 304.

9. In 1948, for example, New York and Pennsylvania had 97 and 73 delegates, respectively (548 votes were required to win the nomination). The third largest state, Illinois,

had 56 delegates. See Richard C. Bain and Judith Parris, *Convention Decisions and Voting Records*, 2nd ed. (Washington, DC: Brookings Institution, 1973), appendices.

10. Bain and Parris, *Convention Decisions and Voting Records*, appendices.

11. Robert Novak, *The Agony of the G.O.P.* (New York: Macmillan, 1965), 19.

12. Willkie had, until recently, been a registered Democrat. Simon Topping writes that Willkie's "liberalism in both foreign and domestic policy was ... alien to the mainstream of the GOP" (Topping, *Lincoln's Lost Legacy*, 79; see also Novak, *Agony of GOP*, 19). Journalist Raymond Clapper argues that a popular outcry over the war had forced Willkie onto the GOP ticket but that the party's politicians had not wanted him. Raymond Clapper, *Watching the World* (London: McGraw-Hill, 1944), 158.

13. This was on the fifth ballot, which occurred after the initial frontrunner, Dewey, had dropped out. Willkie won the nomination on the next ballot by a 655–318 margin over Taft. See Bain and Parris, *Convention Decisions and Voting Records*, appendices, for convention vote breakdowns by state.

14. Kenneally, "Black Republicans," 132–33; see also Sitkoff, *New Deal for Blacks*, 304.

15. "Men Need Jobs, Not Promises: Willkie," *Tribune*, September 14, 1940, 1, 2; see also "Elwood, Ind., Gives G.O.P's Big Welcome," *Defender*, August 24, 1940, 3.

16. Sugrue, *Sweet Land of Liberty*, 49.

17. Ladd and Hadley, *Transformations of Party System*, 60.

18. Simon Topping, "'Never Argue with the Gallup Poll': Thomas Dewey, Civil Rights, and the Election of 1948," *Journal of American Studies* 38 (2004): 180–85. Dewey did end up backing the fair employment legislation that was enacted in New York following the 1944 election.

19. White, as quoted in Topping, *Lincoln's Lost Legacy*, 99.

20. Kesselman, *Social Politics of FEPC*, 210; Topping, *Lincoln's Lost Legacy*, 100–104.

21. Ladd and Hadley, *Transformations of Party System*, 112.

22. "Martin Tips off Negro G.O.P. Leaders That FEPC Bill Hasn't a Chance," *New York Post*, December 26, 1946, 4.

23. Dewey's 1948 victory over Taft depended heavily on the Northeast and Mid-Atlantic states. The New York governor won the Northeast by a 235–42 margin on the key vote, while barely edging Taft in the rest of the country (280–232). See Bain and Parris, *Convention Decisions and Voting Records*, appendices.

24. "Nation's Republican Leaders Select Thomas E. Dewey for President," *Defender*, July 3, 1948, 3; see also McCoy and Ruetten, *Quest and Response*, 122.

25. See Berman, *Politics of Civil Rights*, 130; Topping, "'Never Argue with Gallup Poll'," 189–94; Aronson and Spiegler, "Does GOP Want Negro Vote?."

26. "Dewey Sells Out to Dixie," *Defender*, October 23, 1948, 1–2.

27. Ibid.

28. Ladd and Hadley, *Transformations of Party System*, 112.

29. Bain and Parris, *Convention Decisions and Voting Records*, appendices.

30. Berman, *Politics of Civil Rights*, 209.

31. "Democrats Pressed on Civil Rights," *Washington Post*, July 18, 1952, 1, 4.

32. Berman, *Politics of Civil Rights*, 223; Robert Frederick Burk, *The Eisenhower Administration and Black Civil Rights* (Knoxville: University of Tennessee Press, 1985), 17.

33. "50,000 Hail Eisenhower and Byrnes in South Carolina," *Tribune*, October 1, 1952, 1.

34. Burk, *Eisenhower Administration and Civil Rights*, 17.

35. McCoy and Ruetten, *Quest and Response*, 327.

36. See, e.g., "South Not So Solid, Press Poll Hints," *NYT*, September 18, 1952, 19.

37. Black and Black, *Vital South*, 182.

38. Robert Bendiner, "The Compromise on Civil Rights—II," *Reporter*, September 6, 1956, 12–15.

39. As quoted in James T. Patterson, "The Failure of Party Realignment in the South, 1937–1939," *Journal of Politics* 27, 3 (1965): 605.

40. Both quotes are from ibid., 605–6. From the left, Good Neighbor League head Stanley High predicted a realignment by 1940 in which southern conservatives would abandon the New Deal–dominated Democratic Party (High, *Roosevelt—and Then?*, 268–82).

41. "Urges South Back Republican Party," *NYT*, June 23, 1938, 6; see also Bunche, *Political Status of Negro*, 516.

42. "G.O.P. to Honor Jefferson at Grave July 4th," *Tribune*, July 2, 1938, 3.

43. Ibid.

44. Walter White to John Hamilton, November 10, 1938, Joseph L. Martin Papers, Stonehill College Archives and Historical Collections, Box 7, Folder 1.

45. John Robert Moore, "Senator Josiah W. Bailey and the 'Conservative Manifesto' of 1937," *Journal of Southern History* 31, 1 (1965): 30; "Senators Give Coalition Plea Wide Publicity," *Washington Post*, January 19, 1938, X3.

46. As quoted in Patterson, "Failure of Party Realignment," 607.

47. Even with his overtures to southern conservatives, Hamilton refused to back conservative Democratic candidates in the North and handled southern appeals for help on a case-by-case basis (ibid.).

48. "Republicans Woo States Righters," *NYT*, March 9, 1950, 23; see also Stewart Alsop, "Dixiecrat Party in the Balance," *Washington Post*, April 16, 1950, B5.

49. "Gabrielson Calls South G.O.P. 'Hunting Ground,' " *NYT*, November 17, 1951, 7; "Republicans Map Three Front Drive," *NYT*, October 21, 1951, 54.

50. "Gabrielson Looks to a Two-Party South," *NYT*, November 20, 1951, 24.

51. As quoted in Frederickson, *Dixiecrat Revolt*, 227.

52. "G.O.P. to Run in South," *NYT*, February 7, 1951, 20.

53. See, e.g., "Mundt Speech Hailed," *NYT*, April 11, 1951, 15; "Mundt Urges Alliance," *NYT*, February 15, 1951, 24.

54. As quoted in Scott Heidepriem, *A Fair Chance for a Free People: Biography of Karl E. Mundt, United States Senator* (Madison, SD: Leader Print Company, 1999), 159; see also "The GOP Tips Its Hand," *Afro-American*, June 2, 1951, 4.

55. Heidepriem, *Fair Chance for Free People*, 158–59; see also "'52 Backing of Byrd Offered by Mundt," *NYT*, August 20, 1951, 12. Mundt's Committee to Explore Political Realignment became a reality in October 1951. It included seven Democrats and seven Republicans, with such members as Senator Owen Brewster (R-ME), former Democratic senator Edward Burke (D-NE), former NRA administrator Donald Richberg, and former GOP senator Albert Hawkes of New Jersey. Its January 1952 report proposed to use the name the "Constitution party" for the combination of the GOP and southern Democrats.

56. "Party Alliance Backed," *NYT*, August 1, 1951, 47.

57. As quoted in Heidepriem, *Fair Chance for Free People*, 163–64.

58. Ibid., 162. Mundt's drive received considerable favorable press coverage in the South (see "Mundt Speech Hailed," *NYT*, April 11, 1951, 15; Heidepriem, *Fair Chance for Free People*, 159–61). Prominent southern Democrats also spoke of the importance of developing two-party competition in the region, with Senator Richard Russell (D-GA) stating that he would like to see "a very strong Republican Party in the South" and predicting that "conservatives—those who believe in constitutional government" will eventually join together (*Savannah Morning News*, July 3, 1950; as quoted in Heard, *A Two-Party South?*, 165).

59. Karl E. Mundt, "Should the G.O.P. Merge with the Dixiecrats?" *Collier's*, July 28, 1951, 20, 45, 46.

60. Clifford P. Case, "Should the G.O.P. Merge with the Dixiecrats?" *Collier's*, July 28, 1951, 21, 54, 56–57.

61. See Heard, *A Two-Party South?*, 165. Heard did predict, however, that in the long term, Republicans would capture conservative southerners as southern African Americans' continued movement to the Democrats will "encourage the shift of conservative Democrats to the Republican party and encourage the growth of competitive party politics" in the region (235; see also 247).

62. Burk, *Eisenhower Administration and Civil Rights*, 135–37, 174–94.

63. See ibid., 208–18; Anderson, *Eisenhower, Brownell, and Congress*, 28–43.

64. See, e.g., Anderson, *Eisenhower, Brownell, and Congress*, 42–43, 122–23.

65. Burk, *Eisenhower Administration and Civil Rights*, 222–24.

66. "Ike Jolted by Attack on Rights Plan," *Washington Post*, July 4, 1957, A1.

67. McCoy and Ruetten, *Quest and Response*, 343.

68. Running against the Catholic Al Smith in 1928, Hoover hoped to win over white southerners by siding with the "lily-whites." Hoover favored the lily-whites with patronage and appointed a white supremacist to run his southern campaign. In disputes over credentials at the national convention, Hoover's managers generally backed the lily-whites against black delegates. See Allan Lichtman, *Prejudice and the Old Politics: The Presidential Election of 1928* (Lanham, MD: Lexington Books, 1979), 147–59. Hoover's efforts were at least partially successful, as he won Florida, North Carolina, Tennessee, Texas, and Virginia. By the end of his term, lily-white factions had secured control of most GOP state organizations throughout the South (see Moon, *Balance of Power*, 107–9; Bunche, *Political Status of Negro*, 36; Heard, *Two-Party South?*, 224–25).

69. See David et al., *National Party Conventions*, 396.

70. As quoted in Daniel J. Galvin, "Presidential Partisanship Reconsidered: Eisenhower, Nixon, Ford, and the Rise of Polarized Politics," *Political Research Quarterly* 66, 1 (2011): 51.

71. Michael Bowen, "The First Southern Strategy: The Taft and the Dewey/Eisenhower Factions in the GOP," in *Painting Dixie Red: When, Where, Why, and How the South Became Republican*, ed. Glenn Feldman (Gainesville: University of Florida Press, 2011). See Heard, *Two-Party South?*, 96–114, on the low quality of southern GOP leadership before these efforts.

72. Galvin, "Presidential Partisanship Reconsidered," 51.

73. Daniel J. Galvin, *Presidential Party-Building: Dwight D. Eisenhower to George W. Bush* (Princeton, NJ: Princeton University Press, 2010), 65.

74. Galvin, "Presidential Partisanship Reconsidered," 51–52. See also Mickey, *Paths out of Dixie*, 186–88, on the impact of Little Rock on Eisenhower's party-building efforts.

75. "Operation Dixie: GOP Spurs a Build-Up in South, Has Bumper Crop of Candidates," *WSJ*, June 24, 1960, 1.

76. Galvin, *Presidential Party-Building*, 63–64.

77. Bowen, "First Southern Strategy," 232–34.

78. Lowndes, *New Deal to New Right*, 60.

79. "Goldwater Supporters Hold Key Professional GOP Posts," *CQ Weekly*, October 11, 1963, 1771; see also Philip Klinkner, *The Losing Parties: Out-Party National Committees, 1956–1993* (New Haven, CT: Yale University Press, 1994), 57–59.

80. Galvin, "Presidential Partisanship Reconsidered," 52.

81. Perlstein, *Before the Storm*, 168; see also Lowndes, *New Deal to New Right*, 61.

82. Perlstein, *Before the Storm*, 168–69.

83. Joseph Crespino, "Goldwater in Dixie: Race, Region, and the Rise of the Right," in *Barry Goldwater and the Remaking of the American Political Landscape*, ed. Elizabeth Tandy Shermer (Tucson: University of Arizona Press, 2013), 157.

84. "GOP Campaigning for Jim Crow," *Defender*, October 30, 1962, 13.

85. As quoted in Walter Dean Burnham, "The Alabama Senatorial Election of 1962: Return of Inter-Party Competition," *Journal of Politics* 24 (November 1964), 810.

86. Burnham, "Alabama Senatorial Election," 809.

87. As quoted in Galvin, *Presidential Party-Building*, 67.

88. Galvin, "Presidential Partisanship Reconsidered," 52; see also Lowndes, *New Deal to New Right*, 46–60.

89. "GOP in Dozen States Plans Southern Bloc," *Washington Post*, April 27, 1959, A2.

90. See Perlstein, *Before the Storm*, 15.

91. Galvin, *Presidential Party-Building*, 59–61.

92. "Watch on the POTOMAC," *Defender*, May 5, 1959, 11.

93. "Tags Warren as a Socialist: Justice Unfit for Post, Says Goldwater," *Tribune*, April 18, 1959, 3; "Goldwater Labels Warren Socialist," *NYT*, April 18, 1959, 18.

94. As quoted in Perlstein, *Before the Storm*, 48.

95. Ibid., 48–49; Lowndes, *New Deal to New Right*, 56.

96. Perlstein, *Before the Storm*, 57.

97. Ibid., 63. South Carolina segregationist Workman wrote a glowing review of *Conscience of a Conservative* when it came out, focusing on the civil rights chapter (Crespino, "Goldwater in Dixie," 149).

98. "Goldwater Is Pushed: South Carolina G.O.P. Will Seek to Get Him on Ticket," *NYT*, July 17, 1960, 40.

99. Mary Brennan, *Turning Right in the Sixties: The Conservative Capture of the GOP* (Chapel Hill: University of North Carolina Press, 1996), 33; Perlstein, *Before the Storm*, chap. 5.

100. Perlstein, *Before the Storm*, 83.

101. "This Lively Man Goldwater," *Newsweek*, July 4, 1960, 24–26; "Republican Old Guard Rallying to Goldwater as Its Last Hope," *NYT*, July 23, 1960, 8.

102. "Goldwater Hits Platform Accord," *NYT*, July 24, 1960, 38; "Republican Old Guard Rallying to Goldwater," 8.

103. Brennan, *Turning Right in Sixties*, 35.

104. Novak, *Agony of the G.O.P.*, 23; "Goldwater Rips Pact as 'Munich of G.O.P.,' " *Tribune*, July 24, 1960, 1–2.

105. "Goldwater Rips Pact as 'Munich of G.O.P.,' " 2.

106. "Goldwater Hits Platform Accord," *NYT*, July 24, 1960, 38.

107. "GOP Row on Rights, Defense Planks Seen," *LAT*, July 25, 1960, 1, 4.

108. See "Nixon Leads Bid to Quell GOP Conservatives' Revolt over Platform," *WSJ*, July 26, 1960, 3; "Leaders Reject Plank on Rights," *NYT*, July 26, 1960, 19; "Moderate Says Rights Plank Won't Change," *LAT*, July 26, 1960, 1, 3.

109. Novak, *Agony of the G.O.P.*, 22.

110. Perlstein, *Before the Storm*, 90–91. Nineteen members did not vote. The plank did represent a partial step back from the initial agreement with Rockefeller but was acceptable to the New York governor.

111. Ibid., 86. Indeed, the rank-and-file opposition to the strong platform plank was paralleled in House Republicans' approach to what became the Civil Rights Act of 1960. Despite ultimately voting for the bill, most House Republicans had opposed efforts to force the bill onto the House floor (see chap. 8).

112. Ibid., 93. Crespino writes that it was "the most impassioned demonstration of the convention" ("Goldwater in Dixie, 151).

113. "Goldwater Withdraws His Name," *Washington Post*, July 28, 1960, A1, A8.

114. Perlstein, *Before the Storm*, 93.

115. Novak, *Agony of the G.O.P.*, 12.

116. As quoted in Brock, *Americans for Democratic Action*, 119.

117. See Novak, *Agony of the G.O.P.*, 11–14.

118. Perlstein, *Before the Storm*, 139, 157.

119. Robert Novak, "Shift to the Right," *WSJ*, August 11, 1961, 1.

120. Novak, *Agony of the G.O.P.*, 45.

121. Crespino, "Goldwater in Dixie," 154; Perlstein, *Before the Storm*, 140.

122. "Goldwater Solicits G.O.P. Votes from Southern Segregationists," *NYT*, November 19, 1961, 70.

123. As quoted in Crespino, "Goldwater in Dixie," 161.

124. Novak, *Agony of the G.O.P.*, 56–63, 77.

125. See, e.g., Crespino, who notes that "particularly important is the relationship between national conservative leaders such as Goldwater and the burgeoning southern Republican organizations" ("Goldwater in Dixie," 146).

126. Perlstein, *Before the Storm*, 179–80.

127. As quoted in Novak, *Agony of the G.O.P.*, 136; italics in original.

128. Ibid., 120–24.

129. Perlstein, *Before the Storm*, 181–83; "Texas GOP Boosts Goldwater for '64," *Washington Post*, September 20, 1962, A6.

130. Perlstein, *Before the Storm*, 183.

131. Ibid., 198, 214.

132. Rowland Evans and Robert Novak, "A Rocky Road," *Washington Post*, August 5, 1963, A13; see also "Goldwater's Hat," *Washington Post*, June 13, 1963, D19.

133. Perlstein, *Before the Storm*, 215.

134. Rowland Evans and Robert Novak, "The New Republicans," *Washington Post*, June 24, 1963, A4.

135. Novak, *Agony of the G.O.P.*, 177.

136. Evans and Novak, "New Republicans," A4.

137. Novak, *Agony of the G.O.P.*, 179.

138. See Perlstein, *Before the Storm*, 247–49, 266 on the assassination and Goldwater's stumbles. See Novak, *Agony of the G.O.P.*, 279–92, on the strategic disarray in Goldwater's campaign.

139. Perlstein, *Before the Storm*, 313, 326.

140. While the primary in California was close, the grassroots energy was all on Goldwater's side. The Young Republican convention in the state even voted 256–33 to boycott the presidential campaign if Goldwater was not nominated. When state party chair Caspar Weinberger proved hostile to the far right, the Goldwater backers captured the central committee by recruiting arch-conservatives to run for office. See ibid., 333–36.

141. Bain and Parris, *Convention Decisions and Voting Records*, appendices.

142. "1960 Republican Convention Delegates Now Prefer Goldwater but Expect Rockefeller to Receive 1964 Nomination," *CQ Weekly*, May 3, 1963, 693–96. Goldwater led 115–84 in the Midwest and 105–65 in the West. Rockefeller led in the East by a 145–78 margin.

143. Novak, *Agony of the G.O.P.*, 174. Interestingly, the delegates expected Rockefeller would be the nominee. They evidently continued to believe the northeastern wing of the GOP would dominate the nomination process.

144. Edmond Constantini and Kenneth H. Craik, "Competing Elites within a Political Party: A Study of Republican Leadership," *Western Political Quarterly* 22 (December 1969): 879–903.

145. The 63.5% included 49% who strongly backed repeal; the remainder "somewhat" favored repeal.

146. Rockefeller's failed delegate slate in California registered a position in between the Nixon delegates and the Democratic delegates.

147. Constantini and Craik, "Competing Elites within a Party," 888–90.

148. Thomas A. Flinn and Frederick M. Wirt, "Local Party Leaders: Groups of Like Minded Men," *Midwest Journal of Political Science* 9 (February 1965): 77–98. The sampling frame was all chairs and secretaries of county central and executive committees elected in 1958 or 1962. The response rate was 45% for Republicans and 48% for Democrats.

149. Recent work by political historians has underscored the role of grassroots pressure in feeding Goldwater's rise. For a useful review, see Julian E. Zelizer, "What Political Science Can Learn from the New Political History," *Annual Review of Political Science* 13 (2010): 25–36. See also Lisa McGirr's important study of Orange County conservatives, *Suburban Warriors: The Origins of the New American Right* (Princeton, NJ: Princeton University Press, 2001). Important works on southern conservatism include Joseph Crespino, *In Search of Another Country: Mississippi and the Conservative Counterrevolution* (Princeton, NJ: Princeton University Press, 2009); and Kevin Kruse, *White Flight: Atlanta and the Making of Modern Conservatism* (Princeton, NJ: Princeton University Press, 2005).

150. A majority of Democrats saw the administration's pace as "about right." Given the tendency for partisans to support their own party's president, I focus mainly on the difference in the proportion of "too fast" versus "too slow" responses. A similar share of both party's identifiers had no opinion (16%–17%).

151. By comparison, 24% of economically liberal Democrats believed the administration was pushing too fast in the first period, and 29% held this view from mid-1963 through mid-1964.

152. This analysis was not restricted to Republicans (since many Goldwater supporters in the South did not identify as Republicans at the time). Nonetheless, a higher share of southern Republicans backed Goldwater than northern Republicans.

153. Lowndes, *New Deal to New Right*, 68; Perlstein, *Before the Storm*, 238.

154. Thomas W. Casstevens, *Politics, Housing, and Race Relations: The Defeat of Berkeley's Fair Housing Ordinance* (Berkeley, CA: Institute of Governmental Studies, 1965), 95. Several other referendum battles showed similar dynamics. Harlan Hahn, "Northern Referenda on Fair Housing: The Response of White Voters," *Western Political Quarterly* 21 (September 1968): 483–95.

155. Wolfinger and Greenstein show that Republican voters provided significantly more support for repeal of the Rumford Act than did Democratic voters. However, even Democrats were deeply divided on the issue (though more likely to back fair housing than were the Republicans). See Raymond E. Wolfinger and Fred I. Greenstein, "The Repeal of Fair Housing in California: An Analysis of Referendum Voting," *American Political Science Review* 62 (September 1968): 753–69.

156. Novak, *Agony of the G.O.P.*, 189.

157. Rowland Evans and Robert Novak, "No Hamburgers, No Aid," *Washington Post*, June 16, 1963, A8.

158. Chalmers Roberts, "Politicians Taking a Wary Attitude toward the Civil Rights Question," *Washington Post*, October 20, 1963, A1.

159. Novak, *Agony of the G.O.P.*, 192; see also Perlstein, *Before the Storm*, chap. 11; and Lowndes, *New Deal to New Right*, 68–71, for similar assessments.

160. Crespino, "Goldwater in Dixie," 160, 162.

161. Indeed, close accounts of the 1960 race make it clear that Nixon, on balance, tilted more toward southern whites during the campaign, notwithstanding the liberal platform (see, e.g., Burk, *Eisenhower Administration and Civil Rights*, 258–60). Perlstein highlights Nixon's decision not to reach out to Martin Luther King, Jr., following his arrest days before the election and instead to make a major campaign stop at South Carolina's statehouse; the move "broadcast which bloc he had chosen to court" (*Before the Storm*, 137).

162. On Reagan's rise, see Brilliant, *Color of America Has Changed*, chap. 7.

163. Timothy Thurber, "Goldwaterism Triumphant? Race and the Republican Party, 1965–1968," *Journal of the Historical Society* 7, 3 (September 2007): 349–84.

164. Ibid.

165. Ibid., 378.

166. See Gallup poll 761 from May 1968.

167. Thurber, "Goldwaterism Triumphant?," 371–73.

168. Lowndes, *New Deal to New Right*, 111–13.

Chapter 11: Conclusions

1. See Orren and Skowronek, *Search for American Political Development*, on this idea more generally.

2. Corey Brooks, *Liberty Power: Antislavery Third Parties and the Transformation of American Politics* (Chicago: University of Chicago Press, 2015).

3. See Bensel, *Sectionalism and American Political Development*, 150–52; Bensel, "Sectionalism and Congressional Development," 771–73; Katznelson et al., "Limiting Liberalism," 283–306; and Lieberman, *Shifting the Color Line*, 23–25.

4. Anthony Downs, *An Economic Theory of Democracy* (New York: Harper, 1957). On parties as coalitions of policy demanders, see Bawn et al., "Theory of Parties."

5. Schickler and Pearson, "Agenda Control, Majority Party Power, and the Committee on Rules."

6. See, e.g., the examples in William H. Riker, *The Art of Political Manipulation* (New Haven, CT: Yale University Press, 1986).

7. Kevin Phillips, *The Emerging Republican Majority* (New Rochelle, NY: Arlington House, 1969).

8. Even the party's presidential candidates had to worry about their own nomination prospects and, as a result, were not positioned to allow concerns for the party's long-term electoral success to trump calculations about the current power balance within the party.

9. This resistance to remaking the GOP as a conservative party likely stemmed both from the leaders' personal moderation and from their own power base being rooted in the northeastern wing that was endangered by such a transformation.

10. In thinking about where Democratic leaders stood in relation to this factional struggle, it is striking that the particular individuals who entered the White House were far from the most personally committed civil rights advocates within the party. Yet by the time each left office, he had alienated much of the southern leadership through his actions on the race issue. Roosevelt had deep ties to the South and disappointed civil rights advocates far more often than he satisfied them. Still, many southern elites came to see him as an enemy. Garson observers that, by the end of 1942, southern leaders "felt that the president had turned his back on the South by ignoring its leaders in his decisions and in his appointments policies. He seemed more amenable to the new men of power, such as Sidney Hillman, Walter White, and other leaders of the urban coalition, than to the congressional leadership" (Garson, *Democratic Party and Sectionalism*, 29–30). Following Roosevelt's death, southerners expected greater influence with the border-state native Harry Truman in the White House (ibid., 132). But once in office, Truman had to make decisions on concrete legislative initiatives—and those decisions generally went against the advocates of Jim Crow. By 1951–52 Truman had become identified as an enemy of the South; he decided against running again in 1952 in part to prevent a permanent split in the Party (Berman, *Politics of Civil Rights*, 196–97). Truman's withdrawal reflected the seemingly impossible balancing act facing Democratic presidents even at this relatively early stage of the civil rights struggle: how to live up to the expectations of the northern liberals who had gained control of much of the party without completely alienating the

South. This balancing act became ever more difficult to sustain once civil rights protests dominated the headlines. Kennedy and Johnson seemed to be the national Democratic leaders most inclined personally to find a formula to accommodate both civil rights liberals and southern racial conservatives—yet they each eventually sided decisively with pro–civil rights forces.

11. See Bawn et al., "Theory of Parties"; Cohen et al., *The Party Decides*; Karol, *Party Position Change*.

12. Chen, *Fifth Freedom*; Karol, *Party Position Change*, chap. 4.

13. One might argue that southerners could have blocked the entry of CIO unions by preventing passage of the Wagner Act in 1935. But with just 104 Republicans in the chamber, northern Democrats controlled a majority of House seats. Liberal Democrats also had the upper hand in the Senate, where there were just 25 Republicans, several of whom were Progressives. Southerners likely would have put up more widespread resistance to the Wagner Act had more members shared Eugene Cox's (D-GA) and Howard Smith's (D-VA) belief that it had the potential to transform American politics (see chap. 3). But the labor strife and upheaval of the mid-1930s put intense pressure on Roosevelt and Congress to act, and the overwhelming Democratic majorities made such action feasible even in the face of greater southern opposition. Southerners were also powerless to block the efforts of Joseph Guffey and other northern liberals to woo African American voters in their own states.

14. See Farhang and Katznelson, "Southern Imposition."

15. Cf. Byron Shafer and Richard Johnston, *The End of Southern Exceptionalism* (Cambridge, MA: Harvard University Press, 2009).

16. These results are based on the Cooperative Congressional Election Study. The results are very similar in other surveys. The sample is restricted to non-Hispanic whites. Low-income whites in the Deep South were, if anything, more Republican: 25% of those with a family income under $30,000 voted for Obama, compared to 32% of deep southern whites with an income above $100,000. By contrast, outside the South, Obama won 52.5% among whites with an income below $30,000 and 50% among those with incomes above $100,000.

17. See Green, Palmquist, and Schickler, *Partisan Hearts and Minds*, on the relationship of social identity to partisanship more generally.

18. See Noel, *Political Parties and Political Ideologies*, for an important account that makes several closely related points.

19. Daniel Schlozman's theory of "anchoring groups" in parties offers crucial insights into the post-1960s transformation of the GOP. Schlozman, *When Movements Anchor Parties: Electoral Alignments in American History* (Princeton, NJ: Princeton University Press, 2015).

20. On sectional cleavages and ideology, see especially Bensel, *Sectionalism and American Political Development*; Elisabeth M. Sanders, *The Roots of Reform: Farmers, Workers, and the American State, 1877–1917* (Chicago: University of Chicago Press, 1999); and Gerring, *Party Ideologies in America*. The extent to which parties operate primarily as coalitions of intense policy demanders is likely variable, depending on the nature of the groups and demands prominent in society and within each party. See Matt Grossman and David A. Hopkins on the idea that Democrats tend to operate as a coalition of policy-demanding groups, while the GOP is more ideological. Grossman and Hopkins, "Ideological Republicans and Group Interest Democrats: The Asymmetry of American Party Politics," *Perspectives on Politics* 13, 1 (2015): 119–39. It is worth noting, however, that the northern Democratic Party of the late 1930s and 1940s—exemplified by the CIO and its allies—put forward a strong ideological vision.

21. See, e.g., Edsall and Edsall, *Chain Reaction*; Kinder and Sanders, *Divided by Color*; and Michael Omi and Howard Winant, *Racial Formation in the United States*, 2nd ed. (New York: Routledge, 2014), chap. 7.

22. Tali Mendelberg, *The Race Card: Campaign Strategy, Implicit Messages, and the Norm of Equality* (Princeton, NJ: Princeton University Press, 2001).

23. See Vesla M. Weaver, "Frontlash: Race and the Development of Punitive Crime Policy," *Studies in American Political Development* 21 (Fall 2007): 230–65; and Michelle Alexander, *The New Jim Crow; Mass Incarceration in the Age of Colorblindness* (New York: New Press, 2010).

24. Chen, "Hitlerian Rule of Quotas"; Chen, *Fifth Freedom*.

25. See Sugrue, "Crabgrass-Roots Politics"; Sugrue, *Sweet Land of Liberty*.

26. The tensions over union seniority and security policies that would become especially prominent after 1964 should also not be read back into the pre-1964 period. While provisions of the 1964 Civil Rights Act created serious challenges for some unions (Frymer, *Black and Blue*), labor leaders were among the actors pushing hardest for strong job discrimination provisions prior to the law's enactment (see chap. 9 and Lichtenstein, *Most Dangerous Man*, 387–88).

27. For the more optimistic claims, see Juan Williams, "What Obama's Victory Means for Racial Politics," *WSJ*, November 10, 2008, A19; and Michael Eric Dyson, "Race, Post Race," *LAT*, November 5, 2008, A31. For more pessimistic interpretations, see Omi and Winant, *Racial Formation in the United States*, 3rd ed. (New York: Routledge, 2014); George E. Condon Jr. and Jim O'Sullivan, "Has President Obama Done Enough for Black Americans?," *National Journal*, April 6, 2013, 12–19; and Desmond S. King and Rogers M. Smith, *Still a House Divided: Race and Politics in Obama's America* (Princeton, NJ: Princeton University Press, 2011).

28. See, e.g., Edsall and Edsall, *Chain Reaction*, 12–13; Paul Starr, "How Gilded Ages End," *American Prospect* (Spring 2015): 31–39. Starr writes that "by taking the side of the poor and minorities in the 1960s," liberals made it harder to build effective majorities as "working- and middle-class whites, particularly men, have been suspicious of liberal government as no longer working for them" (39).

29. McAdam and Kloos, *Deeply Divided*, chap. 3, provide an excellent account of these dynamics in the 1960s; see Daniel Q. Gillion, *The Political Power of Protest: Minority Activism and Shifts in Public Policy* (New York: Cambridge University Press, 2013), more generally on the role of protest in influencing politicians.

Index

PRINCETON STUDIES IN AMERICAN POLITICS: HISTORICAL, INTERNATIONAL, AND COMPARATIVE PERSPECTIVES

IRA KATZNELSON, ERIC SCHICKLER, MARTIN SHEFTER, AND THEDA SKOCPOL, SERIES EDITORS

Racial Realignment: The Transformation of American Liberalism, 1932–1965 by Eric Schickler

When Movements Anchor Parties: Electoral Alignments in American History by Daniel Schlozman

Electing the Senate: Indirect Democracy before the Seventeenth Amendment by Wendy J. Schiller and Charles Stewart III

The Substance of Representation: Congress, American Political Development, and Lawmaking by John S. Lapinski

Looking for Rights in All the Wrong Places: Why State Constitutions Contain America's Positive Rights by Emily Zackin

Paths Out of Dixie: The Democratization of Authoritarian Enclaves in America's Deep South, 1944–1972 by Robert Mickey

Fighting for the Speakership: The House and the Rise of Party Government by Jeffery A. Jenkins and Charles Stewart III

Three Worlds of Relief: Race, Immigration, and the American Welfare State from the Progressive Era to the New Deal by Cybelle Fox

Building the Judiciary: Law, Courts, and the Politics of Institutional Development by Justin Crowe

Still a House Divided: Race and Politics in Obama's America by Desmond S. King and Rogers M. Smith

The Litigation State: Public Regulation and Private Lawsuits in the United States by Sean Farhang

Reputation and Power: Organizational Image and Pharmaceutical Regulation at the FDA by Daniel Carpenter

Presidential Party Building: Dwight D. Eisenhower to George W. Bush by Daniel J. Galvin

Fighting for Democracy: Black Veterans and the Struggle against White Supremacy in the Postwar South by Christopher S. Parker

The Fifth Freedom: Jobs, Politics, and Civil Rights in the United States, 1941–1972 by Anthony Chen

Reforms at Risk: What Happens after Majoraaz Policy Changes Are Enacted by Eric Patashnik

The Rise of the Conservative Legal Movement: The Long Battle for Control of the Law by Steven M. Teles